THE SINGULAR
Beast

EUROPEAN PERSPECTIVES

THE SINGULAR

Beast

JEWS, CHRISTIANS, & THE PIG

Claudine Fabre-Vassas

Translated by Carol Volk

COLUMBIA UNIVERSITY PRESS
New York

Columbia University Press
Publishers Since 1893
New York   Chichester, West Sussex

La Bête singulière: les Juifs, les chrétiens, le cochon © 1994 Editions Gallimard
Copyright © 1997 Columbia University Press
All rights reserved

Columbia University Press wishes to express its appreciation of assistance given by the
government of France through Le Ministère de la Culture in the preparation of this translation.

Library of Congress Cataloging-in-Publication Data
Fabre-Vassas, Claudine.
[Bête singulière. English]
The singular beast : Jews, Christians, and the pig / Claudine
Fabre-Vassas : translated by Carol Volk.
p.   cm. — (European perspectives)
Includes bibliographical references and index.
ISBN 0–231–10366–2 — ISBN 0–231–10367–0 (pbk.)
1. Swine—Folklore.   2. Swine—Social aspects.   3. Animals—
Symbolic aspects.   4. Food habits—History.   5. Cookery (Pork)
6. Jews—Food—History.   7. Jews—Dietary laws.   8. Christians—Food
History.   9. Food—Symbolic aspects.   10. Food—Religious aspects.
I. Title.   II. Series.
GR730.S9F3313   1997
398'.369633—dc21   96–50482
CIP

Printed in the United States of America
Designed by Linda Secondari
Frontispiece and part opener illustrations by Martha Lewis

c 10 9 8 7 6 5 4 3 2 1
p 10 9 8 7 6 5 4 3 2 1

For a complete list of books in the series, see page 402.

CONTENTS

ACKNOWLEDGMENTS

Like all research that takes some time, this work is the culmination of a journey full of encounters and interactions. Christiane Amiel, Jean-Pierre Piniès, Dominique Blanc, Josiane Bru, Angès Fine, Marlène Albert-Llorca, Lucie Desideri have long been colleagues and friends. I am, firstly, indebted to the discussions and stimulating debates during the "little seminar" at the Centre d'Anthropologie des sociétés rurales. Jean-Pierre Albert and Giordana Charuty have, in addition, carefully reread one or another of the versions of this manuscript and suggested apt adjustments. Jean Guilaine provided me, in more than one circumstance, with laboratory support. Lucette Bournat guided the text to its final form.

After Jean Séguy, who encouraged a vocation awakened by the ethnography class of René Nelli, those who continued the work of the Toulouse school of ethnolinguistics and dialectology, Xavier Ravier and Jacques Boisgontier, facilitated my task by providing me with the unpublished maps of their respective atlases. I made ample use of these.

This book also owes a great deal to Geneviève Calame-Giaule, for her work, her generosity, her patience, and her friendship.

Daniel Fabre accompanied this research throughout. He followed its successive stages and encouraged its boldness; he remains the first and final reader. Even if propriety dictates leaving out those who played the largest role, it is impossible for me not to mention him. Nor can I help but mention Yvonne Verdier. Her first works, hardly any older than mine, gave me the wherewithal to feel confident on the path—first taken by Claude Lévi-Strauss—of writing an ethnology that, while taking cooking as its primary object, is not limited by its boundaries. A similar theme, a shared attention to "tangible qualities," brought us together initially; more private affinities transformed a relationship that might have remained in the realm of ideas. But Yvonne's proximity made her the most enthusiastic and demanding of readers. During the summer of 1989, as she herself was moving toward completion of her work on Thomas Hardy, she read and annotated the final version of my manuscript, with the exception of the last chapter, the terms of which she knew only verbally. That is why this work, which she so encouraged, is dedicated to her.

To Céline, to return a bit of the time I borrowed from him, I offer this book.

THE SINGULAR

Beast

INTRODUCTION

It is rare, I believe, for an anthropological analysis to faithfully reflect the path of one's research almost step by step. If my own research was more hesitant and uncertain than this book reveals, the latter nonetheless remains the reflection of an exploration, noting as it does the successive horizons through which I had to pass for some of the enigmas that emerged along the way to be clarified. The distance between the relatively limited point of departure and the breadth of the journey may no doubt be surprising; perhaps the simple story of what was essentially a long adventure will suffice to welcome the reader at this threshold.

It all began on the high plateaus of the Languedocian Pyrenees (illus. 1) in the early 1970s. I was attempting to understand something of agropastoral societies through the language of cooking and, in particular, the calendar that divides up its primary tendencies. In the region of Sault the prohibitions of Lent were no longer observed as strictly as they had been, but the memory of that strictness was very present and its opposite, Shrove abundance, was in evidence and easily visible. Since 1950 the carnival games had essentially forsaken the streets and paths, the masks and music, to focus on the death of the pig, which, here, is *the* festival par excellence, the one little boys spontaneously add to the major holidays of Christ, the virgin, and the saints when questioned by the priest at their catechisms. People laugh at this joke, of course, but they know that it masks a sincerely felt truth. This concentration of the festival did not strike me as an impoverishment, a loss. On the contrary, it was extraordinarily revealing: food categories, the ways of the kitchen, table manners, and the space and time devoted to meals were now the

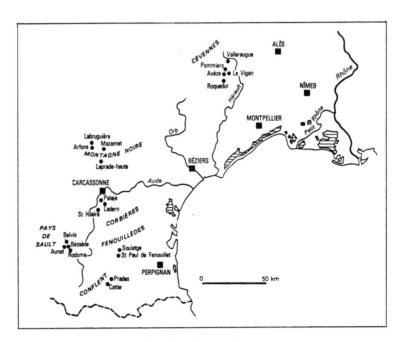

1. The initial area of study.

sole supports of a system of shared meaning. What people said about
these subjects was always rich in memories, anecdotes, and illustrative
stories, always aroused passion and laughter. The social hierarchy—
minus the religious authorities—the relationships between homes, and
the domain of each gender and age group were revealed here with a
transparency that was almost too perfect. In addition, it was an occasion
for each village to express the subtle nuances by which it presented itself
as different and was perceived as such. In this periodic flowering one
could still feel the living, breathing complexity of a culture.

These aspects held me in their thrall for a long time. And since the
pig, killed, divided up, hidden, stolen, eaten throughout the year, was
the tangible center, I recorded, in fastidious detail, the sequence of gestures, the abundance of words that, by manipulating and designating it,
turned the pig into a social phenomenon. I scrutinized variations from
village to village, I observed the vast and complex cooking practices,
attended the meals so rich in rules and rituals. It was intense, often
exhilarating ethnographic research: the strong presence of its object
made contact easy, an ethnological analysis was in the process of taking shape day by day. Rather quickly, in fact, some of the principles that
organized relationships were revealed, enabling an understanding of

what took place around the pig and its festival. Yet these first results left me with a sense of incompletion. I could clearly see the two registers that constituted the warp and the woof of my interpretation at the time.[1] Carnival was an obvious choice, but the pig was quickly lost in a larger bestiary, while the behavior of boys who put themselves on display during the course of this Pyrenean festival called for other analyses, opening a field that I wasn't eager to explore. Furthermore, I knew that while the two events coincided perfectly in the region of Sault, it was not so everywhere; sometimes the pig was killed without games, without pranks, and without a great collective exchange. The link was strong, no doubt, but it wasn't necessary, one could imagine the existence of other networks of meaning, less elaborate, more secret, more enduring perhaps.

The second interpretive register turned out to be more stable, more repetitive, and, soon, more banal. Around 1975 many ethnologists described how the reciprocal gifts of pork brought to light a social structure, made manifest its categories and links. In Burgundy Yvonne Verdier described the two directions of "pig relations," one toward equals, who give back when it comes their turn—"the pig is reciprocal," as they say in Minot—the other toward those who are dominant, who take pride in only receiving. In the Catalan Capcir, in the Gascon Baronnies, in the Provençal Luberton or Romanic Lorraine the functional descriptions varied without the terms being truly different. We were in a necessary period of verification but would soon slip into one of repetition. Between this repetitive "sociographic" work and a carnival that exceeded and displaced my object the horizons seemed to grow hazy.

But they suddenly cleared thanks to a slight shift in perspective. "Doing the pig" for the people of the region, as for ethnographers, meant killing it, cutting it up, and distributing these parts in the social space and time of the year. But didn't it first mean *raising* it, keeping it several months in the house, or in its immediate proximity? This discrete, monotonous, neglected activity, the antithesis of festive commotion, began to grip my attention. This breeding was, in fact, most unusual. It was riddled with tensions never entirely resolved, with contradictions that, for me, would turn out to be fertile: here is an omnivore, an alleged carnivore that is treated like a vegetarian, an adult nourished like a toothless baby, a table companion who is kept yet feared for his potential savagery. This worrisome trait is contrasted with the absolute savagery, with the *salvajum*, with the *ferum* of the beasts of the woods—of the wild boar in particular—since the pig is the only domestic creature who has its woodland double, which it inevitably brings to mind. Until 1980 hunting had fallen out of fashion in the Sault region; the passion for it came later on. Thus, to truly understand the two types of "savages," I had to leave the Pyrenean plateau, descend toward the Corbières and the Fenouillèdes, head back up toward the Cévennes, observe the hunters, and talk with them as they enjoyed the pleasure of domesticating boars and worried about their crossbreeding with stock animals, which would turn them into ordinary pigs.[2] In this new domain I was tracking the difference between the savage one seeks to dominate and the one that's kept "against nature," close to home.

Further, the ambiguous attitude with respect to the pig, a combination of intimacy and segregation, took different forms in each case, in the home and beyond. I saw men begin and end the cycle of this life—from purchase to slaughter—with violence, ruse, and magic; I saw women oversee the daily regimen, which is more subtle than it seems; I saw boys and girls organize strange and forbidden games around or relating to the animal. Yvonne Verdier had already registered the words that are spoken only on the day of the killing, those that keep young women of menstrual age away from this flesh they are in danger of spoiling. Now, in following the details of all these breeding techniques and the daily frequenting of the animal—and not only the technical gestures—I saw distinct sets of relations emerge, all of which have the blood of the pig as their object, as their reference, as their mirror. This blood is treated as a sickly bodily fluid, even as the red, visible symbol of a destiny the stages of which are mimicked by children. All the precautions that, in Mediterranean agronomy, from Aristotle to the Romans to Olivier de Serres, sought to master "the pig and its whole nature" were present before my eyes, still active, their principles alive. Thus I was led to expand my study to encompass this long written tradition. And then, simultaneously, the jumble of ethnographic notations, collections of beliefs, rituals, games, and recipes, the library of rural autobiographies, came alive, confirmed, expanded, sometimes illuminated my field. The first part of this book (chapters 1 and 2) follows these paths; ultimately I had to omit many fine examples and convincing illustrations, keeping only the thread of analogical blood, which led me to cast a different light on the customs of the slaughter. Edmund Leach has shown—in reflecting on the use of common animal names as insults—that bond-forming proximity necessitates this distancing just as the incest prohibition separates us from our parents. This operation turned out to be all the more necessary for the pig, which became "one of the children of the house" whose slaughter risked rousing the unbearable specter of cannibalism. Hence its squalid reputation and the taboos regarding its name: they enable the consumption of pork without eliminating the obligation to give some of it away, the ultimate way of placing its blood at a distance.

Like many other beings, the pig is maintained at the boundary between man and animal. Soon I discovered rich collections of stories that, from Lithuania to Béarn, clearly expressed this transitional quality by harking back to the time of origins, in other words, to the moment of metamorphosis. The pig is thus, as Lewis Carroll's Alice imagines it, a child transformed by a Christ demiurge, an innocent victim of his parents' lie.[3] The circle seemed complete. I had perhaps managed to tie together the major features of the breeding, the obligatory sharing, and the mythical figure. But what could have been an end was transformed into a beginning. In actuality, almost all the European stories on the human origin of the pig have *Jews* for actors and ask the question: "Why don't Jews eat pork?" The response is clear according to the myth: their children were transformed into pigs; they cannot eat themselves (chapter 3). Thus we had a *Christian* discourse on the pig. The play of same and other, of domestic and savage, which characterizes its breeding and consumption even today, took on a new and essential contrast. The investigation reopened.

At first glance I found myself in familiar territory, many times surveyed by historians of religion and anthropologists: that of understanding prohibitions, in particular alimentary prohibitions. The Jewish and Muslim refusal to eat pork has given rise to an enduring debate. Can we, in the footsteps of Maimonides, the twelfth-century Andalusian doctor, stick to a health reason, which emphasizes the easy spoiling and indigestible nature of this flesh? Must we instead opt for more recent and sophisticated ecological, economic, or political explanations? Or should we, rather, seek, with Louis Dumont, "what other type of coherence is likely"? The path chosen by Mary Douglas in 1966 seems more convincing to me. She situates the prohibitions of Leviticus in the logic of a classification of edible animals. For Jews the pig is a hybrid within the category of cloven-hoofed and ruminating domestic and wild mammals. Indeed, though its hoof is split, it doesn't ruminate. It is thus a taxonomical aberration and hence is banished from the vicinity of human beings and their table. But this "cultural reason" becomes efficient only when placed side by side with a cultural antagonism. In a second text, which appeared in 1973, Mary Douglas invites us to reread the Book of the Maccabees. In it we see, after the destruction of the Temple in the second century B.C., the Jews forced by the Greek invader and their chief, Antiochus Epiphanes, to eat pigs, which they must sacrifice on their alters on penalty of death. The Maccabean brothers refuse and are martyred. As Mary Douglas emphasizes, in this founding story refusing to eat pork in the face of those who have come from outside to subjugate the Jews is to affirm that identity, to perform an act of allegiance and fidelity to the ancestral laws that, along with this taboo, have chosen circumcision and respect for the Sabbath as signs of belonging. It is quite possible that this Maccabean episode belongs more to legend than to history, but it allows us to posit one fundamental principle: if forbidden foods manifest the categories of a culture, they also necessarily demonstrate the indigenous distinctions between societies. They are only fully affirmed, and can only be understood, in the context of this confrontation.[4]

Returning to Christian Europe, which I was compelled to recognize as the cultural and historical sphere where the Jewish reference, with respect to the pig, became meaningful, I looked closely at this sign of belonging which, along with the rejection of circumcision and the Sabbath, cut the tie with one's origins, denied a filiation. It was no longer a matter of understanding a prohibition according to the logic of those who promoted and championed it but of choosing something by reaction, electing something out of antagonism. Indeed, very early on, Christianity recommended the consumption of pork "which the carnal synagogue execrates," according to the bishops of the Council of Antioch (third century). One century later, as the new religion progressed within the Roman Empire, the pig began to appear as the incarnation of winter in depictions of the months. The ancient pagans ate pork during this period, but the allegorical relationship would define itself to the point of becoming—after the famous calendar of Salzburg in 818—the rule for cathedral sculptors, illuminators of books of hours, and, later, for more modest image makers. November appears under the sign of the acorn harvest, December under that of slaughter and pork.[5] The pig, now established in Christian time, also developed a strong place in the economy and the society. It could be a unit of rent, an element in the identity of a home.

The Anglo-Norman *Domesday Book* is one such example. Thus named by the common people, who associated it with the big book that was kept by Christ on the final judgment day, it contained a list of every *manse* and every pig.[6] The reality of the "family pig" in the Middle Ages and under the ancien régime was neither ubiquitous nor continuous; the fact remains, however, that wealth and poverty, feast and fasting, lack and abundance were always associated with its presence or absence.[7] Fabliau, farces, and tales are brimming with stolen pigs and ridiculous creatures—the priest, the devil—incapable of "bringing one up." In short, on every level, the pig incarnates a way of life, it is as much a sign of good domestic management as of Christian belonging; one never goes without the other. One might object at this point that this doctrinal elevation of the pig (it was *not* the simple effect of the spread of the new Christianity among pig eaters) sends us to the depths of history, to late antiquity, to the high Middle Ages. The opposition with Judaism would be fundamental, of course, but it would be limited to this distant time, it would no longer really be apparent, in particular when it comes to the consumption of the pig.

Yet European myths on the origin of the animal would suggest, on the contrary, a sustained opposition and introduce us to a third point of view. It no longer has to do with understanding the taboo itself within Jewish logic; it is no longer a question of recognizing the antagonistic choice of the first Christians; it is a matter of analyzing the Christian explanation for the Jewish interdiction. This interdiction would be a troubling enigma for those who lived side by side with the communities of the diaspora and even for Christianity, ever dominated by the biblical reference to the people of Israel and its laws. This, to be more specific, was the direction that presented itself to me and would lead to part 2 of this book. In it we see Jews being associated with the animal. All the features of the porcine nature that I had initially enumerated ended up being imputed to the "deicidal people." Better still, the Jews, in their rituals, in which they were reputed to spill blood, treated themselves like pigs. Furthermore—and this is the great contradiction of their destiny—since they deprived themselves of this meat, they were constantly seeking the closest substitute, the flesh and blood of Christian children. The essence of the Jewish being and customs was thus interpreted with the pig as the key, and what was and is still considered a stereotype became an obsessively articulated reading, ever present in history in one aspect or another. Is this not, in its terrible reiteration, the

logical matrix of the most common anti-Judaism, the basic and seemingly natural justification for all the persecution, for all the banishment,
for all the exterminations?

This systematic association is not without its effect on Christianity.
For the division is not only external, it is not limited to a confrontation
with the Jews alone. It passes through the animal as well as through
every Christian in his body and soul. This discourse on the other
seemed to me to quickly clarify the questions of Christians with respect
to their own habits of consumption—and firstly, that of blood. But it
also objectivizes their questions and doubts, particularly with respect to
the central mystery of the Eucharist, the "spiritual" meal of "flesh and
blood"—of which the Jewish "sacrifice," presented as a parody of
communion, reveals the barbarous underside.

Ethnographers have noted enigmatic conduct and strange names for
things without ever being able to say more about them. For example, in
Wallonia the unconsecrated part of the host that is left for children is
referred to as *Jew bread*. In Minot a sausage is called *judru*, elsewhere
jésus or *jew*, as in the region of Sault the fattest blood sausage is called
breisha, the sorceress.[8] In the Bigouden region all the blood is sprinkled
on the ground and the idea of cooking it is considered disgusting. In an
area that spans from northern Germany to Piedmont a single vertebra
from the animal's spine is sought after: it is the *Jewess*, the *damsel of the
pigs*, which is eaten on Easter Sunday. Every pig contains a Jewish trace,
as does every Christian child. Becoming fully Christian and bringing
the entire pig into one's camp are convergent struggles that everywhere
imply the symbolic slaughter of the Jew. This struggle lasts from baptism to first Holy Communion, sometimes even until marriage, and
occurs during the part of the year dominated by the life of Christ—
from Christmas to Easter. This "conversion" must also occur the day of
the killing, in the handling of the most "animated" part of the pig's
body—the blood and the bone, in which the final reversal of the Jew,
who inhabits every pig and every Christian, is played out. Which is why
our journey ends with this eschatological anticipation of a resurrection
that will once and for all separate Christians from Jews.

No one European society possesses and brings into play all these
relationships, but all engage the logic, which is as protean as it is recurrent. Above and beyond the pig it is this logic that is the object of this
book and that determines the progressive broadening of its horizons.[9]
Now that the road has been traveled, I can clearly see that its development was foreshadowed by a very strange anomaly. We know that all

the world's cultures readily designate others by what they eat; in Europe we call one another frogs, roast beefs, or macaroni eaters. A very rare exception should have aroused suspicion: Jews are called "pigs," imagined to be bloodthirsty, identified precisely with what they forbid themselves. Let's just say this book is devoted to following that anthropological paradox to its most extreme consequences.

PART ONE

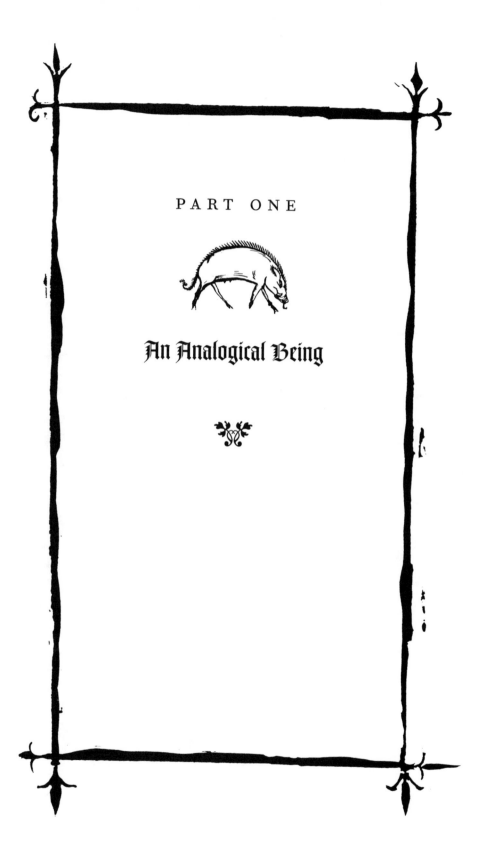

An Analogical Being

CHAPTER ONE

The Red Men

"You are rather afraid of me. Do you know what I be?"

The child surveyed his vermilion figure up and down with much misgiving and finally said, "Yes."

"Well, what?"

"The reddleman!" he faltered.

"Yes, that's what I be. Though there's more than one. You little children think there's only one cuckoo, one fox, one giant, one devil, and one reddleman, when there's lots of us all."

"Is there? You won't carry me off in your bags, will ye, master? 'Tis said that the reddleman will sometimes."

"Nonsense. All that reddlemen do is sell reddle."

—THOMAS HARDY, *The Return of the Native*

On June 11, 1780, a noble breeder from the region of Sault in the Audois Pyrenees, a Mr. Fondi de Niort, alerted the administrator of Languedoc to the mountainous journey of a herd of pigs. A hundred or so animals were traveling the roads single file under the direction of a Mr. Joseph Lafon, swineherd-merchant; they were known to be tainted with "smallpox." Thus alerted, the consul of Rodome sent the merchant off toward Galinagues and Mazuby, where the consuls, also forewarned, forbade him entry to the village. Despite their vigilance, five individuals bought sick piglets in Rodome and fifteen or so in Belfort. Tipped off by these rebuffs, Joseph Lafon split up his herd and disappeared with it. The mounted police arrived too late, the wandering herd remained out of reach; "After death, the doctor arrives," commented the chagrined breeder.

Thus, in the late eighteenth century, the pig already came from elsewhere, probably from Toulouse. In this we recognize a common situation: the cereal-rich plains oversee the complete cycle of breeding, while the other regions import piglets to fatten. Merchants travel, buying and reselling, circulating pigs.[1] This function of the *porcatier* is essential, but two other itinerants are also necessary: the *langueyeur* (who examines pigs' tongues) and the castrator are also men of the road and the square who preside over the pig's entry into the home. All three are important intermediaries with a rank and a role in village societies; each one possesses techniques and knowledge by which he shapes the body of the beast. As the goal of their operations is to profoundly model the pig's nature, it is through these primordial gestures that this nature will first appear to us.

The Commerce in Pigs

Throughout the Languedocian and Catalan mountains, when we asked the question "Where do the pigs come from?" we always received the response "From far away," "From over there," "From the other side of the mountain." In Catllar and in Conflent the merchants are "*gavachs* who don't even speak Catalan." In the Viganais Cévennes the land of the pigs is located "up there, near Meyrueis." Each area nonetheless has its indigenous intermediaries; in the region of Sault, until 1950, "There was one in Aunat, one in Fontanes, one in Rodome, En Candasson from Mirepoix," but their transactions would take place elsewhere, it seems. Every year they went off to visit their clientele: "The one from Mazuby would go all the way to Capcir to sell his pigs, all the way to Cerdagne—he'd go off for several weeks!"

Thus the porcatier is always traveling. In the Languedocian Pyrenees he "comes up" from the plain. The stories allow us to imagine his slow nocturnal ascension, his journey through the gorges—"from whichever side you come, you have to go through them"—and the passage through the village, in early morning, of the silent exhausted herd. The faces of the men leading it are gray with fatigue, their black blouses floating around their bodies. In the Cevenol region the Viganais merchants "from the other side" first head in the opposite direction, north, toward the Causses. Traveling in twos and threes, once there they reassemble their animals, which they distinguish with a red mark on the thigh, on the shoulder, or on the back. They go down again by day or night, walking to the point of exhaustion: "There were losses! These pigs weren't used to it. Just think, leading them from up there, from so far away. They descended by *drailles*, paths in the forest, like wild boars."

The porcatier knew how to lead these animals, said to be stubborn and unfriendly. "That's right! En Porral, from Rodome, his grandfather made the pigs walk on foot! And he didn't know how to read or write. He worked with stones. He had little stones in his pocket and he remembered everything. I saw him several times in about 1920. He was bringing the pigs back on foot—he was pushing them! Since he kept those pigs maybe eight days, two weeks, they got used to each other."

The journeys varied in length. In the early part of the century Aragonais merchants still traveled to the largest Pyrenean fairs, leading pigs who arrived half starved. Others were happy to single-handedly escort a small herd through the wildest regions of the area. Whether they confronted long roads or dangerous paths, the merchant and his pigs were considered foreign by those who greeted them. The animal came from a "distant" land, which could be situated only vaguely and was in any case unfamiliar. Even if he resides in the village, the porcatier is kept at a distance, for the general rule stipulates, it seems, that the pig is bought from an itinerant rather than a neighboring merchant, whenever possible. Which is why the porcatier, unlike the other local merchants—the grocer and artisans especially—is always a stranger in his own home. What social relations are the basis for such a singular status?

In the region of Sault the "pig economy" inspired a kind of ideal strategy that is utterly explicit:

We went to Quillan with the fattened pig, which we carried in the cage, on the cart, and we took a vat of potatoes for him to eat so he wouldn't lose weight, because pigs lose it fast! We had raised this pig expressly to sell it; we generally had two, one for us and one to sell. And then, with the money, we bought the pigs for the next year, but not in Quillan, where we only went to sell the fattened pig to individuals, if we could, to kill it. These pigs weighed two hundred, two hundred twenty kilos, and in the beginning, before the war, we sold them for five francs a kilo. Catalans came, people from down there, others from the area around Quillan. But afterward we bought for ourselves, from dealers. Plenty of those pig dealers came to Rodome or to Espezel. . . . They carried them from Puivert or from Chalabre in vans. But in the past people would go to get these pigs themselves—I heard that the old people went to the fair in Lavelanet or in Bélesta. In Espezel there was a big fair with cows, ox—but no pigs—the pigs were generally further down. Because here there was no stock farming, you had to go around Chalabre, in the Ariège, at the borders of the Ariège and the Aude; in those farms down there they had sows for reproducing, here, no, they didn't have what was needed.

Thus the cycle is self-contained, the sale of fattened pigs allows for the purchase of piglets—"The pig pays for the pig"—and one returns from the Quillan fair with the "pig money." This money is just one point in the circuit, always maintaining its very concrete reference to the animal. But in order to fully ensure the equilibrium toward which these transactions tend, they are carefully projected in space. The fattened pigs sell in Quillan, yet no one hesitates to go to Ariège to acquire the little ones: sell in the east, buy in the west, in the exact opposite direction. When the days of the great Ariegois fairs came to an end, in about 1930, everyone had to accept the local merchants as intermediaries: "The porcatier is a courtier, the intermediary between the breeder and the buyer. He didn't sell fattened ones, only little ones. He went to buy them in Pamiers or in Puylaurens, at the fair, or from a breeder, Cathala, in Puivert, who made them." The separation was maintained even if it lost its spatial dimension. In reality, buying at home and at the local fairs—the number of which increased after the second empire—was only a last resort, which, nonetheless, observed the rule: never put yourself in the hands of a single merchant; the buyer of fattened pigs must not be the seller of piglets. This distrust worsens with respect to the local porcatier, who is always avoided, in any case, at least in the "good houses."

For it is easy to see the price of such a dependency, which in this society defined true poverty. Especially in times of economic hardship many homes of day laborers or small landowners did not produce enough tubers to feed their two pigs. They made do with only one, which they paid for the following year. The merchant brought the new piglet and collected what was due him, most often in kind, thus single-handedly governing the two phases of the cycle:

> When he went to Capcir or Donnezan, or to Escouloubre, for example, where, frankly speaking, it was a rat race, he delivered a little pig to a nice fellow and told him: "Pagarètz quand tuarètz le porc" [You'll pay when you kill the pig]. When he returned he carried off a ham or two. . . . Not

one, both! And he settled the account, as they said. Then he brought the hams to his own village, salted them, and sold them. That was the idea.

On these salted hams the merchant made a second, more substantial, profit by selling them off to the vine growers of the plain, who, after 1875, had gradually abandoned pig breeding. Speculation added to the scandal. This was therefore the most dangerous of dependencies, the true basis for the wealth and power of the porcatier, who quickly became the principal usurer of the village.[2]

Indeed, he is criticized for drawing his power solely from the manipulation of markets, money, and time. He has no machine, like the miller, no specialized knowledge, like the doctor or the notary; what he has is mostly a mastery—and quite a mysterious mastery in truth—of pigs and capital. Widespread hostility serves to justify attacks on porcatiers, which are, in the nineteenth century, an aspect of peasant resistance against the new "lords." By attacking these merchants, one can develop a reputation for being an honorable bandit, like Milou, the "real" hero of Eugène Le Roy's Périgord story. Similarly Pomarèdes, the most famous Languedocian brigand, before being executed one Saturday in February 1843, in Pézanas, in the middle of the market, uttered a curse against Cambachou (ham), his last victim, a pig merchant whose gold-laden belt he had stolen. And the oral tradition further contrasts the worthy bandit and the disloyal porcatier who, despite being left safe and sound, ran to denounce him to the police.[3] Collective attacks bordering on peasant riots sometimes ended up in court; records of some have been preserved in the archives. Thus, in Hérault, in January 1812, a team of merchants originally from Saint-Sernin and Saint-Affrique, in Aveyron, returning from the market of Clermont-l'Hérault, was attacked at the foot of the Escalette by three armed men. The latter fired, killed a porcatier, and demanded money and the leather and canvas belts stuffed with gold pieces that were being transported on the backs of donkeys. The investigation was long, no tips were provided, and the first accused parties had an irrefutable alibi: they were helping each other "kill the pig," for it was prime season. Ultimately the aggressors turned out to be only a gang of peasants sporadically dabbling in crime; they came from Lanet, Cabrières, and Saint-Mathieu-de-Tréviers, near Lodève.[4] Their actions, in these hard times and in the eyes of an entire sympathetic population, represented a legitimate advance deduction.

This sporadic violence suggests the breadth of an insidious domination from which no one could entirely escape, a shared destiny that attributes the porcatier's power to a realm out of reach to ordinary men. His wealth and ease seem the manifestation of a force, an ability, a somewhat supernatural *gift* made apparent by his allure and his fluency of speech.

Cavaillé, from Arrigas, the most famous merchant of the Viganais Cévennes, was nicknamed Polit Pòrc, "pretty pig."

> We named him that because at the fair, when he called to clients, he would catch you a pig [gesture] and he'd say, "Ten! Qu'un polit pòrc, qu'un polit pòrc, as pas jamai vist un polit pòrc atal!" [Look, here! What a pretty pig, what a pretty pig, you've never seen such a pretty pig]. And polit pòrc this, and polit pòrc that. So the name stuck.

But doesn't every porcatier fit this picture? Their physical features are consistent: they are tall and powerful, with a big head of hair, a booming voice, and, most of all, they are distinguished by certain qualities other than their immediate signs of wealth. First, their red belts, the *taiòla*, which they persist in wearing, even though other men abandoned them after 1914. "Cintat de roge coma un porcatier," red-belted like a pig merchant, they would say in the Carcassès; the leather belt swollen with all the money earned is often also fawn- or flame-colored. In the market of Castelnaudary they called the porcatier Còfa Roja, "red beret," because he wore this distinctive sign.[5] "They had red cheeks, the porcatiers, they were chubby-cheeked." These red men also mark their piglets with reddle, a blood-red powder, or rub them with vinegar to make them more lively. This scarlet sign is always impressive and imposes grudging respect, for its source is also deep, *natural*: "Avián la sanc, they had the blood, those porcatiers." This bright blood demonstrates a vigor, a power, a virility that is illustrated by their accessory: a porcatier's stick. Every man who heads for the fair equips himself with a homemade "walking" stick, usually fashioned out of boxwood, but the porcatier's instrument is of an entirely different nature: "It wasn't a stick! A stake! A pilgrim's staff, my friend! A piece of wild bramble that would have killed a lamb in a single blow." Along with this club the porcatier possesses either a kind of flexible stick or a bull's pizzle, a *nèrvi*—quite explicitly, a rod.

Thus strongly and visibly sexed, the porcatiers—who are all more or less skirt chasers—held an attraction for the women of the area. When they made the house rounds, after the fair, to deliver the pig that had been reserved or to present a litter of piglets, "they arranged to appear while the men were out. They preferred to see the women alone." In the region of Ambert, in about 1930, Bouradagné, the main porcatier, was always wearing "a velour overcoat and breeches" and leather boots; he "carried his frizzy head above the crowd" and was endowed with a huge purse, "said to be capable of holding enough to buy all the pigs in the region in one day." He offered credit but deducted both 5 percent interest and a heavy commission. He dealt as much in women as in pigs, seducing the inn servants and later prostituting them in Paris and Lyon. One night, around Saint Martin's Day, the brother and boyfriend of Anna, one of his victims, waited for him and bled him: the first cut of the knife pierced his tongue, the second cut his throat.

> We soon learned of the assassination of Bouradagné on the road to Bordes, at the intersection of the path leading to Veyrat. Everyone had a clear vision of the body of this respectable merchant, lying on the ground, staring at the sky with his dead eyes. We could picture the blood that, following the slanted line of the steepest slope, had flowed all the way to the ditch, getting lost in the dried grass sprinkled with tufts of new growth.[6]

This scene completes the correspondence between the porcatier and the pig. Similarly, Pomarèdes the bandit, at the moment his death sentence was pronounced, murmured for the benefit of the porcatier who betrayed him: "Cambachou, Cambachou se t'aviái salat m'auriás pas dessalat," Ham, Ham, if I had salted you, you wouldn't have unsalted me. They're all pigs, to be bled or salted, or rather, as long as they're alive, strong "whole" boars. In about 1880 "a well-known pig merchant from the middle of Nivernais was nicknamed *Vîhou*, a word that, along with others—*vrat, vîrou, voret, voué*—designates the male pig, the one that presides over an entire section of sows at the breeding grounds.[7] Isn't the Cevenol Polit Pòrc, so persuasive at the fair, just another pretty pig himself?

From this point of view the obscure qualities of the porcatier are illuminated. While the bulk of his social power is based on his control over the economic cycle of the pig, his relationship to the animals is considered more intimate. For, to present them for sale in the region, it is appropriate to have the source of life and strength "in the blood," and this display of a vigorous sexuality suggests that the porcatier is presenting his own offspring, all cozy and warm in the straw, sheathed in thick linen. A Picard witticism plays on this underlying relationship. At the pig market a difficult farmer keeps speaking ill of the young pigs, who are either too fat or too small:

During the discussion, which the merchant was prolonging on purpose, passersby stopped to listen or to put in a word. When the seller considered that he had a large enough audience and that the time had come to make an impression, he said in a loud, clear voice to the buyer: "Since none of the pigs here is to your liking, I can see only one way of giving you satisfaction—I am going to fetch their mother. You'll have her yourself and can then produce the products you desire."[8]

The domination of this "red man" is also considered an effect of his nature: he is gifted with the genetic power of boars. The entry of the piglet into the home, which raises it without having given birth to it, is thus preceded by the laborious process of "bringing it into the world," which occurs within the bounds of the relationship between the porcatier and the animal. All the characteristics that define this relationship illustrate the status of these two beings, their deep-seated singularity. More than any other merchandise, the pig is first a hyperbolic symbol of value. The porcatier, who handles both the animals and the money, bases his power on the circulation of these rare and necessary items. If possible, he gives himself complete mastery over the movement of these "currencies"; the pig is thus the source of his power. It is apparent then that the bond between the animal and the man is of the most intimate sort. They resemble one another to such an extent that the metaphor joining them includes even a suspicion of paternity, casting a disturbing light on the origin of pigs as well as on the nature of the merchants (illus. 2).

In the region of Sault the porcatier's brutality, his cruel violence, often elicits a comparison with animals: "They fight like wolves." "In business they were like wolves, they wouldn't have recognized their own fathers." But this bestiary quickly expands without losing its coherence. In Franche-Comté "the person who sells little pigs is called *guillenier*. The word probably comes from the old French *guiller* (to cheat, to dupe) and from *guilleur* (deceitful, swindling, person of bad faith)." In Catalan today the *guilla* is the fox, the trickster par excellence, the seductive fancy talker. One of the porcatiers in the region of Sault was nicknamed La Loira, "the otter," a strange animal that lives between solid earth and rivers, that navigates between two worlds.[9] And this physical oddity has a moral dimension:

The only ones who came from Galinagues were slick traders and merchants that were famous at the fairs—swindlers. Moreover, "nothing good ever comes from beyond the hill of Jean Blanc," and the village is back there! "De Galhinagues que de canalhas!" [From Galinagues only riff-raff!] They also called it "la crassa dal casset," the bottom of the ladle. When Our Lord baptized the region of Sault, he had only one ladel of holy water left. That's why the country is rough. So he started by putting a little on Belcaire: "You will be named Belcaire, you Roquefeuil, you Espezel!" Next he arrived on this plateau: "You Rodome, you Aunat, Mauby, Fontanes, Compagna." When he arrived at Galinagues there was no holy water left in the ladel! So he scraped the bottom and said, "Galinagues, la crassa dal casset."

This original myth, which turns the region of Sault into the last land visited by Christ, also establishes the classification of its inhabitants. Those from Galinagues, money and animal traffickers, are situated at the bottom of the hierarchy of professions and men. But, most of all, like the peasants of Eboli, in Lucania, another place where Christ is alleged to have stopped, they have a reputation for having been poorly baptized, they are not entirely Christians. And sometimes, as in Gascogny, the savagery of the pig merchant bears a name and a face: he becomes *the Jew*, the stranger within. A well-known proverb in the region of Sault, and throughout Languedoc—"D'un porcatier et d'un pòrc se conèis qu'a la mòrt" (You only know a pig merchant and a pig at their death)—expands its scope as follows:

Dou juiu et dou porc
Saben pas so qu'a ou bente
Que ne sie mort.

[Of the Jew and the pig
You only know their guts
At their death.]

For, in Christian societies, the animal trade even more than the trafficking of money was left to the Jew. He became the emblematic figure of the rapacious usurer, the one Dante has appear in his Hell, bowing under the weight of the purse that hangs from his neck, a purse sometimes blood-red with a sow drawn in its center.[10] By way of money and its handling an analogy is thus established between the Jew and the porcatier as well as between the Jew and the pig itself—a relationship we shall examine more closely later on. For now let us stick to the pig alone. A doubt that only death will dissipate now hangs over its "nature." What means do men possess, during its lifetime, to ward off this uncertainty?

The Place of the Tongue Examiner

Prop open his mouth with all your strength;
Insert the extender from jaw to jaw;
Pull out his tongue to its utmost length,
And, butcher-fashion, inspect his maw,
And whilst his gape is so broad and fine,
See if he's not
The symptoms got
Which show that he's nought but a measly swine.

—ARISTOPHANES, The Knights

At the marketplace the pig merchant was not all-powerful. For a long time he had an attendant by his side, a man precise in his actions, who, with a gesture and a word, would really close the sale:

> Then, when a price had been set, before paying, there was a guy with a little wand like my cane who looked to see that the pigs didn't have white pimples on the backs of their tongues. They called that "measled." This guy went up to the pig, stuck his stick in its mouth, knocked it down, and with the stick he went like this [gesture of pulling a crowbar]. He opened the jaws, pulled a rag from his pocket, pulled the tongue out hard, like this, and looked. Then he said: "Le pòdes crompar, aquel pòrc es pas ladre," You can buy it, this pig is not measled.[11] These guys, you see, were in cahoots with the porcatier. The porcatier would say to him, "I'll make it worth your while." He would buy him a drink afterward—that's how they worked together. That guy was always with the pig dealer at the fairs.

The castrator from Cévennes who is talking and imitating the gesture saw pigs having their tongues checked until the late 1930s at the fair of Valleraugue, at the limit of the region where the technique and its practitioner had continued until then to flourish. For, except for Central Provence, from Limousin to Cévennes the pig tongue examination faded from view everywhere—sometimes as early as the beginning of the nineteenth century—and its memory vanished.[12] In the Pyrenees, Bigorre maintained the custom longer (illus. 3); in the region of Sault a single text mentions it, before 1914: "The *tombaire* gets involved during the sale of the little pigs. He makes himself available to buyers to examine the tongues of the young pigs for sale and to verify whether or not they have symptoms of measles."[13]

The last tongue examiners meant the end of a flourishing corporation, many traces of which have been found since the fourteenth century. By turns proscribed and officially recognized, they checked the pigs at the markets and verified their good health. In the eighteenth century it was even a highly desirable position, and certain guarantees were demanded of the candidate regarding "his life, morals, abilities, Catholic, apostolic, and Roman religion," but the Revolution, by abolishing masters and corporations, caused the profession to lose its official status, hence its slow decline until the 1930s.[14] The practice must nonetheless have been central, since the first veterinarians, in the Viganais Cévennes, still had to check pigs' tongues at the fairs, performing the same actions as their venerable predecessors, reassuring buyers by confirming the good health of the piglets. But what is the tongue examiner looking for in the back of the pig's mouth?

As the words indicate, the man "looks" (*regardar*), "examines" (*examinar*). Sometimes he is called *espichaire*, the one who attentively scrutinizes to establish a diagnostic. The afflictions he detects all reside in the mouth and throat of the animal, which is where he uncovers the growths: the *ta*, the *morèja*, the *grosèlha*, the currant.[15] Sometimes the pig also has "strings in its throat" that are suffocating it, and the tongue examiner's diagnosis is then categorical: "A la sedada," he has the bristle sickness, hairs in its mouth. Whether real or imaginary, still present or an affliction of the past, the defect is anchored in a representation of the porcine body that attributes a wild, festering, and disorderly nature to its most secret recesses. The pig, as we know, "is born with all its teeth . . . two lateral corner teeth or incisors in the rear jaw, two incisive irregular teeth in the fore, four hooked tusks, eight molars, four in each jaw. The tusks are commonly called *wolf's teeth*."[16] It is also up to the tongue examiner to discover these teeth and remove them, but the bulk of his job consists in detecting a more troublesome ill, signs of which appear on the tongue—hence the most common name for this tongue (*langue*) specialist: *langueyeur, lengaire, lenguechaire*, and even *linguiste*.

> He held them with his knee, he didn't need any help! And he pulled out
> their tongues, he scraped them to see, because they have so-called white
> spots. He looked and said: "Es pas ladre." Well, now it no longer exists,
> they don't look at that anymore, but at the time it was done. You could

eat them that way. You kept them, we had kept three or four of them at
the house to kill. You had to cook the meat a little longer but I don't
know if there was really anything. . . . I think it was . . . that it was all a
. . . [gesture in the air].

The story comes up against the indefinable. Yet the etiology of pig
measles was precisely described as early as the late eighteenth century.
It is a disease caused by worms: tapeworm cycsticerus settle in and
develop in the muscular tissue of the pig, forming spots under the
tongue that are sensitive to the touch. While under the ancien régime
contaminated pigs had to be marked by a rip in the ear, or even totally
cut up and discarded, it was admitted early on that a long cooking time
killed the parasites. The fear nonetheless subsisted. Every time a pig
was slaughtered, someone would comment: "Mas que siague pas
ladre!" May it not be measled![17] For *ladrerie* was more than an illness, it
was a social stigma, and the persistence of the fear it inspired resulted
from the status the old word evoked: a *ladre* was also a leper. Beneath
the measled pig lay the specter of ancient human leprosy.

This disease, which was already feared in Mediterranean antiquity
and the High Middle Ages, resurfaced in the Christian West from
the twelfth to the fourteenth centuries, triggering uniformly harsh
defenses everywhere. The leper had be denounced and his body
closely scrutinized by doctors, barbers, or "brothers" who were
experts in the art of reading the signs. He was then solemnly excluded
by the Church from the community of men; in the course of a ritual
that gradually became identified with the service for the dead, the
leper was sometimes even lain in a grave. Thus "separated," the leper
wore the symbols of his difference: a dark cape, a wide brimmed hat,
a pilgrim's stick, and an eta patch or, in Aquitaine, a red crest identifying him as a pariah.[18] He might be shut up—as in northern France
or in large cities—a stone's throw away, behind the high walls of a
maladrerie, from which he could leave only at fixed hours. But in the
South and in Brittany hamlets made up of small cottages, *les bordes*,
set apart on the edge of villages, housed the lepers. They lived from
their fields, gardens, and flocks and also worked with wood and
hemp: the Britons tended to be rope makers, the Gascons carpenters.
When they left to take up collections, their relationships with others
were strictly regulated: clappers or rattles announced their arrival;
they could touch neither bread nor meat, nor drink directly from the

fountains. They always wore shoes on the roads and breathed in the other direction when passing another person.

After the fourteenth century the illness declined and the quarantine stations emptied out. The doctors of the sixteenth century—such as Larent Joubert and Ambrois Paré—were the last to examine lepers. Yet the fear and stigma persisted, and until the eighteenth century, at least, the *cagots* and *crestians* of Aquitaine, the *caquins* of Brittany, the *cacous* of the Bourbonnais, all considered distant descendants of the lepers, still lived on the margins, like the survivors of an extinct race. What relationship can be established between the measled pig and this cursed group?

Whereas the two diseases are now recognized as being entirely unrelated, until the sixteenth century, at least, medicine argued that they were the same. The word *ladre*—after Lazarus, the leper of the Gospels—was applied to them both, and so were its synonyms, the old French *mesel* and the Gascon *gafet*. Pork had a reputation for being easily contaminated, which is why recognized lepers were forbidden to occupy any position that involved handling it: butchers, charcutiers, and especially pastrycooks were pursued by the law—in Bordeaux even until 1520—for ladrerie or *cagoterie*. In addition, overconsumption of pork was thought to communicate the ill, so much did the ever abundant flesh heat up and spoil: "The frequent habit of eating pork brings on measles," affirmed Bouchet in 1592, in one of his *Serées*. In the mid-eighteenth century the *Encyclopédie* still echoed this belief, which, according to Plutarch, explained why the Jews banished pork from their tables.[19] But, most of all, for medieval medicine, one of the signs of ladrerie were "spots under the tongue, under the eyelids, and behind the ears," thus "the leprous tubercle was long confused by the people with the measled spots of the porcine race." When, in about 1845, Françisque Michel traveled from one Pyrenean valley to the next in search of the memory of cagots, he was told, near Argelès, in Bigorre, that "they had ears without lobes and stinking breath, that they had little spots under their skin similar to those of measled pigs." And "it is not unusual," in this valley, "when old women argue with someone alleged to be a cagot, to see them stick out their tongues or show the backs of their ears where it was believed the leprous spots were apparent." This childish gesture of defiance—practiced even by the Romans—thus finds its roots: the pockmarked tongue gives the leper away.[20]

Few such explicit relationships remain: "I never heard *esser ladre* said of people, I never heard of a sickness called *ladre . . . rie*, if one can say that." Only the adjective and fear remain, but they are linked to other words, gestures, and representations that place the pig and its seller—who, as we have seen, form a solidary unit—"at a distance." The allusion to the merchant's possible paternity fits with the etiology of the leper, who is associated with debauchery, incest, and having relations with a menstruating woman. The zesty figure of the porcatier, his active sexuality, the reddle that marks him and with which he marks his animals, evoke the old symptoms and stigmata. He is also the most ladre of men in another of its meanings; he avidly accumulates money. Similarly, his manner of treating the piglet, which is always castrated, squeezed from the time it is received in a narrow cage that in the Montagne Noire is also called the *bòrda*, a separate hut that is a miniature version of the human *ostal*, is reminiscent of the other enclosure, the other segregation. But it is the "visit" of the pig tongue examiner that confirms the permanence of the fear, sometimes until the twentieth century. The pig has long assumed the former curse of the lepers, reinforcing its original outsider status. When he names, confronts, and exorcizes it, it is this curse that the tongue examiner must dispel.

> Fonsagrives, who can be easily recognized by his red hat, which served as his emblem, performed his duties joyfully: taking off his coat, rolling up his sleeves to his elbows, he laid low pigs, sows, piglets, and boars, both indigenous and exotic, with the help of a holly stick. Then he examined the tongues, eyes, and snouts of these animals, which, before concluding the deal, owners and animal traders ritually subjected to his decisive arbitration. A circle formed around him. His sallies were successful. Bombastic and bantering, he performed and pontificated.[21]

Enlightened opinion had it that the tongue examiner was powerless to treat the ills he recognized: "He knew how to diagnose but he didn't know how to heal." Yet, we find him at work, here and there. At the fairground he trims growths, extracts wolf's teeth, and, once the mouth's passage has been liberated, rings the pig. In the days when pigs grazed in pastures, and in the breeding areas where free-running pigs were long the rule, this precaution protected the cultivated land and prevented the animal from burrowing. The practice therefore should have disappeared when the piglet was enclosed in a pigsty. It continued nonetheless and was justified by talk about the animal's savagery:

> We put rings on the pigs. It's a piece of iron, it has a hook and it's pointed. And with that, when you give it a kick or a swipe of a stick, it

pricks them and they move. But it was also so that they wouldn't turn over the dung, because they turn everything over just like the wild boars, and in the old piggeries, when you went in with the pail, they knocked everything in the air, the doors too, even when they were made of metal, whereas when they had these rings they were calm.

These interventions thus introduced domestic restraint; the tongue examiner was required to bridle the excessive vitality, to tame the vigor the piglet was just beginning to demonstrate. He also knew what to do when faced with measles: with his handkerchief and nails he scrapes the mucous membrane and "pops the blisters"; sometimes, with the complicity of the merchant, he makes the pig healthier looking. To heal the infected animal he also knew how to bleed it under the tongue and rub it with salt the way the breeding manuals recommended.[22]

But the essence of his role was not limited to these specific, immediately effective gestures. What the tongue examiner did was referred to as "felling" the pig, which is why he was often called *lo tombaire*, the feller. To open the pig's mouth was a real feat, in everyone's opinion, which transfigured his actions in the eyes of witnesses: "He laid a pig down on the ground and plunged his stick in its mouth." Others speak of his riding it, even reversing the order of sequence. The man "lays the animal low," mounts it, then opens its mouth to inspect the tongue. An epic struggle. It is true that these two spectators dramatize the episode considerably. The animal "cries like a pig being slaughtered," the examined piglets exhaust themselves in long howls "as if they were being bled," ending in true death rattles.[23]

The tongue examiner presents a surprising strong-man image in the face of the animal. "He's a hefty guy, as they say today, he walks around the pig market carrying a strong iron-shod stick under his arm"; "He was built like Hercules, wearing leather boots, a rag tucked in his belt, and a solid club with a strap to keep it on his wrist." Depending on the description, his short stick becomes a fearsome weapon, his clothes a fighter's getup combining several emblems. First, the boots: "Lourgiagas—his real name was Ribart—he was the strongest, he had all-leather boots with big stitching on top, copper inlay, and hooks down the side. They were pure pigskin! The shoemaker of Valleraugue had made them for him special." Then the hat "in black felt, with wide brims like the cowboys on television or rather like that gentleman who sings . . . a big black hat." Finally the red scarf or handkerchief that he tied around his neck and that stood out against his dark clothes, or sometimes a belt that cut a red stripe across his body or some big headgear that, red as well, "served as a sign."

These various elements are the tongue examiner's armor; they are as indispensable to identifying his profession as to his work on the fairgrounds, which is where he shows his stuff. He operates in the middle of a circle of entranced onlookers; as in the theater, the children are in the first row, hanging on his every gesture. Even if the man is highly animated, the seriousness of the stakes sends a hush through the arena, for it appears that this elaborate production aims to do more than recognize a few blisters, to detect some oral anomaly. The pig that is so powerfully and expertly taken in hand experiences a kind of death. He is felled with one blow, cries for a long time, "agonizes" while his victor mounts and displays him. And this victor is as noisy as the pig, "shouting, laughing, grumbling, cursing." He plays on words, playing with his own tongue while unceremoniously working over the animal's: "He'd pull out its tongue and look at it from every direction." The man speechifies, the word that designates him even coming to mean "big talker," "incessant chatterer."[24] Then, suddenly, it's back on its feet, shaking its head, disoriented, reborn amid the laughter and commotion. The examiner's word paves the way for this new existence, but his voice changes tones, emerging forcefully, like a judgment, a sacramental statement: "Es pas ladre!" "He's not measled!" or "Porc sens ladras, sens tara e des plus sans!" or simply: "Es san coma de ferre!" "He's healthy as iron!" This loud metallic voice has the power to restore life.

These ritual dimensions situate the tongue examiner's actions in the line of all the games—such as that of the carnival bear—in which the animal dies and is reborn at the end of simulated combat and following regenerative gestures and words. For the pig this rebirth comes on the heels of an actual cure, which sometimes presupposes that the visible marks of its savagery are erased but always raises the terrible specter of measles or leprosy, based, as we have seen, on the animal's troubling origins. More than a sickly verminous infestation, which is entirely improbable in a suckling pig, the tongue examiner wards off the original evil. Thus life must be restored to this being that, as the habitual carrier of the leprous curse, is dead to the world.

The ritual of tongue examining, which slaughters and then resuscitates, leads the pig on a journey that is the opposite of the leper's journey from life to death. This intervention is necessary to diminish the effects of the pig's fundamental foreignness. The tongue examiner sometimes appears as an adjunct to the porcatier, but his actions—at the expense of the buyer—annul or at least contradict the latter's pernicious influence. Red man against red man, such is the antagonistic relationship of these two roles. One marks the pig with his overly vital and perhaps contaminated blood, the other is strong enough to counteract these stigmas; one is a feared potentate, the other a familiar. Together they are the first intermediaries who "do" the pig and lead it to the threshold of its new life.

But this adoption occurs only after the passage of the final red man, the most unusual, the most skilled, the most nomadic of the three. After the purchase of the piglets, the castrator comes in to operate.

Seasons of the Castrator

To castrate pigs, here, it was Souillet de Lasalle who came because it's a real operation, especially for the sows. The person who spays them is a true specialist. I didn't see him at work often but I know that they cut in with a penknife, they made a knot on the *pocelhièira*, then they put it back inside and took three or four stitches; they sewed it up with a little white thread. It wasn't like for lambs, which everyone knew how to do. The best one for a long time, here, was Pagès. He castrated lambs and steers the same way. With them he crushed the nerve with a special hammer that was nice and smooth, just for this purpose. He used a little hammer to hit the fold, and underneath he put a little triangular plank made of oak, the *soquet*. Later, Auguste also learned to castrate the pigs, and then to kill them, because these guys stopped coming. When the last Valleraugue died no one came here anymore and someone else had to do it.

A Cevenol sheep breeder, providing in this rapid synthesis an overview of the technical and social aspects of castration, thus introduces us to the heart of the problem for pigs. He places their castration at the core of a specialty that is graduated according to increasing levels of difficulty, the spaying of sows being at the summit of this hierarchy. The *castraire* or *sanaire* of pigs is therefore discussed with great respect: "He was a little surgeon" who performed a "real operation."

Yet, while the competency of this specialist is emphasized, doubts are raised as to the effectiveness of his actions: "Sometimes we thought they were castrated males and then, when we killed them . . . " or "We didn't want females because even when they were spayed you had surprises!" Nonetheless, the castrator himself is only very rarely doubted and the causes for what we shall call, for the moment, the "failure" of the castration, tended to be sought among the pigs. Their freakish natures are blamed for certain confusions. Indeed, is it not the only animal whose sex is said to be difficult to identify while it is still a suckling? This argument regarding its indetermination and resistance to the neutering operation may seem, at first glance, irrational from the mouths of breeders, for whom recognizing the sex of an animal is, in principle, a habitual and simple task. It therefore seemed necessary for us to evaluate the basis for this, convinced as we were that it had to be anchored in an interpretation of their true morphology. But what anatomical properties, what common aberrations of physiology are the basis for this ill-defined identity? Is it not to this physiology that the castrator applies his knowledge and know-how, the effects of which apparently go well beyond an ordinary sterilization?

Starting with males, the veterinarian of the region of Sault, in practice since 1950, was the first to give real weight to those arguments regarding the uncertain sex of pigs.

> Among pigs the testicles descend, at the approach of birth, from the loins to the inguinal ring. But it is common for them not to descend completely, in which case the pigs are said to be "cryptorchidous." If you can't get these testicles to come out of the abdominal cavity, if they remain against the kidneys (with which they can be confused, since they are glands of the same texture), the meat isn't good. I remember a farm, in Rodome, where there was a sow that produced only cryptorchidous or monorchodous pigs, with a single testicle out.

All veterinary treatises emphasize this exceptional propensity and Gourdon, a nineteenth-century Toulousian doctor, confirms that the porcine species "offers very frequent examples of this anomaly" identified by the breeders. *Rile*, *pif*, or *hagard* in French patois, *sislce* or *rangolh* in the Pyreneen dialects, *vert* in Dauphiné, are names that designate the animal affected with this characteristic.[25] Thus the castrator first comes to identify the sex of the animal or to detect the anomaly and point out misdiagnoses. This necessity for a *recognition* is in keeping with an operation that always bares the testicles—two sides of the scrotum are cut—and then roots them out to be removed. The piglet must be truly clipped, and the verbs *talhar, copar* refer precisely to this manner of operating.[26]

While the castrator cuts—determining the sex and trimming it—while he detects aberrations, he is also the one who heals them. One such aberration, in particular, requires his services: the inguinal hernia very common to the piglet. Here, again, its anatomical structure predisposes it to this problem, which nonetheless affects only a limited number of males, whereas the most feared instability affects all females and requires complete mastery on the part of the castrator:

> I saw Cazals neuter a sow once at Cambon's. He had bought a pig and it was a sow and this sow wasn't coming along, it was *lhadre* [measled], and every month—oh, the poor thing—it got into a state! They said to themselves: "We have to neuter her or she won't grow." In one day she lost what she gained in a month. They brought in En Cazals and he castrated her (*la sanèc*). He opened her tummy. He went looking for the uterus and the ovaries. And, as he went along, he explained to us: "These are the ovaries, you can't mess with them, you have to know what you're doing" [loud voice]. He disinfected her and sewed her back up and then this sow was fine.

The operation is abundantly and almost scientifically commented upon by the last castrator of the plateau of Sault, yet usually the crucial moment escapes witnesses. The man cuts only one side and digs in the belly, though it's not clear what he is taking out. "With his fingers he went looking for the entrails there; he cut with the knife," because it is preferable to detach a little flesh for the intervention to be obvious and credible. But this is not what's essential, and one operator—a specialist in the tying of tubes—clearly defends what makes his art valued: an effortless and rapid gesture performed in an instant.

> You fell her and, with a razor no bigger than that, pop! tac! it's done! It's a little white thingamajig you have to catch [gesture: hooked pinky]. You pull it, you squeeze it with a string, make just a little knot, cut the thread, and put it back. You have a threaded needle ready, you make a stitch or two, and that's it. Since it's nice and tight, nothing works anymore, it doesn't circulate any more, it's over, she can be with the male as much as she wants.

The men explain in hushed voices: "Sows are like women, they're the same, they get in their mood every month, it stays with them seven or eight days and then it goes away." This similarity itself makes any overt demonstration that causes trouble in the house intolerable. One hardly dares mention the signs, modesty holds back the words: "Sows, when they're in heat, they're . . . you know it by . . . " Others speak of the swelling and the aggressive redness of their "nature." Moreover, these "times," far from following the lunar rhythm harmoniously, last too long and are repeated too quickly: "Every two weeks, she got in her mood! Then, she didn't eat and lost everything she'd gained, it turned red on her and it lasted."

Only motherhood lessens this appetite, which frustration amplifies to the point of making the sow the most insatiable of females: "Often I had two pigs, a male and a sow, and boy, even if the male was castrated, she went with him!" The castrator is thus awaited or, in the most serious cases, called in to exorcize this fever. It's a risky business:

> Sometimes something happens: for example, with me, I go out to neuter, I have one here, I have one in Espèries, I have one in Souillas, but something might happen and you'll wait for me a day or two with your sow who is starting to go into heat. I cut her, it doesn't hurt, but it doesn't help. I do like I told you but her "nature," what we call her "nature," stays the same.

When the sow has already farrowed, it's even worse, the operation is then totally impossible; the castrator reveals his techniques to us like precious secrets:

> Those fat ones, you can't spay them, they have an enormous *pocelhièira*. So what I do [hushed voice] is I give them some lead. Yes, lead, hunting lead. Now that! That's good stuff! The lead goes into the ovaries and it doesn't come out, they don't work and, cold as it is, they don't go into heat anymore. . . . Lead, yes, ten, eight, it doesn't matter.

The females demonstrate, by opposition, the marvelous effects expected of castration. In Piemontais and Swiss French dialects to castrate is called *regulare*, "to regulate," while in western France *affranchir*, to liberate, is the common term; the words suggest that the castrated animal is forever pacified, that it escapes the turbulence of its nature. Moreover, if the castration is successful it erases the traces of sexual appetite while unifying the appearance and taste of the flesh. For the flesh of the incomplete—monorchidous or cryptorchidous—male is as worthless as that of the unneutered adult female; the hot meat is rotten, it's even compared to measled meat. Thus the castrator's final touch completes the tongue examiner's cure. He purifies the animal, makes it "healthy as iron," as cold and stable as metal. To castrate is thus said *sanar*, "to cure." Despite appearances, the castrator doesn't mutilate, he trims only to allow for harmonious growth. He *arranges, fixes*. "Once the pigs are neutered, they grow better, faster."[27]

To be the "master of pigs" a man must possess a good knowledge of bodily rhythms and seasons, anatomical competency, and a fast and steady hand. But his efficacy does not depend on these techniques alone; to be up to the task he must play the part of an unusual character both in his hometown and in those towns through which he passes. His specialized know-how corresponds to a singular social image.

The Man Who Passes Through

When, in his only surviving poem, Raimon d'Avignon, a thirteenth-century troubador, enumerates all the trades that destiny has enjoined upon him, he proclaims that he was even a castrator of pigs. He has not thereby attained the depths of ignominy but, no doubt, the height of itinerancy, for the castrator is, by far, the most mobile of the red men. Indeed, while he still practices in the square, he is neither the familiar bleeder who often examines tongues at the fair nor the merchant who comes from afar but whose social position and origin is known. The castrator is not an intermediary between the village and the foreign world; rather, he belongs to the latter.

Yet it should not be supposed that this foreignness puts him in the same category as beggars, idlers, and vagabonds, whose scrounging is always feared. The corporation of castrators is well known and respected, the long distances they have traveled guarantee their power. In Angoumois, in upper Languedoc, and in Auvergne the common name for the castrator is often Le Béarnais, *lo biarnès*; this professional nickname is reminiscent of the caste that ruled over France and Spain for centuries. With them we are encountering the nobility of castrators.[28] They are, first of all, the most itinerant of all and their journeys have a long history. In 1640 Pierre de Marca, describing the economy of the upper valleys of Béarn, emphasized that the infertility of the land and the inequality of inheritances dictated a seasonal emigration into Spain and Portugal. The migrants remained there six or seven months, from the end of February until Saint Martin's Day, while the women cultivated the fields and the other men of the family tended the flock. Even in the nineteenth century these castrators returned from Spain with double sacks full of gold—the only payment accepted—and their homes in the village were among the most imposing. But this wealth is the opposite in every way of that of the porcatier. First of all, it is collective and shared. It never depends on direct oppression or local domination. During their rounds money is lent and parcels of land are bought and sold, as evidenced by notarized records.

The castrator is thus an honorable practitioner; his proceeds are based on his knowledge. Moreover, he operates on his way out and collects only on his way back, if the operation is successful. The home that provides him with lodgings retains only enough for room and board. When the animal is "failed," or suffers an infection, the castrator not only receives nothing but must pay damages. If he attempts to evade this obligation, the law is informed of the matter. In the Hautes Pyrenees justices of the peace were forced to settle several such conflicts: in Vic-Bigorre, on August 5, 1814, "a castrator having sewn a bowel to the skin was condemned to pay for the animal [a sow no doubt] that died from this operation"; on October 3, 1817, another practitioner was similarly condemned. This time the sow passed away suddenly, during the operation.[29]

There is no faking being a castrator, the profession is always a family affair and three generations are considered necessary to master it fully. This rule is widespread; in Les Pouilles, according to Carlo Levi, pig castrators are rare, for "it is a very difficult art that is transmitted from father to son. The one I saw was a famous *sanaporcelle*, the son and grandson of *sanaporcelle*, and he went from village to village, twice a year, to perform his work. He was famous for his skill: it was rare for an animal he operated on to die."[30] Under the governance of his elders the young castrator undergoes a long apprenticeship, both practical and philosophical.

Each practitioner, of course, possesses his own personal tricks, knacks, or incantations that complete the essential gestures and ensure the success of the operation, but the *secret*, which the last castrator of the region of Sault, according to his own words, refused to reveal to the veterinarian, is so much connected to the profession we should no doubt seek its expression in the castration itself and look to the tools and emblems that commonly distinguish the castrator for the true instruments of his power.

In truth, his tools have nothing in common with the baroque panoply of the surgeon of yore. Several inventories of their cases reveal simply "a selection of knives, some string, needles, one or two lancets." But, in addition to these necessary materials, the equipment also includes "a red and black leather double sack, a boxwood whistle, a pistol." Thus two

2. Castrator's fleam, in B. Boyer,
La Fricassée (Poitiers, 1981).

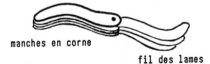

manches en corne

fil des lames

satchels—the case and the double sack—contain two sets of objects: the instruments directly associated with the castration, on the one hand, and, on the other, those required by the itinerant situation: a weapon for defense and a whistle to announce one's arrival. This signal seems to be associated so closely with the personage that one is enough to evoke the other: "Even today, when you hear a sound like that—wheee!—very shrill," a Catalan witness relates, "you immediately think *el xiulet del sanaire*, the castrator's whistle." Every description—even the briefest descriptions—mention it. In Franche-Comté "the castrator came to the villages after the fairs and whistled to let people know he was passing through"; in Champagne, "in Rachecourt, in the past, several days after the fairs, the 'cutter' passed, walking through the village on foot. He alerted people to his arrival with a whistle that had several tones."[31] The last castrator of the region of Sault also had his *fiulet*. His description alone enlightens us as to the nature of the instrument: it was not a mere whistle with a single sound but rather a panpipe (illus. 4).

It is at first glance surprising to see this instrument—associated since Mediterranean antiquity with the world of shepherds and goatherds—in the hands of the castrator, being employed as a professional emblem. In fact, several petty tradesmen may use it as a signal, but they too—the Auvergnat coppersmith, the Catalan sieve merchant, or the seller of Provençal flutes—are also "little surgeons," and it is primarily in this capacity that they carry an emblem clearly connected with that of the castrator of pigs. If further evidence is needed, the words that designate the instrument itself, in the dialects of France, Spain, and Portugal, recall this fundamental relationship. Yet the lexicon of the panpipe is at first approach not very explicit. In Catalan, for example, the terms *flaüta de Pan* and *siringa* are reserved for learned language and it is more common to find *xiulet, xiulit*, or simply *flaüta*. Similarly, langue d'oc abounds in generic appellations, *fiulet, siulet, flaüta*, which correspond to the French for whistle, flute. But, more often, a circumlocution distinguishes this panpipe: *xiulet de sanaire, flaüta de crestaire*, castrator's whistle or flute. Another lexical series—*crestapoarcs, sanaporcs*—specifies that we are dealing with the pig castrator and even, in Spain, Catalonia, and Italy, with the "sow castrator": *capapuercas, sanatruges, sanaporcelle*. Finally, in these countries, the panpipe is still called a "castrator"—*crestadora, capador*—the name identifying it with the function. Could it be that music plays some role in the operation?

Upon arriving in the village or the hamlet, the castrator blows into his flute, and the sounds he produces identify him immediately: "I

3. The merchant of *cresto pouarcs*, in P. Letuaire, *Notes et dessins de
la vie toulousaine* (1796–1884).

would still recognize him today!" we have often been told. According
to Casto Sampedro, who, in about 1940, scrupulously noted eighteen
capadores tunes in Galicia, the profession has its own types of music,
different from those of other itinerants, and passes them down by tradition.[32] Let us examine them.

The high-pitched tone is the first striking element, a function of
the range of the instrument itself. The smaller the panpipe—and the
castrators contrive to produce flutes that can be held in one hand—
the finer its pipes and the higher the sound. All the Béarnais *shiulet
crestaders* we have seen fit inside a square that rarely surpasses twelve
centimeters per side. Its shrillness therefore facilitated the confusion
between the panpipe and the whistle. Yet the castrator plays his flute
as a musician would, his lips producing "an attractive melody with
short repeated themes in rapid tempo and in a high-pitched register"
that is evocative, based on the twenty or so scores available to us, of
true dance rhythms.

GENERIC TERM	SPECIFIC TERM	DETERMINANTS					
"flute" or "whistle"	*"panpipes"*	*"castrator's flute (or whistle)"*	*"castrator whistle"*	*"castrator" (instrument, masc.)*	*"castrator" (instrument, fem.)*	*"pig castrator"*	*"sow castrator"*
flûtiau, F	festeu, P	xiulet de sanador, C	shiulet crestador	chatrou, D	resta-douro, L	cresto-pouarcs, P	capa-puercas, E
sifflet, F	frestel, F	siblet de cresto-porc, OC	shiulet crestader, G	sanaire, OC, L	capadora, C	sanaporcs, C	castra-puercas, E
fiulet, OC	siringa, C, GA	flahuto de crestaire, L	siblet cresta-dou, OC	capador, E		capa-puercos, E	sanatruges, C
xiulet, C	bufa-canyes, C	siulò de crestayre, G					
musica, L	sonaveus, C	gaita de capador, PO					
	pinta, C	silbato de castrador, GA					
	piharet, G	pito de castrador, GA					
	pihurlèc, G						

The abbreviations correspond to the following languages and dialects: C Catalan, S Spanish, GA Galician, PO Portuguese, F French, OC common langue d'oc, G Gascon, L Languedocian, P Provençal, D Dauphinois (Franco-Provençal).

Some are barely elaborated, one or two measures in rapid succession, in the fioritura style:

Melodic line performed by a pig castrator from Carpentras and notated by the painter Denis Bonnet in 1842.

But the castrators of Pontevedra, in Galicia, sometimes develop more protracted movements.

Galician castrators' tune (Pontevedra, Cobelo, Lamosa), notated by C. Sampedro.

Not content to announce himself by hurling as strident a cry as possible, the castrator performed a *passe-rue* in the village. Doors opened as he passed, children followed in the wake of the seductive panpipe player.

Are pigs equally sensitive to such music? In 1850 an artist from Toulon relates this commonly held belief as he comments on his sketch of the Provençal *cresto-pouarcs*:

> This name applied to individuals who sold panpipes would have seemed ridiculous and incorrect to anyone who didn't know that in addition to their little sideline they specialized in castrating pigs. And people claimed that they used their flute to charm their victims and help them withstand the operation. This is one explanation that was given, but I never had occasion to verify it. Whatever the case, these flute merchants traveled the streets producing melodies with the short pieces of reed that constituted their instrument and they stopped from time to time to shout: "Vaqui lou marchand de cresto-pouarcs!"thereby announcing both their business and their sideline! I also must admit that at certain moments the high notes of their flutes sounded a lot like the cries of the pigs![33]

The harmony between the castrator's music and the porcine sensibility is thus effectively put to use in the castrating operation. The panpipe is thereby elevated to the ranks of those orchestras whose pacifying sounds accompanied the most painful operations until the eighteenth century. As it was most often used to facilitate cutting the bladder and extracting a stone, we might well wonder whether this aristocratic musical surgery was not simply transposing the practice of the castrator.[34]

But this melody, adds Letuaire, culminates on a note so high it almost "sounds like" the cries of the pig. Is the song of the panpipe not playing on this mimicry, captivating the animal by this powerful decoy? We know that the flute was capable of producing a shrill cry, hence one of the Béarnais names for the instrument, *pihurlet* or *piharet*, from *pihet*, to howl. This is the panpipe's *roidʒos* that we hear in *Daphnis et Chloé*, the Greek pastoral. Pigs can't resist it; Pliny the naturalist recounts how stolen pigs jumped from a boat to respond to this voice, while a panpipe was sometimes used to call wild boars during Roman hunting parties.[35]

The shrill sound produced by the panpipe is not just a cry. The pig, which generally grunts—*renar, rondinar*, they say in langue d'oc— reaches this pitch on only two occasions, "quand le sanan e quand le sannan, when it is being castrated and when it is being killed," they say in Languedoc, this minute phonetic variation allowing for the play on words. To imitate the sound of the castrator's panpipe, our witness from Catllar, in Conflent, produces the same "wheee!" he uses to imitate the outburst of the final agony, when the knife has been planted. The cry of the musical instrument, the cry of the pig whose throat has been slit, and the cry of the pig being castrated thus echo one another; in the Audois Pyrenees the language plays on this equivalency. *Arrincar un sisclet* is to let out a piercing whistle, but *sisclar* is also to cry like a pig being bled, and a *siscle* is none other than a male with hidden testicles. By modulating this cry does the panpipe not announce the imminent castration?

As sharp as a blade, more pointed than a needle, as suggested by the Catalan *pinta*—both point and knife—the piercing cry of the panpipe does more than just prefigure the events to come. If we look at the word's lexicon, there is no doubt about it. The flute, *châtreur* or *châtreuse*, operates musically. It emerges from the core of this itinerant surgeon's limited equipment as the essential object. More than a simple accessory or a sign of recognition, it is closely linked to the castration operation. Thus, to become a castrator, to access the secret of the profession, is to learn both the gestures that alter the animal's genitals, the fabrication of the panpipe, and the art of eliciting from it those shrill, stinging, throbbing melodies. One cannot exist without the other, and, ultimately, it may be the music that cuts, "Mes que xiula, capador," he who whistles best is a castrator, affirms the Catalan adage. The scene of the castration will henceforth resonate with the magic that affects both animals and spectators, and each of his actions will better reveal the breadth of the personage and his role.

We find the cry of the animal, which the flute captures and modulates, reproduced in his mouth: "cridar coma un sanaire," to cry like a castrator, says one Languedocian metaphor, along with "cridalhar coma un porc que san(n)an, to cry like a pig being castrated (or bled)." By assuming the vocal power of the animal the castrator also appropriates its vital force, the sexual energy the operation confiscates. *Crestaire*, as the name suggests, designates that which is *acrêté*, pungent or acrid, while the verb *crestar* designates, in Languedoc and in Provence, both castration and the sexual act from the male point of view. The one who *creste* is the one who "covers." The term first applies to the cock who wears his virility in the form of its red crest, which the women cut off along with the testicles when they castrate it. "Red like a castrator" is a common comparison, which Mistral glosses as follows: "Scarlet red; in order to be recognized, professional castrators wear red jackets."[36] We are again confronted with the insignia of the porcatier and the tongue examiner. Like them, the castrator is noted for his bright jacket, belt, or head of hair, but his redness is deeper still. Custom calls for ample libations at the time of the pig's castration. The castrator is often partially paid with a meal and drink upon his arrival and departure. He therefore has a reputation for being a drinker, unlike the porcatier who cold-bloodedly pushes others to drink. The warmth of the castrator shines on his face and sometimes in his hair, a flaming mane that attests to his being intimately marked with red. The sana-porcelle of Les Pouilles is the "redheaded man"; one Breton "gelder" has a red beard; a castrator from Diois, in Dauphiné, is called Red.

Now, redness is not usually positive. The redhead, like the woman of menstruating age, can, for example, spoil the flesh of the pig; his hands are always feverish and, in this case, putrifying.[37] Thus, to ward off the risk to his patients, the red surgeon performs purification rituals at every step of the way. He is careful where he breathes, recites a prayer over his knife, sometimes deposits the testicles he has cut in pure water for a day and a night.[38] All this so that the wound will heal without infection. But the fire that inhabits his body is also a favorable quality. Indeed, the castrator operates on living beasts whose instability is a known fact. It is necessary that the weather be calm and cool, but direct contact with the cold could affect them: either the cold of the metal or the cold of the hand. Thus personal warmth, bolstered by a little drink, makes him better suited to the pigs, ensuring an equal temperature, a necessary warm-bloodedness. And, in return, his constant digging in their bodies fuels his heat.

The castrator thus simultaneously possesses the singularity of each sex or, in any case, cultivates great familiarity with what constitutes their differences. Endowed with his own qualities, he completes the actions of the red men. If the merchant is the "boar" who engenders the piglet, if the tongue examiner, by exorcizing measles, causes the pig to experience a ritual of death and rebirth, the castrator consecrates a kind of bond. So long as it has not been operated upon, the pig is not part of the household, and the passage of the castrator, in fact, has many wedding-like qualities. The village, first alerted by his professional arpeggio, opens its doors; the elders remain on their doorsteps, but, caught up in its enchantement, the others form a train. He leads a procession like the musician of the church festival, like the leader of old-fashioned marriages. He then fixes the animal's genitals and, by the power of his flute, reduces its fantasies, bringing it into unison with the house. But, at the same time, he occasionally borrows one of the tongue examiner's mouth treatments: fitting it with irons, buckling the snout, which in Venetia is designated by the expression "spozare il maïale," to marry the pig, to place the nuptial ring.[39] Finally, the meal that brings closure to this day of castration has, at times, the quality of a ceremony sealing a conjugal union. The castrator attends, just like the matchmaker. The terms designating the two roles sometimes overlap: *adobar* and *arengar*, in Languedocian, mean both to castrate and to arrange an affair, to plot a marriage. More specifically, the *adobaire*, in the region of Foix, is the intermediary in rites of passage, dressing the dead and performing marriages. The rich and varied names for the matchmaker clearly associate him with this world of itinerants: in Savoie he is a *traîne-manteau*, in Lyonnais a *bâton-brûlé*, in Berry a *chien-blanc* or a *tête de loup*. In the north of Gascogny, in several Girondin communes, his quality as a red man is clearly asserted: when a marriage is concluded the wealthy families who employ his services offer him scarlet socks, breeches, gaiters, or boots, *caussas rojas*.[40] The castrator plays this role for the pig, the only animal so intimately incorporated into the home. Which is why it is not surprising that, in the second half of *Laʒarille de Tormes* (1620), he was invited to "make music" for the future groom after the latter, washed and shaved, was delivered to him by the women of the house, feet and wrists bound, on the nuptial bed.[41]

Yet this triad, through which the year's pig is progressively adopted, also carries an antagonism that remains, for the moment, mysterious. Let us simply note the adjectives and attitudes that represent its extreme poles. The merchant handles an animal that, like money, grows without effort, becoming for him, among other things, a very lucrative unit of value—the image of the piggy bank is not in the least bit arbitrary. This go-between is necessarily deceitful and a usurer, he is not a Christian and is called *Jew*. Even though real Jews traded, say in Alsace, in every animal except pigs, making the porcatier a Jew is in keeping with one of the most emphasized features of the image of the Other. At the other end is our third red man, the castrator, who regulates moods and who, despite the secrets of his magic, must be an excellent Christian. Is this because castration is one of the absolute prohibitions of Judaism? In any case, Jehan de Brie in the fourteenth century specified that any castration, including that of lambs, required the purity of the officiant, who "must be without sin, and, for that, must have gone to confession," while in about 1830 Denis Bonnet drew a Provençal castrator, "praying in the church of the Observance" in Carpentras, where a Jewish community lived.[42] Our contemporary castrators never fail to make "the sign of the cross" before operating. But let us leave aside this division for the moment, which the mere arrival of the pig seems to create, to follow the animal inside the home whose doors are now open to it.

CHAPTER TWO

Children's Stories

The baby grunted again, and Alice looked very anxiously into its face to see what was the matter with it. There could be no doubt that it had a very turn-up nose, much more like a snout than a real nose: also its eyes were getting extremely small for a baby. . . . Alice was just beginning to think to herself, "Now, what am I to do with this creature, when I get it home?" when it grunted again, so violently, that she looked down into its face in some alarm. This time there could be *no* mistake about it: it was neither more nor less than a pig, and she felt that it would be quite absurd for her to carry it any further.

So she set the little creature down and felt quite relieved to see it trot away quietly into the wood. "If it had grown up," she said to herself, "it would have made a dreadfully ugly child: but it makes rather a handsome pig, I think." And she began thinking over other children she knew, who might do very well as pigs, and was just saying to herself "if one only knew the right way to change them—"

—LEWIS CARROLL, *Alice's Adventures in Wonderland*

Sometimes in fairy tales it happens that a pig is the son of a king and queen; he develops in the womb and is born in the royal chamber of the palace, surrounded by an astonished court. Storytellers enjoy this unusual birth, which, much later, gives rise to an amorous metamorphosis, the prince being revealed beneath the bristles and pigskin. In one variation, attested from Queyras to Romania but particularly present on the Italian peninsula and islands and noted for the first time in the mid-sixteenth century by Giovan Francesco Straparole in his *I Piace Voli Notti,* a pig loves the youngest of three daughters. He is quite dirty, however, and even killed the elder sisters, who acted too repelled to be by his side on the wedding night. But let's stick with the introduction to the story, when the piglet appears.

While some storytellers give us the hard facts—"Once upon a time there was a father and a mother who had a little red pig for a child"— most offer a specific explanation for this surprising birth. The queen was enchanted, either by fairies, in Straparole's version, who decide that Hermésile, the beautiful Hungarian wife of Galiot, king of England, would have a son "covered in pig bristles, with the countenance and bearing of a pig," by the devil, in the version from Queyras, in which the king declares to a stranger, "I would like a male, even if he has the head of a pig," which is subsequently what happens, or by a beggar who had been insulted by the arrogant queen, in a Florentine variation. The powerful desire for a child, the obsessive anticipation of an heir can be such that the filial pig is awaited as a kind of last resort: "If only I had a little piglet for a son!" says the sterile lady seeing the sow and her "six little red piglets." "And so she did, she had a piglet for a child!" adds the Corsican storyteller before her snickering audience. In one Romanian tale an old man and woman resign themselves to adopting the first creature they meet: it turns out to be the most sickly of a litter of "twelve piglets, who were wallowing in the mud and warming themselves in the sun."[1]

But why, specifically, is a *pig* born to the sterile woman? No doubt part of the answer should be sought in the representations of sows for which these queens and ladies serve as substitutes. For the sow is widely recognized for its marvelous capacity for fertility: "It has as many little ones as it has udders, twelve, fourteen, sometimes more!" Anthropomorphic comparisons still pervade "scholarly" texts of the sixteenth century: in the same chapter, and at the same time, Ambrois Paré addresses both the fecundity of sows and of those "women who carry several children in one bellyful."[2] He nonetheless fights the anatomical confusion according to which, in women as in animals, multiples births are prefigured by a partitioning of the womb: so many "cells," so many children —or piglets. Although medical treatises since the Renaissance rejected this image of the female body, we find it quite alive, in the region of Sault, in the discourse on the sow, whose belly is opened with a curiosity that verifies the belief: "It's quite a load! The womb weighs five or six kilos. With kinds of tiny chapels on each side like little pockets. And in each pocket there is room for a little pig." Which is why, in

Albigeois, at the end of the sixteenth century, women stricken with "womb disease" would ask the pig castrator for the dried organs of a virgin sow, the *pousselière*, which they wore dried on the left side of their belts to reestablish order in their bodies and endow them with a harmonious fecundity.[3]

This gives us a better understanding of why, in several Breton legends, "the girl who did not want to have children," and who took every precaution to avoid or expel them, would be viewed after her death in the form of a sow "followed by as many little pigs as she would have had children if she hadn't prevented them."[4] Porcine prolificity is thus the exact opposite of feminine sterility. In an exceptional situation fate—chance and sorcery combined—or simply an irrepressible desire sends the women, in a seesaw movement, to the other extreme. Thus she gives birth to a pig-son—only one, it is true, but one that appears under the sign of abundance, excess, as well as great social distance, which, on another level, adds to the dissonance: contrary to other fabulous births in which the progenitor uses the skin of the bear or the wolf to engender a furry boy, this Mediterranean fable always stays on the side of the mother; the king has nothing to do with it.

This sowlike fecundity is not the domain of fable alone. The relationship first manifests itself in the realm of the cravings and fears that are thought to make an impression on the mother and mark her offspring. The belief is old, very much alive and widespread, but the pig has a very particular place among the repertory of examples. Let's first look at the vocabulary. The child's body bears a "spot," they say, a "mark," a "sign" that may also be referred to as an *envie*, a *desig* in Catalan, a *lunar* in Castilian—words that associate the marks with their believed cause. But the word may also designate the objects of the craving or fear, which Karl Jaberg classified into series for the Romance languages: the first includes fruits (strawberries, raspberries, grapes, cherries, prunes), the second wine, the third fire. A final series evokes the mark of the animal: "voglia di contenna, crodie, voglia di porcello," craving for pigskin or desire for pig are specified, for example, in several villages of the Italian alps. For the pig and the wild boar, while they are not the only animals that leave marks, are very commonly considered to be responsible for hairy moles.[5]

In principle, the pregnant woman craved fruit or wine and feared fire, but the emotion that marks her child with a tuft of bristles varies. Thus, for instance, a lunar of his mother's earns Don Quixote, in Cervantes's novel, a "brown mark with a few hairs like sow bristles . . . right in the middle of his spine." But mere contact, without any manifest emotion, suffices. In Wallonia, in the middle of the nineteenth century, it was recommended that pregnant women "not eat pig meat during their pregnancy so that their children will not have 'bristles,' the milk crusts that cover the head of an ugly 'pigskin.' "[6]

Finally, unlike other influences, the sway of the pig sometimes goes beyond this visible sign; its mark is deeper, it transforms the body: "It was during the harvest. A pregnant woman was standing at the vine, her legs apart, between two rows. A pig came up behind her and ran between her legs. She had a child with a pig's snout! Every year someone told this story at the grape harvest in Lespignan."

This lexical fixation, this plurality of possible causes, this amplification, from a mark to a snout, confirms the primordial place of the pig among animals who "imprint," since the mere sight of it risks leaving a mark. Another group of stories proposes a different explanation for these porcine marks, one in which maternal sensitivity is no longer the only thing at issue:

> There is a fancy restaurant in Saint-Agnès [in the Var], and I remember not long ago, in the summer, a fellow arrived who was being carried in an armchair and whom they seated at his table, with cushions. The people from the village said that he was one of the last offspring of the Rothschild family, the big bankers, and that he had a pig's tail!

An identical theme runs through Gabriel García Marquez's novel, *One Hundred Years of Solitude*. From time to time, the Buendía have a child endowed with "a cartilaginous tail in the form of a corkscrew with a tuft of hair at the end." This secret blemish of the "important families" has a long history behind it. Already in 1578 the Montpellier doctor Laurent Joubert, as much a collector of "popular errors" as a crusader against them, delighted in an etymological legend regarding an Arlesian family called Porcelets, Piglets. Cursed by a beggar to whom she had refused alms, the mother gave birth to eight children in one shot. She became a sow, but only in the number of children. Angry and disconsolate, she sent her chambermaid to drown the creatures and had her husband informed that they were only "piglets." The story spread, producing the surname that became their insignia and patronym.[7]

This is the first set of stories regarding the tale of the pig-prince, but they don't stop at conception and birth. Following this well-received birth, the child is always reared by his mother the queen. Indeed, from the moment of his adoption, the child piglet receives the most ritual care: "Instantly alert as a young girl, she prepared the wash, heated a bath, and as she was well-acquainted with the midwife's profession, she took the piglet, bathed it, rubbed it with good oil in all its joints, squeezed its nose, all the while covering it with kisses so that her little treasure would not catch the evil eye," relates the Romanian Ion Creanga. As for Straparole, an Italian, he lingers over the mothering scenes:

> This little child was diligently fed, came often to his mother, and raising itself on two legs, placed its little snout on her lap, and its little hooves on her knees. And the good mother never tired of caressing it, placing her hand on its fuzzy skin, and kissing it and hugging it just like any human creature. All the while the little son waged its tail, showing by evident signs that these maternal caresses were highly agreeable to it.

In all these tales the sow and the mother enter into a metaphorical relationship by way of a third element, the sterility of the wife, which initiates all the action. But her desire for a child is but one cause among other possibilities. The slightest disequilibrium at the time of conception is enough for the attraction to manifest itself, as if, invisible but ever present, it was lurking in the wings. But then, what is the source for this ever present correspondence if not the daily language of the women who rear the real pigs? By placing the animal in a state of absolute dependency on its foster-mother mistress, the fattening process pushes the correspondence between animal breeding and child care. True, it's not like in Melanesia, where the adoption is made plain by the woman breast-feeding the piglet, baptizing it, and welcoming it, castrated, into her bed: here, in order to exist, the adoption must be mediated in various ways as well as *denied*. We have therefore created an inventory of these equivalencies and these acts of distancing— found in gestures and words—to map the complete spectrum of relationships between the child and the pig. It is here that the tales and beliefs about this motherhood—both human and animal at once—are rooted and experienced.

The Nursling

The piglet to be fattened generally enters the pigsty at about the age of two months, just after it has been weaned: from then on it will be separated from the company of its peers and will have regular relations only with its hostess and cook, who immediately replaces its mother. Of course, it has passed the point of confusing her entirely with its progenitor, the way Konrad Lorenz's little greylag goose did, but the words used to call it, to name it, show evidence of the shift. In Provence, *lo mess*—redhead or carrot-haired—is the young pig sold at the market to be fattened; *rojanilha* designates both the litter of piglets and the "little scamps." *Garri* is used both for rats, pigs, and little boys with an affectionate connotation; it is one of the names most commonly used to call the pig, along with the simple *petit* or *pichou*. The same polysemia still exists today for *noirigalh* and *noirigat* in the dialects of upper Ariège. The uniformity of terms can only be based on an equivalency of growing stages: every animal goes through this smallness, this fragility, this dependency for nourishment. Yet the pig does not have a series of names denoting a change in category every year, as do sheep and cows; it is either a pig or a piglet (*porcèl, tesson*), and these terms could easily be applied to an adult, a relative synonymity that can cloud the age scale, as in the region of Sault for example.[8] For the state of nursling, which several of these words denote, is not just transitory for the pig.

Once a day the grandmother, or the oldest woman in the house, cooks for it. Morning and evening, she pours it a liquid mash—*abeural*—using a *massa*, a long wood pestle, to crush the tubers and stumps that could, even cooked, interfere with its unctuousness. Though its original teeth have been extracted and a new set of teeth fill its vigorous jaws, it is treated like a toothless baby. Stuffed with soups and gruel, it is rigorously maintained on a weaning diet. While its natural mobility calls for this soothing preparation, the association is nonetheless evident: in the consistency of its meals the pig is a perpetual infant. The explanations furnished in response to children's questions further root this correspondence. In several Catalan villages it is in the troughs (*naucs*) and pigsties (*cortals*) that babies are said to be found. In Cerdagne, where outdoor breeding was long common, they are alleged to be discovered in the woods, under oak trees, among the acorns.[9] In the region of Sault, through indirect channels, the similarity is further developed. The midwife—the "nice lady," as they say there—gets newborns from the attic, from the *caisha de la civada*, the oat bin. This same storeroom, next to the salting tub, is where the sausages are stored, warm and dry. The tale of origins passes by way of the most precious porcine product: the delicate meat wrapped in the finest entrails. As for the rudimentary cradle, it bears the name of the wood or stone trough, the *nauc*, of the same shape. Connected through food, anchored in a common origin, the association is further affirmed by a similarity of illnesses.

Once it's "brought in," the pig is safe, in principle, from the strange ills the red men exorcised. It therefore is incumbent upon the women who feed it to watch that it "comes along," "develops" without incident. The cereal paps, the starchy foods necessary for its fattening expose it to one danger: a "thickening" of the blood, which is reinforced by its retention in a narrow loge. This "binding" food must be balanced with "herbs," with "greenery," which is why the women continue to gather for the pig, ensuring a nutritional compliment, a reequilibrium:

> When we went into the fields, we also gathered for the pig. Nettles on the edge of the road, *caucidas*, thistles—in the spring, when they're soft, they're like artichokes. Wild spinach. We called it *galhinas grassas,* "fat hens." All this greenery was cooked for them, chopped up and put in the *farnat.* Some people gave it to them raw, but we've always cooked it for the pig.

Depending on the informant, wild greens were added—dandelions, sorrel, oyster plants—but also plants known for their blood-cleansing virtues, "blood plants"—red poppy flowers, artemisia tips—that the women use as a cure in the spring and "when their periods don't come, at that critical age. It lightens the blood, makes it circulate." But this green seasonal diet is not enough to ensure the equilibrium of humors, the threat of which always persists, for disease enters into the very substance of the pig's body, expressing its original defect.

The Red Sickness

The most feared of these fevers, so unpredictable was its outcome for so long, is the red sickness, *rouget*, erysipelas or diamond skin disease. "They turned red and all patchy and you had to keep them warm, they had a devilish fever! And it came over them regularly when they were fat. Inside, they'd have plaques just like on the outside, that's right! You'd give them a sack soaked in very hot water on their backs, you'd cover them in straw, and that's how you treated it." This meant waiting in a state of uncertainty, with the anxiety of seeing the entire meat provision disappear: "But sometimes, they got better by themselves, just like that." Let's attempt to outline the etiology of this red sickness. It doesn't come on all at once: heavy heat, they say, favors it—"it came to them often in summer, when it was hot"—or at least aggravates it. The sickness "comes out" in plaques and the conclusion is that "it's the blood that must do it to them." The emblematic sickness of the pig therefore comes under the sign of fire that boils the blood and casts it to the periphery of the body in the form of spots of varying reds, from bright pink to violet. For one woman the connection is obvious: "Rouget is like the measles!" Reduced to a single symptom that makes them "red sicknesses," the eruptive illnesses of childhood are often confused and, consequently, treated in the same manner. Efforts are made to chase away, to draw out the "bad elements," the two perceptible qualities of the illness: *heat* and *redness*. While waiting is in order, symbolic action is not ruled out.

Being covered is an efficient method for warding off the "fire"; children and pigs are buried, one in feathers, the other in straw, wrapped in blankets or sacs. Both are treated to herbal teas. But the heat of the antidote counts more than the power of the plant used for the infusion, hence the choice of "gentle plants such as mallow, Aaron's rod." The effects can be accelerated by bleeding the patient. This course of action is common for pigs; in regard to children, a debate as to its appropriateness raged until the mid-nineteenth century. Hence the preference for provoking a natural flow of blood without wounds, such as a bloody nose. Antoine Fueldez, a Languedocian specialist on this "true scourge among children," advises using the kind of prickly lawn grass herbalists call Dactylis and the Tuscans *Sanguinella*, stuffing it in the nostrils and pulling to make it bleed, or using milfoil or horsetail.[10] In western Vendée and Poitevin, until 1910, one "herbed" the child as one "herbed" the pig. In Loudunais, one put a *sainbois* on the arm, a plaster of pretty wood (Laurier Daphné). The abscess that formed was sustained by applications of ivy leaves rubbed with lard, and the pus that flowed out purified the blood. In Aunis the abscess was set in the ear, as was most commonly the case for pigs. But, usually, a red cure sufficed. "For measles, you put red curtains on the window of a room, a nice warm eiderdown of red fabric, if you have one. You give them cherries, strawberries, mulberries, and red seasonal fruits to eat." Certain red flowers, geraniums and erodiums (*erba del mal roge*) in the regions of Sault and of Saint-Pons (Languedoc) or the red poppy in Sicily and in the province of Grenada (Andalusia), have the same power.[11] The pigs, for their part, were "rubbed hard with vinegar"; the attraction of the color combined with the repulsion effect and, here and there, the same red flowers, especially geraniums, were used to heal them. Thus the symptoms and remedies of all these red sicknesses offer a homogeneous and coherent picture that should allow us to advance further, toward representations of the young body and its physiology, in which these actions and arguments are rooted. The unusual nature of these fevers is a help to us: while they represent a movement of the blood, they are nothing like "blood attacks," those unpredictable, devastating tempests that require the men of the house to intervene. They are specific to the young and enter within the competency of women. Since through this red sickness the pig is always *like a child*, perhaps we should ask where this unexpected disturbance comes from in children, this humorous fire that reddens the skin.

> Gordon suspects that in some children this corruption of the blood (from which measles result) may come originally from a conception and generation occurring at the time of menses. It can also come to those who are forced to eat fleshes or meats that are corrupt or are easily corrupted. The Ancients, especially the Arabs, attributed a more universal cause to it, namely, the food the fetus absorbs while inside the mother for several months, that is to say, the blood that was accustomed to flowing out every month, and that is retained for the duration of the pregnancy, a part of which is beneficial but the other part of which has some impurity that remains in the constitution of the child's body. This less pure portion stays in the pores of the body until nature is strong enough to reject this old leaven, which is consequently the origin of these eruptions we call measles and pox.

In his invaluable *Dictionnaire Oeconomique* (1751, vol. 2) Noël Chomel thus recalls, and ultimately refutes, the three explanations on which doctors were long in agreement.[12] The two main explanations pointed to the unseasonable menstrual blood of the mother, at the moment of conception or during the pregnancy, as the cause of the ill. Through measles or erysipelas the child and the pig are thus expressing a disordered state on the part of the mother. But within what cluster of signs are these attacks inscribed?

In the womb the fetus feeds off the blood that is retained, or, rather, uses it as a "leaven." Now this diversion disturbs the pregnant woman. She "instinctively" moves toward her blood, gravitating toward particular meats and tastes. First, red fruits—strawberries, cherries, currants, prunes, wild cherries—whose color is generally in keeping with tartness, a taste she also seeks in vinegar, pickles, capers, and all acidic preparations. This association of redness and sourness evokes and reminds her of menstrual blood. Young girls awaiting their periods have similar tastes; they too enjoy the sap of tendrils of the vine, chew bitter herbs, such as wild sorrel, called "vinaigrette." The best known of the playing songs says it well, "sorrel soup for the young ladies."

They gather berries and wild fruits. Any absence in their periods, any delay, inspires the same cravings, while menopause also brings a return of these tastes. Thus the pregnant woman's cravings serve less to feed herself and her child than to bring back her "stray" periods.[13]

This irrepressible desire is so predictable that one never fails to cultivate such regulating fruits within sight and reach. In the region of Sault and in Cévennes the gardens, women's sites par excellence, are bordered with currants, and, yet, "we don't like them plain very much; they're too acidic." The Mediterranean agronomers of the Renaissance, noting the custom of fencing in the *hort* (garden) of these hedges of red berries, provide the explanation: it is the "meat of pregnant women," the answer to their cravings. This compensation can also take the conscious and applied form of a ritual. In several Spanish provinces pregnant women never lose sight of their ordinary physiological interval and mimic their periods in various ways: by a monthly purging, by a bloodletting at the ankle, by the preparing of a liquid in which a black stone and some iron filings restore the menstrual "rust." For if the craving is not satisfied the child suffers and is born *marked* with signs, the repertory of which is familiar to us. Most women remember the red fruits they craved, even out of season. We should add that it is considered risky to refuse the request the pregnant woman expresses through her captivated gaze; to anyone who says no to her she inflicts a mark in return, temporary but painful, a sty, a red sickness of the eye.[14]

This initial disequilibrium may affect the child in the initial phases of the pregnancy; after seven months, however, "the baby is finished." But an equally dangerous disturbance still threatens his life. It can happen that the diverted menstrual blood is so strong and so abundant that it spoils the child and expels him, which is why when miscarriage—considered the anticipated return of the destructive period—is anticipated or feared, one must keep away from the habitual objects of desire. Women thus avoid contact with "red": they exclude it from their clothing, they neither consume nor touch berries, wine, vinegar, bloody meats, and, especially, in Galicia as in the Catalan Terra Alta, the dangerous spleen (*melsa*) of the pig.[15]

These precepts, fueled by experience and examples, control without eliminating the disequilibria of gestation. All women have cravings of which their newborns bear the mark; their diverted blood always bathes the being coming into existence in some excess; which is why all children must pass through the red sicknesses. It is here, in this original disturbance, that the measles of children and pigs takes its meaning. This passing eruption purges the offspring of the excess blood as soon as it is strong enough to shake off the maternal ascendancy. The passage is successful when the sickness comes out—"those kinds of illnesses, you have to have had them." They are even said to accelerate growth.

For they are only truly serious and leave lifelong scars if the menstrual flow "sullied" conception. This is the second explanation for the red sicknesses that Ambroise Paré also noted in his 1573 general theory of monsters:

> The child conceived during the menstrual flow feeds and grows, being in the belly of his mother, on a defective, dirty, and corrupted blood, which, with time having rooted its infection, manifests itself and makes its malignancy appear: some will suffer from ringworm, others from gout, others from leprosy, others will have smallpox or measles or another of infinite illnesses. The conclusion is that it is a dirty and brutal thing to have relations with a women while she is purging herself.

Of all the disfiguring illnesses measles is both the most benign and the most visible: it, along with red spots at birth, which Joubert discusses, red hair, and, we may now suggest, certain quite obvious porcine metamorphoses reveal the transgression.[16]

Thus this "attack of redness," which manifests the original corruption of the blood, marks the incompatibility between menstrual excess and the fetus, and then between the child and maternal menstruation, whether it accompanied conception or was "seen" after birth. This is hardly the ancient argument of an archaic medicine; an entire series of precautions keeps babies away from the menstruating woman, for, later, the sight of her can still inflame the blood and skin of children. In Sicily, according to Giuseppe Pitré, a menstruating women does not kiss an infant, for he would be marked with crusts on his face, which, for nine months running, would become exacerbated at the time of her menstrual cycle. Women are also sometimes at the origin of rouget, erysipelas: "Was the red sickness fate or not? People were wary, they were wary of it because anyone who had a sign, who had a red spot, who had something on . . . [the narrator points to his face], they were wary, they said, 'Aquò es un brèish,' that's a sorcerer, and so they avoided him."

The necessary distance between offspring and menstruation is not always formulated in such explicit prohibitions, but a metaphorical detour strongly imposes it. It passes by way of the red poppy (*Papaver rhoeas*) which, in many aspects, is the flower of measles. It appears in May, spotting with red fallow lands, uncultivated ditches, the still green wheat. To avoid walking on the spikes, children were prohibited from making bouquets of them, which were quite ephemeral in any case: "Don't gather them, it's poison and it dies right away." But the prohibition lies elsewhere, as evidenced in the language. While several French dialects have recourse to the image of the rooster's crest, red and mobile like the flower at the slightest breeze, other forms dominate and designate a special semantic field. The flower is called rouget, *rougerole* and in langue d'oc *rogèla, rosèla*, terms very close to those designating the red sicknesses. In old French we find *popelure*, which now, in Lorraine, designates measles: *popelieure*, the purple sickness. From this comes the series of descriptive names that Rolland, in his *Flore*, enumerates and that evoke fire, the burning boiler, hell: *tsodere, maison brûlé, feu d'enfer, feu volage, feu sauvage*, and, in the Comminge region of Gascony, the witches who make potions: *posoèras*. The threat is thus clearly expressed: in upper Brittany, notes Paul Sébillot, playing with red poppies results in the sickness called *feu sauvage*. Now, children everywhere play at defying this risk; they produce little dolls by turning back the four petals of the stem, shaved-headed choirboys, babies in red dresses. In Wallonia the name *marque*, given to the flower, alludes to the game that consists in popping it noisily on one's cheeks or forehead to "mark" one's face, while, in these same dialects, to menstruate is to "mark." These variations on the metaphor bring us back to the central image: the red poppy, with its delicate, almost wrinkled-looking petals, whose redness erupts in green fields, is a sex-flower, a sex in "flower":

4. The "choir boy" made from a red poppy flower.

Jo veig taques pes rostoi
¿Que tens sa paprovina?
Allota ¿que t'hes ferida
amb sa fauç en es genoi?

[I see spots in the straw
Who has the red poppy?
Young girl, who wounded you
on the knee with the scythe?]

says the Majorcan song.[17]

A child must neither look at nor touch the woman who "sees," who "marks," or the red poppy, her floral equivalent, for, if he does, he again runs the risk of fire and eruption. The cures we have described refer back to this origin. The young patient drinks infusions of poppy, his forehead is haloed in red, his neck wrapped in scarlet silk, but, most important, the lights are reddened around him since the inopportune menstrual blood first affects one's vision. Joubert informs us that in Languedoc "the red poppy flower" is called *langagne*, "because it brings on red, rheumy eyes, *laganhoses*, to anyone who looks at it attentively and who has tender, delicate eyes, such as a child." In Arles, Aix, and Avignon the red poppy is called *mau d'iue*, eye sickness.[18]

The "red" cures given to pigs confirm the source of the ill. They are rubbed with a vinegar all the closer to blood, since it bears a dark and nourishing clot inside, the *mother*, that only certain women who have a "good hand" succeed in transmitting to their neighbors. In Albigeois the old woman who collects the blood as it spurts from the slaughtered animal constantly stirs with her arm and gathers a large fistful of fibrin. Elsewhere it is thrown to the dogs and hens; here, in perfect keeping with the ritual logic, it is slid under the roof of the pigsty. The "blood mother" of the former pig must protect the little one to come from rouget.[19]

The pig, like the child, thus lives in the maternal aura, from which it is liberated by erysipelas, but often at the risk of death. It should not surprise us that the acute form would be more common among pigs, for the sow, as we know, is the most irregular of females. The time is so short between its rhythmic cycles that, as we have seen, it forms the basis for the peasants' wariness: "The sow is in heat all the time!" The pig, marked for life by its mother's irregularity, is therefore always threatened by the most archaic of children's illnesses. According to some, this is the source of its original measled state, as it is for leprosy among humans. Which is why, in about 1830, in eastern France, piglets that were excessively blond, red, or mottled were drowned, for their coats betrayed an irregular conception and suggested a measled future.[20] Isn't this feverish meat, so close to that of a sow killed while in heat, and thus "easily corrupted," also responsible for giving measles, according to the etiology cited by Noël Chomel? This pig meat, of which so many ancient doctors were wary, is not good for children and pregnant women, who are nonetheless attracted to it.

The hot blood that rises to the skin with the redness of May's red poppies can only come from the mother or from her double, the sow; through erysipelas and measles the bodies of the child and the pig experience one of the great crises of childhood emancipation, their skins scaling as during a moulting, "La picòta te despelhòfa, le serrampiu te dèisha tot viu," they say in the region of Sault of this red sickness through which the child has to *pass*. "Smallpox 'peal' you, measles leave you full of life." That the pig, too, so often had to pass through it adds to its definitively childlike image.

Melancholy

"If you get a pig in the habit of having milk or something good and you take it away from one day to the next, it realizes it (animals understand) and feels hurt, it *s'anaïgue*." The term is common and specific cases abound. *Anaigament* comes out of a situation of lack: offspring separated from their mother, a drop in the quality of the food—an animal that is well fed before being sold *s'anaïgue* at its new owner's house—a habitual indulgence or caress that is suddenly refused. From that day on the animal languishes (*languiment* is a quasi synonym), refuses to eat, "drags." It then becomes urgent to reestablish the previous favor or to invent a compensation. Among farm animals only bovines, pigs, and beasts of burden fall prey to this problem. The sheep, which are more numerous, form a society that is less supervised in this respect, the animals of the farmyard are oblivious to this psychological trouble due to unsatisfied appetites, to suppressed cravings. This first level of meaning well established, the interview continues:

> And *anaigament* is used only for animals?
> No, you can use it for children when they don't have something they want. There was a little kid on public assistance who was fed here, she was placed with a poor family, and, when she got out of school, she had

some dry bread and the daughter of the house had chocolate. *S'anaigava aquelha petita* [this little one *s'anaïguait*].

Children are indeed prime targets for this "sickness of lack" whose etiology we are developing: beyond frustration and its specific object, there is always the implication of the affective relationship with the one who provides nourishment, uniting the child to its mother and the pig to its mistress in the same manner.

The word itself, whose specificity is so clearly perceived and described, is not used in the plain; it is limited to the Pyrenean dialects—Donnezan, Sabarthès, Sault, region of Foix—where it represents a continuation of the Catalan influence. From Perpignan to Valence, it is part of the common language. Young children are always the designated victims, and it is always to them that the cure is addressed:

> We treated that, there was a supreme remedy, it was jam of *espollas bolitras*, of hip, of rose hip. That was the universal remedy. Every year, we went to gather some! It took a long time to make. You had to pass everything through a very fine strainer to remove the pits. It was excellent, that jam, it was really good. They don't make it anymore because it's too much work. Every home in Catllar had a jar or two, in anticipation of anaigats . . . and from time to time a neighbor came by: "You wouldn't happen to have a little *espollas bolitras* jam for the little one who is anaigat?" It was a remedy![21]

This fruit of the wild rose (*Rosa canina*) bush is connected in its descriptions and uses to the world of children's appetites. In Quercy children like to suck the soft fruit as if drinking from a bottle; they call them *chuca-barlets*, sucking barrels. Just about everywhere the handful of berries is used to represent barnyard animals: the hens and, especially, the pigs. "The children line up their fruits and call them their pigs"; they add white match sticks for legs and leave the green stem for a tail to complete the resemblance. Hence the common riddle "What has a black head, a red body, a green tail, and white guts?" In Wallonia "the young wild rose shoots are good to eat, they have a sugary taste and

5. A pig made of the fruit from the wild rose
(*Rosa canina*).

children call them *crä lär*, fat bacon." The metaphor refers back to the mother flower, often called the "pigs' rose."[22] This fruit is thus the quintessential meat equivalent, so much so that parents have to deal severely with the little gatherers' passion for "hip," whose brambles shred clothing. On the imaginary horizon of its uses, the most complicated of jams takes on the value of a panacea, converting a metaphorical meat into a sweet. It is apt to revive the most disappointed of appetites.

Anaigament, etymologically, designates liquefaction, deliquescence: the young disgusted patient loses all energy, grows pale, and "dissolves into water." So doing, it assumes a position opposite the red sickness that inflames the blood and vividly colors the surface of the body. The redness of fire contrasts with the cold aquatic transparency. As much as rouget noticeably "comes out," so anaigament is slow and secret. One is an attack, the other can become a state.

In the case of red sickness the child and the pig suffer from a direct and excessive union with the menstrual blood of the mother. In anaigament they suffer from an overly abrupt separation from her milk. Symmetrical but opposite, these two ills involve a difficult but necessary separation. There remains the gaze, the agent common to all these cravings and repulsions whose destructive and curative force we have noted; sorcery will dictate the conditions and effects of its power.

The Evil Eye

There was one of them here who had come as a manservant. He was called En Licart, and he was a *brèche*, a sorcerer. He stopped the carts; he must have read the *Grand Albert*! Once he had bewitched a pig—he had cast a spell on it, and the pig was sick. But they didn't tell him they thought it was him, they told him: "We have a pig we can't cure"; then supposedly he went and looked at this pig: "But this pig isn't sick, you're joking!" He touched it: "There's nothing wrong with it!" It seems that the pig started eating again.

The pig being fattened is one of the vulnerable points in the living household, its being charmed is but one of the uncontrollable effects of *envie*. For anything that is in a state of growth, a nursling especially, is a possible victim: the child at the breast loses the taste for milk, the veal refuses the udder, the pig rejects the trough. It suffices, for this to occur, that a passerby or visitor strongly desire this abundance; without thinking of it clearly, his mere gaze could stop the natural flow of things or, rather, inspire an inexplicable distaste in the nursling.

In the Causse de Blandas, in the southwest of Cévennes, when the pig showed the first such sign one pretended to sell it to a neighbor or a friend. The latter ostensibly gave a coin to the animal's owner and "declared in a loud voice: 'Auquel porc es tieu, lo te vendu' [This pig is yours, I sell it to you]." In Perigord Georges Rocal, who witnessed this type of transaction one day, specifies that the fictive sale was concluded with a shoeing smith, who for a long time acted as a veterinarian.[23] Using only slightly different methods, the same ritual was long applied to children: this is probably the practice that Father Amilha vilifies when he speaks out against the double baptisms given in the upper region of Foix in about 1670. The most precise description comes to us from the Balkans and clearly confirms the similarity:

> The woman who, for example, has no luck with daughters, seeks out a woman who has had several, all grown to adulthood. The latter goes to the window [of the house where the unlucky woman lives] and asks: "Would you happen to have a child [to sell]?"
>
> "Yes, we do! responds the woman who is in the house, but we're not lucky enough to see her live!"
>
> "Sell her to me then, for I, thank God, have enough luck!"
>
> "Okay, I'll sell her to you. . . . What can you offer me?"
>
> "What are you asking?"
>
> "Well . . . what can I say! . . . A lot, for she's a child beautiful as a flower, truly!"
>
> "I can only give you this, not more!"
>
> "Give me the money!"
>
> The foreigner passes a hen or a little money through the window. The mother of the daughter takes the money and gives her the child, still through the window. The foreigner, with the child in her arms, walks around the house and enters through the door. Upon entering she says, "Could you offer me shelter? For I am a foreigner come from afar and I don't know where to go . . . and, what is more, I have this child with me and I can't carry her anymore."
>
> "Yes, we will house you, why not!" responds the mother of the child. . . . "Come closer."
>
> The woman puts the little girl on the bed or on the ground if she is a little bigger; she sits on a bench or on a chair, simulating great fatigue. "What's the little one's name?" asks the mother. The woman now says the [new] name she has given her.[24]

But the most difficult moment is still the visit, governed in every detail by etiquette. It is in poor taste to ask too insistently for news of the health of a pig who remains out of sight. A simple "Is it well?" or "Is it coming along?" is enough, to which the reply is a "Yes, it's coming along, *va plan*," or a very evasive "It's profiting."

As with any creature that grows and fattens, there is also a taboo with respect to gestures and words of measurement, to weighing and counting, which can "cut off" the natural progression of the body. You never step over a pig; you measure one only at the risk of seeing it perish, for the number fixes, immobilizes, stops development. The pig's nature is always to grow, never to regress. The envious gaze perturbs or arrests this movement. The household must therefore protect its living enterprises and, certainly, not exhibit them without taking precautions. Between these beings who "are rising" and the gaze of others ritual defenses are erected—objects and words—as well as barriers of enclosure. The biological progression is kept secret.

Thus a first equivalency develops between the pig and the child around food and illness, an equivalency that continues to be dominated by the ambiguous effects of the maternal presence. With respect to this presence, growth and regression are defined by a discourse that first passes through the woman and that the young child—jealous of the pig or sick like it—amplifies. However, this conjunction is not only temporary: when the child, at about seven or eight years old, asserts his independence, when he forms groups with their own initiative that, far from adult eyes, elaborate and transmit their own customs, he does not break with the pig. He performs real work, speaks of other things, plays other games, performs other rituals in which the pig plays a role for some time still and in which new aspects of its cultural position are revealed.

The Time of the Swineherdesses

Curly locks, curly locks
Wilt thou be mine?
Thou shalt not wash dishes
Nor yet feed the swine,
But sit on a cushion
And sew a fine seam
And feed upon strawberries
Sugar and cream.

—Nursery rhyme

The pigs' keepers are often little girls. Throughout the Catalan Pyrenees this was the case; in upper Pallars this relationship was the rule:

> Pigs have always been raised by little girls who also took care of the gardens from which their food was procured. They were very proud of their flourishing, tidy gardens and of the clean fat pigs they could present to people. Which is why the elders said: "Els horts i els porcs son de la noies." Gardens and pigs are girls' business. They managed . . . to have cabbage all year, and, in the fall, pumpkins, beets, and other vegetables on reserve for the pig. In the spring, while protecting their hands with a stocking, they went to gather nettles to give them pap, in the summer they prepared the leaves of the young elms that were planted in almost all the gardens (illus. 6).[25]

These attentive swineherdesses, whether they feed them in the yard or lead them into the woods, are diligently attentive to their pigs, as to their younger brothers and sisters, and exercise an authority that is fastidious to excess. Despite certain moments of covert complicity, this period increasingly marks the break between the well-behaved little girl and the stubborn, gluttonous, and boisterous animal. The early similarities dwindle and disappear. Nonetheless, the time comes when even this unequal contact is no longer possible.

In the old langue d'oc pastoral, at the very sources of this poetic genre, the courting of the young peasant girl by the passing noble gallant involves a language whose sexual precision depends on the animal she oversees. Shepherdesses inspire a tender heart, the herders of cows are solicited by more direct, pressing words, while swineherdesses arouse the crudest obscenity. The description of one, in an anonymous fourteenth-century poem, is a ferocious caricature. When she refuses the ironic propositions of the lover, it is in the name of her cowherd, for "I love him more than the pig loves acorns," she says, "And than a sow who has farrowed loves cabbage."[26] The swineherdess chases away the lovers. In the Breton legend the young girl transforms herself into a sow to put an end to the attentions of her followers.

One ballad of beloveds, which developed on Mediterranean shores—from Piedmont to the Baléares—before spreading into the interior of the continent all the way to Savoy, Poitou, and Nivernais, makes explicit the custom that precisely defines the proper time and length of the frequentation of pigs.[27] A lord, whose name varies, marries a very young girl *que sap pas cordelar* (who doesn't even know how to sew); called to war, he entrusts her to his mother with these instructions:

Vos recomandi maire
de li ren fiare far
la fètz pas anar a l'aiga
ni fielar, ni pastar.

[I ask you mother,
Not to make her do anything
Don't make her go to the well
Spin or knead.]

But once her son is gone, the mother does just the opposite:

Al bot de cinc setmanas
los pòrcs li fa gardar
[At the end of five weeks
She has her watch the pigs.]

The swineherdess then sends her plaintive song echoing through the mountains and across the sea, far and wide, all the way to the warring spouse. The return of the lord takes seven years in the Provençal version; on the way home to his castle he encounters a swineherdess but doesn't recognize her as his young wife. There follows a portrait of her decline: no one waits for her at dinner, she never eats at the table, she can only offer the cavalier some bad oat bread and rotten soup the pigs don't even want. Her daily herding is accompanied by crushing tasks: spinning seven spindles, gathering seven bundles of dead wood. . . . But in the end, by virtue of the name the girl mutters and of the ring she never ceased to wear, the spouses recognize one another and the cruel mother-in-law is walled in alive. The plot of the entire poem revolves around the description of this unfortunate condition, while implicitly describing the ordinary rules of apprenticeship. This noble young girl did not follow the necessary steps: she married knowing nothing of pigs and without ever having touched a needle or spindle.[28] The mother-in-law reestablishes the normal order of things, an order that was absent at the castle, but cruelly locks her daughter-in-law into this transitory state, setting her up with the herd of pigs despite the recommendations of her loving husband.

The question of love is thus at the heart of this delicate relationship. But does this sudden separation from the pig not suggest that the latter possesses real power over this time in a girl's life? We find this idea confirmed by certain divinatory rituals. On Christmas eve in the Vaudois Alps, in the region of Chartres, for Saint Andrew's Day, November 30, and in Germany on the same day, the youth—girls and boys—camp out near the doors of the pigsties or delegate one among them, the "pigpen listener," to heed and interpret the sounds being emitted. In the satisfied grunts, in the stirrings of sleep, they decipher the name of their future lovers and spouses.[29] Everything, in this rare instance, is reversed: the pig abandons its silence and speaks to the girl, and it is important to listen, for it speaks of love to come. But nothing will happen for sure without the temporary but absolute separation of the animal and the female lover.

Castrator, Castrated

It would be going too far to make an absolute distinction between the pig of the girls and that of the boys, who are also charged with watching over meals in the pigsty, the meadows, or the forest. In the same way, their association alternates between periods of rational authority and playful fantasy, but the relationship between the two attitudes is entirely reversed, and herein lies the difference. Mischievous laughter dominates in the memories of boys, for whom the animal quickly becomes a participant and companion in games. Ten-year-old boys bring a hint of folly to their task, like the magic shepherd in the story and the song, making the pigs dance or, if they are already locked up, taking their places. A langue d'oc memorialist, Henry Mouly, has compiled a list of pointless tricks imagined by young guardians to master the animals. He himself, one day, attached his pigs by the tail, two by two, thereby mutilating them without really meaning to, like the evil swineherd of the fable who, having become the devil's servant, shows his master the tails of the animals he claims have sunk when in fact he has just sold them.[30] This aggressive attachment, this ludic violence against a fraternal animal that is as restless as the boys themselves is illustrated and, perhaps, explained in more secret games. When children turn against themselves or against one of their own with gestures that hurt, mutilate, or draw blood, the pig is again the model. But it is no longer fixed in the state of a nursling being fattened; rather, the most tumultuous moments of its fate, those moments when its body is subjected to a harsh and alien violence, capture the boys' imaginations.

When, in the spring, the pig castrator announces his presence in the village, he finds he has an automatic following: once school lets out, the children never leave his side. His actions inspire many questions on the part of those who don't understand. The adult responses refer either to minor childhood surgery—"It's having an appendix operation"—or to the more secret equivalency with other porcine alterations—"It's having a ring put in its nose." But in lower Vivarais the man with the red vest and the strident whistle has a special name in children's slang: *lo rospaliaire*, the one who scrapes, who extracts, who removes.[31] The term is laden with fear and shame. It puts the castrator in the role of an underhanded monster who could subject the child watching him to a similar fate. This, in any case, is the function the elders assigned him in the region of Sault: "When you couldn't get a boy to listen, when he was being a rascal, we would tell him 'A tu! Veiràs que te sanarèm' or 'Te farèm sanar' [Oh you! you'll see, we'll castrate you or We'll have you castrated]. I heard this in Munès from an old, but I mean a very, very old man, from the father of En Cyrille, who was not the most refined guy, you know, a little crude."

But this intervention by the red man on the child's genitals is not limited to adult threats and childhood fantasies. The castration of boys really and truly existed and was even a fairly common operation. Ambrois Paré again put us on the trail. In his discussion of "the treatment of bad tempers," of testicular hernias that afflict little boys when they won't stop shouting and coughing (*crier et toussir*), he reacts vehemently against a flourishing and undiscussed mid-sixteenth-century profession. Scholarly surgeons from that time on would periodically anathemize those "radical surgeon's knives," which were constantly resurfacing.[32] They scoured the Angoumois at the dawn of the seventeenth century when, "under the pretext of a profit rather than a cure, they cut indifferently, for all hernias, the testicles of a *miliace* [thousand] little boys." In the mid-eighteenth century note was made in the Swiss cantons, in Breslau, of "a [surgical] operator who passed through this city and mutilated over two hundred boys." From its foundation in 1776 the Société royale de médecine, alerted by the administrators of Paris and Languedoc, launched an investigation into these singular "charlatans." They received detailed responses from Beauvaisis and from the Languedocian dioceses of Montauban and Saint-Papoul; the knife wielders were therefore still practicing, whether as established "surgeons," simple "operators," or as unknown "itinerant charlatans." They treated a very common ill in the peasant societies of yore, the hernia, by applying to boys the efficacious remedy recommended for the *gorets à bourse* (piglets with testicles), common victims of the same problem. Is the specialized healer not then a simple pig castrator? The affair of the hernia operators who, on the eve of the Revolution, combed the Toulousian Languedoc with impunity furnishes us with the elements for an answer (illus. 5).[33]

At the end of the year 1777 the bishop of Saint-Papoul, in Lauragais, protested against the passage through his diocese of "operators or charlatans who trumpeted that they had an infallible cure to heal the most chronic hernias. The remedy consists, when the hernia has reached both sides, of performing a full castration, and, when it is limited to a single side, in performing a half-castration, and they demand for each operation a sum of thirty pounds." At this time "more than five hundred children" between the ages of one and seven had already undergone the operation. The investigation launched in person by the administrator of Languedoc quickly led to the village of Gaillac-Toulza, in the diocese of Rieux, south of Toulouse. Two families of castrators lived there, the Joffres and the Latapies. The latter would fill the legal chronicles until 1786. They were castrators of boys, or rather "hernia surgeons," from father to son. It was an itinerant and seasonal profession. From November to April they combed mostly the countryside, going from farm to farm. In 1786 the father, who was questioned, recounted something of his travels in the Lauragais. He went where clients called him and sometimes collected what was owed him only on the way back. His tools were quite simple. A "horn" as a signal, along with a few necessities: "Two boxes of white iron containing sazilicum ointment, a pair of scissors about seven inches long and a knife with a black horn handle, a case containing a lancet and sewing thread." The entire inventory was seized from the son, in Castelnaudary, in April 1786. His technique merits close scrutiny. Jean Reverdy, head valet, one of the parents who called on him, in December 1784, for his little three-year-old boy, described it in detail:

> Having lain out the said child with his head at the bottom, he told him to comfort himself and to hold his hands. And he saw that the said Latapie made an incision at the extremity of the lower abdomen and . . . having placed his fingers inside he cut something with the scissors that he could not identify and, having strongly attached the end of the bowel with a waxed string, he placed a plaster on it which he make up of the ingredients he carried and an egg yoke. During this operation . . . he had Gratien Falcou hold his fingers next to the incision he had just made, telling him to squeeze with all his might.

But, by the castrator's design, the crucial moment of the operation escaped the attentive and experienced gaze of Jean Reverdy. Indeed, this art depended on sleights of hand, as a second witness confirms: "having cut the extremity of the bowel or of the cord that held the testicles (he cannot be sure), he saw him throw it on the ground and he noticed that a testicle the size of a fava bean was attached to it." The clients respect this dexterity, as did the judges, since no law condemned it. They simply issued a warning and demanded an oath on the part of the operator.

Both admired and feared, the operator had all the features of the pig castrator or, rather, of the sow spayer, whose techniques he borrowed: he cuts the groin, extracting the cord and the "ulcer" with the tip of his hooked pinky; like the spayer, he never cuts on more than one side. The success of the operation established his prestige. The parents of problem boys had visited every surgeon and truss supplier "without obtaining any relief"; after Latapie's intervention, three out of five fathers were satisfied, their sons felt nothing more. Only one remained "weak in the area" and suffered "from changes in the weather." The man worked miracles.

This competency and the near complete confidence it inspired were based in fact on the similarity of the two morphologies: he who was adept at "fixing" the pigs also knew how to "fix" the boys. The cases were identical, the gestures and operators as well. A same overlapping is observed in Italy, for example, where the pig castrators—*castraporcelli*—originally from Norcia, not far from Assisi, in Umbria, were called *Norcini*, as elsewhere they are called *Béarnais*. In Florence, the meaning of the word broadens to include the pig slaughterer, a colorful character of the Florentine streets in the nineteenth century who carried the killed and opened animal on his back to the charcutier's shop. Now *norcino* also designates a castrator of children, long presiding among Italian operators. At the end of the sixteenth century, according to a surgeon at the time, one Horace de Norcia single-handedly castrated nearly two hundred children a year. Throughout the eighteenth century many comedies made comic allusion to these castrati-makers and, in 1804, a Montpellian doctor recalled that "this operation was performed in Italy by barbers known as norcini. We even know that there were shops in Naples with signs that said, "Qui si castrano ragazzi a buon mercato, Boys castrated here cheap"; one can imagine that few made operatic careers.[34] The *norcino* who specialized in pigs could logically also castrate boys, and it happened, in fact, that from time to time, far from Italy, a famous animal castrator would be solicited to operate on men convinced that his power *had* to extend to them. The sad story of a Breton carpenter made the headline of the newspaper of Rennes in 1888. Suffering from a "mysterious ill," he had solicited the help of an *affranchisseur*—as the gelder was called in upper Brittany—to obtain relief from his sickness. He died of the operation and the castrator was called up for "homicide by negligence."[35] More recently, in 1930, the story of a hernia operation in the French Vexin brings us an echo of the enduring relationship between the operations and operators:

> I assisted in a hernia operation; it was awful. The doctor came with the surgeon from Gisors. They needed someone strong to hold the patient down. They came to get me at the workshop. He was tied down like a pig. I passed a sponge over him, I lifted his head. He was buckled down, hung up, his head below over a pig stretcher, in the dining room. A pig stretcher is like a ladder, with two poles, bars, and hooks to tie the pig's hooves when it is being killed. This guy weighed at least ninety kilos; they'd fixed his arms on top. They'd given him a local anesthetic, but he was shouting, "Unstrap me, you pigs! I'll break your necks, you beasts."[36]

But the castration of children included more than just these real mutilations. The "exhausted," "broken" children, victims of "effort," of "descending bowels," of a hard and painful stomach, also felt the curative powers of rituals in which castration had a place, but only a figurative one.

The cure for stomach pains practiced by certain Corrézian blacksmiths throughout the nineteenth century struck Vuillier, the visionary sketcher of Limousin magicians, as quite spectacular. He relates how the *metge* Chazal invited him one evening to his forge to witness the "hammering" of a child. The man "girded in red" activates his flame, the two women hold on the anvil a "skinny young boy, almost anemic, his eyes "rolling with terror." The hammer strikes the iron twice, a third time it "stops short above the patient's belly, then gently brushes against the epiderm." An increasingly powerful cry, a "howling," writes Vuillier, accompanied the three simulacra. The child trembled, his mother cried.[37]

While it is, in effect, possible to see this cure as a new example of the powers of the blacksmith, who remakes bodies whether animal or human, and of the forge, this eminently collective site that reintegrates the patient into society, the gestures and words invite us to go one step farther, to examine the relationship between this practice and the "radical cures" for the child's belly.[38]

Martelage and *martellement*: both words mean hammering, but not in the same way. *Martelage* designates not just the generic action of striking with the help of a hammer, but, in these same regions, the castration technique that consists in crushing the sperm passages with the help of a special hammer and anvil, over which the scrotal envelop is stretched. The Littré dictionary, in fact, gives only this specific meaning of the word. We have seen Cévenol shepherds apply this method to sheep. That the blacksmith is the one who executes the procedure is not surprising; he performs this operation on horses, bulls, boars, and others. He is often the one to ring the noses of piglets and, in Périgord, he is also the one who buys them back in the fictive sales that trick the evil eye. By thus hammering the belly of the child, he reestablishes the proper disposition of the organs and subjects them to a castration that is just barely displaced, a regenerative castration.

A second ritual, by situating the cutter's gesture within a more complex whole, sheds light on its many dimensions. Throughout Mediterranean Europe, and in the south of Italy to this day, a ceremony is performed that was described as a medical cure by Marcellus Empiricus, a fourth-century Narbonnais doctor, and denounced as superstition in the seventeenth century by the priests Amilha and Thiers: a ceremony involving a tree and a child with a hernia.[39] We shall borrow Julio Caro Baroja's description from Aragon:

> During the vigil of Saint John a gathering is held outside a hermitage dedicated to the saint of children who suffer from hernias. Oak trees are split with axes, one for each patient. A great fire is lit in front of the porch of the hermitage and the children await midnight, dozing in the presbytery. The crowd is large. At midnight the priest sings a hymn and the sick undress. Two men pass them through the branches, while two others hold open the breach in the tree, which is later tied up and firmly bound after the wound has been covered with a mud plaster. Those who pass the child recite the following formula in the form of a dialogue:

> "Dámelo, Pedro."
> "Tómalo, Juan."
> "Lisiado te lo doy."
> "Sano te lo devuelvo."

> [Take him, Jean.
> Give him to me, Pierre.

I give him to you ruptured.
I return him to you healthy.]

The ritual takes place everywhere on the night of Saint John's Day, when the solar year reaches its peak, at the high point of all vegetable magic. The plant employed varies—oak, fig, walnut, water willow, or rush—but the operation is always identical: the trunk is split, then closed up with a plaster and a binding. It is often specified that the hernia is cured when the body of the tree has joined, since the sweeping cure has been transferred to it. Furthermore, to trim a tree, to top it, to shape it, is one of the meanings of the verb *châtrer,* to castrate. His hernia closed up, the child is healthy, *sanado,* which means "healed," of course, but also "castrated," for in Aragonais the word has a double meaning and signifies *castrated like a sow.*

Castration symbolized in this manner is accompanied by a rebirth. New progenitors take over the child, godfather and godmother replace the parents, but they often must exchange their first names: Juan is called María, and vice versa. They also take on—except in the case of a perfect coincidence—the names of the great apostles and of the mother of God. Thus "disguised," they incarnate the celestial intercessors who pass the naked child to the previous world, from which he came, to bring him back to earth *sanado,* closed up:

"Un niño quebrado
¿Quién le sanará?"
"La virgen María
Y el señor San Juan.

[A ruptured boy
Who will heal him?
The Virgin Mary
And Sir Saint John.][40]

The gesture that cuts, separates, and reforms the tree, opening and then closing up the living body, and the one that passes the child through the gaping wound, coming and going between the two worlds, are complementary and equivalent. Castration thus appears less as mutilation than as physical passage, a stage in growth of which the castrator, who splits the trunk and clips the animal or the child, is the master.

Boys are therefore sensitive to this personage's secret role. If they hover around him so much, it is because they sense the importance of this moment in which the pig is fixed in its very being. Which is why their fear is accompanied by a real passion for the event, in which they sometimes play a role. In upper Pallars, when the *curandero* came to castrate the pigs, the boys, the *mainada*, gathered the testicles that had been removed, fried them in a pan, and ate them all together, proclaiming, "We have eaten the flesh of a living animal."[41] The castrator's instrument, the flute by which he announces his arrival, a combination of his tools, his technique, and his magic, is avidly sought after by the boys. In lower Provence, in 1830, they bought them from peddlars of *crestapouarcs*, pig-castrators, or, in Catalonia, they made them themselves and called them *xiulit de sanador*, castrator's whistle. In Fougax, at the foot of the plateau of Sault, the whistle consists of a small willow whose opening one blocks to varying degrees that is called *crestadora*, the castration panpipe; with it the boys modulate the enchanting arpeggio. This very particular flute, whose shrill register we have discussed, is in fact but the instrument and sign, par excellence, of the *right to whistle*, which the boys assume at the age of eight or nine, when they begin creating these sounds with their mouths and then with whistles of willows, hazel wood, elder, or reed carved in the spring when the sap rises. The young whistlers thus recognize in the itinerant red *whistler* all the seductions of a virility they are in the process of conquering. Which is why the boys appropriate his gesture, akin to that of a "dubber of knights," shaping the most secret parts of bodies, and integrate it into their own customs. In the Cévenne hamlet of Vigan, in about 1910, the rule was to *crester*, to "castrate" all newcomers; the ten-year-old André Chamson, a new student, learned one day that he was threatened with a "simulacrum of this torture." For one week his mother unknowingly protected him by picking him up from school, but, faced with disturbing mockery—only girls were accompanied home—he decided to confront the ordeal. At the end of the day forty rogues were at his heels, shouting "Cresto-lou!" He was "forced back" toward the avenue, from which the "pack" then pushed him toward the "fair grounds," the pig market:

> They spread into a half circle and forced me, like a wild boar, into the
> most solitary corner of the chestnut trees. When I felt them breathing
> down my back, I faced forward, my hands out in front of me, my head
> low. But, at the first push, I fell to their numbers. Someone tripped me
> and made me stumble, a blow was enough to make me lose my balance.

The back of my head hit the ground and I felt bunches of my school-mates on top of me.

"Cresto-lo!" they shouted, piling one on top of the other . . .

Wrists clamped by ten hands, ankles nailed to the ground, held down by the hair and shoulders, I underwent my torture, squealing like an animal. It was a hard twist, painful but careful, the gesture of a shepherd who doesn't want to spoil his livestock.

"He's cresté!" shouted the little boys, accelerating their elfin dance.

"He's cresté!" responded the older ones, wiping the sweat that ran down their faces with the backs of their hands.

They had all moved away and were looking at me, forming a half-circle.

In a few seconds I was standing, winded, ready to fight.

"He's a strapping one!" said the strongest among them, looking at me sympathetically. "A real strapping one of the strong breed."

A half-century after the ordeal the memorialist subtly situates its place and meaning:

> We never had an inkling what these games meant. We castrated new-comers. It was the custom, and this custom had existed for centuries. Our elders had to do it before us, but they seemed to have forgotten it, as if the tradition had been lost after them. . . . It was not a matter . . . of humiliating the newcomer but of checking his virility. He had to prove that nothing could harm it.[42]

Moreover, the gang of young Protestant and secular Viganais in which André Chamson was thereafter accepted didn't "castrate" the Catholics, their enemies. Castration was thus, for boys, replayed, relived, and reversed. They pretended to perform it to confirm their manly force; this semblance of mutilation, in which they played every role in turn, paradoxically introduced them to their virility.

This enables us to gauge the depth of a wordplay common in the east of Gascogny. "Dieu te cresque!" May God make you grow! one says upon greeting a child for the first time, which, when someone sneezes, jokingly becomes "Dieu te creste!" May God castrate you! The phonetic chance that created the similarity between the two verbal forms was only exploited in this way because the connection between castration and growth fit in with the concept of the developing virile body.[43]

This is the first scene in which the boys refer back to the pig or, rather, to an essential moment in its history governed by the castrator.

The sexual organ is the site and object of these transformative games. However, we will now consider a second sphere, whose substance is the blood—of pig and child—and whose figurative characters are the red men, in association or mixed up, for it is beneath their nails and their blades that the blood of the pig flows on several occasions. The boys never lose sight of this.

Blood Games

A first set of games refers to the purchase. In Provence, in a variation of hide and seek—*li porc*, the pigs—one player chosen by chance plays the pig merchant—*lo porcatier*—who rests his head on the knees of the *maire*—the mother, the mistress, the game's arbiter, played by one of the children—while his friends, acting as pigs, run to hide. During that time the mother and the pig merchant talk:

> "Monte son ana ti pòrc?"
> "A la riva de Malamòrt."
> "Que son ana faire?"
> "Manjar d'aglan."
> "Si lis agantes, de que ie fas?"
> "Testa au sòu."

> [Where have your pigs gone?
> To the ravine of Malemort.
> What are they doing there?
> Eating acorns.
> If you catch them, what will you do to them?
> Head on the ground.]

The pig merchant goes in search of his dispersed flock and as soon as he touches a pig he rubs its ears, but any player who reaches the "mother" before being caught escapes the punishment. "Head on the ground" (*testa au sòu*) becomes *Titassa* in another expression that evokes both the tongue examination and bloodletting: "Titassa la lia bachonada, Titassa la gòrga lis, Head on the ground the mud [the dregs] muddied, Head on the ground the throat flows [or, the throat clean]."[44] The scene virilizes—this is not a girls' game—and seems to mimic the physical alterations that punctuate the life of the pig until its slaughter.

This slaughter is at the center of a rich Catalan ritual in which Joan Amades participated, in about 1900, in his childhood: "The kids of

Barcelona, in my time, set up a cross made of two twigs of straw on the ground and tickled their nostrils with a branch of *mil-en-grana* *(Chenopodium botrys)* singing:

Herbeta de Sant Tomàs
Sang a terra, sang a terra
Herbeta de Sant Tomàs
Sang a terra i sang al nas.

[Grass of Saint Thomas
Blood on the ground, blood on the ground
Grass of Saint Thomas
Blood on the ground and bloody nose.]

Comic song accompanying the ritual bleeding on Saint Thomas's Day, noted by J. Amades in Barcelona, transcribed by J. Tomàs.

"With all that rummaging we managed to make blood flow and we tried to make it fall on the center of the straw cross." Joan Amades specifies elsewhere that this "game" took place in the fall, but especially around Saint Thomas's Day, on December 21.[45] The child, his nose, his blood, and Saint Thomas's Day are in this ritual connected by a concept that all the participants are aware of and that a well-known seasonal proverb makes explicit. "Per Sant Tomàs qui ten un bèl pòrc i pòt fotre aquò sul nas, For Saint Thomas Day he who has a pretty pig can tap it on the nose," they say in the region of Sault; in Catalonia we hear: "Per Sant Tòmas gafa el porc pel nas i per Nadal posa'l a la semal, For Saint Thomas's Day catch the pig by the nose and for Christmas put it in the salting tub," or, in a shortened version that superimposes the two rituals: "Per Sant Tòmas sang a terra i sang al nas, For Saint Thomas's Day blood on the ground and blood in the nose." The long eve of Christmas begins the period of slaughters in several villages of Languedoc and Catalonia. But if the mimetic flowing of blood furtively seals the fraternity of the children and the pigs, this is not its only effect; it introduces us into a more complex relationship centered around the crisis of

6. The plants of flowing blood: Milfoil (*Achillea millefolium*), Persicaria
(a knot grass: *Polygonum Persicaria*), (*Galium aparine*).

growth that upsets the boy's body at swineherding age. The bloodletting is but one aspect of the experience, which is broader than the childhood uses of blood herbs lead us to grasp.

The *Achillea millefolium* (milfoil), queen of the sanguinary plants,
stops and provokes blood but also favors dreams and delirium, as suggested by its names in the dialects of northern France, from Picardy to
Jura (*anrêve, indove*), and attested as early as 1530 (*enrêve*). Here are the
ceremonies that illustrate this power: at Provenchères-sur-Meuse
(Haute-Marne, in about 1895)

> the children play a game that is a form of sleepwalking. They gather
> in a meadow; one of them stretches out on the ground after having
> removed his shoes. His playmates put milfoil in his hands, his ears, his
> nose, his mouth, on his eyes and on his feet, then they dance in a circle
> around him, clapping their hands or noisily knocking their shoes
> against each other. The boy, giddy from the smell of the plant and
> from the noise, soon *falls into a dream*, in other words, into a half-sleep,
> dazed. Then another one takes his place.[46]

According to the oldest description known, in the region of Lusigny
(Aube), the *herbe à entrôler*, nostril or bloody nose grass, provokes an
alternation of sleep and violence:

Entrôler is a popular expression, synonymous with bewitching, that has lent its name to a children's game. This game consists in putting the leaves of the plant into one person's nose and ears; the leaves seem to make an extraordinary impression and, after remaining some time in a real or imagined state of somnolence, in the middle of the noise his playmates are making around him, the subject suddenly dashes after them, trying to grab them, but the latter flee his approach and avoid getting caught. In Montargis they call this plant *enrêve*, attaching the same meaning to it as we do here to the word *entrôler*.[47]

In Saint-Omer (Pas-de-Calais, 1858) the same process, *endoverie*, seems to lead to the point of possession:

The one who consents to be *eindovèy* lies down on his back, having removed his shoes. His companions, those who must perform the incantation, first place some *endovoir*—some milfoil—in his nostrils and ears and in between his fingers and his toes. Then they place a large stone near his head that one of them strikes in double time, but at measured intervals, with another stone, singing in a monotone these mysterious and cabalistic words:

Eindove, eindove li martinet
les quate-r-pieds sur un cavet
Eindove, eindove li martinet, etc.

and he continues like this for ten or fifteen minutes without interruption until the eindoverie, the charm, has produced its effect. When the *eindoveux* consider that the operation is finished, that the eindovèy seems to be sleeping, they withdraw silently.

Gradually the eindovèy, left alone, seems to revive. Suddenly he stands up, but has a hard time staying on his feet, he stumbles like a drunken man, supposedly prey to a magic sleep, to sleepwalking. An occult power has come over him and posesses him, *deux ecce deux*, that's the rule of the game. Soon the irritations of the little charmers who observe him from a distance behind the trees and bushes, posing a string of ironic questions, make him mad; he bellows, he foams, he pronounces inarticulate sounds, *baccatur vates*. He advances, still sleeping, his eyes closed, toward the sound of the voices that are prompting his outbursts. He supposedly doesn't see where they are but enjoys a supernatural lucidity that allows him to gather stones and throw them at his joyful companions, for whom each of his movements, each of his spills (for he must fall several times—another rule of the game), sets off fresh bursts of laughter and joking.[48]

One of the effects of milfoil, which is also the grass of flowing blood in these same regions, is thus to prompt a trance. The young participant in the middle of the circle, ears and nostrils full of milfoil, surrounded by the rhythm of the striking rocks and of the song, falls into a hypnotic sleep, visited by invisible forces. He hears questions, sometimes provides answers, struggles violently, rushes toward his companions. This loss of consciousness, this drunkenness that turns into aggression against oneself and others possesses the same characteristics as an extraordinary illness: the epileptic seizure. The subject never loses contact with the earth, he is lying on the ground or falls back down as soon as he sits up, making it the *mal caduc*, the *mal del sòl*, the *mal de tèrra*. Furthermore, the boy hears voices and no longer seems to be in control of himself, as if inhabited by another being. Aimé Courtois, of Saint-Omer, seeking an analogy, came up only with the magical sleep of the "Lappish shamans." And this is how epilepsy was long explained: the body is open to the presence of a saint (John, Donatus, Francis, or Loup, according to the region) or to wandering spirits.

The treatments implemented are quite familiar to us, among them bloodletting. It was used mostly for children, according to Noël Chomel (1740): "With respect to those who have passed the age of seven, if at the first attack blood is drawn, they no longer fall back into epilepsy, or else we'll cup them between the shoulders, or make them a cautery." In southern Italy, in the Abrruzzi, until the 1900s at least, the remedy was as follows: to calm the convulsion one wounded the ear of the patient with an iron point—a rusty one if possible—or even bit it until blood was drawn. If the patient was then "liberated," the person who saved him became his parent, and, from then on, he had to call him "godfather" or "godmother." Naturally the hemophiliac plants were called upon first, to stimulate the nostril and cause a violent sneeze; later, to calm the attack or even prevent it, various preparations were recommended of which the most common was "milfoil water." The rhythmic sounds with which the boys surrounded the one they *envornent* also echo this dimension of the cure, as attested by a Bourbonnais doctor in 1935: "Not long ago in this region, when a patient had an attack one cut the earlobe with scissors and everyone in the house, armed with noisy instruments, household utensils, tools, made a deafening racket around the patient 'to make the blood flow.' "[49]

This bloodletting is not effective simply because it works against the epileptic seizure but *because it resembles it.* The blood and the body that flow and fall to the ground lead to the same wasting of vital energy, to the same lethargy of the senses alternating with the same visionary euphoria. Like the loss of blood, the trance of the mal caduc is an experience of the unconscious, an exploration of the limit between sleeping and waking, between life and death. The cure thus displaces the disorder to a different part of the body; it changes its form to control its progression. Further, the other common treatment—the metal key slipped over the nape of the neck and the back—was used to cure both hemorrhages and seizures, affirming their partial resemblance. This resemblance is confirmed by the application, in both cases, of the same medicinal herbs, in the same way and to the same places. But these herbs have the power to provoke as much as to heal both the mal de terre and the hemorrhage, and, here again, the children play on this reversibility. The milfoil that heals the mal caduc also sets it off, the loud ruckus that calls on the blood to calm the attack precipitates the attack in the game. This antagonism is even a component of the children's ritual, which alternates between moments of apathy and fury.

By leading us to these trances, has the repertory of children's uses for the bloodroot plants not caused us to stray from the pig, even though the trials of its life furnished the blood games with a very explicit model? Looking back on the details of these rituals will verify that the analogy continues to this depth, where it is, no doubt, clarified. If we return to the "cabalistic" formula that, in Saint-Omer, helped put the boy to sleep: "Eindove, eindove li martinet / les quate-r-pieds sur un cavet," its meaning can only be understood, in our opinion, in light of its relationship to the pig. He whom they eindove is called *martinet*, or "little Martin," one of the names for the pig, Saint Martin's Day being one of its slaughter dates. Grasped by his comrades, the martinet is perched on his *four feet*—his four pig's feet naturally—on the *cavet*, a Picard-style stool. Using these dialectical and archaic words and its highly elliptical syntax, the incantation superposes the magic sleep of the eindoverie and the preparations for a slaughter. Similarly, the most recent account of this ritual, which we owe to Achille Millien, who practiced it when "it was widespread throughout the Nivernais" as a game "of shepherds and swineherds," highlights the place of the pig and its guardian:

> One of the children, consenting to allow himself to be envorné, laid
> down on the ground. His playmates gathered leaves of envorne (*Achillea*

millefolium), rolled them into balls, and placed some in his mouth, nostrils, in the corners of his eyes, in his ears, between his fingers and toes. Then a shepherd shouted into a shoe at the patient's ear; a second struck the flat side of a clog with a stone, and all the shepherds sang at the top of their lungs:

Envorne, envorne, my little swineherd
All the pigs are in my wheat
Except the big two-colored sow
Who is up there in the salt pans.

The envorné seemed to fall into a dream agitated by spasms, then, when he came to, was shaky and dazed for an instant; or else he stood up abruptly, his eyes haggard, seeming delirious, and, punching, kicking, and throwing stones, he made his companions disperse.

In the dialect the word and its derivatives (*envorne, envorner, envornement*) unite the movement of the blood and giddiness into a semantic field the children's rites activate. One would say "this man has *envournements*" to indicate that the blood is rising to his head," which also happens when one *s'envorne* by twirling a long time in place.[50] *Envorne*, finally, is the name of one of the herbs of Saint John's Day, milfoil; "In Nivernais we also call it 'tongue bleeder' or 'nose bleeder.' The children pass the leaves over their tongues to make them bleed or place them in their nostrils and lightly rub their noses, which immediately bleed." In the same cultural region a *gaillet* (yellow bedstraw) treats epilepsy or Saint John's disease, which is also cured by bleeding the left pinky. The exploration of the Nivernais system, which ensures echoes and connections between words and things, rituals and their actors, sharply highlights the context in which these games are to be understood.

Without attaining the same coherence, the constant relationship between the child, the pig, and epilepsy on which the northern rituals are founded is confirmed in Languedoc. In Saint-Hilaire, in the Aude, children are advised not to mount the pigs or "they might catch the mal del sòl," epilepsy. In Toulouse, in the mid-sixteenth century, according to *Las ordenansas e costumas del Libre Blanc* (vol. 295), the cry the child emits preceding the attack, and, by extension, the onset of epilepsy itself, was called *siscle*, a word that commonly referred to the piercing cry of the pig as its throat was being slit. Finally, these conjunctions are rooted everywhere in a daily reality. If epilepsy in children is somewhat rare, it is quite common in little pigs. In the region of Sault, according to the veterinarian:

> There were quite a few, even many cases of epilepsy. When I started I treated them with intravenous vermifuge and calcium. And that's not very convenient, because they're constantly moving. There was yet another one in Marsa, three years ago. The animal falls on the ground, starts struggling for a moment, squeeling, then it all goes away. It's a little dazed but then it comes around.

This is a common sight, for the pig, weaned too early or worm-infested, periodically has attacks within sight of children. They recognize the cry, the agitation, then the dazzled look triggered by the intervention of the red men, as well as the blood, which the man of the house draws from the tail or the ear as soon as the attack begins.

Having started with games that violently manipulate a figurative pig, we have now run through, guided by blood plants, a set of children's rituals in which the provoking of blood and the experience of epilepsy as a magic trance combine to bring us back to the destiny of the pig and its regular bloody intervals. But it is clear that this childhood interpretation of the pig's story is inscribed in children's behaviors, preoccupations, and experiences, in everything that physically and socially defines this period haunted by the obsessive presence of flowing blood. Between the ages of eight and twelve many explorations, games, and confrontations have bloodletting less as an unfortunate consequence than as a result to be appreciated and sought after. If, by bleeding from the nose, ten- or twelve-year-old girls anticipate the advent of their periods, we have seen in the many wounds that the boys inflict upon themselves a voluntary and theatrical marking of their puberty.[51] While the girls are preparing for the monthly rhythm of their blood, the boys are experiencing a defining moment, a break between two stable states of their bodies upon which their relationship to the pig sheds light. The animal is the growing being par excellence, its physical progression is spectacular, visible to the eye; it corresponds closely to the age when the body changes too quickly, has no time to adjust to its own shapes, to its own image. But the pig is also a being whose destiny is marked by a succession of deaths and rebirths, all translating into high-pitched cries, convulsive movements, blood on the ground, and a final pacification. At the market the tongue examiner fells and then liberates the pig, renewed. When it is "brought inside" the slightest "blood attack" or apoplectic fit ends in a bloodletting. Finally, on the day of its death, all its strength flows out, but, in truth, it doesn't die; in principle it is already replaced; a new growth begins with its anonymous successor—the calendar of its consumption provides for overlapping among cycles. The boys thus appropriate this constant alternation governed by the seduction and sexual power of the red men.

The most explicit games refer, however, to an accidental break in this relationship: the little swineherds lose their animals. In Provence they take off for the "banks of Malemort," in Nivernais "for the meadow," except for the *truie garelle* (the two-colored sow) "in the salt pans." As we are dealing with games of initiation, this loss becomes meaningful: the age when the metaphorical closeness is most intense will lead to a real separation.

It is also the case for boys that the frequenting and guarding of pigs lasts only for a time, which Emile Guillaumin precisely situates in his *Vie d'un simple*: from seven to nine years old, the sheep, from nine to eleven, the pigs, beyond that, the oxen. This customary progression is never quite so rigid, the breaks spread into slow transitions and the animals one watches proclaim one's true age group. But in Bourbonnais and in the Pyrenees, as soon as one "touches the oxen" without the help of an adult, childhood is over. Then, confides Tiennou to Emile Guillaumin, "the winter after I turned fifteen, having stopped watching the pigs entirely, I had to act like a man. They set me to thrashing with a flail, to participating in the cleaning of the stables."[52] Elsewhere this break can take the form of a "banquet of passage" in which the child offers an animal to his family, his neighbors, his boat; the ship's boy from Audierne, in the nineteenth century, symbolized this manner of definitive accession to the sea.

The ritual is divided into two sequences, both symmetrical and successive, that illustrate the two sets of relationships we have seen develop around castration and the flowing of blood. First, one evening, the father announces to his son that he has "put him on the list" and that he will be baptized the next day; "armed with a pickaxe and equipped with an old clog, at low tide he joins the group of ship's boys below the port, in the riverbed, to unearth the silt worms the fishermen use for bait." His comrades overwhelm him with their politeness, offer him tobacco, sing *The Pleasures of the Drunken Man* to him in the form of a hymn.

Once the song is over, the baptism occurs. The neophyte is surrounded. If he doesn't undress on his own, the elders strip him by force. Then the ceremony begins. Some rub his entire body with grit; they scrub him, *briquent* him, according to the commonly used term; the others *salt* him. With big fistfuls of silt worms, they knead his genital parts, often until he faints or swoons. After which he is given a nickname he will keep for the rest of his life.

Next comes the first voyage, the first salary, and, six or eight months later, a very special pig slaughter:

> The ship's boy's first profits had been put aside: ten crowns to buy a piglet at the Pont-Croix fair. The animal was coddled by everyone, walked on the shore at low tide, given baths in the sea every day of summer. It had grown large and today was its *fête, fest en oc'h*. All things, in this world, have their destiny, and the pig had followed its own. Yesterday they had lifted him up and sat him on the wooden bed, which had been carried and set up on the doorstep. The ship's boy, in the place of honor that rightfully belonged to him, since he was sharing the benefits of his first earnings with everyone, had held its ears, while his father, with the knife he used to gut the fish, had, with an inexperienced hand and after much jabbing about, put an end to its existence. Meanwhile the ship's boy's younger brothers imitated the animal's cries of suffering, applauded the final spasms of its agony, and covered themselves with its blood. Today is a holiday. The table is full—the boat's entire crew, close relatives, intimate neighbors. Twenty-two people, not counting the children and the curious onlookers roaming about under some pretext and invited to enjoy a morsel on their way. Meat and eau-de-vie! A first-rate meal among the sailors.[53]

To become a ship's boy the young boy is put to the test: he lives as in a dream, the hymn of the drunken man charms him, his skin is irritated until it bleeds, his genitals kneaded with a precision reminiscent of the "crestage" of the little boys of Cévenols. But here the "baptism" is not the final step in the integration process, which occurs through the offering of a pig, who truly *represents* him. Thus, the two sides of the ritual correspond to one another, element for element. Like the boy, the pig takes on sailorlike airs, he becomes a creature of the shoreline, his daily bread becomes algae and kelp, he is bathed by the waves. Like the pig, but at a faster pace, the aspiring ship's boy is coddled, then bullied, his body, naked and white on the sand, is "castrated," "scraped," and "salted." Just as the anonymous pig dies under the "fish knife," to become a varied profusion of prepared meats that are named and shared, the boy dies as a child to be reborn a sailor, endowed with a new name. But the succession of the two rituals also demonstrates the end of the similarity. Between the ship's boy's baptism and the slaughter of the pig the first voyage has taken place, the first salary has been received, the child no longer exists. The killing of the animal makes this difference plain. The younger brothers mimic the squealing agony, play with the spouting blood, the elder virtuously holds the head of this pig he has earned before becoming drunk with the men in a celebration that will take up the afternoon. To share one's pig, for the young fisherman of Audierne, is to offer one's childhood to the family and work society that now "counts on him." Just as, inland, according to Emile Guillaumin's Tiennou, one leaves behind the pigs to "act like a man" before returning to them at the end of one's life.

But what then happens to the swineherd who stays on, who doesn't leave his pigs at a reasonable age? Like the swineherdess, he is marked by a stigma that indicates, first, his low social standing. In the regions where the flock of a vast property is entrusted to a specialized domestic—which is the case in the Balearic Islands—the latter is the lowliest of farmhands and is quite poorly paid:

Porqueret de sa pellissa
Mentres tu serà porquer
No guanyaràs cap dobler
Ni seràs a temps a missa.

[Swineherd with the fur-lined coat
So long as you remain a swineherd
You will earn no doubloon
Nor be at Mass on time.]

But most of all his function is trivial, unworthy:

Per amor de Deu, no faces,
Estimat meu, de porquer
Ni tampoc d'endioter
Son ses dues arts més baixes.

[For the love of God, my friend,
Keep neither pigs
Nor turkeys
They are the vilest of trades.]

And the swineherd becomes the butt of all the youth's jokes, as evoked by many *cansos curtas*. But this social disgrace is compounded by a very uncertain identity. This grown-up bachelor boy is but a little child: "Lady Curta nursed him / behind this pile of stones," one sings maliciously in Campanet.[54] This suspicion has its source in the social image of the trade: he who always lives in the company of pigs cannot really be a man, as if he had not, through them, in reference to their cyclical destiny, passed through the stage at which one experiences one's new virile body.

"It's Only a Pig"

According to a Sicilian fable, a farmer sent his son to school, but the teacher found him such a bumpkin he sent him home, saying: "I'd rather teach a pig!" The farmer, hearing this, took the wish literally and put his pig in school in place of his son. He even gave him a book, the pages of which he garnished with soft fava beans so that the animal would skim through it with pleasure! The strategy failed and provoked laughter, to the chagrin of the farmer, who thought he was only following instructions. He had given his pig some *fava* beans so that he would acquire *favelle*—stories, words, language—but he came up against an unbreachable limit: even with good accompaniments, words cannot be eaten. Which is why "mimologisms," phrases that translate animal speech into human language, ignore the pig or cite it only to mock the poverty of its vocabulary—the one Sicilian pig that tries to speak can only say: "Un! Un!" Even the one time during the year when all the domestic animals speak distinctly, on Christmas night, the pig is not included in the miracle.[55] The pig will never be anything but an *infant*. Its destiny, which one might have thought parallel to that of little humans, stops at this state and at this age.

A being of silence, the pig is necessarily left unspoken, as witnessed by Simin Palay, the Béarnais linguist and writer, in his autobiography:

> At the Palay house, we don't produce enough corn and potatoes to sustain *one*. This *one* always intrigued me; it is the only word in our language that means "pig." I think this comes from the fact that the word *pig* is considered one of the most vulgar words, to such an extent that when forced to use it, one adds the following excuse: "That's the only name for it," or "as it's called." To feed *one*, to skin *one*, everyone knows what that means.

A little further on, the memorialist specifies that, in houses that are rich enough, "there is a 'mister' in the pigsty." These are the rules of appellation we find more or less all over Europe. They allow for elision,

enabling the speaker to place the generic name for the animal in quotes
by using an indefinite pronoun (*he, one, him*) or a metaphor borrowed
from the realm of social rank (the *Mister*, the *Noble*, the *Magistrate*, the
Guest, and, especially, in the region of Sault, *Vestit de seda*, a play on
words suggesting both "Dressed in Silk" and "Dressed in Bristles")—
euphemisms that veil the crudeness of the name.[56] It is generally
accepted that these evasive terms diminish the obscenity of the subject;
they translate the disdain for an animal removed from policed society.
Yet, as we have demonstrated, perhaps no other animal is as assimilated
into domestic life, as close to being confused with the offspring of the
house. Should these evasive names, this roundabout language, not be
seen, therefore, as an attempt to distance the animal, to reaffirm its ani-
mality, while humorously playing on the antiphrasis by granting the
reputedly lowly animal a title of nobility? This respectful expression,
this aristocratic attribute, facilitated by a play on words—from bristles
to silk—denotes a social difference that excludes the guest from the
community, designates it as a stranger who cannot be "of the family."
Once the pig has been "put in its place" its common name falls into the
stock of "vulgarities," and we find it flourishing amid the ranks of
insults and curse words. *Pork, porcàs, sow, pig*, often preceded by
bloody, are common invectives, hence the excuses that surround the use
of what has become an injurious term; the semantic circle closes. Even
in the highly unusual cases in which an individual chooses to more fully
adopt a pig by assigning it a personal name, this name is relatively
generic. Several of these family pigs are named "Joseph," and the name
is ironic, affectionate, friendly. One woman named hers "Martin," like
the patron saint, but also like the donkey or bear who performs at
the fair.

The pig is thus tainted by a twofold stigma: in principle it has no
proper name, and its common name is often not fit to be spoken. Hence
it joins the ranks of the large flesh-eating animals, the bear and the
wolf, whose "real names" are replaced by metaphorical periphrases for
fear they will "come out of the woods." Included by virtue of these linguistic precautions in the most savage category of predators, the pig is
all the more removed from the household, its deliberately blurred identity situating it as far as possible from the domestic universe.

The peremptory, almost scandalized response—"You don't baptize
a pig!"—that we received in answer to our onomastic questions no
doubt summarizes this verbal exclusion, while adding another dimension to it: since *to baptize* means "to name," a name confers a quality

that both includes and surpasses personal identity, ensuring by means of the baptism ritual the spiritual and corporal protection of the new Christian. The naming of stock animals borrows some aspects of the Christian baptism, and particularly godfathership, the fashion for which now seems to be extending to cows in the region of Sault. When the name is no longer simply descriptive (*Calhòla*, the two colored one, *Corbet*, the one with upright horns), when it is taken from among the names commonly in use ("Jacqueline," "Martine"), it is an indication that the godmother chose to lend her own name to the young calf. But the pig is symbolically too close to the child to permit this transfer of rituals; by refusing to name it one excludes it from being implicitly converted into baptized flesh—*carn baptisada, carn de crestian*—which designates a person in many Mediterranean incantations and, especially, for the monster, the tender, delicious, and highly desirable body of the infant:

Carn de crestian senti
Morirai se n'en mangi.

[I smell the flesh of a Christian
I shall die if I don't eat some.]

If names presuppose baptisms, the reverse is not always true, for the canonical signs alone, imitated and interpreted, suffice to ensure the defense of the being threatened by evil. When, in 1952, Ernesto de Martino investigated the magic world of Apulia, in southern Italy, everywhere he went he encountered a belief in the protective efficaciousness of the gestures, words, and objects of the baptism, to such an extent that, "when it's a pig that is touched by the evil eye, meaning it is losing weight or not gaining enough, it is baptized with water and salt as a preventative measure."[57] But the baptized animal is still not named, and this essential difference is brought into relief in the fictive sale rituals that, as we have seen, thwart bewitchment. When a child is sold, he changes names; he is called "Bear" or "Wolf" in Romania, or simply "Sold" in Turkey, whereas his porcine homolog remains as it was: an anonymous pig.

Intrigued by this manner of debasing the names of the most familiar animals by converting them into insults, Edmund Leach saw in it something of an extension of the metaphorical prohibition against incest, which also forbids, and thus distances, close relatives.[58] For the pig this rule takes on particular keenness. "All it lacks is speech," according to Sicilian fable; it also lacks a name to more fully become a child being raised. Other stories and experiences justify the distance and aggravate it. The pig is not only distinguished from the child, but becomes his most dangerous adversary.

"It is so voracious it eats everything it finds that is moist and fatty: you cannot safely raise them within reach of children, whose hands or feet they mutilate, either out of voracity and the brusqueness with which they help themselves to the food they see in these innocent hands or by attacking them in their crib if they can get to it," writes Collaine in 1839. In his work entitled *Moyens de préserver la santé des cochons* (Ways to preserve the health of pigs), he includes a word of caution to families against a danger that is mentioned constantly ever since the ancient agronomers wrote treatises "on the pig and its complete nature." Centuries later, the same argument can be heard today:

> There is no question that pigs are ferocious. When they're hungry, they're ferocious. At night they howled in an extraordinary fashion. They ran when we opened the door! Everyone gave them food at seven, and in all the *corts* we heard the pigs crying. And there were quite a few pigs who attacked people, especially children. . . . Some say they'd even eaten them in the past!

The pig comes to embody the domestic bogeyman, the *pòpòia*, the *babau*, the *bòbòta*; the shapeless creature that designates fear in the minds of children takes form in the pigsty, a site of darkness where supernatural evil can be imagined.[59] Strict enclosure no doubt enables a more rapid and better-controlled fattening, but, most of all, protects the household from this latent ferocity. As soon as this strict enclosure fails, the savagery is reawakened:

> We, in Campagna, had the "passade" all the way in the ground. We used a room with nothing in it. We kept only the donkey and the pig there. The donkey came up every day by the stairs to go to work. The pig was killed down there, he only came up dead. He was safely locked in a large "enclosure" . . . or else he might have eaten the donkey! Once, at another farmyard in the depths of Campagna, they put a pig in one, and there was a ewe who had given birth to a little lamb but didn't want to love it, didn't want to feed it, so they stowed her there, next to the "enclosure," and the pig opened it and ate the sheep, not entirely, but the *pit*, the utter, he smelled the milk and started there. He devoured it.

This terrible drama is constantly repeated, but, as if to make it more present, the child who helps feed the pig must experience this danger daily; numerous precautions accompany the opening of the loge.

> Pigs are quite ferocious, particularly with children, so at night, when we gave them their food, we had to be careful. Because, in their pigsty, *la cort dels pòrcs* we called it, there were two parts: the "night" part, where we enclosed them behind a locked door, and the "day" part, which was lighter, which had running water and troughs, *els naucs*. When they were big we couldn't even give them their food while they were in the room; we had to lock them in the second part. We came in and put their food down. Grandmother left the outside door ajar, opened the other one while holding onto it, and very quickly left. There was a child who locked the door behind her right away.

In this house in Conflent the two-room pigpen—"the bedroom and kitchen" as they jokingly called it—ensured a safe incarceration, but the pig was still granted a certain freedom by day. This freedom disappeared entirely when a trough with a mobile hatch allowed the provision of food without even opening the door; the animal then lived in a loge that was always closed. This new tool, imitated from the large collective piggeries, eliminated even the daily gesture that liberated the

7. Trough with hatch developed by a Munès carpenter.

animal somewhat, that tamed it for a moment while dispensing its rations; it pushes the logic of incarceration to the limit and reveals its profound contradiction. The morning of the killing the pig emerges furious, for *its prison makes it a savage*. The prison serves as protection from a ferocity it deliberately creates. Like the reduction of its diet solely to vegetables, it pushes the limits of nature and creates duplicity. In the darkest corner of the stable, the house thus chooses to raise a real bogeyman in its midst.

The space in which the confusion between the child and the pig is refuted is thus filled with scenes of gruesome deaths and scandalous meals. As if the question of cannibalism were on the horizon of this metaphorical exploration, which glimpses one being in the reflection of the other, as if, faced with this logical conclusion, it became necessary to step back, to establish solid, symbolic, and coherent barriers. The two gestures that always separate the child from the pig are complementary. If baptism is refused, the similarity is incomplete. Thus the one that is killed is not a familiar being, whose flesh could not be eaten—since it would be considered a peer—but an anonymous meat. The reputation for being a man-eater imputed to the animal reinforces these effects: it casts the pig as among the worst flesh-eaters *that must be killed* to protect the house. Indeed, they say in Minot "that the pig is becoming mean" when the slaughter is approaching—claiming to require this vigilant distancing of the children, the most "tender," fragile possessions. Denying the evidence of a similarity between these infantile beings, hiding the cannibalistic temptation from view, allows one to make the companion to and mirror of childhood fit to be killed and eaten.

CHAPTER THREE

The Circle of Metamorphoses

In the days when the demiurge lived among men, the latter asked him if they could taste wild pigs, which didn't yet exist. The Grandfather (the name of the demiurge) took advantage of the absence of all the Indians, when only the children under ten were left in the village, and changed the latter into young wild boars. When the Indians returned he advised them to go hunting. At the same time, however, he sent all the young wild boars to the sky via a tall tree. Seeing this, the men followed the little boars and, having reached the sky, began killing them. . . .

Upon returning to the village, the Indians feasted on the flesh of their children transformed into wild boars. They beseeched the Grandfather to descend from the sky (where he had followed the children) and to return to the village, but he wanted to do nothing of the kind and gave them tobacco to take his place; they called it Badzé, and this is why they make offerings of tobacco at certain times.

—CARIRI MYTH REPORTED BY MARTIN DE NANTES (1706) IN CLAUDE
LÉVI-STRAUSS, *Le Cru et le Cuit*

The first collection published by the Brothers Grimm in 1812 contained a strange and scary story. Was it really a tale? Could it be told to children? Achim von Arnim, a writer and friend, didn't think so, and, in a second edition, in 1819, omitted the following narrative:

One day a father killed a pig in front of his children. When, in the afternoon, they wanted to play, one of them said to the other: "You be the pig and I'll be the butcher." Whereupon he took a knife and planted in the throat of his little brother. The mother, who was sitting in the upper room bathing her youngest child in a tub, heard the little one's cry, instantly ran downstairs, and, discovering what had just happened, withdrew the knife from the child's neck, and, in anger, planted it in the heart of the one who had been the butcher. Thereupon she went back upstairs and hurried to the child she had left in the tub to see what he was doing. But, in the meantime, he had drowned in his bath. The woman was so overcome with despair that nothing and no one could console her. She hung herself. When the father returned from the fields and saw what had happened, he died of sorrow.

This story is not entirely unknown. In the third century the Roman orator Aelianus gave a fairly close version of it in Greek, in which the sons of a priest of Bacchus mimic a sacrifice on their father's alter to the very end. Starting in the 1550s variations in collections of anecdotes abound, and, from then on, it is the killing of the pig that is enacted, the confusion with the child that is pushed to its tragic end. It can of course be seen as a simple cautionary tale: Wilhelm Grimm, in his childhood, had heard it from his mother in this context, accompanied by a lesson of caution.[1] But, more than a blunder, a mistake that can be excused by the age of the participants, it is a serious infraction, a transgression. Oral literature indicates its importance by returning to and amplifying the theme, casting it in new directions.

It all starts with children, a boy and his sister, in the oral version of Hop-o'-my-thumb and in the Brothers Grimm's *Hansel and Gretel*. Their poverty-stricken parents abandon them by losing them in the forest. They arrive at a house that, depending on the version, belongs to the devil, an ogre, or a witch. Upon his return the master, who is very sensitive to their smell, recognizes the children's presence. "It smells like fresh meat here!" "You know we killed the pig!" replies his wife in a Dauphinois version in which the ogress protects the children. But this answer is a lie, for in principle there is no pig in the diabolical house. In several tales from Morvan and from Dauphiné the devil keeps a sow, a *caye*, that he uses only for riding; he mounts it to attempt to track down the escaped children, albeit unsuccessfully. He has a pig-pen, but it is always empty. His home, in fact, does not really reproduce itself, since he always has girls whom he inadvertently kills or who are stolen from him, never to return, by young heroes. Nor does it produce anything else; it seems to feed on what comes from the world of men.

The children are therefore welcomed as a godsend, as in this version from Velay:

> The husband says: "Good for us, we should eat them." The wife responds: "No, mustn't eat them, not fat enough. Look what little fingers!" showing Jean's hand. "We have no servant," says the wife, "we have no pig. We'll make the little boy into a pig, the little girl into a servant. We'll lock the little boy up in the *trio* [the pig's pen] and when he gets a little fat we'll kill him. And the little girl, who'll be the servant of the house, will prepare his meals." They brought the boy to the little *trio* to fatten him up and took the little girl as a servant. She prepared the meals for her brother. It was a meal for pigs. The boy couldn't eat it. He ate only a few pieces of bread and cheese that the little girl passed to him on the sly.[2]

The same sharing of roles is found in Aubrac: the boy is placed in the pigpen, where "the ogre went every day to see whether *the pig* was fat enough," finally deciding, when the moment arrived, "Oh! you're fat enough, I'm going to the city and I'll bring back what we need to salt you, and we'll put you in the salting tub." The ogre thus treats the boy the way the local pigs are treated. In Corsica and in Italy he fattens him with figs, as is the custom in the Mediterranean countryside.

The child uses a subterfuge to delay the moment of the slaughter; he passes the foot of a mole or rat through the slot in the door to show that he is not "gaining," but the ogre gets tired of it and decides one day to bleed "his pig." A debate may then occur with his wife, when she is his accomplice, on the way to prepare the meat. For the ogre or the devil doesn't just eat raw meat. In fact, the comparison continues further since the young flesh will be treated according to the rules for cooking pigs. They plan to made the traditional blood sausage, to place the good pieces in the salting tub. A Vendeen version includes a full accounting of these gastronomical plans. This time a werewolf and his maid have gathered up two little girls. One is placed in the "pig pot," the other must feed her.

> When she was fat enough, the werewolf said to his maid:
> "Do you smell fresh meat?"
> So the werewolf killed the little girl and cut her into pieces, and the maid put her in a larder, like a piglet. After which, her little sister took her place in the pigpen, and the maid brought her food. The little girl figured she would be eaten. One fine day, when the larder was empty, the werewolf said again:

"Do you smell fresh meat?"

He killed the other little sister, and they salted her in a larder, and they ate her all up too.

In all other variations the devil's culinary plans fall through. At best he cooks his own daughters. Incapable of recognizing his own "blood," he realizes his mistake too late. But, most often, he and his wife burn up in the fire or oven they light to cook the child.[3]

The two story cycles we have just heard are mere variations on the same metamorphosis. In the Brothers Grimm's censored version the children are deluded, they kill each another for want of being able to distinguish themselves from the pig who is so close to them, and their father—by killing the pig before their eyes—did not maintain the proper distance. In Hop-o'-my-thumb, from the oral tradition, the ogre's wife methodically tries to transform children into pigs and almost succeeds, though she is still unable to eradicate the curse that makes her home sterile. Thus, in both cases, the same boundary is involved, the boundary that embodies the paradoxical precepts of domestic breeding. Furthermore, we learn that, in our pig-eating societies, this vacillation between the child and the animal is *essential* and results from the origin of pigs—at least according to the only myth in Europe that reveals this origin. Jean-François Bladé, the Gascon ethnographer, noted it in the 1860s in Lectoure.[4]

Christ, Saint Peter, and Saint John were traveling on the Earth and came to knock "on the door of a poor farm" where they asked for bread, giving rise to a first miracle: the dough expanded magically in the oven. But "while they were eating the three children of the sharecropper's wife had hidden in the pig stable and were yelling. "Sharecropper's wife," said Our Lord, "what have you in this stable?" "My poor man, they are three little pigs." When the meal was over Our Lord left with Saint Peter and Saint John. But when the sharecropper's wife went to look for her children in the pig stable, she found three little pigs." The storyteller can stop there, and sometimes does. The individual miracle then takes on universal value; it accounts for the appearance of pigs—even if it seems to suggest that they already existed, it's the second genesis that counts—for their native affinity with children and for the risks of familial cannibalism inherent in their breeding. But the Gascon storyteller continues. We see the sharecropper's wife run after her holy visitors, admit her lie, and thus recover her children in their original form. It was all just a good lesson, which, in the process, shows that only Christ can cross the fragile boundary in both directions: something a diabolical creature cannot do successfully, something man cannot do with impunity.

In the vast majority of European versions of this story, however, the transformed children remain pigs and the story doesn't reverse itself. But the foreignness of the heroes or, rather, of the victims of the metamorphosis, is always specified. Here, for instance, is a Swabian story:

> Once, Jesus and Peter crossed over fields and arrived in a city. A Pharisee was seated in front of his house. He said to himself: "I would like to ask a question of these two wise men." "Hey! Lords," he called, "tell me what is under this vat." That day the Pharisee had slaughtered a pig and the tub had been turned over to dry. However, the children of the Pharisee had gotten underneath it to play. Our Lord replied: "Your children are underneath." The Pharisee began to laugh and said: "Not at all! My pigs are there!" Our Lord replied: "Very well, let them be pigs!" And at that moment the Pharisee's children escaped from the tub grunting, tranformed into little pigs. This explains why Jews do not have the right to eat pork and why pigs have entrails similar to the intestines of men. Moreover, from that day forward, pigs had a vertebra in the shape of a tub in which a young girl was seated, "the damsel of the pigs," which one naturally looks for at meals.[5]

According to the various versions, about thirty of which have been assembled by Oskar Dähnhardt, the Jews put Christ to the test by hiding one of their own in the oven or the tub, sometimes a rabbi but more often the wives and their children. Thus, in Latvia,

> the pig used to be a Jew. When the Lord walked the earth the Jews asked him one day to guess what was found beneath two tubs; under one was hidden a Jew and his children, under the other a sow and her piglets. Jesus responded by reversing them: "Here there is a sow and her piglets; there a Jew and her children." The Jews laughed at him for guessing wrong. But when they raised the tubs, the Jewess had become a sow with her piglets and the sow a Jewess with her children. Ever since then, Jews don't eat pork.

It is generally considered that the story took form in the seventh century, in the Arab version of the gospels of Christ's childhood (illus. 7, 8, 9). Christ appears as a restless child who subjects his playmates and passing adults to terrible pranks. Which is why the Jews, who see him approaching, fearfully, from inside their homes, shelter their children or even hide them. In one of these stories this precaution is justified as follows: "It is said that Jesus told children what their parents ate. They went to them afterward and asked them for some of this food. 'Who told you that?' the parents would ask. 'It was Jesus!' When Jesus would inquire after his companions and ask if they weren't in the house nearby, the parents would respond 'there are only pigs there.' And it was true. When they opened the door, the children had been transformed."[6]

From Béarn to Lithuania, from Catalonia to Provence to Poland, Christ is the revealer, the one who states the correct order of things by doubling the fragile boundary between children and pigs with another far more solid one between Christians and Jews. All the questions that, as we have seen, inform the everyday breeding, the slaughter, as well as the consumption of this so human animal are resolved at once by virtue of the myth. It was the Jews who originally confused their children with pigs, who committed this most serious error in classification, and that is why they are forever separated from the animal. Thus, contrary to the universal rule that associates the other, the foreigner, with what he eats, Jews are associated with the flesh they are forbidden. Sameness and prohibition are reconciled in one stroke.

If, in myth, this ultimately elegant solution is satisfactory, in history, which sometimes places Christians and Jews face to face, Christianity and Judaism have always generated more elaborate—and more violent—constructions. For it was always necessary to reaffirm the association between the Jew—the entire Jew—and the animal he judges unclean and, at the same time, to make the pig, with its shady origins, again become the meat that proclaims the difference of Christians, the Christian meat par excellence. This symbolic manipulation of every instant is possible only by reference to the pig one feeds and eats; in return, it marks the words spoken and gestures made surrounding it. No one escapes. The usurious merchant and the devout castrator already entered into this inevitable divide, which must, logically, intersect the lives of boys, the lives of young Christians.

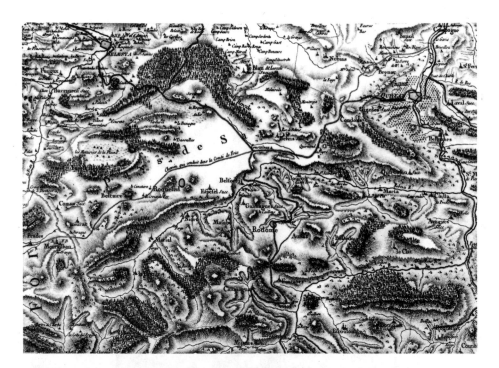

1. The region of Sault in the eighteenth century, map by Cassini, circa 1780.

2. *The Pig Market of Carpentras,* by Denis Bonnet.

3. *Castrator Playing the Panpipe at the Market of Carpentras*, drawing by Denis
   Bonnet, 1842.

4. Ordinance of 1779 against castrators.

DE·PAR LE ROI.

ORDONNANCE

DE MONSEIGNEUR L'INTENDANT
DE LA PROVINCE DE LANGUEDOC,

Du 12 Janvier 1779.

QUI défend à tous Charlatans ou autres, d'exercer la méthode de guérir les Hernies par la Caſtration, ſoit ſur les Enfans ou autres Perſonnes qui en ſont attaqués, à peine d'être arrêtés & conduits en Priſon.

JEAN - EMMANUEL DE GUIGNARD , CHEVALIER, Vicomte de Saint Prieſt , Conſeiller d'Etat ordinaire , Intendant de Juſtice , Police & Finances en la Province de Languedoc.

LE ROI ayant été informé qu'il s'eſt répandu en Languedoc différens Charlatans, ou Gens pratiquant la Chirurgie ſans titre, qui ont introduit & pratiqué la cruelle méthode de guérir les Hernies par la Caſtration, particu-liérement ſur les Enfans qui en ſont atta-qués ; Sa Majeſté nous auroit donné ſes ordres pour les faire arrêter, en nous chargeant de lui en rendre compte, & de lui envoyer les noms de ceux qui auront été arrêtés : Et pour que perſonne n'en ignore,

IL EST DÉFENDU à tous Charlatans, ou autres, d'exercer la méthode de guérir les Hernies par la Caſtration, ſoit ſur les Enfans, ou autres Perſonnes qui en ſont attaqués, à peine d'être arrêtés & conduits en priſon, pour y attendre les ordres de Sa Majeſté : Enjoignons à tous Maire & Conſuls des Villes & Communautés de cette Province, de faire arrêter ceux qui pratiqueront cette cruelle méthode, de les dénoncer à cet effet à la Maréchauſſée, & de nous inſtruire des captures qui auront été faites, pour en ren-dre compte à Sa Majeſté ; comme auſſi à nos Subdélégués de tenir la main à l'exécution de la préſente Ordonnance, laquelle ſera lue, publiée & affichée dans toutes les Communau-tés & Paroiſſes de la Province. FAIT à Montpellier le douze Janvier mil ſept cent ſoixante-dix-neuf. *Signé* DE SAINT PRIEST, *Et plus bas ;* Par Monſeigneur, SOEFVE.

A MONTPELLIER, De l'Imprimerie de JEAN-FRANÇOIS PICOT, ſeul imprimeur du Roi, Place de l'Intendance. 1779.

LA VIE AU GRAND AIR
A LA FOIRE — LE LANGUEYEUR

5. *The Tongue Examiner,* postcard circa 1910.

6. The pigs' mealtime in Munès, in the region of Sault, January 1983.

7. Jewish children transformed into pigs. Illuminated manuscript illustrating an English version of the *Evangiles de l'enfance,* infancy narratives of Christ, thirteenth century. Egerton manuscript, British Museum, ms. 2781.

8 & 9. The same scene, in a manuscript from the Bodleian Library. Selden manuscript supra 38, f 22 v and f 23.

10. The Jew's sow, early sixteenth century.

Pruneta. Israhel. Coluab. Beatus SIMON. Samuel.

Mayr. Vitalis.

Zu Trent. 1474

Moyses. Engel.

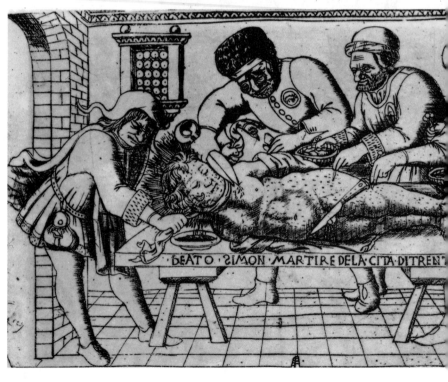

BEATO SIMON MARTIRE DELA CITA DI TREN

2ᵉ page du 5ᵉ feuillet.

Est depeint vn champ auquel y a vn Roy couronne habillé de rouge a la Iuifue, tenant vne espée nue : Deux Soldatz qui tuent des enfantz de deux meres qui sont assises a terre pleurantz leurs enfantz ; Et deux autres Soldatz qui jettent le dit Sang dans vne grande Cuue pleine dudit Sang, ou le Soleil & la Lune descendant du Ciel ou des nuées se viennent baigner, a soin six Soldatz armez d'armure blanche, & le Roy fait le 7.ᵉ Et Sept Innocentz mortz & deux Meres, l'vne vestue de bleu qui pleure s'essuiant la face d'vn mouchoir, Et l'autre qui pleure aussy vestue de rouge.

11. *The Martyrdom of Simon of Trent,* engraving on colored wood, German school, fifteenth century.

12A. *The Martyrdom of Simon of Trent,* as popularized by a Florantine engraving circa 1490.

12B. "Second page of the fifth leaf. Depicted is a field in which there is a crowned King dressed in red in the Jewish manner, holding a drawn sword. There are two soldiers who are killing children and two mothers who are seated on the ground crying for their children. And there are two other soldiers who are throwing the blood into a large vat full of said blood, in which the Sun and the Moon are descending from the sky or from the clouds to come bathe, and there are six soldiers armed with white armor. The King makes the seventh. The seven innocent dead and two Mothers, one dressed in blue, who is crying, wiping her face with a handkerchief. And the other also dressed in red." Ink drawing based on the *Livre de cabale* by Abraham le Juif. Paris, bibliothèque de l'Arsenal, ms. 3047. Photo courtesy Gallimard.

13 & 14. Two German engravings from the seventeenth and eighteenth centuries combining the theme of the Jew's sow with the martyrdom of Simon of Trent.

Anno 1475. am Grünen Donnerstag war das Kindlein Simeon
2 Jahr alt als es von den Juden ist umgebracht worden
Cet enfant nommé Simeon agé de 2 Ans, fut tué par les Juifs,
le jour du Grand-Jeude de l'An 1475.

Diese Abbildung stehet zu Franckfurt am Mayn
am Brucken Thurn abgemahlt.
Ce portrait est peint sous la porte du pont de Francfort
sur Le Mayn

Dieses ist
der Juden Teuffel

O weih Rabb: Anschl, au au Mausch, au weih au au!
O Veh Rabbi Anschel. au. au Mauche o Veh. au. au.
Sauff Mauschi sauff die Milch friß du Rabbi den Dreck
es ist doch alle Zeit euer bestes Geschleck!
Bois Mauche. bois ce lait! Manges Juifs ces ordures!
Ces sont friands pour vous. de bonnes confitures.

15. A Barcelona manger early in the century. Among the fruits and sweets are the *neules*, the large scalloped hosts consumed by children until January 6.

16. Palm Sunday, in Romón Puiggari, *Costumbres populares de Barcelona* (1860).

17. Palm Sunday in Barcelona early in the century.

18 & 19. Judas returning the coins and the hanging of Judas. Eglise Saint-Martin, Jenzat (Allier). These murals are part of a fifteenth-century passion cycle.

20. The hanging of Judas. Mural painting. Notre-Dame-des-Fontaines. La Brigue, Alpes-Maritimes, fifteenth century.

21 & 22. On the island of Procida (Bay of Naples), the morning of Holy Friday, the little boys "hang Judas" before taking part in the procession, dressed in the blue and white garb of the brotherhood of Turchini. Procida, 1992.

23, 24, 25 & 26. On the island of Procida, Holy Friday, the procession of the "mysteries" takes place. The most important and the most often reproduced represents the passage from the Jewish seder to the Christian supper. On the Jewish side note the presence of lamb, unleavened breads and bitter herbs. On the Christian side Lent is signified by fishes, lettuce, and raised breads. All of it is consumed after the procession by the members of the brotherhood and their families. Procida, 1992.

27. Examination of the intestines for making blood sausages in Munès, in the region of Sault.

28. The *kalikandjarai*. The native Cypriot painter M. Kashales chose to represent the nocturnal ritual during which women prepare pancakes and sausages to make the unwelcome visitors leave.

29. The auctioning of pig's feet, on January 19, Saint Anthony's Day. La Maçana, Andorra, 1983.

PART TWO

Two Bloods

The Jew's Sow

They maintain that the four persecutions they suffered are marked by the four impure animals of Leviticus. The camel marks the empire of the Babylonians; the hare that of the Medes and the Persians; the rabbit that of the Greeks and the Romans under which they agonized for a long period of time, but the pig, which they despise above all, represents the Christians under whom they are suffering more than under the idolaters.

—JACQUES BASNAGE, *Histoire des Juifs*

The Pig's Ear

Regarding the daily cohabitation in the Gascon towns of yore between Christians and those of the race of Abraham, a trivial fact my paternal grandmother often told me comes to mind, a memory of her Bordeaux childhood in the final years of the last century. She was living then in Bacalan, in the popular neighborhood on the banks of the Garonne, near the port and the docks. At that time, in this section of Bacalan, a peddlar often passed, a shabby old Jew. If some young men happened by while the man was occupied with a transaction, they never failed to grasp the corner of their coats with one hand and twist it sharply with the other, very openly, in the face of the old man. And, at the same time, they produced a kind of guttural, nasal grunting sound—a swinish grunt to be exact: "Oink! Oink!" The gesture and the grunting infuriated the old merchant, who responded with insults and threats, filling the jokers with delight! The piece of twisted cloth represented the pig's ear. The symbolism was perfectly clear to the offended party, to the offenders, and to all witnesses to the scene, including little children. These events occurred in about 1900, at the time of the Dreyfus affair, but it is clear that all this had nothing to do with the kind of anti-Semitism that was poisoning French political life at the time. It is more than likely that the young boys of Bordeaux were repeating a gesture that dated from long ago, a gesture their fathers and ancestors made before them and that must have perpetuated itself for many generations in this town, where an original and tightly knit Jewish community had lived among Christians for centuries.[1]

Let us now travel a half-century back, to the shores of the Mediterranean. Régis de La Colomière, who carefully compiled popular Provençal expressions, noted the insults with which the children of Marseilles addressed the Jews whom they awaited outside the synagogue:

> Complaints were lodged, and the police, who intervened on several occasions, brought an end once again to this disgraceful ploy; but they were never able to prevent a certain class, little children and even bigger ones, from shouting *aurilho de porqui!* or *pouarc!* (pig's ear!) upon seeing a poor Israelite pass, simulating a piece of an ear with the tail of their garments. These shameful expressions have fortunately gone out of fashion.

Many other Provençal witnesses have recorded the scene; Frédéric Mistral cites the following gibe under the word *auriho*, "Negre bardaian, vaqui l'auriho de toun paire, Black infidel, here's your father's ear," and he comments, "Insult that the little rascals call out to the Jews while imitating a pig's ear with the tail of their garment." As for *bardaian*, that "injurious expression one uses for Jews," it derives from *bard*, the mud or silt where pigs like to wallow. Armand Lunel also notes the gesture and the jeer, specifying that they constitute "the exorcistic expression employed in the past by children upon encountering a Jew." Alsatian, Italian, and Catalan witnesses refer to the same situations with the same words, using the same mimicking gestures, bolstered by language that exploits the analogy in greater detail.[2] In the region of Barcelona Joan Amades reports a belief in a difference between Jews with "high ears" and Jews with "low ears." Thus we find a criteria being applied to Jews that is ordinarily used to determine the "race" of a pig. In many French provinces *oreillu*, "low ear," designates the pig. What is more, in the Pyrenees, the pig with big ears is considered to be the indigenous race, while the foreign specimens have such tiny ears there is nothing to hold on to on the day of the slaughter. If you can tell a pig by its ear, the Jew who originates from the animal must share this distinguishing feature.

In a novel by Ladislas Reymont, *Les Paysans*, the Jewish merchant who runs a small café in the little Polish village where the action takes place is greeted several times by the men who constitute his regular clientele with the epithet "Jewish pig," without any other information being given to explain this manner of speaking. But, in addition, the recent work by Ludwik Stomma on the representation of foreigners in Poland, basing itself on material previously collected by Jan S. Bystron, drew attention to the recurrence of morphological traits borrowed from animals to define the *other*. The Jew occupies a special position within this group: he is born, they say, *de culo*, for the Jewess—who is compared with a sow, carrying for six months, while the pregnancy of a noble Christian has been known to last as long as twelve—has a vulva "split crosswise." In addition, he is red-headed, smells bad, has a black palate and rear end, and pointed ears that "stick out or hang."[3] All these attributes account for the iconographic theme that appeared on cornices in Germanic Europe, toward the end of the thirteenth century, in which Jews with big ears are being nursed by enormous sows (illus. 10).[4] To illustrate the proximity between the man and the beast, obscene variations are provided: Jews straddle the animal, drink from its sexual organ, collect its excrement. But the category of "satirical allegory" under which these figurations are classified seems insufficient to account for their content: Jews and pigs placed together illustrate far more than a metaphor. When a sculptor represents sows with human heads in the midst of piglike Jews, is he not using these hybrid creatures to portray the transformation the myth pushes to its conclusion?

This affinity writ in stone is enacted by the preacher, in the midst of the Counter-Reformation, in the form of exempla. Camerarius recounts that

> in one German city a sick Jew arrived at the home of an old woman one day to ask her for milk. The latter thought to bring him that of a sow, which she went off to milk for this purpose. The milk was not long in taking effect and the Jew, noticing that he was starting to grunt like a pig, refused to drink the rest of it, but just then all the pigs in the vicinity died.[5]

Many more texts could be mentioned, all of which rehash the idea that the metamorphoses of Jews is merely the revelation of their "true nature." For the analogy doesn't stop at appearances, as the story of the ear might lead us to believe. This morphology reveals a hidden identity that a detour by way of the Pyrenean *cagot*, another marginal being, will enable us to clarify.

In the last part of his large work devoted to the *Histoire des races maudites de la France et de l'Espagne* (History of the cursed races of France and Spain, 1847), Francisque Michel provides a collection of original Gascon songs on these cagots.[6] This local lyric specialty explores every situation, from the grotesque to the pathetic, in which the hapless Pyrenean outcast is forced to disclose a defect that he tries to hide as much as possible. The songs therefore abound in "recipes" for revealing the hidden flaw. "Here is how one recognizes the cagot. First one casts a glance at his ear. He has one larger, and what is the other one like? Rounder and covered on all sides by long fuzz " (2:151). Dissymmetry, pilosity, and the absence of an earlobe constitute, according to the doctors, presumptive evidence of *cagoterie* but, most of all, this is where one detects the spots of ladrerie, or leprosy, those irrefutable signs one suspects the cagots of hiding by keeping their ears out of sight. Here is the reproach an inhabitant of Béarn addresses to an alleged cagot:

> Qué tas'tu heit dé l'aüreillou
> Jean-Pierre, lou mey amigou?
> 'as-tu dat a l'enchère?
> Tan tira, hère, hère!
> Ou bien l'as dat dé grat a grat,
> Pa poudé presti lou müssat.
>
> [What did you do with the lobe of your ear
> Jean-Pierre my little friend
> Did you put it up for auction?
> Tan tira, hère, hère!
> Or did you give it away bit by bit
> For the corn soup to be prepared.] (2:148)

Thus the cagot shares the pig's most secret illness. Let's recall the gesture of the tongue examiner: he explores the snout, around the eyes and the tongue, to ascertain the presence of those infamous "measles spots." The bearers of the illness possess this skill "naturally." According to a medical topography of the Basses-Pyrénées, many of them exercised the profession of tongue examiners and, in the canton of Orthez, several families of pig slaughterers were considered "descendants of cagot tongue examiners." Which is why the songs noted by Francisque Michel associate a custom of the cagots—they travel in groups, like "herds of pigs"—with the ill particular to them: they are, according to the songs, "measled up to their necks" and "have scaling skin"; one can grab "fist-fulls" of "measled spots" off of them.

Cagoterie and measles overlap, and the marks that designated them—in actions and words—were for a long time identical. They bring us back to the ear, our point of departure. A fourteenth-century Béarnais text of law discovered by Francisque Michel designates cagots by the term *échaureilhadz*, or *ischaureilhatz*, cropped; he himself collected the confidential testimonies of an honorable family of car-penters from Montréjeau whose nickname was Short ear. Now, while the absence of the lobe was recognized as a symptom of cagoterie—until the dawn of the twentieth century, doctors would continue this research on the subjects they examined with stupefying regularity—it could also be its consequence: at the market the tongue examiner ripped or cut the tip of the suspect animal's ear in order that henceforth it would visibly bear the mark of its stigma. By being "cropped," the cagots received the same sanction that designated the measled pig. This was so prevalent that in Béarnais the noun *chaueilh*—derived from the name of this punishment—became synonymous with *penoun* or *penderilhou*, terms designating the earlobe. The elimination of this little piece of flesh, the *eschaurelhade*, properly speaking, was in the Middle Ages a less serious punishment than complete cropping, and we find a euphemistic variation of it in the custom of "pulling" or "fub-bing" the ears, a bullying now reserved for children, a form of ritual penalty generations of schoolchildren have experienced.[7] Thus the name that stigmatized the cagots made this auricular detail both a nat-ural trait and the result of a punitive action: from this twofold per-spective they appear as a "cursed race." The marked ear made visible the interior vice of the body, but what can we say about this body? Where do the *échaureilhadz* get their measles?

It seems that any discourse on cagots gets caught up in the fascinat-ing mystery of their origin. This "mystery" has troubled historians and scholars to our day. The hypotheses are highly varied: are they descendants of the Goths, converted Saracens, Jews, Cathars? And this first line of questioning is supplanted by another: what is the nature of the illness that affects them? Do they really catch it? Is this disease, which is at the source of their exclusion, truly hereditary? All these questions have been discussed since the sixteenth century, espe-cially among doctors, some of whom, even today, insist that the unfortunate cagots are descended from distant lepers, "cagoterie" elevated to the status of a race, constituting an attenuated form of the terrible ill. The work of Francisque Michel should have swept aside these ideas, for it was the first to demonstrate, by comparing the situation of cagots with that of other "cursed races," that they were no more lepers than Goths, even if the society and local scholarship presented them as such. Collecting the arguments—from a surname to a narrative song—that posit the relationship between the cagot and the leper and between the cagot and the Jew invites us to update the logic that unites these cursed figures.

In Béarn a song states that the "father of the cagots" was the leprous lackey of King Gripput, prince of the kingdom of Galimachia, a fantasy monarch related by name to the devil. But from one song to the next this leprous footman becomes the well-known figure of Gehazi. In upper Chalosse the cagots are even called *géʒitains* and the "error" of their unfortunate eponym is readily recalled. Based on the biblical tale, the story is told of this servant of the prophet Elisha, who was punished for his greed. Whereas the prophet cured Naaman of his leprosy, asking nothing in return, Gehazi caught up with the illustrious personage and asked for and received—unbeknownst to his master—precious goods of gold and silver. To punish the thief, God transferred to him the leprosy from which Naaman had just been delivered. By making cagots the "descendants of Gehazi," the punishment is extended to the "race" of the guilty party, now marked by the disease that recalls the misdeed. They are *ladres* in both senses of the word: thief and leper. They are accused of being "crooks" and of having "hooked" fingers. Was it not mainly these offenses, in fact, that in the Middle Ages sanctioned the ignominious mutilation of the ear?[8] The cagots thus resemble the Jews in their most commonly disgraced representation. A ballad from Béarn even portrays them as descendants of the carpenters accused of making the cross on which Christ was tortured, when all other artisans had refused. Their disease punishes this contribution to deicide.

Jews, pigs, and cagots, united in a circular relationship, hiding in the fold of their ears the irrefutable mark of the stigma they all carry, that which in the case of the pig and the cagot can be named ladrerie. Though the Jew does not exhibit this ill so crudely, we shall see that his intimate vices form a coherent picture solely in the light of this disease, other signs of which we shall now enumerate, each of them solidifying and enriching the fabric of these connections.

The Bad Smell

When in about 1320 Bishop Jacques Fournier began questioning the inhabitants of the region of Foix in order to single out the heretics among them, he was quickly captivated by an unusual personage: Arnaud Gélis—alias Bouteiller—from Mas-Saint-Antonin, in Pamiers, who occupied the position of "messenger of souls." The inquisitor questioned him about his ideas on the beyond and the penitence of souls but wished to know more regarding the post mortem status of those whom the Church automatically considered to be the damned—in other words, the Jews. "What does Bouteiller teach on this subject?" he asked Mengarde, the seamstress, and Bouteiller's principal client. "He tells me that the Jews who die travel the paths like Christians," she replied, "but not with them, and that they worship on a mountain or on a plain, and that the defunct Christians make fun of them, calling them dogs." Questioned in turn, Arnaud Gélis confirmed that he could see the souls of Jews quite well: "I have often seen dead Jews, some of whom were walking backward, others heading straight ahead like the others. But I did not see them enter the churches. They travel the paths, not with the Christians, however, but among themselves, and I don't know if they go to the place of rest." But the bishop, knowing that there were few Jews in these Pyrenean regions—only one, from Toulouse, in fact, would be questioned by him—and familiar with dialectical subtleties, pushed one point that proved decisive: "How could you distinguish the Jews from the Christians?" To which Arnaud Gélis provided this firm and immediate response: "Because they stink and keep away from the others." A stench Raimonde de Pamiers seconded, completing Mengarde's testimony: "The same Arnaud said, speaking to me and in my presence, that the souls of Jews went with the souls of Christians, but they walked curved like pigs. Many of them were saved."[9]

The "bad smell" of the Jew is certainly the first and most constant feature of anti-Judaism, and the most universal one as well. This smell, stigmatized again and again—to the point that medieval literature, which cultivated epithets, always attached that of *pudent* to the Jew—received a recurrent explanation in medical treatises, which expanded on the image provided by our Pyrenean witnesses: "It is this stench [of the Jews] and the filth in which they wallow every day in their homes, like a pig in its trough, that makes them subject to inflammations of the skin, to flushes, and to other stinking illnesses that cause them to lower their heads all the time."[10]

By living like pigs—recall the epithet *bardaian* used by the Provençal boys—the Jews were alleged to develop the illnesses that commonly affected the animal as well as its bearing. In this world, and beyond, they walk "curved over," "heads lowered," a stance that, according to breeders, is one of the first symptoms of measles in the pig. Their odor and bearing are also indications of the illness that corrupts their flesh and their breath more deeply, predisposing them to various afflictions that are apparent in the disorder of bodily fluids, particularly of the blood. The doctors who treated the "discharges" of Jews and cagots, who were also afflicted by these strange "flushes," perfected an infallible test to decide if they were leprous or not. They bled them, collected the blood in a basin, added salt to it—the exact proportion of which was even specified—and watched. If the salt "melted," it was due "to the excessive heat of the fluid," leading to the conclusion that the patient was infected.[11] In so doing, the doctors were close to applying to humans a reading still used for the pig: "The meat of the measled pig, it doesn't take the salt; it doesn't coagulate. It dissolves in water, and then, it stays red, it can't be preserved, it rots."

The smell, a new shared symptom, which in both cases results from a single ill, triggered interesting etiological constructions. As always, they manipulate while reversing causal relationships. Indeed, specialists consider porcine measles to be endemic. As Jews are particularly "predisposed" to this illness, it is considered quite appropriate that they should abstain from a "flesh" so close to their own. The ancients were the first to support this thesis, which Plutarch, in his *Table Talk* (4, question 5), made the backbone of his explanation of the Jewish prohibition against pork. But, generally, consumption of the flesh of the pig has always been regulated among those who eat it. From the Latin agronomers to the *Maisons rustiques* (guides to domestic economy found in peasant homes), it is advised in small quantities; moist and hot, it is recommended only to dry temperaments and counterindicated to hot ones. In all cases it is preferred salted. Consequently, the sale of "fresh meat" is subject to rigorous legislation, with certain regions prohibiting it entirely. In lower Navarre, for example, in the fourteenth century, "salted pork could only be sold after a certain time in order to allow the salt to penetrate the flesh. Certain unscrupulous butchers sold as *carnbielh* (aged meat) pigs that had been salted two or three days before, fresh pork fetching four liards a pound and salted pork six liards from Christmas to Ash Wednesday, and eight from Easter to Christmas."[12]

Is this to say that Jews, too, need to be salted? This is at least what came out of the debate on the "bad smell," the arguments of which were reexamined in the seventeenth century by Thomas Brown in his *Essais sur les erreurs populaires*. The French edition states that "Hucher and Cursius after him attribute this odor to their habit of abstaining from salt and salted meats, which is difficult to prove for modern Jews and hardly seems founded with respect to the ancient Jews, who certainly salted their victims and offerings, of which the priests ate a large part."[13]

Deprived of the meat of the pig and its "salt," the Jews, who, according to Christian commentary, thereby believed they were protecting themselves from leprosy, found themselves paradoxically exposed to it. For them there was no escaping it. One couplet says it clearly, commenting on an old German engraving entitled *Das grosse Judenschwein*, "And as we do not eat roasted pork, we are lustful and our breath stinks."[14]

The Red Jew

The following riddle is asked in Saintonge: "Why do Jews have red beards?" There is no real response, for the question makes plain a cultural understanding that can only be illustrated by way of an entire analogical and explicative thought process we shall now follow.

Allusion has been made several times already to the "flush of blood" of the cagots or Jews, to the "secretions" of their bodily fluids, to their internal warmth and sexual ardor. Meanwhile, these same features mark the porcine species and, among the possible causes of leprosy, there is one that deepens the similarity of the two "natures." We have already mentioned the precautions relating to the consumption of pork; it is now fitting to add to that list the distinction between "male meat" and "female meat." If the castration of most males succeeds in regulating their bodily fluids, this is not true of females, who are operated upon less frequently, so as to preserve their reproductive capacities. But, one day, the cast sow—impossible to neuter, say the castrators—ends up on the market. In the Middle Ages this meat was sold at a special stall. It was strongly prohibited to sell "trueja pria per de porc, trueja porcelina o grossa per prima, ni vielha per novela," as stipulated by a Lauragais ordinance of 1333, the terms of which also appeared in other regions of France, Spain, and Italy. In all cases a distinction was made not only between the young sow and the male but between a pregnant sow, or one that had just given birth, and a young sow, between old and young. The latter, as long as it had been castrated, was viewed with a certain indulgence, whereas the meat of the older animal, or one that had been covered—if only once—was strictly forbidden for sale or joined the meat considered measled on a separate shelf. The two meats, in fact, were gathered together and combined under the single name of *carn corrupude*, which was purchased cheaply by the poor, who were believed to be at lesser risk of "contamination." If offenders were caught selling it mixed in with good meat, it was seized; the many Gascon texts devoted to these insalubrious meats ordered "que la carn sie dade aus gafets, that the flesh be given to lepers." The Scottish rules in force in the twelfth century brought into play the same principle: the "corrupted" pigs placed on the market had immediately to be sent to lepers, or, if there were none nearby, entirely destroyed.[15]

The association between the meat of a sow and measled meat might seem surprising should one forget the hot and passionate temperament of an animal—the most dissolute of females—reputed to permit herself to be covered by the male when already pregnant. Permanently in heat, she marks her progeny, as we have seen, with a redness that only a total body eruption can cast off through the surface of the skin, via erysipelas, accompanied by a fever that either brings down or liberates the pig but, in all cases, "heats" its flesh and makes it inedible. We have previously described the analogy by which this disease and children's measles are considered to belong to the same category. Fueldez, a doctor in Rodez, discussing the "difference that can exist between the menstrual infection that produces syphilis (comparable, according to him, to a strong measles) and that which produces ladrerie," adopts the old theory of Arab doctors: "Thus Alzaranius, in the chapter on leprosy, decides the heart of the question when he says that the child becomes measled if it is engendered with the mother's own menstrual blood and develops smallpox, through an infection that occurs during the residence within the womb with the menstrual blood." If children are *marked* by menstrual blood—on which they "feed" throughout the pregnancy—until their liberation via a red sickness, conception during menstruation sullies them with an indelible leprosy that is far more serious. Ambroise Paré, Liébault, and, before them, the great doctors of the fourteenth century were all in agreement on this matter.[16] Might leprous Jews be the fruit of an "unnatural" conception?

Offspring produced by such a conception—to complete the picture—were set apart by unequivocal signs on which an entire body of literature provided abundant commentary. Throughout Europe red hair indicated fertilization during menstruation, along with an entire set of features casting the redhead as a disturbed being whose smell was strong and breath too hot. It was thus a discredited color that obviously did not spare the pig, which passed through a radical selection process at times. "In various places people are so far from preferring blonds that if a specimen of this shade shows up among a litter it is quickly drowned, for all those with such skin are imagined to be measled: the red and the mottled are highly subject to the same sickness."[17] Which is why Jews were said to be red; they were commonly nicknamed Father Jaundice or Egg Yolk in Poland, Carrot Hair in Germany, where one avoided sowing carrots on Saturdays, the day of the Sabbath, or their roots would be "like Jewish beards." All the "cursed races" whose images we have outlined present this feature, which even lends its name to a small marginalized group that Francisque Michel discovered in Angoumois: the *reds*, the *russets*. Of course, the doctors who examined the cagots all noted "the reddish color of their hair," and in the Asturias the peasants of the plain, evoking their highland neighbors, the *vaqueiros*, told the ethnographer that they were *demasiado rubios*, too red or too strong, which is also true of redheaded and menstruating women. It is this deeper redness—beyond physical appearance—that is betrayed by the foul breath, the smell we have already noted, and the burning touch. A petition of 1517 against the *agotes* of Navarre presented proof of their leprosy as follows: "We see it clearly, for the plants they trample while walking dry instantly and lose their natural qualities and also because an apple or any fruit they hold in their hands or place at their chest rots." Ambroise Paré, examining lepers, adopts the belief that "sometimes, if one of them held a fresh apple in his hand for the space of an hour, the fruit appeared as dried out and wrinkled afterward as if it had been eight days in the sun."[18] Menstruating women were also alleged to desiccate flowers and green plants by touching or even by merely looking at them—when they weren't condemning conserves, salting tubs, and wine cellars to rot by the putrefying power of their breath. We should not be surprised, then, to learn that the cagots' "skin became quite red, especially during the phases of the moon" or that they were possessed, on the nights of the full moon, by a strange ill, the *cagoutille*. As for Jews, whose calendar is guided by this star whose rebirth they celebrate, first with their new moon festivals, then with their Sabbath, it is in the image of the feminine star that they "bleed every month."[19]

Jews and cagots, by sharing the intervals of women, participate in their sexuality, but their redness also betrays a "disordered state" that feeds the "strange heat" said never to leave them. Florimond de Roemond, who, in the seventeenth century, pleaded the falsity of the physiology attributed to Jews and cagots, reported, skeptically, "It is claimed, for example, that they all have foul breath, that they feel no need to blow their noses, that they are subject to a continual fluctuation of blood and semen, that they are born with long tails."[20]

As red men, Jews are subject to desire and to blood in the manner of red females, the reddest of which is the sow. Let us return to the *Judensau* iconography, certain aspects of which we have already explored. The depiction is of Jews being nursed by the animal. Now, of all the mammals consumed by Christians, the sow is the only female whose milk is not put to use. Like the milk of the redheaded wet nurse—who, it is feared, will transmit her qualities to the child—the milk of the animal would put one at risk of contamination. Already, in *On the Characteristics of Animals*, Aelianus asserted that "merely tasting sow's milk caused one to become covered in skin patches and leprosy."[21] The image of the Judensau, therefore, also asserts a bond "of nature" between the Jews and the red female and allows us to draw the consequences as to the sexuality of those who are produced by such a mother. Medieval iconography, in fact, takes this one step farther: lustful Jews mount the animal, fornicate with it, performing the crime of bestiality, the prohibition against which was, as we know, strictly enforced. The "strange heat" that reappears in the writings of doctors who treat cagots and lepers, this "singular heat" alleged to maintain their sexual organs in a permanent state of turgidity—to such an extent that castration is recommended— is thus explained. But popular imagery adds a particular significance to this sexuality. By coupling with their progenitor are the Jews not acting as *gens incestuosa*, a qualification that also haunts them? The songs noted by Francisque Michel suggest a similar propensity among cagots: one of them, married to a "Christian" woman, so exhausted her that she died, and he continued to marry, his wives succumbing one after the next in the face of such demanding vigor. Moreover, they are said to be "equally hot for their mothers as for their sisters." As for cagot women, they need as many men as children; they reproduce "like cats."[22]

As concerns Jews, the Middle Ages produced a mythical figure of the false messiah that was brought to the stage. In Savoy, until the early seventeenth century, his spectacular birth was represented in the *Mystère de l'Antéchrist et du Jugement de Modane*. A messenger first announces his arrival:

In Babylon the city
An abominable rake of a Jew,
Prompted by lechery
By the temptation of the Devil,
Would carnally know his own daughter
From which the false wretch would be born.

And throughout the sixteenth century it was repeatedly asserted that this false messiah was in the image of a pig.[23]

The Mark of Judas

If, in the eyes of Christians, the entire Jewish nation is marked by incest, among the red figures it includes (and they are ever so evocative, from Esau, to Saul, to Cain, those fratricidal red men), there is one who accumulates and magnifies the features whose grouping we have just proposed, raising them to the status of a singular destiny, and that figure is Judas.

In France, the expression *poil de Judas* designates a redhead. In Germany, "Judas" or "soul of Judas" suffices. This is equally true in Bavaria, in Swabia, in Franconia, and to such an extent that the Catholic Church itself had to defend redheads against this slanderous identification. We should add that, throughout Europe, freckles are called "marks of Judas." And it is also often Judas—and sometimes Cain—who is recognized in the spots of the moon. In Catalonia Judas is always said to be "redheaded, with unkempt hair," which is why in the Passion theater, during the Holy Week and Corpus Christi processions, he is a grotesque character, distinguished from the others by his disheveled scrubby wig. And the wealth of iconography purposely increases his redness: from red hair to an abundant red beard, from the emblematic red purse he wears around his neck or carries in his left hand (since the traitor most often poses in profile) to his red clothing or the gaudy fox fur he sometimes wears around his shoulders.[24] A common tradition attributes this universal redness to Judas's betrayal on the Mount of Olives; this, in any case, is the assertion underlying the spell against burns, skin irritations, inflammations, and red sicknesses:

Fire, fire, lose your heat
As Judas did his color
When he betrayed Our Lord.

But the *Lives of the Saints* furnish far more detail, noting that, on February 24, Saint Matthias's Day, he "was put in the place of Judas," who had been crossed off the list of apostles for his heinous crime. Jacques de Voragine, echoing an earlier tradition, which many medieval Passion plays adopted and illustrated after him, composed a biography that, while offering a coherent reading of Judas's fate, invites us to reread the significant episodes. It begins, almost as in the myth of Oedipus, with a dream that reveals to his mother that she will give birth to "a son, who will cause the destruction of the Jewish race." At his birth he is therefore abandoned, like Moses, in a swaying basket, the currents carrying him to Iscariot. He is taken in by the sterile queen, who receives this newborn as a gift from the sky, even simulating a pregnancy at the end of which she "brings him into the world" in a second birth. And he does indeed bring her fecundity, since shortly thereafter she becomes truly pregnant and gives birth to a son. Judas feels such jealousy for this younger brother that he brutally kills him before fleeing to Jerusalem, where we find him in the service of Pilate, governor of Judea. Judas reigns over his friend's palace, but Pilate governs his heart. One day Pilate sees some beautiful apples in a nearby garden; he calls Judas and tells him, "I have such a desire for the fruit of this garden, if I do not have some, I shall die." So Judas heads off in an emotional state and hastens to take some apples.[25]

We know what follows: the orchard belonged to Ruben, the father of Judas who, like Oedipus, fulfills his destiny: he kills his father and marries his mother. The Passion plays treat the events narrated here as a counterpoint to the life of Christ. Even today the "despair of Judas" constitutes one of the highlights of any representation: in a long monologue he reviews his life and crimes. The Catalan theater of the fourteenth century was the first to develop all these episodes. We learn through Judas that his mother abandoned him, after having "marked him with a red iron," so that he would escape the massacre of Innocents commanded by Herod. A detail that, focusing the emphasis of this ill-fated destiny, contributes to dramatizing the story, which unravels over the course of hundreds of verses in the great European Passion plays of the fifteenth and sixteenth centuries, turning this scene into a veritable "Passion of Judas." But sometimes the emphasis is focused on the cynicism of the character, his choice and responsibility replacing the tragic blindness. In such cases the sequence of events may be reversed without compunction: he sins with his mother first and admits to killing his father later, "per poder [se] més folgar," for fun. While this variant is a late one (eighteenth century), it is not unique; a fifteenth-century Catalan text upbraids him in these terms: "O traydor! Per qué no es remembrant del pecat de la tua mare la qual fou causa de la mort de ton pare! O traitor, how can you forget the sin of your mother, who caused the death of your father!" Whichever the case, death, always represented in very realistic fashion, brings an end to these revelations.[26] In the Passion of Jean Michel (1486), the scribe who indicates the scenic effects specifies that "the soul of Judas, being perverse, could not pass through the same mouth that had kissed Jesus; it therefore finds another path, for the traitor, having hung himself, dies by the gut and his intestines hang out, making way for his evil soul." A German version even specifies "Judas must have animal entrails that fall when the devil opens his robe."[27] We can bet that they were often pig entrails—as we shall see, many were killed during this Easter period—that slipped to the feet of the illustrious hanged man (illus. 18, 19, 20).

The moral leprosy of Judas, fallen like Gehazi for his greed, and his ambiguous redness—in Spain, dummies are sometimes burned at Easter called "Judas" and "Judasse"—find an expected outcome in this singular death. We are familiar with the sexual effects of hanging. According to the medieval belief, the executed criminal gave birth to vegetable species with dual forms, virtues, and natures: the mandrakes that were long sought at the foot of gallows. Was this the case for Judas? According to the most widespread tradition in Europe, his meanness, his "corruption," first passed into the tree or the vegetable species from which he hung himself. In Catalonia it was the *baladre*, the rose laurel, that traded its white flowers for poisonous red ones. But other versions point to the fig tree, which became sterile, the trembling poplar, which caught a fever and "trembles more," or the elder tree, which acquired its black berries and its bitterness. This malodorous tree, treacherous for climbing—its branches break like glass—also shades a variety of mushroom that lives in symbiosis with it and of which Rolland writes, "*Fungus sambucinus*, this mushroom is called *sambucinus* because it is mostly found attached to the elder, and 'ear of Judas' because tradition has it that Judas hung himself from an elder tree."[28] This ear of Judas brings us back to our starting point. Judas, according to the European tradition, is the father of all red-headed boys and all "easy" girls, a fact of which they are reminded by the same formula. In Bordeaux and its environs one sings to the red-headed boy:

Carrot top, do you remember
When your father was hung
from the end of a rope.

To the girl, in Belgium, one says:

Impudent one
Your mother burned
Your father was hung
By the branch of an elder

And, from Liège to Arles, one decorates her come May with a branch of this tree, which signifies, in Picardy, that she is a whore—as explicitly stated by the maxim, "Moé de chenï, ch'est enne truie, Elder May, she's a sow"—that her blood is too hot or that she had a bastard. In Languedoc it means that she "stinks," that one cannot and should not trust her . . . features that define all those who, we have seen, share the nature of the red men and the "hot" women.[29]

"Pig's ear, your father's ear," repeat the Provençal boys to the Jew exiting the synagogue, while in Majorca the Christian schoolboys slip a piece of pork into the pocket of the *xuetas*, then, circling around the children (accused of having remained "Jews"), pretend to be looking for something on the ground. When questioned, they answer, sarcastically, "Venim a cercar es testament de'n Judes, We are looking for the testament of Judas."[30]

The equivalency between the Jew and the pig, initially posited with the brutality of an insult, gives way to a first branch of relationships that, passing by lepers, cagots, and red men, culminates in the figure of Judas, of whom we shall later sketch other profiles. But what constitutes the Jew in his "true nature"—the morphology, physiology, and pathology of a pig—also serves as a matrix of interpretation to account for the difference in lifestyle and, especially, for rituals whose veil of mystery is thereby instantly lifted.

The Pigs' Baptism

"Oh him, he was baptized with a pruning knife!" That is how one designates the Jew in Languedoc today, just as one says of the Protestant that he is "baptized under a juniper," by allusion to the clandestine ceremonies of the desert. This "baptism" of Jews—circumcision being understood only with reference to the Christian sacrament—is certainly the ritual that inspired the most intense curiosity. Sixteenth-century travelers visiting Jewish communities—such as Montaigne during his sojourn in Italy, Platter during his medical studies in Montpellier, where he boarded with a family of Marranos—witnessed circumcisions and gave very precise descriptions of them, which may be compared with those emanating from Jewish milieus.

Let us recall, very quickly, that the operation takes place in three stages that correspond to three essential gestures. The first is the moment when the operators, using the ritual knife, cut the foreskin, properly speaking. In the Roman community, according to Montaigne, it seems that every precaution was taken to cut only the necessary minimum: "He takes the member and pulls the skin back over it with one hand, pushing the glans and the member inside with the other. At the end of this skin which he holds toward the said glans, he places a silver instrument which stops the skin there and, in slicing it, prevents him from injuring the glans and the flesh." The final stage of the operation, which Montaigne and Platter both recognize as the most "violent," concerns the rupture of the glans' frenum by the circumciser: "He grasped the foreskin with the two long nails of his thumbs, separated it violently and pushed it behind the glans, which remained completely naked." Between the two gestures the *metsitsa* takes place, the repeated sucking of the member, intended to stop the bleeding provoked by the cut.[31]

This ritual, to which we shall later return, provoked the mirth of the Provençaux, who called the Jews *sucabarigoula*, mushroom-suckers. What the epithet implies, facetious remarks, "jokes," or spectacles even, trivially represents. A highly popular and often performed pantomime—though delicately left unmentioned in most works devoted to the Italian theater—persisted in the seventeenth century "among the people" where, according to Bragaglia, a specialist in the genre, it had the same effect on the Roman audience as a "grain of pepper." French travelers in the eighteenth century—De Brosses, the Abbé Coyer— evoked these "comedies full of sacrilege and indecency," such as *Puclinella fatto ebreo* (Punchinello plays the Jew) that Coyer summarizes as soberly as possible: "I saw one in which Punchinello becomes a Jew. The songs, the prayers, the ceremonies of this religion emanating from God are turned to ridicule. A Rabbi, the circumcision knife in hand, frightens Punchinello, causing the girls to ask, What will the Rabbi do to him? As early as the fourteenth century a theatrical genre was born: the *giudiata*, which, as its name indicates, depicts Jews, most often endowed with priapic noses, as attested by the masks that have reached us in the form of engravings. The "rabbi" maneuvers among them bearing a "coltello grande per la circoncizione," which he brandishes menacingly in the direction of his coreligionists' monstrous appendages, to the audience's great amusement.[32] This play on a displaced castration speaks to us about the nature of the ritual attributed to Jews and about its anticipated effects. A glance at the spectrum of scattered terms that designate Jews, but also cagots or lepers, brings out the common reference to the well-known operation. Thus, the cagots find themselves referred to as *crestias*, among other names, and Francisque Michel—wary of scholarly etymological justifications—sticks to the popular gloss that recognizes the verb *crestar*, to castrate, in this word. "There can be no doubt that the belief according to which the cagots are descended from the Jews owes its origin to this interpretation. The latter were called eunuchs or capons because of the circumcision they underwent, an operation that the people understood no better than they do today."[33] Whether they are considered castrated or fit to castrate—let's not forget the debate as to whether lepers should be castrated—Pyrenean cagots, lepers, and Jews are "treated" by the Christian in the image of the animal of reference. And one cannot help but note the redundancy with which this relationship is put forward. Cagots are also called *capots* (from *capar*, "to castrate"); Guy de Chauliac, discussing lepers in his *Grande Chirugie* (1383), also gives as a synonym of *ladre* (leprous or measled): *capots* and *cassots*. The term is certainly defamatory. It leaves a threat hovering over its unfortunate targets to which other outcasts were equally subjected. Such was the case of the *vaqueiros*, the "cursed race" of the Asturias studied by María Cátedra Tomás. These mountain people, whom their neighbors of the plain considered "too red," were said to descend from the Moors who refused to obey King Pelagius. It is said that they took refuge in the highest mountains to escape expulsion and massacres. This is what the *aldeanos* of the plain tell the ethnologist:

> They always sleep on their stomachs because they are afraid of being castrated (*capan*). When Pelagius expelled the Moors, it was said he wanted to castrate them, and there was one called Diego, Diego de la Capona, who did castrate them. And one woman said "better to leave them in the highest mountains of the Asturias, where they'll die of hunger." And that is why they were banished there—why they live in the mountains, at the highest point.[34]

The *vaqueiros* thus survived and prospered, but the ancestral fear remains.

The threat implied by the words and legends was, in certain cases, acted upon. Indeed, a very real castration sometimes awaited Jews accused of having had sexual relations with Christian women. In the fourteenth century residents of Avignon denounced such a crime; the guilty parties were emasculated and their organs exhibited for the edification of the public. In Spain Jews who were convicted of having performed circumcision on Christians were also castrated. The punishment speaks volumes, in this case, on the nature of the alleged crime. In 1652, in a Parisian section of secondhand dealers, when rumor took hold that a murder had actually been a ritual crime, "the Jews" were quickly accused of being the culprits. From one lampoon to the next we can see the development of the representation of the greedy, heartless Jew, leading up to the ultimate play, entitled *Le jugement criminel rendu contre la synagogue des fripiers partant que ceux de leur nombre qui se trouveront circoncis (qui est la marque de la juiverie) seront chastrez, ric à ric, afin que la race en demeure à jamais éteinte dans Paris* (The criminal judgment rendered against the synagogue of second-hand dealers [by virtue of which] those among them who are found to be circumcised [which is the mark of Jewery] will be thoroughly castrated in order that the race will remain forever extinct in Paris).[35]

For Christians circumcision evokes castration, and the latter is always present in the mythical background of the Jew, even if, in reality, it figures as an exception. We find it euphemized and displaced in a custom still alive in Provence in the nineteenth century and recorded by Armand Lunel: "When the kids of Carpentras met a Jew on the street, they threw stones at him and bullied him, shouting *capo! capo!* until he took off his hat." According to other sources they also said *faire cavo* to designate the custom by which any Christian, merely by saying *fai cavo!* (or *fai capo!*), could make a Jew kneel before him, his head down and hat in hand. But hat in Provençal is *capèu*, and even if the gesture that accompanied the hazing may have brought about a redefinition of *capo* into *capèu*, we would tend, based on all the preceding information, to recognize the meaning already apparent with respect to cagots. Moreover, Mistral permits us to see the development around the word and expression of a semantic field familiar to us. *Faire la capo* means to become corrupted, whereas *capo* means a libertine but also a ladre and a cagot. Finally *a sei cavo* is said of a woman who has her "business," who is menstruating. As the pig is at the heart of this network of meanings, its mere evocation in a neighboring context suffices perhaps to verify that the relationship was not forgotten. An old Jewish man, a contemporary of Armand Lunel, relates: "And I always heard that an alms collector in Leghorn, encountering my uncle the rabbi outside the ghetto, pulled him by the beard and forced him to kneel: *Porco! Porco!* he shouted . . . knocking his forehead into the dust."[36]

We must pursue this line of inquiry for the relationship to the castration of the pig to become clear and for the interpretive use that is made of it with regard to the Jew to be further refined. Let us return to the Italian theater, which has the advantage of being blunt in what it says and shows in this area. Between the fourteenth and seventeenth centuries a series of genres followed one after the next that had the common feature of defining themselves around their central characters, as had the *giudiata*. In the fifteenth century, according to Bragaglia, a new burlesque genre was born, the *norcino*. Its name was derived from Norcia, a city in Umbria whose peasants furnished a comic type of incomprehensible, dialect-speaking commoner. But this character was also an artisan, a professional we have already encountered: the *norcino*, in Italy, is a castrator of pigs and children. Itinerant by profession, he first emigrated from this poor region toward Rome, where we find him taking on the added roles of slaughterer and pork butcher in winter, straw hat merchant in summer. Soon the theater, drawing from life, integrated this model and the norcino appeared, dressed "as a pig castrator"—*castraporci*—a large knife in his hand to better signify his role; he calls to the passersby, who respond with gestures reminiscent of those employed in the giudata. He represents the most primitive of characters; his appearance on stage triggers gibes: *villano codicone, porco brodigone*. Though he brags in a highly realistic monologue of the "marvelous" effects of his operations, he also confides to the pit the reason he had to flee his region: *una mala capata*, a bad castration, a dirty business.[37] Unfortunately there remain only a few fragments of these plays—the plots, as we know, were often slim—and some evocative titles: *Il porci, Il castraporcelli*. The giudiata and the norcino, each while pursuing its own course, could not help but merge. Are they not, after all, complementary, depicting the potential eunuchs, the Jews, and the professional castrators? Don't rabbis and castraporci reveal two aspects of the same gesture? The norcino maneuvers in the animal sphere, with all its extensions into the human realm that we have seen, while the rabbi acts on beings whose humanity is less than certain. They are depicted with the same pantomime, waving their respective weapons. As a result, the Jew and the castrator encountered one another in the theater through the mediation of a comedic author, Giovanni Briccio, who seems to have made a specialty of the genre. One of his extant plays, composed in 1627, *Li strapazzati* ("The Mistreated," "The Tattered"), contrasts the figure of the Jewish merchant, who is ridiculous in his amorous pretensions, and that of the norcino.

The crude norcini, which the *commedia* associates with circumcised Jews, strengthens the parallel: whether they "castrate" themselves by the hand of the circumciser or are threatened with being castrated by the man no longer adept at his art, are Jews not always, in this theater, the badly castrated ones? No doubt, for well beyond the Italian stage, the metonymy that leads from circumcision to castration is always nuanced by this failed effort, by this incompleteness, opening new horizons for satire. The games of castration in which Jews are sometimes the participants and sometimes the victims combine two registers. First, the reading of the circumcision with which they provide us confirms the Jew in the image of the pig. Like the latter, his sexual indetermination is both a fact "of nature" and an effect of the culture (the *xuetas*, who are alleged to be recognizable by their voices, which are "shrill like those of women," are still called *homes-dones*). Though they may possess their own professional castrator in the person of the rabbi, in the eyes of Christians the latter cannot claim to successfully perform the delicate operation that regulates and harmonizes, the secret of which only those who raise pigs may know. This makes a frequent insult noted in Provence by Mistral and Lunel more comprehensible: *macasse* is shouted at Jews, or, speaking of one of them, *es un macasse*. Both authors are at a loss to explain the insult. Lunel sees in it a deformation of *kasher*, alluding to the Jewish dietary laws, while Mistral considers it a derivation of the curse word *macareu*, "pimp," still present in the latter form in Provence. Yet we need only recall that *casse, cassato, cassot* formerly designated lepers and Jews as well as the measled pig and the castrated sow. *Casse* in Provençal also refers to the male sexual organ that has been "fixed" and the prefix *ma (mau, mal)* introduces the pejorative nuance: the Jew is "poorly castrated." In Provence an analogy arises with the lepers, who during the same period were commonly called *rascassetos*. Let us recall the popular Parisian prosecution demanding the strict, "ric à ric" castration of Jewish secondhand merchants, in other words, perfectly flat and not halfway.

In addition, Jews and lepers appear together in Corpus Christi processions in Aix, and the association induced by the term designating them is more than phonetic, as demonstrated by the "games" in which they are united. First, during the nocturnal march, the two groups, lepers then Jews, follow one after the other. Then, in the course of the daytime procession, each group plays a specific game. According to Gaspard Grégoire, who in 1777 furnished the best description of the ceremony in Aix, and accompanied it with images, the Jews played *juec daou cat*, throwing and catching a cat wrapped in a canvas sack, a mysterious game Grégoire interpreted as a parodylike transposition of the cult of the golden calf. But the Jews were distinguished mainly by their clothes: "They are dressed in black, with little black coats that reach their knees. Their earlocks, on either side of their heads, protrude enormously, making for a rather ugly hairstyle." If the Jews stand out by their unusual "heads," the lepers are distinguished by the equally surprising game played on the head of one of their own: "One has a large comb, the other a brush, the third a shearing scissors. These three are almost shorn." They gesticulate around the fourth, wearing "a dirty, old wig," and pretend to comb his hair, to brush it, and especially to *sheer* it. We shall leave out the etymological lucubrations of scholars invoked by Grégoire to attempt to understand a scene about which he concludes: "It's hard to say what that might signify." Yet these lepers are acting out the very name that stigmatizes them! If the Jews are poorly castrated, their leprous brothers are cleanly castrated: shorn, razed.[38] We know that there is an equivalency between shaving and castration, which rituals such as the "barber's game" or "shaving the bear" periodically recall in the peasant societies of Europe. Next to the right of *faire capo*, another ritual hazing, related by Armand Lunel, was maintained in Provence: "The Israelites traditionally cared about their beards. Knowing this, the captain of the Catholic youth group, during the carnival, at the helm of his mad squadron, fell upon a Jew and had permission to shave him completely, brutally, savagely, with a jagged knife, an affront known by the name of *droit de barbe* that was finally atoned for in the seventeenth century with an annual fee paid in crowns."[39] This same right was long the privilege of Toulousian students who marked the Jew by shaving him halfway.

Let us stick to our own context in order to better establish the equivalency we have just posited. The Jews employ it when they find themselves in the difficult situation of re-Judaizing one of their own who has passed for a time into Christianity. Here, on this subject, is the confession of Baruch, a baptized Jew, suspected of having fallen back into sin and, thereby, liable of heresy. He describes to the Bishop of Pamiers the ritual by which the Jewish community reintegrates someone who cannot be circumcised a second time: "The baptized Jews who return to Judaism do so in the following manner, according to Talmudic doctrine: the nails of their hands and feet are cut, their hair is shorn, and their entire body is washed in clear water."[40] The correspondence is thus put into practice; the right exercised by the Christians also borrows from Jewish ritual: a bad shave ("halfway," "with a jagged knife") equals a bad castration. But since we have passed to the side of the Jews in examining this question of the re-Judaization of a defector, let us also, conversely, look at the solutions possible for someone who wishes to definitively erase the mark of Judaism from his body—and such cases exist. Christian surgeons were, it seems, more than once solicited for this purpose. Laurent Joubert, in the second part of his *Erreurs populaires*, explains the rationale for a certain number of "vulgar words." Of the Languedocian *retalhat* he writes: "It's a Jew or a Turk who has left his religion and whom his people have since named *retalhat*, just as we say defector. But the meaning is different—it's for a different occasion. Namely, it is when the Jew and the Turk, having been circumcised, subsequently leaving behind their group and no longer wishing to bear the mark, have the head of their virile member recovered." The method immediately follows: "To remake a foreskin, one must cut the skin of the virile member against its root all around. When it has thus lost its conduit, one pulls it little by little from below, as one strips a branch of willow, to make a trunk, until the head is covered with it."[41] The langue d'oc term that designates someone who has undergone this operation is clear: *re-talhat*, twice castrated. For Christians, then, Jews cannot escape their destiny. By the same logic, a Christian can never entirely become a Jew. Basnage, the seventeenth-century historian, relates that in France, under Philip the Fair, "an order was established of re-Judaizers or apostates, who, after having voluntarily left the synagogue, returned to it through ablutions and had their heads shaved. There were Christians who became Jews and who were circumcised in a manner different from the others in order that they might always be distinguished from the truly circumcised."[42]

A Small Difference

The operation that gives Jews their identity is therefore only possible on a Jew. Thus, in Provence, in the early twentieth century, the word *retalhat*, for which Joubert gave us a concrete meaning, is still applied to the Jew who becomes a Christian, to any Jew who has rejected his origins. The analogical treatment of this ritual thus expresses an essential idea for Christians: the Jew remains a Jew no matter what; any attempt to escape his state only reinforces it. By a surprising reversal, circumcision, a deliberate act, a cultural fact, "naturalizes" the Jew, and this naturalization, as we have shown, always brings him back to the pig. This logic is best demonstrated when we look to the *conversos*, and particularly to the two large groups of Jews, Majorcan and Portuguese, who converted to Catholicism: the *xuetas* and the Marranos.

The xuetas of Majorca have inspired and continue to fuel an abundant literature, but they are first known to us through the registers of the Spanish Inquisition and the work of Baruch Braunstein. Converted to Christianity in the fifteenth century as the price for maintaining their freedom and their lands, they continued to practice the major Jewish rituals—aside from circumcision, which was too visible—and to abstain from pork, until the Inquisition decided to hunt down this crypto-Judaism. The worst period for them began in the seventeenth century. Torture, autos-da-fé, confiscation of goods, and expulsions recurred until 1691. These persecutions had the effect of exalting a Jewishness that, throughout the two previous centuries, had learned to come to terms with Christianity. The xuetas rediscovered themselves as Jews; one of the first victims of the auto-da-fé of 1675, Alonso López, became a "martyr." The end of persecution, for those who remained there alive, brought about a redefinition of their status. They had to be Catholics; they could no longer be Jews. The era of the xuetas began in earnest, and continues to our day.

The word *xueta* appeared for the first time in an official document in 1688. Called upon to furnish their genealogy in the name of the infamous *limpieza de sangre*, purity of blood, those who had been forewarned declared themselves "de casta y generación de xuetas de la Calle." *Chueta* or *xuyeta*, according to Braunstein, is both a deformation and a diminutive of the Catalan *jueu, jueta* and thus means "little Jew." Now, these "little Jews," of whom the inquisitor Don Juan de Fontamar, in 1672, outlined a thirty-two-point portrait intended to facilitate their identification and denunciation, were, in the eyes of the magistrate, the very model of duplicity. Such duplicity manifested itself particularly in the realm of food:

> Not only don't they eat animal fats, but they even abstain from meats cooked with it. And they observe this to such excess that they stop eating sheep on the days when the pigs are killed because they are slaughtered at the same butcher and are cut up on the same tables. For added dissimulation, they buy some pigs, of which they later sell the fat and

the leanest meat, make a few grilled meats, adding a great deal of cow and lamb meat and so much spice that one can barely tell if there's any pork; moreover, they eat it ostentatiously and manage to be seen by the Catholics, whereas when they eat other foods they hide from them.[43]

This disdain for pork and even more so for lard exacerbates the hatred of their neighbors, who consider it a desire to denigrate what is for them the most desirable and precious part of the animal. But the xuetas make themselves even more odious still by their "dissimulation" and by the display—induced, no doubt, by inquisitional practices—of a false adhesion to a Christianity they thereby doubly ridicule.

We find the same accusations brought against the Marranos, the Portuguese Jews expelled in 1487. Having passed into Spain, they were subsequently chased from that country in 1492. From there they emigrated toward the south of France (to Bordeaux, Languedoc, and Provence) and to Italy to escape persecution. As a distant echo of this time, the Portuguese today call a sausage, or a blood sausage, described as containing neither blood, nor meat, nor pig fat, as a *chorizo de marrano*. And oral tradition has it that at the time of the Inquisition the Marranos kept one of these "fake sausages" that still bear their name in reserve at all times, in order to present it during an anticipated search as proof that they were "good Christians." Indeed, Cecil Roth, whose important work is devoted to the religion of the Marranos, emphasizes their, as well as the xuetas's, rigorous maintenance of Jewish dietary prescriptions: "From pork, the Marranos of the earlier generation would try to abstain, going so far as to destroy any dish in which it had inadvertently been prepared."[44] Thomas Platter, during his stay in Montpellier, noted that his hosts ate neither pork nor lard, an omission that sufficed to identify them and that their Catholic neighbors stigmatized once a year in spectacular fashion: "Not a carnival goes by without the most notable among them being represented by dolls stuffed with hay and garnished with lard, which are suspended on the squares and in the streets, sometimes with rhymed identification markers."

The testimony of the Swiss schoolboy, living with the family of the Marrano doctor Gilbert, is extremely valuable. It reveals that the "duplicity" of which the conversos were accused evidenced their inability to break away from the Judaism of their fathers. The "double baptism" was a frequent practice intended to preserve both the belief of the religious authorities and the good Jewish faith; the child, after having been "secretly circumcised and baptized" according to custom, in the home, underwent a Catholic baptism in the eyes of the world, but the obligation to practice Catholicism led many Jews to sincerely adopt some of its forms of expression: "Finally I informed my father of the Marrano religion. Gilbert would be obliged to return to Mass and to confession when he returned to Montpellier, for the Marranos, while conserving the practices of Judaism, attached great importance to the Mass and cared more about the Virgin Saint than about Jesus Christ."[45] Xuetas and Marranos were thus accused, under the pretense of conversion, of flouting the Church and the saints and sullying the Christians' "purity of blood" through marriage. In Spain and Portugal the *marranía* came, popularly, to signify the occult observance of Judaism, even though the registers of the Inquisition favored the terms *confesso, converso,* and *tornadizo.* But who, in reality, were these "re-converts"?

On the Island of Majorca the centuries have not erased the distinction between xuetas with "high ears" and xuetas with "low ears." Even if, generally speaking, they are commonly recognized as "Catholics," their church is referred to by the Majorcans as the "synagogue of the xuetas," and, until 1930, a xueta priest did not have the right to preach at the Cathedral of Palma, nor could his followers participate in the Holy Week, so persistent was the myth of the deicidal people. *Matacristo* is still the insult most commonly addressed to a xueta, the one he would hear most often, beginning in childhood on the school benches. The argument, even if it no longer links the difference in "nature" of the xuetas to the crime still imputed to them, gives those who have long been qualified as *capados* and *retallats* a murky identity; a seventeenth-century theologian described them in these terms: "Since they crucified His Divine Majesty, some have little tails that extend from their bodies at the base of the spinal column, others lose blood every month from their shameful parts as if they were women." We have seen them referred to as *homes-dones*; they are men "without trousers" according to another expression, sometimes accompanied by an "Argenter, argenter te l'han tallat, i no en tens, Silversmith, silversmith, they cut it off, and you don't have one," in answer to which, according to contemporary sources, more than one xueta found it necessary to respond with demonstrative gestures and language.[46] In Provence, where in the course of the sixteenth and seventeenth centuries anti-Marrano sentiment raged, as confirmed by the popular literature and theater, the converted Jew was qualified as both *manjalard* and *retalhat.*[47] Thus the implicit references to the pig and to its castration are further connected, but we must look farther, question the words, to see the "hidden face" of the converted peoples revealed. Two philologists, one Italian, the other Catalan, furnish us with decisive arguments.[48]

Farinelli first followed the word *Marrano* and its use in literature through European testimonies. While the word simply means "new Christians," it is always accompanied by a nuance borrowed from the image of the Jew, in the manner we have shown. In Provence the term is now an adjective synonymous with bad, difficult, mean. In Italy the Marrano is an incarnation of treachery and vulgarity. It refers to someone who leads "una vita sudicia, maialesca e libidinosa" (a life of filth, beastliness, and debauchery). In France the Marrano is imputed with the ill said to be "French" in other European countries. And because it represents a special cursed figure just about everywhere, a long philological tradition had it that the word *Marrano* was derived from the expression "anathema maran atha sit," by which Jews and the first Christians mutually anathemized one another (Cor. 16:22). Farinelli put an end to this: according to him, the word *Marrano* simply means pig. The term was already present as a synonym to *cerdo* in the contract for sale of a monastery in 965, in which it appeared with the particular nuance of "young pig" and referred even more to "the animal that had just been weaned." By extension, it came to designate "the fresh meat of the pig." For Farinelli it is related to the Andalusian term *maharrana*, fresh lard, a form that already allows the origin of the word to be surmised. Its Arab source is *moharrama*, which quickly became *máhram*, *mahrán*, signifying "the thing that is prohibited." This demonstration clearly shows the filiation; an ethnologist would not be surprised that the forbidden animal should be named by the word signifying the interdiction itself.

After having verified the data proposed by Farinelli, Corominas in turn examined the word *xueta* with the same perspicacity. Here, too, he overturned convention, declaring the term closely linked to the vocabulary relating to the pig. Even today, in Majorca, *xulla* (which is pronounced "xuia") signifies "lard, fat meat of the pig." The term has a Catalan origin Corominas detects in the Valencian *xulla* and its diminutive *xuelleta*, which passed into the Spanish *chuleta*, where today it more broadly designates the chop of any butchered animal ready to be grilled. *Xulla*, before signifying the flesh of the pig, was more narrowly specialized (like *Marrano*) in designating the fat of the pig, *tocino*. And Corominas looks back further still, to old Catalan, searching medieval texts to find the oldest form encountered, *ensunya*, for which he provides the following definition:

Ensunya: fat, particularly that of the pig, passed into **enxunya*, then to **enxulla* by dissimilation. As for *ensunya*, it has the same origin as the Portugese *enxulha* and the Castillian *enjundia*, namely the Latin *axungia*: "pig fat."

Thus from the words to the gestures that give them meaning—whereas their primary meanings were lost—a similar coherence occurs. The carnival doll stuffed with lard representing a Marrano in Montpellier, the furtive gesture of the little Christian boys, placing a piece of lard, even today, in the pocket of a xueta schoolboy, mean to say that both are pigs. This conclusion is not universally accepted. Many Jews reject what seems to them to be the height of absurdity: "Since Jews detest pigs, they cannot be called that." The argument advanced by Braunstein is of the same order: "It was spelled either *Chuetas* or *Xuyetas*. The Chuetas used it freely in speaking of themselves, lending credence to my feeling that they would not refer to themselves by the interpretations advanced by some scholars." Yet, pressed by the Inquisition, "the child João Carvalho, who at the age of twelve denounced his mother and other relatives at Goa in 1627, relates how he was told that those who ate pork were turned into pigs."[49]

With the xuetas and Marranos the porcine nature of the Jew was further refined, while the name designating them referred to the particular status of those who were "in between Jews and Christians" and who manifested even more clearly the duplicity of which the "race" was accused. Indeed, between the Marrano "just weaned piglet" and the xueta "little lard," or "bacon," as one says familiarly of a child, lies the identity created for the new convert. At a time when being a good Christian meant being an "old Christian," *cristan vell* in Catalan texts, the conversos, barely weaned from their Jewishness, could claim this title. They were therefore like the piglet just separated from its nursing mother, whose flesh, being "too fresh," was removed from consumption or sold at a low price at a separate stall so as not to be confused with *carnbielhe*. Two hundred and fifty years of Catholicism were thus powerless to make the converted Jews into Christians, at least in the eyes of those who were striving to "send them back"—a paradoxical effort if there ever was one. Even in 1860 a xueta had to seek special authorization to marry a Catholic. Questioned in 1976, one of them explained: "Even today, we have access neither to the table nor to the bed of a *butifarra*." In Majorca, *butifarra*, "blood sausage," designates the Christian elite, the old families who, to express the purity of their blood, also borrow from the pig: "Sa botifarra i sa xuia tot surt de's porc, Blood sausage and lard, every kind of pork," they say today, smiling.[50]

Returning from Portugal, a Turkish Jew, whose family had emigrated long ago to escape the Inquisition, was sitting next to a Portugese priest to whom he revealed his origins. "So you're a Marrano, well, a poorly baptized one," he was told. Thus, ironically, the Catholic minister himself was questioning the sacrament performed by Christians, as if this sacrament were powerless to act upon a Jew. Is this not the meaning of the word *tornadiço* applied to Jewish converts? Returned, cast back, "castrated," we are tempted to say, playing on words that, we have seen, were consistently taken literally. Jews remained Jews by virtue of a "baptism" of blood that could not be erased. From the "castrated Jew" to the "circumcised pig," the route of the cursed always led back to the animal from which they hailed and from which they could not be detached.

Hanged Pig

Do you know what becomes, after his death,
of the terrifying body of a rabbi?
His head turns toward the rising sun,
His legs hang from a ladder.

—J. SLOWACKI, *Ksiadz Marek*
(The Abby Mark), act II, v. 527–530.

These words, whose primary meaning had grown hazy, were brought into play in carnival pantomimes and children's bullying. But for a long time there was a sphere—that of the law—where their true meaning must have been solemnly demonstrated. Indeed, after inheriting Roman law, the Middle Ages were keen on diversifying the punishment according to the nature of the crime and its author. Thus the parricide was drowned in a sack in the company of a rooster, a snake, and a monkey, and Jews were hung between two dogs, who were sacrificed along with them. Hanging, which initially sanctioned theft, became the "punishment of the Jews" in the early fourteenth century, regardless of the crime with which they were charged. It was then necessary to introduce a variant to distinguish them from Christians, to whom such punishments were also applied, and from the higher animals—bovines, hide animals—who also received such punishment if they were recognized as guilty of homicide. The *Coutumes de Bourgogne*, written between 1270 and 1360, after having examined the two preceding cases, concludes in these terms: "but if other animals or Jews do it, they must be hung by the hind feet."[51] Now, among these "beasts," the pig was condemned on many occasions, until the first half of the eighteenth century, as evidenced by the numerous ancien régime trials. Thus, in 1457, in the region of Compiègne, a wild sow—whose piglets were in fact acquitted—"committed and perpetrated murder and homicide on the person of Jehan Martin, age five"; it was "confiscated to be brought to the final punishment and hung by the hind legs from a tree." It was, in fact, mostly for glutinous infanticides that the red female paid with her life, and we know in detail the story of the sow of Falaise, another child-eater, whose spectacular execution occurred in 1386 following a trial in due and proper form. The animal appeared dressed in a jacket, breeches, and gloves. It was executed in this outfit after its snout was slit and its face covered "with the mask of a human face"; it was hung by its hind legs and abandoned at the gallows for the edification of the public.[52] This upside-down hanging, used for pigs and Jews, humanizes the former while animalizing the latter, dispensing with the need to add dogs or monkeys for this purpose. The punishment is ignominious and cruel, which is why, in 1315, the Jewish community of Majorca addressed a petition to King Sancho requesting its abolition. Yet we continue to encounter it until the seventeenth century: in Mantua, in 1603, five Jews were punished in this way "for blasphemy."[53]

If the Jew is a pig and must die like one, his mother is a sow, by whom he is intimately marked and to whom he remains scandalously close, as seen in the Germanic iconography of the Judensau. This relationship would be further illustrated by legal ceremonial beginning in the thirteenth century. We are familiar with the oath *more judaico* by which the Jew who appeared before a Christian jurisdiction called upon himself and his descendants the worst calamities—among them leprosy—if he committed perjury. This ceremony, which we find in nearly identical form "between the tenth and twentieth centuries, from Byzantium to Provence, from Germany to Romania, by way of the papal state of the Comtat Venaissin," follows a ritual that has often been judged "extravagant." In Romania, where, curiously, it was established in 1844 and maintained until emancipation in 1919, even as the struggle initiated by Adolphe Crémieux led the countries of Europe to abrogate it, the Jewish witness was led to the holy arch in bare feet, dressed in the funerary shirt (the *kittel*) and holding a candle in each hand, in a death ritual—the words he pronounces against himself tended in this direction—reminiscent of the lepers' *separatio*. In earlier centuries the Jew swore an oath standing, balancing on a three-legged stool, and, after having "wreathed himself in brambles and spit on the circumcision," he called upon himself the anathema and abolition of his race. Sometimes a goat skin was placed beneath him. But in the fourteenth century the German legal code, the *Sachsenpiegel*, stipulated that henceforth any Jew appearing before the court "must stand on the skin of a sow having farrowed within fewer than fourteen days. The skin will have been split up the back, and will be spread with udders on top. The Jew will stand on it barefoot."[54] It is further specified that the skin must be "bloody," which suggests that the sow was skinned for the occasion. This measure is all the more ignominious when one considers that during the same period the Jewish criminal—who would be hung by his feet—was led to the site of his punishment "wrapped in a pigskin."[55] But, by choosing a female who had just delivered, by taking care to place the Jew's body in contact with the engorged udders of the animal, the judicial rite was endowed with a supplementary nuance, attesting to the widespread circulation of this filiation myth in all social spheres.

It is true that the symbolic violence of these penalties gradually dwindled; the communities obtained the elimination of terms that crudely sent the Jew back to his "nature": thus, in 1784, the tax of the "cloven foot," which every Israelite had to pay upon entering Strasbourg, was abolished, but not without difficulty.[56] The underlying continuity of this representation, however, the vast field of signs it unifies and governs, its capacity to produce new images, lends it the inexorable weight of fatality, leading one to doubt the possibility of emancipation for Jews in a Christian world that places them as close as possible to its most intimate animal.

Sacher-Masoch took as his theme for a harsh yet realistic short story the obligation that Jews were under to adopt "Christian" names—a corollary to the right of "naturalization" the countries of Central Europe recognized one by one between 1785 and 1912.[57] He recounts how, in Galicia, the prince's functionaries sold their services and tells of the disappointment of one poor man who, for lack of money, was unable to obtain the beautiful names of which he and his family had dreamed—the Goldenbergs, the Rosenthals—acquired for one hundred florins by the smarter set. And because the less lustrous Zucherhut ("sugarbread") or Eisenstein ("iron mine")—valued at two ducats— were still too expensive, he was, at the culmination of a tragicomic bargaining session, called a leper and ousted by the commissioner presiding over the attribution of patronyms, but not before having a chance to decipher the name he was finally assigned. Back home, everyone surrounds him:

"Well, what's your name? asks his wife impatiently. Why aren't you speaking?"

"Alas, responds Absalom, resigned to his fate, what might my name be? Look at me, my good Rachel, and pity me. Woe is me! From now on my name is Absalom Saufuss. Sow's foot."

CHAPTER FIVE

Red Easter

Swan's father was an associate stockbroker—the fact that he was a Jew didn't enter into the equation because he frequented only Catholics and, at most, prompted a desire in curious women to ask him whether he was forced to eat the flesh of Christian children on certain days, a question that their husbands, with a certain ill humor, discouraged them from asking.

—MARCEL PROUST, *Du côté de chez Swann* (Paris 1987), sketch 12

In the middle of the Holy Week in 1472 the city of Trent, in northern Italy, was rocked by a tragic affair. A two-and-a-half-year-old child disappeared from his home while his parents, who had gone to the Tenebrae service, were away. Despite searches, he could not be found for several days, at which point his cadaver was fished from the river that bathes the city.

This "affair" might seem to be just another news item if we had not taken it, and presented it in summarized form, from a contemporary *Lives of the Saints*, where it appears on the date of March 24. But our surprise and curiosity only grew when we discovered a nearly identical account on March 25: the year is 1144, the place Norwich, England. It is still Easter week, and a young twelve-year-old boy, William, has disappeared under equally mysterious circumstances. He would be found dead, three days later, hanging from a tree in a neighboring wood. William, like Simon, was "horribly mutilated." Soon investigations made it possible in both cases to "illuminate" the affairs. The accused, each time, were Jews, who kidnapped the boys in order to subject their bodies to various brutalities before killing them in as cruel a fashion as possible during the days when Christians were commemorating the passion of Christ in sadness and faith.

The Holy Innocents

Little William was the first "affair" in Europe in which charges of *ritual murder* would lead to the canonization of the presumed victim. With Simon, or "Simonet," as he was called, a little more than three centuries later, the cycle of sanctifications of children martyred to Jews would close. Simonet was certainly the most "popular" among them. The city of Trent worshipped him faithfully until 1965, when such worship was abrogated by the Catholic hierarchy. Between these two dates lie other cases, all following the same pattern. The most famous include Richard de Pontoise (1163), Dominguito de Saragoss (1255), Hugh of Lincoln (1255), and Werner d'Oberwesel (1287). The last marks the close of the period of canonizations resulting from these affairs, while the accusations of ritual murder broadly surpass these High Middle Ages on both ends. The chronology goes from the fifth to the twentieth century, in which it has been rekindled at every anti-Jewish eruption, giving shape to persistent rumors. But these rarely turn into concrete affairs; the glory of the Holy Innocents is over.[1]

The phenomenon was of rare breadth in Europe and inspired many debates, particularly since it went against the current. At a time when the Church was attempting to introduce greater rigor in the election of its saints, these child martyrs were bothersome. Indeed, over the course of the second half of the thirteenth century it strove to establish a distinction between "saints" and "the blessed." Canonization crowned Christians who had died struggling for the faith, responsible beings who had chosen the path of martyrdom. Beatification honored more dubious martyrs, often swept along by popular groundswells. That was the case with the young "victims of Jews," who usually attained only this lesser recognition. But while the Church may have merely beatified them, the people made them saints. André Vauchez, investigating the "mental representations" underlying this phenomena, writes, "Two aspects of the popular mentality combine in these devotions, both of foreign origin: a valorization of childhood, considered the age of innocence and perfection, and a virulent anti-Semitism, which justifies itself by launching accusations of ritual murder and host profanation against Jews."[2]

We sense that this encounter had to occur and that it extends well beyond the sphere of the "popular." But let us look at the facts as they emerge from the primary cases gathered. Among this group the Simonet affair, accompanied by a wealth of iconography, is the most complete model of the genre and will serve as our guide. To begin with, here is how the events were related by the Benedictines of Paris:

> In 1472, on the Wednesday of the Holy Week, Jews from the city of Trent, had asked one of their own named Tobie who practiced medicine to obtain a Christian child as a victim. The latter took advantage of the moment when the Christians were gathered in their church for the Tenebrae service to entice a small child named Simon or Siméon, aged two years and several months, to follow him.[3]

The status of the victims and their tormenters is the first point to be noted. We are talking about young boys whose ages range from three to twelve years, with a distinct tendency, over time, toward younger victims. This feature exalts an innocence made palpable by the choice of diminutives. "Simonet," "Dominguito," and "Niño de la Guardia" are tender prey for Jews, whose cruelty appears all the greater as they gather around the little victims in large numbers. The leader is strongly individualized, and we should note his capacity as a "doctor," a "rabbi," or a "cook." It is important, too, that the crime take on a collective dimension: the entire "Jewish nation" bears the weight. But let us return to our story after the "procurer" has succeeded in luring the child away and the unfortunate parents have noted his disappearance:

> Meanwhile, on the night of Holy Thursday to Holy Friday, the Jews took the child to a vestibule contiguous to their synagogue. An old man named Moses took him on his knees: a kerchief was placed over the victim's head, while the wretches made various incisions on his little body and collected the blood that flowed from them in a basin. During this time some held his legs and others took his arms and spread them in the form of a cross. He was then placed on his feet, and two tormenters held him in this position as the others pierced his body with awls and chisels.[4]

Putting aside the crucifixion with which the crime ends for a moment, let us consider the details of the operation. In all the stories death is merely the outcome of a long series of gestures performed on the body of the child by each of the participants, in a "ritual" the hagiographer's story invites us to examine. The position is surprising, initially, but soon we recognize the posture of the Jewish circumcision. Moreover, in the version furnished by the Bollandists, translated here word for word, the confusion is rather adroitly maintained:

And there, sitting on a chair by the fire, he took him on his knees. And all gathered around him, they lowered his clothing to the navel and to the elbows, turning them inside out, and pulled up his light tunic on the sides. Then Moses, having drawn a knife from its sheath, pierced the end of the child's penis and, grabbing some tongs, ripped the right jaw near the chin. The pieces of flesh he thereby removed were deposited in a receptacle."[5]

Among the wood engravings of the fifteenth century a Roman print depicts Simon on a Jew's knees, and the images clearly demonstrate what the text suggests. A colored German engraving of 1480 represents him standing, surrounded by seven torturers with Hebrew names— care was taken to inscribe these names beneath each one. The most active ones pierce Simon's naked body with pins and chisels. A sharp-nosed woman hands the instruments of torture to them, a man kneeling on the floor collects the blood in a receptacle, while another observes the scene, arms crossed. In the foreground, with his long white beard, is the elderly Moses in the process of operating on the child's genitals. The gesture is precise, and a rapid review of our cases confirms the intention. The young Hugh of Lincoln was first "circumcised," we are told, before being eviscerated. So, too, was Louis Van Bruck, tortured, with the help of a same "Moses," by the Jewish family in whose service he was employed, and his torturers "also performed a kind of sacrilege on the genital parts of the child: an ignominous practice that was part of the death ritual" (illus. 11).[6]

That the martyrdom of little boys begins with circumcision confers added meaning on the operation. The castrating knives, with their sharp blades, which the comedic rabbis manipulate on the theatrical stage, are first a threat to the Jews themselves; the large kitchen knives, distinctly visible on engravings that represent the sacrifice of Christian children, depict the circumcisor as the priest of a bloody cult that requires the execution of others' children. By replacing the ritual knife with a "kitchen" knife an interpretation is already offered. The widely disseminated image of Simon's martyrdom and the preservation in situ of the objects of the crime remind us, if need be, of the end to which the initial gesture was a prelude. In Trent one could see, long preserved in seven reliquaries, the "sacrificial knife," the glass from which the Jews drank the blood, the basin in which it was collected, the little gown of the saint, and two containers filled with his blood.[7] After the "circumcision" came the bloodletting; the receptacle intended to collect the blood is always present. Indeed, these ritual murders speak a language that is well known to us. Let us continue, nonetheless, with other texts.

In 1490, in the midst of the Inquisition, the Niño de la Guardia affair exploded in Toledo. The conversos were hunted down; as one can imagine, an accusation of ritual murder constituted a weighty argument if one wished to strike a major blow. The operation was painstakingly prepared and all the elements were present: a family of conversos, the Francos, felt fearful and threatened; they had recourse, therefore, to a Jewish "wise man" named Yuça Tazarte, who suggested an infallible means of obtaining the death of the inquisitors and reestablishing the supremacy of Jews over Christians. But a host and the heart of a Christian child were needed. The Francos kidnapped Cristobal, a three-year-old boy, and cut him up in a grotto in the Guardia section of Toledo. The murder was discovered. A long trial ensued in the course of which the accused "admitted everything" before being burned for the edification of the conversos. The minutes of this trumped-up trial were discovered and published in 1887 by a scholar, Father Fita, who, as a conscientious historian, prefaced them with an account of the story written in 1544 by Damián de Vegas, a Toledan doctor, entitled *Memoria del Santo Niño de la Guardia*. Isidore Loeb based himself on this text to prove—if further proof were necessary after the critical examination to which he subjects the trial itself—that the entire affair was "an invention of the Inquisition." But, according to all appearances, the incident sparked a legend that had circulated earlier and that the famous account readopts in turn. Here is the version advanced by the chronicler, claiming to have received revelations of a first effort on the part of the Francos:

> Some Jews who fled Spain at the time the Inquisition was established in that country had gone to reside in France. There lived a knight who was poor and burdened with children; the Jews offered him money if he would accept the murder of one of his sons, giving them the victim's heart. He refused, but his wife, who was shrewder, arranged to take the Jews' money and keep her child: on her advice the knight killed a pig and supplied the Jews with the heart of the pig in place of the heart of the child. A diabolical old woman sold them a host, and they made a mixture with the heart, which they threw in the river, and the Christians would nearly all have been poisoned had the knight not revealed the mystery. The said Jews then passed into Spain with Christians and settled in Guardia.

It was there that they allegedly kidnapped the young Cristobal and killed him, "after having hidden him for three or four months to contemplate the manner in which they would put him to death."[8] The substitution of the pig's heart for the child's heart speaks of their proximity, which we have analyzed from the facts but only fiction pushes to the extreme. The Jews had to be the ones to put the analogy into action, since, deprived of the flesh of the animal, they were forced to find a substitute for it in that of Christian children. From then on the infamous "ritual crime" can be read as a "slaughter": a "castrated" body that is bled—with care taken to collect all the liquid, as evidenced by the pots, basins, flasks, and glasses—and eventually boiled—a woman heats water in a kettle for William of Norwich—eviscerated, and cut into pieces laid out on platters. Often the victim is hung "head down"; this is the case for Werner d'Oberwesel and André de Rinn. Sometimes, of course, the stages are shuffled, the order and progression of the sequences disturbed. The Jews are bad butchers: Simon of Trent is immediately "cut up" by Moses, who attacks one of his jaws with prongs. The carving is not always mentioned and the consumption of the flesh is not systematic; sometimes the heart is salted and, most important, the blood is used to make cakes to send to Jews of neighboring or distant communities. Finally, this singular treatment is sometimes explicitly identified by text and image.

The crime of Hugh of Lincoln, who at the age of eight was "circumcised and crucified" by the Jews in Gloucester on March 24, 1255, inspired numerous ballads, the most famous of which was reprinted many times until the nineteenth century. But we find oral variants, next to this literary version, such as that noted by Jamieson of Scotland and those from the north of England. One of them presents the young boy playing ball with his young friends, a ritual Easter game that was highly honored in clerical circles, practiced in the Middle Ages within the bounds of the Church itself. Hugh, with an awkward kick of the knee, sent his toy "to the Jews." Lured into the ghetto in pursuit of one of their daughters, who tempted him with a "beautiful red and green apple," he found himself at the heart of her dark dwelling. There, the ballad tells us:

> She's laid him on a dressing table,
> And stickit him like a swine.
> And first came out the thick, thick blood,
> And syne came out the thin;

And syne came out the bonny heart's blood;
There was naemair within.
She's row'd him in a cake o'lead
Bade him lie still and sleep.[9]

A rather crude Florentine engraving similarly caught our eye: one depicting a new Simonet. His martyrdom gave rise to three types of representations, which we have mentioned in part: sometimes the child is seated on the knees of his executioner and subjected to what we have recognized as a "circumcision"; sometimes he is held in a cross position on the model of Christ. But another group of images shows him lying on his back, his body riddled with puncture wounds, surrounded on occasion by the instruments of his passion. At the heart of this picture is a curious scene. Simonet, one may note, is lying on his side. The emphasis is placed on the treatment of his genitals, which are being cut with a large knife. A gaping wound is opened at his throat, from which blood is flowing into a receptacle set in place for this purpose. Sheering scissors are ready to cut into his chest and needles pricking his skin contribute to bleeding him white. Everyone is wearing, on their chests, backs, or heads, not the simple circle that designates them as Jews but, quite visibly, a badge with a pig at its center (illus. 12).

Thus, just as he is being presented to us in his role as a cannibal butcher, and as we are offered the spectacle of the child being bled, the Jew shows his hidden face. With this porcine mark he sports the secret of his "true nature." And this seemingly misplaced sign makes the image of the piglet behind that of the slaughtered child all the more obvious. It is not surprising that in Germany, much later, between the seventeenth and eighteenth centuries, engravings and text would combine to associate the iconography of the Judensau with the evocation and representation of the murder of Simon of Trent (illus. 13 and 14). In one of these images the criminal Jews are made to present themselves one by one: "Butcher is my name; I hold the sow by the rope," says one of them. And another adds, "Judas betrayed Christ, so it was for the child of Trent."[10]

The accusation of ritual murder thus plays on the relationships that in these societies unite pigs, children, and Jews. For pig eaters the Jew performs in reality the action that is always on the horizon of their own pork consumption, the action revealed by the metaphorical games of breeding. What is left unspoken is spoken only with respect to the other and what the other forbids himself. By a complete turnaround the Jew bears the burden of the question that is always hovering over Christian homes, where issues concerning the consumption of this so human-seeming animal are definitively unsettled. Would it not be appropriate, therefore, to further examine the argument by which Christians construct what "makes" Jews different? Do their most secret fears not surface in this discourse on the other? And, first, those regarding blood—both the blood one eats and the blood one discards.

The Taste of Blood

Though it initially maintained the Jewish prohibition concerning blood, the Church quickly showed proof of tolerance in this area. Next to prescriptions aiming to control the consumption of so-called *de sanguine* animals, the reading of synods allows us to gauge the favorable treatment afforded the pig. The animal that had absorbed human blood, for instance, was not exluded from the table; the Irish penitentials simply recommended postponing its consumption for one year. We know that barbers were in the habit of fattening their animals with the blood of their clients—a practice that for a long time bothered no one—this breeding constituting a complement to their role as "bloodletters." Not until 1336 did the Benedictines take issue with this and offer as a gift to the barbers of the city of Bruges a plot of land where they could dispose of the residues of their bloodlettings and of the minor surgical interventions they performed instead of giving them to their pigs. Thus, from the first centuries, the Christians maintained a paradoxical relationship with blood, which is highlighted by the status afforded the pig.[11] In the process they accused their neighbors, who utterly rejected the pig, of enjoying it in secret, in keeping with the "nature" they constructed for them, finding confirmation of this hidden appetite in the Jews' outward distaste for the pig, for its flesh and blood, and for everything connected to this bodily fluid, including their own blood.

Christians also drew this conviction from the Jewish law rigorously proscribing blood. Indeed, where the Talmud meticulously legislates on the precautions to take to prevent it from flowing—we are familiar with the round-edged razors used by Jewish barbers to eliminate the risk of bloodshed—where Maimonides questions whether swallowing one's own saliva when one's gums are bleeding is a contravention of the law, and where, after him, many wise rabbis in no less scholarly glosses addressed this question without ever deciding it, Christians have read "obsession with blood." Through an already abundantly illustrated transposition, such an absolute prohibition constituted an additional argument against the Jews. Anti-Judaism fed on this and succeeded in making it known, to such an extent that those in more recent times who dared not openly express it alluded to it, at least hypothetically. This was the case of the insidious *Dictionnaire apologétique de la foi catholique*, which, in 1916, posed the question in these dubious terms: "And is the prohibition of Leviticus against eating unbled meat not a precaution against the Semite's particular penchant for blood?" More generally, in fact, Christians employed an equivalent but differently formulated proposition: the "privation" could not help but bring about a lack, resulting in the Jew's avidity for blood. The outward rejection masks a secret presence, which manifests itself in the ritual murders that constitute the very essence of the Jewish "cult."

This is the conviction that has regularly been embodied in recurrent accusations throughout history. These accusations have been conveyed from society to society, from religion to religion; Christianity itself was accused of such heresies in its early years, only to take them up and stigmatize each of them one by one.[12] But it is the Jews who are struck by them with remarkable constancy; it is for them that they are effective. Among Christians the accusation of ritual murder is part of the residual effects of an ever difficult conflictual proximity to Jews. It bases itself on an ample and rich discourse regarding the Jew, his practices, his rituals, and those who perform them. In addition, it induces action on the part of Christians—the struggle against the Jew—in response to the "offensive" attitude of the "enemies of Christ." Does it not thereby offer itself as a relational and conceptual model that enables one to grasp the longstanding ideological confrontation between Jews and Christians, at least in the form given it by the latter in order to conceptualize their differences? And since the Jew is present—visible to Christians—everything that constitutes his relentless singularity will be the object of intense and lasting interpretive activity.

So it is for the "circumcision" that, in almost every case, inaugurates the torture of the young martyrs and that, curiously, does not seem to have surprised analysts of ritual murder. It's true that it is not a matter of making the victim into a Jew, of invalidating the baptism by virtue of this operation. If Christians positioned it at the beginning, is that not primarily because, since they themselves ceased to perform it, they no longer considered it anything but a bloody mutilation that verified the barbarity of the Jews? Even when humanists such as Montaigne explain the procedure certain practices nonetheless remain "strange." Let's go back to the metsitsa, the rapid suction of the organ intended, it is said, to stop the bleeding provoked by the cut. The officiant, having first filled his mouth with wine, performs three short suctions on the penis and, each time, spits the liquid into a receptacle. The young boys and men who are present then share the wine, a libation in which the circumcised boy also shares as the cup is brought to his lips. At this point Montaigne, despite his knowledge of the custom, cannot keep himself from noting that the circumcisor, to separate the frenum from the glans, had earlier operated "with his nail" and "ripped," and that finally, after the sucking and until the end of the ceremony, "he nonetheless always has a bloody mouth."[13] In addition to the cutting knife and the ripping nail, one can imagine that the image of the operator with a reddened mouth, which, well before Montaigne's description, must have worked its way into Christian homes, offered ammunition for this concept of a "taste for blood."

We cannot help but read in the description of the crime itself and even down to its details an amplification of each of these gestures. But while we have recognized the sequence of this ritual operation, it is also important to identify the participants. In the hagiographic trials and legends they are presented as the "cook," the "doctor," and the "rabbi," the last title falling most often to the Jew who officiated over the child's body. Does this mean that, for Christians, Jews make no distinction between their doctors and butchers, their cooks and their priests? That the role of each is reduced to a single function—that of drawing blood? Where does such an association come from? What elements inherent to Jewish culture could have fed such an image, and what consequences can we draw with regard to these so-called ritual murders?

Strange Red Men

"What's it called, the Arabs' temple [*sic*], you know, the synagogue. They don't want us inside."

"No one knows what they do there, but it's full of weapons."

—Conversation overheard on a train, Toulouse, 1986

Three individuals occupy central positions in every Jewish community, and the roles they play are, at first glance, clearly defined. Let us simply review the basics. The rabbi is the spiritual leader, and his duties mainly cover all religious and ceremonial functions that occur within the walls of the synagogue. It is in this capacity that he attends circumcisions, often chosen to be one of the child's "sponsors," for his presence and protection honor the family. But the operation is performed by the mohel, the circumcisor, who is not a religious man in the usual sense. Any Jew, therefore, can attain this status, and, in fact, according to Montaigne, "everyone wishes to be called to this service because they consider it a great blessing to be employed in it often." A father can operate on his child himself, and this was often the case among the Montpellier Marranos described by Thomas Platter. Today the officiant is required to be an "observant Jew," and this quality carries far more weight than others, if combined with manual dexterity. The ceremony was long performed in private homes as well as at the synagogue. With the medicalization of birthing the role is also tending to become professionalized, and in our day, in France, the mohel has come to practice circumcision at the hospital itself. The third individual, the shochet, or ritual butcher, is the person who, using a specific slaughtering technique, bleeds and cuts up animals considered fit for consumption according to the law. This, along with the process of cutting it up, is an indispensable precondition for it to be kosher—in conformity with the rules of kashrut.[14]

At first glance, each of these practitioners maneuvers in his own particular sphere: the rabbi in the synagogue, the mohel in the home, the shochet in the slaughterhouse. There is no cause for confusion between the three individuals, their duties and places—the one where men pray together, the one where they are brought into the world, the other where animals die. Yet certain overlaps blur the established distinctions, encroachments that Jewish culture has long authorized but that the Christian, for whom the rabbi is automatically a "priest," the shochet a "butcher," and the mohel a "surgeon," has a hard time accepting. Let us attempt to see how things really work in order to better grasp the singularity of this system.

Take a Comtat Venaissin community between the sixteenth and eighteenth centuries. Notarized instruments have recorded the contracts that the street counsels—the *carriera*, the street, designates the neighborhood reserved for Jews in Provençal—established for various rabbis. As noted by René Moulinas, who studied these records, rabbinical powers often surpassed strictly sacerdotal functions. A contract of 1688, for instance, stipulates that the rabbi engaged by the carriera of Isle must *sagatar*, slaughter, all the livestock of individuals twice a week and perform circumcisions. The carriera of Cavillon, in 1744, requires that its rabbi perform only the latter role, while in other, more frequent, cases the rabbi is engaged solely as a *sagataire*. Even if, as René Moulinas emphasizes, these are cases in which special powers were granted an individual, the frequency with which the three duties were combined means that it cannot be considered a simple emergency solution.[15] We can see the development around the person of the rabbi of a configuration based on the tight bonds woven by custom between the three men and their respective tasks. Proof of this can be found in the teaching provided in rabbinical schools today: the student still learns to circumcise and to slaughter animals.

That one could give the ritual butcher, in these same Provençal communities, the title of "rabbi slaughterer," or that the rabbi could be called on to perform the function of butcher teaches us something about the concept of the sacred in Judaism. The Christian hierarchy of men and trades, which places the priest at the top and the butcher at the bottom—the butcher being, in the Middle Ages, associated with the executioner and deprived of a certain number of rights—is not valid for Judaism, which places these men and these functions on the same level.[16] The shochet, even when he is only a butcher, is a respectable man, a man of honor, and must therefore respect certain demands that clearly situate his gesture on a noble and sacred register. He must be in good health, clean, pious, moral; to be approved by a community, he must also pass the examination of the college of rabbis, which alone is qualified to bestow the diploma of shochet that is always displayed by Jewish butchers. Before performing any slaughter he must say a short prayer and perform the act with a sure hand, for which he is equipped with a *halef*, a long rectangular-bladed knife with a keen flawless edge. Each animal, cow or lamb, requires a certain posture; whichever animal it is, however, the slaughterer must obey the custom according to which its blood must flow down to the last drop and be covered with earth.[17] How was this particular slaughter, the development and maintenance of whose sacredness we have seen, interpreted by Christians? First of all, in a culture that attempts to reduce the gravity of the act by banalizing it—anyone can kill his own animals—or by hiding it, the solemnity of ritual slaughter stands out. An ostentatious and mysterious ritual, in the eyes of Christians it came to seem an end in itself. The technical refinement involved, the concern with spreading the blood until the last drop, the protocol of gestures and postures of the slaughterer seem to them to speak of a complacent theatricality. In the aftermath of the Nazi genocide a Jewish veterinarian devoted his thesis to the defense and illustration of the "Jewish method of slaughtering butcher animals." In it we learn that, while throughout history this method was regularly condemned and stigmatized by Christians, the anti-Semitism between the two wars revived the attacks, which, beginning in 1855 in England, Switzerland, and Germany—through animal protection societies in particular—were alternately virulent and "racist." France followed much later, prohibiting Jewish slaughter on its territory for reasons of "cruelty" during the Occupation. In 1939, within the framework of their propaganda, the Nazis produced a film in Lodz denouncing *The Crime and Barbarity of the Jews* that represented a ritual slaughter scene dramatized by ss filmmakers.[18] A similar spirit animated the Hitler Youth section leaders responsible for indoctrinating young Germans. In the story by Hans Peter Richtel *My Friend Frederick* the narrator, a ten-year-old Jew, attends one of these conferences with his schoolmates. The narrator describes ritual slaughter as follows:

> Armed with a big knife as long as my arm, the Jewish priest approaches
> the cow and slowly lifts the knife of sacrifice. The animal feels threat-
> ened with death, it lows and seeks to break free, but the Jew knows no
> pity. With lightening speed he thrusts the knife into its neck, the blood
> spurts, everything is sullied by it, the animal struggles furiously, its eyes
> roll back in agony. . . . The merciless Jew does nothing to shorten the suf-
> ferings of the bloody animal, he wallows in it, he needs blood, he is there,
> watching the gradually bloodless animal perish miserably. . . . This is
> what they call a sacrifice. . . . This is how the God of the Jews wants it.

And this long description is but a pretext for leading up to "the slaughtered Christian children" and other crimes perpetrated by the Jewish nation. It concludes that "our misfortune is the Jews."[19] Thus Nazism was able to use a venerable old idea to justify and trigger the anti-Judaism of the populations it dominated.

In fact, the first crime of living Jews, despite the borders of the ghetto, of the carriera, or of the *call*, was their absolute attachment to a ritual that separated what could be consumed from what could not. This was an injurious separation for the Christians, who were thus reminded of their own slaughter practices and of their dietary customs considered unclean. In Italy, Spain, and Portugal inquisitional trials against the Jews denounced their customs to the same extent that the "race of Abraham" held Christian customs in contempt. In a tit-for-tat measure Christians prohibited themselves from consuming the food of the Jews, especially their meat. An article of the statutes of Avignon treats in a single section "De carnibus viciatis vel a Judeis interfectis vel macellatis." The "meat of law"—the sacred meat—and the flesh "of animals who died of illness, measled pigs, that of calves and lambs extracted from the body of a dead female or themselves already dead," are to sit side by side on a separate stall.[20] Doesn't this suggest to all that the flesh that undergoes the ritual is bad, as is, necessarily, the incomprehensible ritual itself?

This explains the derivation to which the Provençaux subjected the Hebrew word *shachata*: to cut the throat. It was borrowed and Provençalized into *sagatar; sagaire* meaning, as we have seen in the contracts, the rabbi slaughterer. But *sagatar*, beside the other verbs meaning to kill in Provençal, is used familiarly in the sense of "to fail," "to do something in a dirty fashion." Based on this example, we can imagine what kind of image the title of rabbi slaughterer, applied to a man who is primarily considered "the priest of the Jews," might suggest to people outside the communities. Did such an association, carried here by words, elsewhere translated into facts, not contribute to spreading the belief, to nourishing the conviction that a religion that makes its priests butchers, and vice versa—its "killers" the ministers of its worship—can only be a religion of blood, in which any celebration of worship must take the form of the bloody sacrifice it offers as a model? Is this not what the accusation of ritual crime is saying, in its own way? Thus, the three individuals and roles we began by recognizing and distinguishing exchange attributes and characteristics to the point of melting into a single actor; he who is most often referred to as the rabbi "circumcizes" the child before "slaughtering" him and officiating like a butcher over his bloodless body. The Christians, combining rituals and moments in time, have thus played off the overlapping roles, the blurry edges that Jewish custom allows.

The ritual butcher, it is specified, "wears a silk belt like the pious Jews and the mohel who practices circumcision." Just as the latter habitually maintains "long, sharp nails on each thumb," before the operation the shochet "tests the blade of his knife on his nail, which he keeps long for this purpose"; this is an old habit of Jews who are genealogically destined to the priesthood, if we are to believe the hagiography of Saint Mark, according to which the saint amputated his own thumb in order to escape this obligation.[21] Yet another ritual posture—a far from negligible one—further unites the Jewish operators: "Some of these circumcisors, in order to better access their knife at the moment of the *milah*, the ritual circumcision, have gotten in the habit of placing it between their teeth, in the manner of the *shochtim*, or the ritual slaughterers."[22] In Majorca, in the seventeenth century, engravings were still circulating of "the child sacrificed by the Jews": Simonet appears crucified, crowned by thorns, while two Jews are playing cards for his garment. But as two others stand at the foot of the cross holding a basin to collect his blood, on either side, perched on ladders, two Jews are leaning toward the child. One is extending his arm, a long-bladed knife in his hand, the other is climbing the top steps, the ritual circumcision or butcher knife between his teeth.[23] Who are they? It matters little, since for the Christians the gesture of the first implies that of the second, the operation that "bleeds" is an extension of that which "makes one bleed": the two are equivalent.

Do these very different Jews not occupy precise places in people's beliefs? Let's listen to Armand Lunel's description of the feared yet respected figure of Chanaan, the circumcisor of his childhood, in Carpentras, in the year 1900:

> This lovely old man, square, crude, and full of maxims, was still distinguished by the stain on his right hand to which he owed his nickname, Red Hand, a large, bright sign, colorful and solemn, that we gazed at with religious fear; it gave us to understand that we not only had the greatest dealer of red dye in France, now in retirement, before our eyes, but also the still active performer of the milah for all the young Jewish males of the Comtat Venaissin area.[24]

But while the pig seems to offer itself up to the knives of our "red men," the direct relationship between the mohel and children's bodies seems intolerably violent. For Christians, once again, the Jew gives concrete form to the ever veiled horizon of their own practices. If circumcision had to be part of the "death ritual" in the course of which Jews were alleged to kill, bleed, and share the blood of Christian children, as expressed and shown by the ritual crime imagery, it was because this minute ritual bleeding inherent to Judaism—the only one it allows, since neither animal castration nor therapeutic bloodletting for humans is authorized—is for Christians in a metonymic relationship with the other blood ritual. From this perspective every Jewish ritual is criminal and the various Jewish "ceremonies" are the images of an ever repeated murder, an incessant quest for blood.

Blood Against Blood

Throughout the torture of our "innocent" saints we have noted the care with which the blood was collected, the zeal with which it was made to flow through a thousand tiny wounds and by means of small pointed instruments—reeds and feathers, probes and needles—so that nothing should be lost. Emphasis was also placed on the extraction of the heart, the receptacle of "good blood," the possession of which in many instances was alleged to motivate the murder. From this perspective "ritual murder" also appears as an act of black magic. This at least is what we are led to believe by these bodies riddled with needle pricks, while in confessions the preponderant role played by a "doctor" or "wise man" comes up repeatedly. This blood, initially shared immediately in a libation restricted to the ones making the sacrifice, generally found its consumption spread to the local Jewish community— even to more remote communities among which it formed a bond, since each one was designated in turn to perform the killing for the benefit of all. This idea, which had already been carefully noted by the scribe who related the murder of young William of Norwich, reappears as a leitmotif throughout the trials of the Inquisition. In addition, the inculpated, in the course of adroitly led interrogations, admitted using this blood "for their evil doings." The Jew was thus a sorcerer. In the case of Jews this allegation, a corollary to that of cannibalism, which we know plagued marginalized social and religious groups, gave substance to the myth of the quest for power, which we have seen resurface right up to the twentieth century. This suspicion of sorcery was shared with women, a fact that can be understood in reference to their common nature. Beings of blood, Jews and witches—who were also "red"—were accused of the same heinous crimes: murder, cannibalism, profanation. Jews, moreover, "associated themselves" frequently with lepers, with whom they were seen as acting in concert against Christians.

Any Jew could be a potential sorcerer, of course, but, particularly at the end of the Middle Ages, this quest for power was incarnated by the Jewish doctor.[25] He was one of the special figures, revealing the dark side of a medical world that still touched on the secret arts. Many stories, of lasting posterity, circulated throughout Europe. A German chronicle of the sixteenth century reports that a "Jewish doctor," under the pretext of needing a human heart for his medical practice, hired a Christian to obtain one for him. The latter, who was wary, delivered a pig's heart instead, which the Jewish doctor burned in the middle of a field. Immediately, all the neighboring pigs dashed to the spot where fire had consumed the heart and frenetically killed one another. Another story, situated for greater verisimilitude at a specific time, 1535, and in a specific place, Jägersdorf, in Silesia, developed the same theme:

A Jew offered to buy milk from a Christian wet nurse who instead sold him the milk of a sow. He then got a poor peasant who owed him money to execute his orders on the promise that his debt would be erased. He brought him to the foot of a gallows, made him cut off the head of the hanged man's corpse, and had him place it to soak in a receptacle filled with the milk. Afterward the Jew ordered the peasant to put his ear to the head and asked him, "What do you hear?" The peasant responded, "The grunting of a herd of pigs!" "Woe is me!" the Jew then cried, "the woman tricked me!" The next day all the pigs within a radius of eight kilometers gathered at this spot and killed one another.

And the exemplum ended with this question: "What would have happened if the good Christian had obtained human milk for the Jew?"[26] In every case the pig is introduced as a substitute, serving to denounce the Jew and showing what might have come to pass, yet without granting the sorcerer the benefit of success. The pedagogical nature of these fables meant that those who heard them were offered both a terrifying glimpse of the Jew's underhanded practices and the recipe for foiling them and causing their power to fail.

Several remarks should be made about the first category. First, we should note the consistency with which the pig is used to concretize the beliefs, though this fact was never noted by those who recorded the events. Thanks to the pig, we know how the magic of the Jew would have functioned had the Christian not guessed his bad intentions. Once again, the latter proves able to manipulate the double analogy to his benefit: by transferring onto the animal the evil intended for himself, he ultimately causes the Jew's action to affect only a creature in his own image, his porcine double. Jews therefore turn out to be powerless to change the order of the world and to destroy Christianity, even though the belief in their responsibility for major epidemics remained very much alive. More commonly they attempted to employ the blood of Christians for the transformation of their natures.

The Jews needed this blood for their "illnesses." "Rednesses," "discharges," "inflammations" can be reduced to a common cause of which we have attempted a preliminary sketch; still, we must go further and seek the underlying principle of this emblematic Jewish illness. Circumcision, once again, will serve as our guiding thread. Jews were said to be hemophiliacs, of which the paleness of their skin served as proof. Wasn't the bleeding provoked by the cut of the circumcision, as minimal as it might be, therefore exceptionally risky? The answer is again found in the trials for ritual murder. Many of the accused admitted to having performed the crime "for their circumcisions." More specifically, as revealed in 1492 by Jews pursued in Mecklenburg, the blood of a Christian was "an excellent remedy to mend the wound to the foreskin." Moreover, since "Jewish men have regular blood flows like women, this blood helped to relieve them."[27] The catalog of secret Jewish illnesses, which a specific Christian tradition disseminated for nearly two centuries throughout Europe, is illuminating. Here is one, established in 1602 by an alleged convert to Christianity, Franciscus de Patience.[28] In keeping with the vast oral tradition that classifies plants, animals, and men based on the two high points of Christ's destiny— the Nativity and the Passion—but also of Christ's stay on earth, the "infirmities" of the Jews are associated with the particular but always hostile gesture that each of the twelves tribes of Israel performed, in the person of its eponym, with respect to Christ. A coherent whole is thus revealed. Aside from the "incomplete" or "mutilated" Jews, we find those who affect a porcine nature ("to those of the tribe of Naphtali, which as we know hid its children in a pigpen upon Christ's passage, the presence of four pig's teeth, pig ears, and a pig's smell"), those who burned with an unusual heat ("to the members of the tribe of Ruben, who seized upon and beat Jesus on the Mount of Olives, the property of making pale [of drying] all vegetables they touched within the space of three days"), those marked by bleeding ("to the members of the tribe of Dan, who cried 'his blood will fall back on us and on our children,' the appearance each month of bloody wounds that smell so bad they have to hide"). While the latter group is particularly affected, the others are also afflicted by "hemorrhages," whether seasonal (the tribe of Simeon is "afflicted with bleeding" four times a year), or chronic (all Jews and cagots, it was claimed not long ago in the Pyrenees and in Brittany—where they are called *cacous*—"bleed even more strongly on Holy Friday"). A calendar-bound bleeding of which, in a medieval exemplum, one passionate Jewess takes advantage to fix a safe date with her Christian lover, a young canon, given that "on that night, the Jews are busy suffering a flow of blood" ("fluxum sanguinis patientes").[29]

Even if leprosy is nominally absent from this picture, we can easily recognize the features that elsewhere constitute the clinical signs of the "Jewish disease." Until now we have attributed this to the Jew's "nature," a nature constructed by Christians to better anchor the disease. Indeed, it was important that this sickness be incurable and hereditary. At this point the ethical and metaphysical dimensions of this "original sickness," reactivated at each birth, are fully affirmed:

> Many medical treatises assert that Jewish children are born with their right hand soiled with blood and held against their forehead, as if attached to the skin, to the point of necessitating an operation to free it. In addition to this position of the hand, the presence of blood blinds Jewish newborns when they come into the world, for the delivery of a Jew is laborious and difficult. And here too, of course, Christian blood comes in handy to bathe the eyes of newborns and restore their vision and to bathe the genital organs of the mother and facilitate the delivery.[30]

This sickness reactivated by every birth, this blindness by excess of blood takes on an allegorical dimension. In it we recognize the allegory often represented by medieval iconography as the "blind Synagogue," a blindfold covering the eyes.[31] Stricken with a physical and moral blindness, infected by impure blood, the Jews subsist in order to offer Christians—cleansed of their original leprosy, their eyes opened by the blood of Christ like the centurion Longinus—the spectacle of their impurity and of their unfortunate attempts to escape their destiny.

The widespread belief among Christians that Jews take "blood baths" has its roots here. But the founding myth of these legends took shape in the story of Constantine. According to the hagiography, Constantine was sticken with leprosy while fighting the Christians, and a blood bath was prescribed for him by his Jewish doctor. It was then, guided by the vision of the cross—the very cross that his mother, Helen, later "invented"—that he received the baptism of Pope Sylvester and was cured upon his immersion in the vat, as depicted in the vast iconography on this miracle.[32] Following his example, his daughter Constance, also a leper, converted and was baptized with the same result. Thus, baptism by Christ replaced the bloody sacrifice; it alone could "cure" the body and soul of those who submitted to it. Henceforth, every Christian cleansed himself of the original stain in the baptismal pool, while the Jew attempted to incorporate the virtues of the sacrament by immersion in the blood of the purified Christian or by annointing the body of his freshly circumcised newborn with "Christian blood." This too was among the details that Jews confessed when pressed by the Inquisition, emphasizing how indispensable this "unction"—*crisam* was the word they used—was to them at the moment of circumcision to erase their leprosy.[33] One cannot be more explicit as to the anticipated effects of this "baptismal chrism" that, from Jews to Christians, would change in nature alone.

The spectrum of uses Jews were alleged to make of Christian blood, revolving around circumcision, the "Jewish baptism," went on from there. Once the mechanism that caused this fundamental sequence of Jewish life to be considered a model ritual was understood, it was easy to extend this model to all Jewish holidays. With the development of inquisitional trials and polemical works addressing "Jewish customs" it was asserted that all transitional moments (births and circumcisions, marriages and funerals) as well as all major moments of collective life, Sukkot, Purim, Passover, and Shavuot, required the blood of a Christian child. If, according to Christians, none of these rituals could occur without recourse to the blood of the other, it was because ever since the killing of Christ, by which Jews placed themselves on the other side of the dividing line traced by his blood, they have continually repeated the gesture that separates them. First, from a reading of rituals based on an ensemble of representations that depict the Jew as a being "of blood," Christians developed the conviction that Jews were obsessed with blood and gave meaning to this concept in the ways we have noted. From this perspective the *ritual crime* would make manifest the Christians' pseudoknowledge of the Jew, with the coherent ensemble of diseases, practices, and beliefs attributed to the Jew forming the foundation of this crime. But, just as the accusation of cannibalism that is at the heart of this ritual crime is illuminated when one looks at the questions posed to pork eaters by the so human and childlike flesh of the animal, so the specifically metaphysical dimension of this use of blood, which has been progressively revealed to us, prompts us to now look at the most intimate beliefs of Christians, at what makes *them* so different from Jews.

Running throughout the entire Middle Ages is a dialectical relationship between the Jew of the Old Testament who applies the divine prescriptions *stricto sensu*—as incarnated in alimentary prohibitions, the practice of circumcision, respect for the Sabbath, and sacrifices to Yahweh—and the Christian who has in some sense "passed into the spiritual." In their sermons and diatribes the champions of the anti-Jewish polemic revive and adapt the commentaries of the Church fathers on "the letter that kills": while Jews circumcise their bodies, Christians "circumcise their hearts." While the former sacrifice "victims of flesh and blood," the latter, by the New Covenant, rise to the spiritual sacrifice. Yet at the same time the very real nature of the change produced in the Eucharist is affirmed. By a mystery that constitutes the central point of the dogma, the host becomes "the flesh and blood of Christ."[34] Does this mean that, despite their best intentions, Christians are unsuccessful at separating the spirit from the letter? Is it no wonder then that they should ascribe to this same Jew, in the context of ritual crime, the use of the object that supports their belief—the host—the ingestion of which is the vehicle for participation in the divine?

Let us recall the circumstances under which the young Werner was put to death. "On Holy Thursday, April 19, 1287, he attended services and received holy communion. Upon returning from church he was seized by a gang of Jews who, in order to make him vomit the holy host, persecuted him, opened his veins in several places, and ended up causing his death." We already encountered the host in the Niño de la Guardia affair. There, too, it emerged as a necessary ingredient in the mixture that one of the "participants" in the plot, for which Jews and lepers were jointly accused in 1321, described to the Bishop Fournier. Guillaume Agasse, a leper from Pamiers, confessed in effect that to ensure the poisoning of wells and fountains one had to have subscribed to the conditions, revealed to him during a gathering, of "denying the faith of Christ and his law, and [of] taking a powder found in a kettle that will be brought here soon, in which what the Christians call the Body of Christ has been grilled, then pulverized."[35] Is this capturing of the host a mere accessory detail in stories that are already filled with horror? Does it simply complete the analogy between the Jew and the sorcerer—a renowned employer of sacred objects, who puts them in the service of infernal powers? We might be tempted to stick to this explanation if, beginning in the second half of the thirteenth century, and with increasing intensity until the sixteenth century, Jews were not also pursued for profaning the host. Both the chronology of the two accusations and the personality of those involved invite us to make a connection between them, guided by the blood that colors the unleavened bread and the Eucharist.

The Host That Cries and Bleeds

In the exempla, starting in the thirteenth century, profanation of the host began to emerge from among the numerous sacrilegious acts that could affect sacred objects: statues, crucifixes, and holy images were also attacked, either because the nonbelievers or heretics were determined to sully and destroy them or because naive individuals attempted to confiscate them for their own profit or to use the powers attributed to them to harm others. The exempla relating these profanations are far fewer than the ones developing the various misappropriations to which the host could be subjected. The illustration of this is furnished by the miracle, which became the theme of an apiarian legend or tale, of a villain who placed a host in his hive to increase its production of honey— or simply for it to be devoured by his bees. When he opened it he found a chapel of wax and an alter on which gleamed a glowing chalice. Through this materialization, the host demonstrates that its powers are spiritual in nature; the naive profaner who was so touched he fell to his knees, imploring forgiveness, immediately received its good graces.[36]

The pedagogy of the exemplum was addressed first to peasants, to women, to "simple minds," all of whom sinned by an excess of credulity. So it was with the widows and abandoned lovers who carried in their caps or aprons a host intended to bring back the beloved or unfaithful one. But all Christians, even the wise, expected wealth and health from the host. It was said that Pope Alexander VI "wore a host placed in a gold box on his neck, with the assurance that it would protect him against evil and death." Indeed, in the face of death the host was a passport to eternity, administered to the dying in the form of the last sacrament; as early as the first centuries, however, the Church had to fight abuses consisting, in the case of a deceased who was unable to take communion, of placing it between the lips of the cadaver as a "guarantee of resurrection."[37]

This rapidly sketched picture of the powers Christians attributed to the host includes, oddly enough, that which the Jews were alleged to attribute to Christian blood. Knowing these usages and beliefs is important, therefore, to a better understanding of the specificity of the stories concerning Jews. Unlike Christians, who were hungry to capture a bit of its power, the Jew disdained the host. While the exempla that depict the Jew obey the rules of the genre and the period, which have it that the profanation must end in a holy revelation, they nonetheless always unravel, in a particular fashion. Taking advantage of the trust of a Christian friend, a Jew procures a host so that he can "adore it," he claims, before being baptized. This reverence is only simulated, however, since once his Christian neighbors are gone he surreptitiously throws the sacred host into the trough of the pigpen. But the pigs begin tramping down earth and grunting furiously, refusing the gruel, or else "kneeling" before it, the sight of their devotion prompting the conversion—unfeigned this time—of the Jewish provoker.[38] This model quickly replaced the exempla in which pigs uncover the hosts that "thieves," having stolen the ciborium to resell it, emptied on a pile of dung or buried before fleeing with their booty. The newer version of the facts places the Jew in an unprecedented relationship in which the pig betrays him against his wishes, affirming its Christian nature. At the turn of the fourteenth century the exempla took on a new tone. This change was brought to light by Jacques Le Goff with respect to the *Alphabetum narrationum*, an anthology that, though composed at the start of this century, nonetheless compiles earlier stories. When the Jew is one of the protagonists, he continues to receive divine clemency by way of a miraculous conversion, but he is more and more ridiculed and vilified by Christians, particularly by clerics, who become true heroes in the face of the active enemies of the true religion.[39]

This move toward intolerance is equally perceptible when one compares the literature of the exempla with the neighboring literature of *miracles*. Our Lady, for example, is credited with saving a Jewish child thrown by his father into an incandescent oven as punishment for having taken communion with his young Christian friends. The first-known version dates from the sixth century, when it was put in writing by Grégoire de Tours; the story, initially intended to sing the glory of Mary, which spread throughout Europe by way of anthologies, was later revamped, with the emphasis shifting from the figure of the child to that of the father. Berceo, in his *Milagros de Nuestra Señora* (twelfth century), Alfonse el Sabio, in his *Cantigas de Santa Maria* (thirteenth century), calls this tale *El niño judío*, the Jewish child. Both linger over the sweetness of the child and the mother, tenderly describing the baptism of the child saved by the virgin and the conversion of Jews that followed. But, already with Gautier de Coincy, the tone begins hardening in France. His *De l'enfant à un Gui qui se crestiena* emphasizes the violence of the father—of the Jew—thus preparing the reader for the long final diatribe against his coreligionists.[40] The child moves into the background so that no sympathy should temper the harshness with which Christians should now view the Jews. When we rediscover the miracle under the heading "Eucharistia" in the *Alphabetum narrationum*, it is entitled "The Eucharist Taken by an Infidel Protects Him from the Fire."[41]

The same bias is at work in the "eucharistic miracles" scattered throughout the European Middle Ages as so many founding events— they are at the origin of cultural celebrations, of the establishment of an order, of a church's construction. The legends digress considerably in order to place the Jew in the role of profaner in the foreground. A single example will suffice to illustrate this shift.

The Italian city of Lanciano, in the Abruzzi, was singled out twice by a miracle. Already, in the eighth century, it was said that a host began dripping blood on the alter for the priest who doubted that it contained a real presence. The miracle repeated itself in 1273, this time for a woman who had put the host up "to cook," at the advice of a female friend, in order to reduce it to powder and concoct a potion to bring back her husband. The first event was related by a Franciscan monk—the order settled in Lanciano in 1258—as follows: "In Lanciano, one can see the very holy sacrament that changed into flesh and blood when a Jew struck it with a knife"; the scribe finishes with a vicious couplet: "May the sacrilegious tongues of the Jews be silent." It is of the Jews, in fact, that the local memory has been maintained; it is their crime that is recalled during the May celebrations that exalt the miraculous host. Meanwhile the heroine of the second miracle, Ricciarella, appears as a victim. A series of paintings based on the legend, which became official in the sixteenth century, show her listening to the advice of a servant girl with dark skin and a hooked profile. Henceforth the imputation of sacrilege is transferred to the Jewish sorceress; she is the one we see "frying" the host, under the timid gaze of the innocent Christian.[42]

When the hagiographers of the holy sacrament established this new version of the facts, it was necessary, for the sake of consistency, that only the Jew be the instigator and actor, in keeping with the movement that then linked the revelation of the eucharistic mystery to his profaning action. We shall see how this was done by returning to the most famous case of host profanation—a model for all those to come—the Billettes affair, in 1290. We are now in Paris. A Jew, a Jonathan or a Jacob, depending on the version—a usurer in any case—proposed a deal to a poor Christian woman who had hocked her skirt with him and, though penniless, wanted to take it out "for Easter." He would return it to her on the condition that she give him the host upon her return from communion. The deal was made. Once in possession of the host, Jonathan went home and began performing violent acts on the Body of Christ—which started to bleed—finally plunging it into a boiling cauldron. A crucifix appeared above the water. A Christian neighbor, alerted by the Jew's son, salvaged the host intact and informed the religious authorities of the act and miracle. The Jew was arrested, judged, condemned, delivered to the executioner, and burned before a large crowd. His house was destroyed and, in its place, the church of Carmes Billettes was built, within which the host and the knife were displayed. These objects were since venerated as relics by Parisians who carried them every year in procession, while *The Mystery of the Jew* was performed on a chariot.[43] In his *Journal d'un bourgeois de Paris* the chronicler describes the representation given on May 15, 1444, before a large crowd, but we owe the most precise account of this *Jeu et Mystère de la Sainte Hostie par personnages*, which was still performed in 1513, to a spectator from Metz, Philippe de Vigneules. To follow is the moment that must certainly have constituted the climax of this fantastic theater:

> The Jewish traitor, wishing to test whether God was inside it, took the said holy host, placed it on a table, and struck it with a knife. Then, by a secret means, a great abundance of blood squirted high above the said host, as if a child were pissing, and the Jew was all fouled and stained by it, which suited his character well. Afterward, still not content, he flung the said host into the fire and, by a mystery, it rose up and attached itself against the hearth of the chimney. The traitor pierced it thereupon with a dagger, and by other means and secrets it instantly spurted abundant blood. When this was done he took it back and attached it with two nails to a post and struck it with a hunting spear and the said host shot blood abundantly behind it, and the blood splashed all the way to the middle of the floor; the entire site was all bloodied. And then, as if in a rage, he took the host and flung it into a cauldron of boiling water, and it rose into the air in a cloud and became a small child while rising upward, and all this occurred by secret devices.[44]

What is striking about this description, of course, is how closely the progression follows the preestablished outline of ritual murder. The Jew's obstinate violence against the host, the various tortures to which he successively subjects it, do they not produce an effect of humanization that the long streams of spurting blood and, especially, the final metamorphosis "into a small child" make even more stunning?

Further, this transfiguration does not always constitute the finale; certain accounts bring it into play very early on, using it as a dramatic twist in order to accentuate the horror of the crime. The profanation of the host then becomes the murder of a child, or the attempted murder. In his *Histoire des juifs* Basnage, the seventeenth-century Protestant historian, records this same miracle of the Billettes as it was narrated sixteen years after the event, an event we know was abundantly exploited by Philip the Fair when he decided to expel the Jews from France in 1306:

The Christian historians attribute it to the miracle that occurred inside a host that had been purchased by a Jew. He threw it into a caldron of boiling water and at that moment a child of extraordinary beauty appeared. Instead of being touched by such a tangible miracle, he wanted to slay this miraculous child, but the child fled and ran from one end of the cauldron to the other as the Jew chased him, knife in hand. The sight of this moved his children, who went to tell their mother and later opened the doors of the house and made it known. The people and the clergy entered and saw the miracle of the host preserved, for the child had already disappeared.[45]

It is thus the murderous obstinacy of the Jew that is retained, the "bleeding" host that, in certain cases, "cries and groans" but, usually, becomes a "beautiful child," a "small child," so alive that the sight of him seems to redouble the fury of the Jew; "blinded by the blood," knife in hand, he chases his prey "to slay him." Sometimes, as evidenced by the rich European iconography of profanations, the Jews band together to perpetrate their crime. Thus, the analogy with the ritual murders becomes even more vital. They fuss as if over a child: one raises his weapon, the other holds the host on the table where it seems to be struggling, a third tends to a cauldron, while the host bleeds from the Jews' repeated blows.

If we allow ourselves to see these two structurally inseparable accusations as the panels of a diptych that, when opened, display parallel scenes, and when folded, overlap perfectly, would we not be led to think that making blood the motive for ritual murder and placing the host at the center of profanations means questioning the latter through the former? Does this not imply that in the thirteenth century, when the figure of the "criminal" Jew was added to that of the "profaning" Jew, the dogma of the real presence was not entirely secure?

Unleavened Bread and the Host

The reading of any dictionary of heresies will present this period as one of theological controversy. At the same time the Jew was progressively associated with the pagan, then with the heretic, against whom struggles were also being waged in Europe, where Waldenses and Cathars agreed to contest the point of dogma that until then one was permitted to discuss with the Jews. Indeed, the *Dispute of Barcelona* (1263) was the death knell for a debate that, while always ending in the victory of Christianity, manifested a spirit of tolerance that was no longer in vogue.[46]

Jews, once assigned this doctrinal position and vindictive attitude, had to be separated out, in the image of the "excommunicated" who were cut off from the Church. This was what the Lateran Councils put into effect through the mouth of Pope Innocent III, by declaring, on the subject of "Jews or Sarrasins," that henceforth, "in every Christian province and at all times, these people, of either sex, will distinguish themselves publicly from the dress of other populations." While the Lateran Councils recommended a "distinct, very apparent color," they seemed to leave complete freedom in the choice of shade and form. At first a yellow circle was imposed almost everywhere, which, in the course of the fourteenth century, became scarlet. How should this change be interpreted? In his *Practica* of the inquisitor, Bernard Gui, who officiated in Toulouse at the start of the fourteenth century, compiled a precise list of defamatory marks: to those who "perpetrate spells and evil deeds by means of the Eucharist: two hosts of rounded shape are imposed." Thus, at the moment when accusations were mounting against the Jews, it is easy to imagine that a parallel was being made between the Jew's circle and the profaner's host. Should any doubt remain, the lexicon common to the host and to the mark confirms the relationship. Both were called *corona, circulus, rotula.* When, in fifteenth-century Turin, a "red circle ringed in white" won acceptance, how can we help but interpret it as the pure heart of the host from which the divine blood is rising? Henceforth the circle, the "mark of the Jew," designated the enemy of the faith, the unshakable adversary of that which became the symbol of Christianity in these centuries of affirmation and combat, its most central and most contested mystery.[47]

It is thus in the face of the Eucharist that the heretical split was brought to light, a split of which the Jews paradoxically incarnated the extreme limit. But this founding difference was not enough, and the host itself would be responsible for maintaining the constant repetition of the gesture of separation. From its inception Christianity was confronted with a twofold requirement. First, in order to affirm itself, it had to deny its Jewish roots by abandoning rituals (such as circumcision and the Sabbath) and lifting major prohibitions (that of consuming blood and pork) which it saw as constituting the very essence of Judaism. This effort at detachment, the progression of which may be followed through the councils, was effected over the course of the first centuries. At the same time the Easter celebrated by Christ became the central founding ritual of Christianity. It was necessary, therefore, on the occasion of the holiday and of the meal, to make the difference as radical as possible, with the bread of communion becoming the first focal point for this work of disjunction. And yet, after some oscillation and concessions, in the eleventh century the western Church went strictly unleavened—adopting an unleavened host—as opposed to the eastern Church, which celebrated Easter with a "raised" bread. These antagonistic choices, as we know, tore apart the Christian world, fating Roman Catholicism to multiply its signs of distinction with respect to Judaism and its unleavened bread.[48] Yet the event that caused the break was the religious eruption of blood. The accusation of ritual murder, that of the profanation of the host, according to which a repeated "Passion" became the essential and secret ritual of the Jews, established a division at every Easter where before there had been filiation between Judaism and Christianity. But, in addition, the Christians maintained the myth that the Jews were constantly attempting to appropriate this "blood of Christ," an effort that led them to maintain the practice of the "bloody sacrifice" with which Christians also broke.

The accusation of ritual murder, like that of profanation, but crueler in its own way, shows the ambivalent position the Christians attributed to the enemies of Christ, who both attempted to capture the "sacraments" and performed violent scornful actions on them and their powers. In both cases, however, the Jews provide the proof and counterproof of the combined powers of blood and host, even if, by adding Christian blood to their unleavened bread, they are absurdly attempting to repeat the miracle, which they trigger despite themselves by piercing the host. For the Jew—and this is not the least of paradoxes—is the one who *makes the miracle appear* to the Christians, who brings to light the very mystery that is the foundation of the Christian faith. Does this mean that the "believers," for whom the exempla and miracles are intended, are not fully convinced themselves?

Just as the Jews sometimes treat the host as an ordinary food, cooking it in various ways—fried in holy oil or boiled in a cauldron—all those who cannot accept the miracle of real presence reduce it to its material nature as unleavened bread. The Pyrenean heretics of the fourteenth century, in their debates, speak of it in circumlocutions— "that dough cooked between two fires"—while the doubting priest in the *Miracle of Bolsena*, presented in Florence in 1405 for the Festival of the Holy Sacrament, exclaims:

Io per me no credo
Che questa asima
Carne e sangue sia.

[As for me I do not believe
That this unleavened bread
Is flesh and blood.][49]

As for women, when they appear among the Jews as profaners they perform actions—undoing and remaking the host, even adding leavening to see whether it will behave like dough—that confirm their nature:

> A woman tempted by the Devil decides to test the Eucharist, brings it home in a napkin, and tries to cook it in the oven. She hears the voice of a child calling its mother, and sees the Virgin removing the Christ child from the oven. Stricken with remorse, she is on the verge of hanging herself, but the Virgin places her trust in her.[50]

A similar curiosity tempts Jewish males. With regard to the Billettes affair, the account of Philippe de Vigneules specifies that Jonathan acted to "test" whether the host was God, while in 1453, in Breslau, Jews stabbed a host "to see if God is really present in it."[51] The similarity of the words, gestures, and intentions is clear: the Jews put into action what constitutes for each Christian the limit of his belief. In its own way the ritual crime—the bloody ritual alleged to be at the heart of Judaism—offers only the sham image, the barbarous backside of the Christian miracle.

Those who dismantle the mechanism to attempt to reproduce it, those who doubt because they cannot picture the truth of the dogma other than in the form of a "cake of blood," are equally caught in the trap of the carnal illusion. The very illusion that, according to the exemplum most often told, sent a young boy into frenzied flight upon seeing his brothers "eat a child" during Mass, or of the Jew who enters a church and finds each of the Christians "eating a bloody child." To them the mystery of transubstantiation was revealed.[52]

Such are the questions that arise with respect to this dimensionless body, this diaphanous and translucid being—the paradoxical host that is known to be flesh. Henceforth, the mystery is inseparable from the tests to which it is put. Jews and sometimes even Christians—women and children mostly—cannot grasp the spiritual nature of the "divine ferment" that inhabits the Christian host and manifests itself in the form of this "bloody child," which is how they designate the Body of Christ. Even though it is through the Jews that proof of the incarnation occurs, it is still necessary that they remain shut off to this sublime reality, incapable as they are of seeing it with the eyes of the spirit, blinded as they are by the blood. They will therefore be forever deprived of this knowledge, for which they will remain forever thirsty.

How do things stand today among Christians? The questions triggered by the ingestion of the host explicitly reveal that by wishing to make the mystery present one runs the risk of falling into heretical negation. Indeed, barely thirty years ago this secret constituted the main preoccuption of those who were preparing to experience it for the "first time." Our personal memories, those of readers if they are willing to go back in time, and the spontaneous comments the mere mention of the host inspires "among children," which many of our interlocutors related to us with the same naive tone that memorialists attentive to this moment in their childhood recreate, are in agreement. All give the same image of their anticipation of the event, of the beliefs discussed. Take, for instance, this dialogue between two old women from Cevennes who attended parochial school: "The nuns had told us, 'If you chew the host, you'll get a mouthful of blood!' A friend asked, 'And if we bite it, do we die?' After that, we were all jittery when we had this host in our mouths! And then, it was hard to swallow, it sat in our stomachs, and we were afraid of 'vomiting' it because it was a mortal sin." From beliefs we move rapidly to experiences. The "rehearsal" that takes place before the Holy Communion was the site of the host's transmission. In the 1950s, in Béziers, one prepared for Holy Communion with the *sembla òstia*. "What if it sticks to your palate?" The sister explained, "You moisten it properly with saliva and it comes off. Gently, with the tip of your tongue. Sometimes people choke." "And if it touches your teeth?" "You must be very careful! Some have bitten the host and it began bleeding. They say they had a mouthful of blood."[53]

This fear of bloodshed upon mere contact with one's teeth is also motivated by the terrifying image of the retribution it incurs. Through the writings of Ramón J. Sender, Paco, a little peasant altar boy who is also preparing for Holy Communion, evokes the climate of anxiety among the novices several days in advance: "They talked about the Holy Communion, among themselves, inventing strange dangers. They said that, to receive Holy Communion, one had to open one's mouth very wide, because if the host touched the communicant's teeth, he dropped dead and went straight to Hell."[54] It is thus among neophytes that the secret is revealed as the mysterious ritual approaches.

A strange power, that of the host, henceforth limited to the sphere of childhood; strange, too, is the power of the young Christian, who knows that at any moment he can put it to the test. But the host is well protected: "If you bite it, it bleeds," "If you make it bleed, you die." A twofold belief that, like the safest of the tabernacles, prohibits transgression while leading those who accept it and who, consequently, act with caution, to always feel on the edge. To verify the reality of the dogma is the ultimate profanation, for which one pays with one's life. This is the teaching that is carried down to children taking communion to our day. It appears only at the end of a long journey, which, to impose the "truth" of the mystery, required making the belief act from the outside—and this was long the role that fell to the Jew. This belief, internalized in the form of a prohibition and provisionally shielded from and at the mercy of each individual, continues to live in the secrets of hearts and, more precisely, among those who first played the role of innocent victims of the sacrilegious trial.

CHAPTER SIX

Old Jews, Young Christians

I remember one thing that annoyed me a lot: not being able [as a Jew]
to receive first communion. I would have liked to be dressed like a
princess like the other little girls. My mother bought me a white bracelet
watch and a ring like they had. . . . There was also the fact that, at my
middle school theater, I couldn't play the Virgin, my mother forbade
me, so I had to be happy as a tree or a little angel.

—MERCEDES FERNÁNDEZ MARTORELL, *Una communidad judía*

Ritual murder should thus be understood as the Christian's
overall interpretation faced with the enigmas of Jewish culture. Does it not enable us to shed light on both the major prohibitions—that of pork and of blood—and the rituals that mark the
times of the year and the times of life, while illustrating the differences
in nature that separate the two "races"? But this fable also draws its
strength from an imperious necessity: the Jew must test the eucharistic
mystery faced with which every Christian risks crossing the fine line
that would cast him on the side of the profaners. It is for this reason that
every calendar of Christian holidays—Christmas, Easter, Pentecost,
and Corpus Christi—is accompanied by confrontations in which the
cutoff is starkly exhibited. Nowhere in Christian Europe have Jewish
communities been spared. Avoidance of and silence toward the Jews, at
the very least, mark the period of the Holy Week, not so much to recall
the act of deicide as to signify the fear perpetuated in the irrepressible
gesture by which the Christian child is sacrificed on this date. Ida, a

Jewish woman who spent her childhood and adolescence in Salonica in the 1900s, recalls it in these terms:

> The most tragic night is the night of Easter, the Greek Easter. Always, the Jews killed a child, we put the blood in the unleavened bread. Every year it was the same story. We would see that the young people were in foul moods. The night of Easter, the Greeks were bad as could be. It was a bad eight days, both with the friends we had and with all the youth. We went out with Greeks, we talked with them; who knew if one day we might marry one? And yet the eight days of their Easter, it was the end of the world.[1]

The story has been told of the alternately aggravated and euphemized situation to which this separation ritual gave rise. In Rome, for instance, where the Jews lived in pontifical states like witnesses to the violent origin of Christianity, until 1312 an old Jew was made to tumble down Mount Testaccio in a barrel spiked with points: his broken body, whose blood had escaped through a thousand wounds, initiated the period of Lent. The payment of a tribute of ten florins replaced this cruel execution, but in the mid-fifteenth century Pope Paul II raised the fee for each of the one hundred and ten synagogues in his states and added, "in memory of Judas," thirty florins destined to pay for Masses. Still the Jews were not free and clear; in place of the old Jew in his cask the people were offered the spectacle of pigs, decked out and seated two by two in ornate carriages, "as a sign of disdain," they said, "for the Jews who couldn't touch them." Led in a procession surrounded by notables and prelates whose dress had been paid for by the Jewish dues, the escorted carriages and their occupants mounted the flanks of the Testaccio. There they were cast off the mountain peak, crashing down to the great joy of the gazing crowd. The murderous ceremony was thus doubly abated—the Jews paid with their own money and the pigs replaced them in their roles—but this abatement was no doubt illusory. In the fifteenth century the carnivalesque *palio*, during which Jews formed a procession between youths and elders under a red banner, became a humiliating ordeal: when Montaigne visited Rome in 1585, the Jews were running "naked," alone with the prostitutes.[2]

These scenes of violence and derision, which were more than just local improvisations, always ended up incarnating the Christians' image of the Jew by means of familiar attributes—the pig, Judas, the body that's been bled, the color red. Moreover, they always took place around the holiday that was disputed by the two religions: Easter. We have seen how the logic that gave form and meaning to these aggressions based itself on the existence of a Jewish community and on daily interaction—familiarity mutating into a hostile distance during these days. Yet the absence of Jews or of conversos did not eliminate the antagonism, furnishing new proof that it was a constituent element of Christianity, of its advent, of its sacred history and its symbolic system. But if one no longer had recourse to the Jew to play the ancestral role in the drama of Christ, what forms would it take? How would these roles be distributed? And, most of all, by virtue of what differences, which now had to be found within the very core of the "Christian people"?

The Christians' Jews

Until recently the Museum Giuseppe Pitré, in Palermo, offered visitors a surprising glimpse at two colorful statues of armed warriors known by the name of Giudei di San Fratello, the Jews of San Fratello. They were there, it was said, to preserve the memory of the days when several men so dressed gave a performance of the flagellation of Christ during the Holy Week for city residents. Today in San Fratello "dressing up as a Jew" has become a tradition, giving the annual and appropriately named "festival of the Jews" its particular character. It was also their representation in large numbers that led Aragonais communes to designate the large nocturnal procession of Holy Thursday, the one followed most by the population, as the *procesión de los Judíos*, the procession of the Jews. The latter lead the train. Their faces hidden by penitent hoods, barefoot and dressed in tunics, they advance to the clinking of heavy chains. Sometimes they blow mournfully into a horn, sometimes they whip themselves to the muffled beat of the drum.[3] Throughout almost all of southern Europe, the Easter stage is divided among such representations: armed Jews in San Fratello, Jews in chains in Aragon, Jews whipping or being whipped. But, while the street spectacle most often shows us one or the other figure, the Church, which also enacts its liturgy within its walls, restores coherence to this fractured vision. Let us listen to the testimony of one of our Catalan interlocutors concerning Conflent in the 1910s:

> On Holy Thursday they had lain Christ before the high alter and the devout women had decorated him with flowers; candles were lit and all of Catllar paraded past to kiss his feet, and especially the nail. There was one special thing: two Roman soldiers—life-size statues with spears—were placed on either side, and the people called them *els jueus,*

the Jews. They were no Jews, those Roman soldiers, but for the people of Catllar they were *els jueus*! And on Sunday, at the moment when we struck up the hymn to the risen Christ, the Jews were pelted until they fell. Everyone waited for this moment.

The church scene first brings together the two antagonistic images of the Jew and illustrates them by the two sequences, in which they appear near the sepulchre, standing, then fallen. No doubt the "confusion" between the Jews and the Roman soldiers, which our interlocutor attributes to the absence of historical awareness on the part of his fellow citizens, is characteristic of more than this particular Catalan village, especially since the catechism has long taught that the Jews killed Christ. Renaissance paintings of the mounting of Calvary liked to juxtapose and contrast the face of Christ with those of Jews and soldiers mixed together.

Moreover, an enlargement of our perspective confirms this connection between "Jews" and "Romans." In Majorca the centurions stand guard around Christ on Holy Thursday. Their attire is startling: knit coats of mail, helmets crowned with ribbons and feathers, spears and swords at their sides. They stand frozen like statues. But on Sunday, at Mass, when the archpriest intones the Gloria, they come to life and play at spreading terror, running in the church, wreaking havoc in the bays, frightening even in their defeat—after being overcome they continue to smash their spears against the ground as a sign of powerlessness and fury. In San Llorèns d'Escardesson, in Catalonia, the same "centurions" who openly snore during the first part of the service—in keeping with the teachings of the sacred history—awaken one by one at the first measures of Ad Regi and cast off in search of Christ in the rows of benches, which they knock over, hailed by the assembly of the faithful to the cries of "Els jueus! Els jueus!" thereby confusing the ethnographer who related the scene and who noted that they were occasionally called jueus romans, Roman Jews.[4] As for the *giudei* of San Fratello, although they were always dressed in a military jacket with epaulets, they are more commonly qualified as "diabolical." Today their faces are blackened and partially hidden by red pointed hoods with fox tails at the end, a fat tongue of black fabric hanging from their mouths. Blowing noisily into horns, they pass through the village streets, attempting to enter homes, and are quickly caught and placed in chains by the Christians. These games, which are still acted out in San Fratello for the children's amusement—they scared them and made them laugh—preserve the memory of the scene that was played out more completely in the past and that is still acted out on occasion.[5]

In Esterri, in Catalonia, while the jueus romans guard the Holy Sepulchre in the church, the "Christians" attempt to kidnap Christ from them. They get as far as the *Monument*—the name given here to the sepulchre—but are immediately pushed back by the armed Jews. The result is a mass of confusion: the church resounds with the commotion of slamming and shouting, especially since neither of the forces present weakens until a jueu, from the gallery of the church or from a nearby balcony, loudly proclaims the victory of the "Christians." The "Roman Jews" are run down, forced to disappear.[6] In every instance, as one may note, defeat characterizes the difference of the Jew. This is the case in the Abruzzis, where we encountered the most demonstrative form of this principle. In Roccaramanico, on Holy Friday, twenty-four men act out *I farisei*, the Pharisees, in the parish church. They divide up into two teams, *I Rossi*, the Reds, and *I Verdi*, the Greens. All are indiscriminately decked out in worn women's garments, to which an attempt has been made to give a warriorlike quality through an accessory such as a spear or a helmet, creating an absurd appearance. From Holy Friday until Sunday the two groups take turns next to Christ, who is never left alone in the sepulchre. At the same time the church becomes the theater of the Passion, the most significant episodes of which are acted out. But now the ending approaches. In perfect unison, as the Gloria in excelsis begins, the Reds—who, of course, are the Jews, the bad ones—fall to the ground, while at the same moment Judas, who has just taken his own life, is abruptly lifted into the air by the branch from which he hung himself. This is the signal for the Greens to come in, who are now in charge, and cut him down; the overturned Reds—in Pescocostanzo, where they fall violently and comically, they are said to "take a tumble" (*fanno la cascata*)—are unceremoniously transported outside the church and with them all the "Jewish" extras in the spectacle: Caiaphas and Judas. They will nonetheless reappear in the solemn procession of Christ's resurrection that closes the Easter cycle; defeated, deprived of their weapons, wearing women's clothing, stripped to the bare essentials, they are completely and clearly Jews.[7]

Among Christians the identification of a particular group with the Jews extends beyond the theatrical stage, even if it maintains a close connection with the latter. In Catalonia, according to a very active oral tradition, coalmen, carpenters, tailors, and cobblers were "Jews" because they contributed to the crucifixion by furnishing the thorns of the crown—the tailor's needles—the nails—the cobbler's awls—and the carpenter's wood for the cross. Cobblers, in particular, are punished in the person of the Wandering Jew, condemned to walk to the end of the earth for having refused to help Christ on the path of Calvary.[8] The tailors certainly remain "the most Jewish" of these accursed artisans because Jews themselves often exercised this profession or trades that had to do with fabric, such as that of secondhand clothes merchant. The *armats*, those Roman Jewish soldiers we have encountered, were recruited from among their ranks. Their captain's banner, decorated with the famous initials of the Roman legion, S.P.Q.R., has always inspired facetious interpretations, including that of "Sastres Pobres Que Roben," poor tailors who steal.

Esparreguera, at the foot of the Montserrat, is known to this day in Catalonia for its Passion. Whereas, in their current form, the first large-scale representations date back no farther than 1875, the date of the great vogue of Barcelona theater prompted by the Carlists, this wool-working hamlet had long been famous for its "Jews." Indeed, according to the local blazon:

> A Terrassa bona raça
> Quasi tots son bona gent
> A Olesa son dimonis
> I a Esparreguera son jueus.
>
> [In Terrassa a good race,
> Almost all are fine people
> In Olesa devils
> And in Esparreguera they are Jews.]

But, our informers tell us today, with a smile, "they call them Jews because they played the Jews." Oral tradition has it that for many years the monks of Montserrat recruited the Jews and the Judas of their Mystery plays from this city close to their monastery, where they celebrated the Easter holidays with great pomp by means of a large production. Thus the residents of Esparreguera climbed the famous mountain every year to go "play the Jews" for their pious neighbors. In 1588 Esparreguera built a church and its residents began acting the scenes at which they excelled among themselves, for themselves. The residents of Esparreguera took advantage of this past as "Jews" to proclaim the superiority of their theater and of their actors, and in particular of their Judas: the one in the Gospel, they assert, "was from Esparreguera."

The visitor is shown his house or, rather, what remains of it, for it was burned down several times. The site is called "cal Judes."[9]

Judas's Fire

"Burning Jews," "Burning the red Jew," "Burning Judas." These expressions are used to designate, in northern France, the great blaze that is lit on Holy Saturday.[10] It is a ritual fire, a purifying fire, they say, since in it are consumed old sacerdotal garments and dried palms from the past year. But sometimes one also burns the above-mentioned personage. This is the case in Catalonia and Majorca, where a Judas is fabricated for this purpose: "The doll was made of rags to be extra repulsive and strange; he was necessarily red-headed and red dominated his clothing. He held a purse full of broken glass in his hand, so that, when he moved, it jingled like the thirty coins obtained from the sale of Jesus. He was hung by the neck to show that he had hung himself."[11] Detached from the context of the representation of the Passion, of which it was but one episode—albeit a major one, as we have seen—the putting to death of Judas, represented by this ignominious punishment, takes on new dimensions when inscribed within a scenario in which children are the protagonists. In Spain and the New World the Función de Judas, the "game of Judas," one might say, constitutes one of the highlights of the Easter cycle. It goes from Holy Thursday to Easter Sunday, taking various shapes and breadths but always requiring the active presence of young boys.

In Barcelona, where it is called the Hallelujah festival, the ceremony is dominated by a giant Judas, similar in every way to the model found elsewhere. Before being burned it is paraded through the courtyards of the homes, followed by a crowd of boys carrying burning torches, which they throw into the fire where the puppet is consumed. Before or instead of burning it, the children, bearing long sticks, energetically strike the dummy, hung by a rope in the air. In upper Extremadura the scenario is more sophisticated. After constructing their Judas in secret, the boys bring him out and parade him through the streets, to the jeers of the crowd and the local children. They carry a highly visible placard marked "Traitor, he will be hung and burned." Or he might even be locked in the town prison until Saturday afternoon, as in Montehermoso. On Sunday morning, beginning as six o'clock, the children gather and proceed to the prison. Judas is escorted to the square and hung. The small group then joins the procession of the Encuentro, so named because it marks the reencounter of the Virgin and the risen

Christ in the person of their statues, which are made to "meet" and greet one another halfway between two churches. Then, once this homage has been rendered, they return to their Judas and, armed with rods, attack him with redoubled blows before burning him to the cries of "death to Judas Iscariote." Sometimes, as if this weren't enough, his remains are thrown in the water and dispersed.[12] Imprisoned, jeered at, hung, struck, ripped apart, burned, and drowned. The list of punishments shows the retributive nature of the roles that fell, in all these cases, to boys. The ceremony of Judas's Fire thus serves as a reminder of the odious part that the Jews and Judas played in the Passion. The customary role played by the boys is sometimes augmented by the memory and direct evocation of this "crime." The game then grows more violent, as emphasized by witnesses: "Luckily it was a puppet, or else . . . " In Jaffa, in about 1840, lengthy preparations were made for what seemed like a punitive expedition:

> Every evening, during Lent, the little children from Greek families go to the doors of Christian homes and, with monotonous cries that sound like plaintive ballads, ask for wood or for *paras* (some liards) to buy wood. "Give, give," they say, "and next year your children will be married and their days will be happy, and you will enjoy their happiness for years to come." The wood these children solicited was intended to "burn the Jews." The night of the Greek Holy Thursday is when the fires are lit. Each little group lights its own. A straw man is constructed wearing Jewish dress, and the effigy of the victim is led before the fire, amid clamoring and shouting. The children deliberate seriously over the type of torture to which they are going to condemn the Israelite. Some say, "Crucify him! He crucified Jesus Christ." Others say, "Cut off his beard and his arms and then his head!" Finally, others say, "Split him open, tear out his insides, because he killed our God." The leader of the group then speaks, "Why bother with all these forms of torture?" he says. "The fire is all ready. Let's burn the Jew!" And the Jew is thrown into the flames. "Fire! Fire!" cry the children, "don't spare him! Eat him up! He slapped Jesus Christ, he nailed his feet and hands!" Thus the children enumerate all the sufferings the Jews caused the Savior to endure.[13]

But in addition to this Judas, consumed in the blaze that is fed by the entire community, Judas and the Jews die in yet another, more secret manner at the hands of the young boys. The particular relationship uniting them has produced a special dramatization culminating in an unusual practice.

"Kill the Jews"

Not long ago young Catalans armed with rattles and *martelets* announced
the Tenebrae service as follows:

> Al ofici dones
> Poques i bones!
> Al ofici anem
> Garrotades als jueus!

> [To Mass, women
> Few and good!
> To Mass, let us go
> Blows to the Jews!]

Here is the story of this custom, transcribed by a participant in Céret
in the 1880s:

The Holy Week had barely begun when we went, all of us, to get sledgehammers for ourselves, *la massa*, large or small ones depending on how
strong you were. Why these sledgehammers? Hell, it was to make a
racket at the end of the Tenebrae service and especially "per matar els
jueus"! As soon as the bell for the evening service sounded you would
see us emerging from every part of town, each one carrying his instrument on his shoulder and heading to the church square. Some preferred
the rattle, the *criquette*. The first one to arrive rushed to count the candles lit in the choir, on both sides of a wooden triangle extinguished
every night. "How many are left?" we asked the messenger. "An
manque un i la lloque, There is one missing and the 'clucker.' " The
lloque [brood hen] was the candle that was lit at the top of the triangle of
wood. Immediately, our noisy games ceased and, despite the protests of
persons responsible for maintaining order, we swept into the church and
divided up among the lateral chapels until the signal was given. Finally,
after several moments of waiting, we heard the priest strike his book.
The Mass was over. At that moment a deafening noise broke out from
all sides. The alter steps reverberated under our hammers; the raucous
sound of the *criquettes* was heard. Those who were unarmed grabbed a
praying stool and knocked the seat against the frame.[14]

Let us remain in Catalonia, where the practice continued until the
Second World War. In Conflent our interlocutors performed the
patrico-patraca using rattles. In Catllar each boy had his own, with
which he "killed the Jews" in front of the two statues representing them,

which were toppled at the end of the service. In other communes of Roussillon, whether they went so far as to strike the interior walls of the church, as in Vernet, or to beat the stalls and paving stones with long rods, as in Las Illas, the actions that took place, after the twelve candles of yellow wax referred to here as the "twelve Jews" had been blown out one by one, were performed, we have repeatedly been told, to "massacre the Jews and avenge the death of Jesus Christ." In Czechoslovakia, where we discovered this ritual—it is attested throughout Europe—the children encouraged each other, to keep the rhythm of their rattles, with this couplet: "The infidel Jews are black like dogs. They dug a hole in Jesus Christ to hang him and crucify him. They placed him in the sepulchre on Holy Friday, and exhumed him on Holy Saturday. Judas the infidel, what have you done, delivering your master to the Jews? As punishment, you now burn in hell, where you dwell with the devils."[15] In Majorca, where the racket is resumed on Holy Saturday for the Hallelujah, the boys, bearing rattles, terra-cotta bells, and rifles, exclaim at each shot or blow, at each broken bell, "Un jueu menys," one less Jew.[16]

Thus the boys fight the Jews with their noise-making weapons, and if such weapons suffice to "kill the Jews," their effectiveness is augmented, in the eyes of the participants, by the tangible proof they provide of their belligerence. Joan Amades remembers the "wooden mallets" whose name, for the artisans who used them, referred to the biggest of hammers: "The boys in my day walked around with their sledgehammers attached to their belts like swords, or we carried them tied around our necks and walked around like that, as triumphant as if we were carrying real weapons." These sledgehammers, in fact, were tampered with by the young warriors to increase their deadly powers. They tinkered with them guardedly, spiking them with nails to make them more hazardous. Furthermore, "Every year before beginning to strike with the hammer, we dipped it in the holy water. And those who were christening one dipped it longer, stirring it up, as if they were baptizing it."[17] Once it was "Christian," the instrument was all the more suited for "killing Jews." In Conflent the boys put the rattles under their shirts so that they would be blessed at the service of Palm Sunday, the week before. In Rousillon, added to the *martelets* were sticks, mostly leafless laurel branches whose heads were left intact. These blessed branches were also called *fas*. A bunch of green palm branches sufficed, but strips of poplar bark or of any other green fresh plant could replace them.

Yet in Ponç and its region the *bastó de sanguinyol*—the stick of corneltree or dogwood—was the accepted, obligatory weapon. In order to obtain one the boys thought nothing of plunging deep into the brambles and thickets bordering the river Segre, where the bush grew.[18] Let us consider the species and its selection for a moment. The *sanguinyol*, otherwise called the *saigneux* (bloody one), the *sanglant* (bleeding one), is so named for its red wood, a feature that has determined many of the bush's names throughout Europe. And while red in appearance, it also produces abundant sap, which has earned it the name *piche-sang*, blood-pisser. Furthermore, the plant is alleged to "smell bad," this odor being suggested by the Langudocian *pudis* and the Creusois *pudin* as well as by its names in Vosgian dialects, where the "bloody" corneltree—the dogwood—becomes a smelly or fetid wood, thus joining the elder or bloodwort tree whose connection to Judas we have seen. In the region of Belfort children are kept away from the corneltree and its fruit, termed the "Jewish cherry," in the name of risks we also noted in Languedoc: "It's a poison," "It gives you rabies," "It hurts your stomach."[19] Thus humanized as bloody fetid flesh, the dogwood, the wood used to "kill Jews," is also chosen for its aptitude to exhale the tangible signs—a stench, flowing blood—of bodies expiring under repeated blows. Nothing is explicitly said about these properties, which we may suppose are revealed only by the children's violence. In Roussillon, where they whip the floor of the church with the tender spongy fibers of the *fas*, the boys like to call the large wet spots left on the tiles "the Jews' blood," just as they hear the clamor of rattles, which are sometimes shaken at the same time, as "the voices of the Jews," their mad cries, raging and gasping beneath the blows.[20]

Come Easter, then, the boys mobilize against the Jews like true soldiers. But as they amass the concrete signs of their struggle and victory—in the image of the open confrontation depicted by the adults—it is through the power of a ritual that belongs to them alone that the Jews "really" die. Thus the boys seal while reversing the bond that unites them to the Jews—the children become killers, Jews victims—but this reversal requires a specific place and time: the church and its Easter liturgy. By making this commotion at this particular place and time, what inherent right are they affirming?

The ritual, we have said, generally takes place at the end of the service on Holy Thursday, known as the Tenebrae service. Participation for the boys can become an absolute requirement, taking the form of a punctual invasion of the church by the armed group for the purpose of the commotion. This commotion can be repeated—this is the case in Catalonia and on the Balearic Islands—during the course of the triduum, the three days between the death of Christ and his resurrection, but it can also start up again on Holy Saturday. The liturgy assigns it a single time and a single occurrence:

> When the oration is finished the ceremoniarius strikes a bench or a book and the choir makes a small noise the same way, until the cleric who is holding the hidden candle makes it visible. Then the noise stops and the cleric extinguishes the candle and rests it on the credence table. The clergy withdraws in the order in which it arrived.

This is how the last manual prior to the new ordo understands it. On this same Holy Thursday, during the service, the small liturgical bell sounds the Gloria. This bell, like the larger bells, will then remain silent until Saturday. The same canon specifies that the use of the rattle is reserved for announcing the Mass, that at no time should it sound during a service. Thus a moment—when the final candle is hidden behind the alter—an act and a time—the brief clap of the hand on the bench or on a book—situate the ritual at the heart of the liturgy. The participants are the officiating priest, to whom the gesture properly belongs, and the choir, to whom the custom is extended by allowing it the right to make "a small noise in the same way." This is all one can draw from the liturgy, which, in practice, accepts the large rattle, in place of the large bell, to call people to services.[21] Only the reiterated requests of the synods to reduce the commotion enable us to make headway in our quest for the identity and meaning of the objects and actors.

More than prohibiting the acknowledged commotion, the Church aims to temper it, to reduce its excesses, initially attributed to the nature of the instruments employed. The Italian synods of the fifteenth and sixteenth centuries offer us a rich typology of rattles. Even their names evoke the strident sounds that reverberate under the vigorous shaking of their bearers. *Raganelle* and *taccole* are reviled, due to the noise they produce in church, which is considered excessive. Some people, emphasize the synods, like to shake them longer and harder than they should. Numerous restrictive regulations are directed at such individuals, recommending the use of wooden sticks or smaller, "less noisy" sticks. But recourse is made to prohibition pure and simple—pleading adherence to the letter of the liturgy—to reduce the constant and continuous use of rattles.[22] And these efforts to impose "temperance and solemnity" on the ritual fail all the more surely as the incriminated instruments are already in the hands of a group that is powerful and recognized by the Church.

The Voice of the Rattles

The altar boys, actors in and masters of the ritual, appear in the synods when it comes to condemning the use of rattles. We hear exasperated clergymen entreating parents, in the name of the authority they have the right to exercise over their children, to prevent the youth—*adolescenti*—and children—*pueri*—from making this racket. Now, *puer*, in Medieval Latin, more commonly refers to altar boys. For us, since our first exposure to the ritual was through the words of those who practiced it, the relationship is immediately apparent. Even in Catalonia, where the commotion is the domain of all boys between the ages of seven and thirteen, the altar boy maintains a special prerogative. One of our interlocutors, who was an altar boy in the village before becoming a chorister for over fifty years, recalled this time and its privileges very clearly: "Everyone waited to be the first altar boy to have 'the rattle.' When the priest closed his book, it was his signal; he started making a racket with this rattle, and everyone started in!" The instrument in question was the property of the church and was also of a particular size. Thus a scale of values linked the object to the one who wielded it—the largest one went to the first altar boy—according to a relationship that needs explaining. To do so we must become acquainted with these acolytes, on whom few ethnographers have focused. A contemporary study in Lorraine—the only one, to our knowledge, in this area—will serve as a counterpoint to our own fieldwork. In it we discover that the altar boys are designated only by the expression *altar boy/rattlers* or as *trételeurs*, based on the name of the rattle in Lorraine.[23] And this name, here and, more broadly, in northern France, marks a ritual role to which they are particularly attached and will bitterly defend if need be. It is true that at Easter they collect and distribute the unconsecrated hosts and call people to Mass with the sound of their rattles, but the Lorraine testimony emphasizes their power both inside and outside the church:

> In Foulcrey, between the two wars, there was a group of organized and hierarchical altar boys overseen and governed by the one with the most tenure in the position: *the first altar boy*. He established the schedule for that year. Each one had his week; an elder with a younger one under his wing was responsible not only for serving the Mass and services but also for sounding the daily Mass at seven in the morning. He called up the

number of servers necessary for Sundays and holidays. During Holy Week he divided up the tasks of the rattlers in the village, which was partitioned into four neighborhoods, with a leader in each one: Groffes, Nombourg, Pâquis, and Bout d'en Bas. In Assenoncourt there were two groups: the Bout d'en Bas and the Bout-Haut.[24]

The altar boys "ran" the village, and this continued until the thirties, when, in these same communes, the instructors of the Republic formed parallel teams of "rattlers," recruited from among their students over the age of ten. This caused new zones to be drawn up and new groups to confront one another, each with either an altar boy or a boy from the "secular" school as its leader. The stakes were possession of the rattles and the privileges that ensued, but also that of collecting and distributing the large hosts, which the headmasters began producing themselves.[25]

Moreover, in this region, where the custom of "burning Judas" continued until the sixties, the altar boy/rattlers maintained a stranglehold on the "Judas walk" and on the traitor's punishment. The preparation of the fire was strictly under their aegis and they gave it their all: "In Dannelbourg, even after the Liberation, on the eve of Holy Saturday the altar boys/rattlers made off with bundles of wood. The fire was lit at four in the morning at the church square. Around it and against the public fountain, which is visible from all sides, they scattered the blood of a pig killed the day before to show that Judas had been executed."[26]

In passing, we should note this evocative detail and retain from this first grouping the unity of meaning found in these two regions. Both in Catalonia and Lorraine, the altar boys practice the custom of "killing the Jews." By reserving it for themselves, by practically confiscating it for their own usage, they designate themselves as the best equipped, among all other boys and Christians, to confront the ritual in its most violent aspect: the putting to death, even if symbolic, of the Jew. How do they come by this aptitude?

First, they establish a familiarity with the sacred, as related in the account of a Castillian memorialist. As a new altar boy, he was dragged along by an elder who initiated him to the church's most secret recesses, as if he owned the property: "When they were together in the attic, the other altar boy pushed his familiarity with the statues. He straddled the apostles and knocked them on the head with his finger to see if there were mice, he said. He put a piece of rolled-up paper in the mouth of another one, as if he were smoking. He went up to Saint Sebastian and tore out the arrows from his chest in order to cruelly plunge them back in."[27] This apprenticeship was both aggressive and transgressive: exorcising one's fear by "playing" with the statues—despite their formidable and well-known capacity to become animate—was the first stage. The second stage occurred when one mastered the sacred objects. In the privacy of the vestries the altar boys all learned to eat hosts washed down by the wine for the Mass—shakily at first, then with a feeling of perfect impunity.[28] Those who told us these stories brought the same jubilation to them: "Yes, you had to pass through that stage. We drank straight from the altar cruet, we chewed the hosts, we wiped ourselves with the altar cloth." Are they not thereby developing the immunity necessary to manipulate the ritual objects, these objects that convert substances? "Once the priest tipped over the ciborium. The hosts fell. I ran to pick them up. The priest gestured me to stop: 'Don't touch them, my boy! One must never touch them.'"

Indeed, as an assistant to the priest in his daily practice, "passing" chalices, altar cruets and linens, the altar boy ran the risk of profanation more than anyone else. Yet he was also aware of holding a certain power: during the elevation, while the priest, arms extended, represented the erection of the cross, and while the faithful bowed their heads, he rang the "bell." This jingling represented "the trembling of the earth produced at the moment when Christ breathed his last" by virtue of liturgical symbolism—the Mass "reenacts" the Passion and the resurrection—of which each altar boy knew the code and the meaning. This familiarity with divine death was broadened by visits to the dying, on which he accompanied the priest, always ringing the little bell at the sound of which Christians bowed down and crossed themselves at the passage of the Holy Sacrament. And, of course, he was at every funeral. In an autobiography from Lorraine dating from the beginning of the twentieth century, a former server highlighted what an "impression" performing these services made on him as a young child—he took on his duties at the age of seven, for Easter—and the part played by young altar boys in ceremonies he qualifies as "fearsome," particularly viewing the dead, Corpus Christi, and the services of Holy Thursday and Friday. He concludes, "But as compensation we had the rattles, a privilege reserved for the servers."[29] Under the ancien régime this encounter with death was a quasi rite of passage. Custom had it that the youngest altar boy—the newest one—sang the Lamento of Christ's death alone on the pulpit during the Tenebrae service.[30] That was how he marked his introduction into the choir. But within the group itself other trials are reserved for the neophyte. Let's go back to the story of our chorister as he evokes the ceremonies of the Holy Week in Catllar, in Conflent:

> For the patrico-patraca we altar boys had larger rattles and it was a matter of who could shake his the loudest. The others, those who didn't have rattles, shook the benches. That raised the dust in the church! And on the steps of the alter was Christ lying under a black cloth and on each side a jeu. When the commotion was over, we put the statues to rest. We said they were dead and toppled them over. And afterward, when the service was finished, people passed in front of them—those who weren't afraid, anyway. Whereas we swaggered, we kicked them to see if they were really dead. We spit on them. Because I should mention that afterward these jeus disappeared. Before the service of Holy Thursday we took them out and put them way in the back of the church, in the dark. Later we locked them in a closet until the following year. Back when I was an altar boy they were in the bell tower and we scared ourselves with them. Because we would mess around in the church. All of a sudden, one of us would shout: "Gar'als jeus, Look out for the Jews!" and there would be a stampede down the stairs—especially among the newcomers, the little ones who didn't know.

The confrontation thus became operative in the privacy of the church, where the altar boys also learned, by their "games," to tame their fears, giving them the face of the Jew. But the former altar boys who imparted the memory of their innocent amusements to us are unaware that these games involving Jews, ritual games recognized as secret, brought to light something of the official position they were conceded. This position was even granted them as a right during the Middle Ages, a period during which the symbolic fabric of their relationship to the Jews was woven strand by strand.

The Return to the Holy Innocents

It was at the dawn of the fourteenth century that the institution of altar boys, several times moribund, was reborn throughout Europe.[31] Indeed, while from the first centuries of Christianity the necessity of having children participate in the services was established—a participation based on principle, their presence signifying the place the young religion granted children, in keeping with the teachings of the Son—a job was also soon found for them. First reading, then singing—mobilizing their inimitable voices, which signified "purity" and "innocence," in the service of the faith—would turn the altar boys themselves into the guarantors and representatives of these fragile qualities. The fifteenth century saw the growth in prestige of an art that also had to be preserved. The Church was then at the height of its musical glory. Services were performed with great pomp, with the contribution of string and wind instruments, including the organ. Within these broad-ranging sophisticated concerts the human voice had to find its proper usage, assert its singularity. Choral schools were founded and young boys, the *clerici chori*, took over the vocal segment of the services. But their duties soon surpassed this initial function.[32]

Between the fourteenth and the sixteenth centuries the pueri appeared in the liturgical theater alongside the clerics. For Christmas in Bourges they played shepherds and angels. In Narbonne they sang at the Nativity services dressed in their albs, two wings attached to their backs, a red band around their foreheads. But it was the great Passions that anointed them the first child actors. In Mons, in 1501, the children of the choir of Saint-Nicolas-en-Havré distinguished themselves in the angels' choir. Already, almost a half-century earlier, Arnoul Gréban, who directed the choir of Notre Dame between 1450 and 1455, had worked at developing the singing segment—that of the altar boys—in the Passion that he composed and directed and that constituted almost a bible for works to come.[33]

The children, who were vocally instructed by singing masters, were also educated by illustrious pedagogues. In this capacity Gerson was concerned with perfecting their "state of grace," composing for the edification of his young students and of their future masters a Doctrina in which he recommended that those whose mission it was to guard their souls seek to preserve the "angelic" part.[34] And "their status as altar boys is mixed up with that of the angels they incarnate in the theater, to such an extent that in the rubrics the word *angeli* is often replaced by pueri."[35] Just as often another term was also used to designate them, topping off the "character" attributed to these little singers: in the circumlocution of one synod, they are sometimes evoked as "Pueris cantoribus, quos innocentes vulgo appelant."[36] "Innocents"— a title that the common people were fond of but that the altar boys also adopted just about everywhere, as in the fifteenth century in the choir school of Chambery. But, more broadly, the entire community of altar boys identified with this patronage and placed themselves under the protection of saints of the same name. As a separate corporation, they instituted a festival day whose celebration they set for December 28, that of the children sacrificed by Herod, whom the church inscribed on the list of martyrs under the name of Holy Innocents.[37] Let us consider the stages of this identification and the forms it took.

The Middle Ages had chosen this date and this patronage to celebrate its clerics at the time of the January 6 Fête des Fous. Condemned by the Church, it evolved, giving altar boys a growing place. The Council of Basel (1431) designated it as their holiday, "festum fatuorum vel innocentium seu puerorum."[38] In Sicily, according to Giuseppe Pitré, who followed its history well after the council's interdiction, the celebration continued at least until 1736, despite the fact that a synod of the province of Catania recommended that the choirboys be prevented from dressing up in sacerdotal garments and making themselves ridiculous at the vespers of the Innocents. Another Sicilian document from 1550 brings to light the role played by the altar boys, here called *chierici rossi*, the red altar boys, or, even better, *russuliddi*, the red-headed or red-faced, who turned this day into a holiday by dressing their leader with a miter, a cross, and the episcopal robe, but, in this case, it was a matter of garments made to measure for whoever was elected. Until the eighteenth century these emblems of the young bishop for the day were piously preserved. The child prelate solemnly officiated until the final benediction, which he generously granted the crowd of gapers who hung, according to the chroniclers, on his every word.[39]

In passing authority from the young undisciplined and violent clerics to the more docile group of altar boys, the Fête des Fous usually grew tamer, because of which it was allowed to remain within the precincts of the Church. This is confirmed by the Catalan monastery of Montserrat. In this eagles' nest was perpetuated the tradition of an *escolanilla*, and the training school for the altar boys—the *escolanets*—functioned according to the model we have just described. The boys officiated over the services and maintained the privilege of electing their young bishop "in as dignified a manner as possible."[40] In the north of France, where the altar boys were formerly numerous and powerful, they elected their "king," who would preside over the collections on Holy Saturday, while on the Thursday before Lent a pupils' holiday occurred in the same fashion.[41] These shifts, both spatial—from church to school—and social—from the clerics to children in general—was long accompanied by an increased presence on the calendar year. Where it subsisted the holiday took place during the period from

December 6—Saint Nicholas's Day—to January 6—the Twelfth Night—delimiting what Claude Gaignebet has rightly called a "Kingdom of Childhood."[42]

Yet these ephemeral monarchs usually preserved the memory of the event that founded their sovereignty even as all these shifts were occurring. The medieval altar boys had already developed a specialty of playing the "Innocents," along with angels, in the great Passion plays that realistically incorporated this episode in their depictions. But they also participated in the liturgical drama that was still presented in churches, in the fifteenth century, until January 6. In the Offices des Mages de Rouen they had to lay down, as if dead, on the stones of the cathedral to embody the young victims of Herod, who would be played, as in Bourges, by a cleric on horseback.[43] In Brittany, at Christmas and the Twelfth Night, the custom of performing *La Tragédie d'Hérode* lasted until the nineteenth century. These Mystery plays, collected and known as the *Bible des Noëls*, are contained in a text printed for the masses. In one of these widely distributed works there appears a *Massacre des Innocents*, which was acted "by characters" in the form of dialogues. The play was still put on by the children of an outer district of Saint-Malo in about 1860, and, at about the same time, in Dinan, the main publication center for these popular booklets. When Paul Sébillot wrote about the custom, it persisted as follows: "The day of Twelfth Night young people go to recite *The Life of Herod* in verse; there is an *innocent* who represents the Jewish children, and they pretend to cut his throat with a wooden sword."[44] This "throat cutting" is equally important in Spain, in Valencia; between December 28 and January 6 a Misteri de la Degollació del Sants Innocents is performed. The moment of the *degolla*, as it is familiarly called, is the highlight of the production, when it has not been reduced to this scene alone. In Barcelona, where the text of the sermon given between 1383 and 1566 by the *obispillo*, the little bishop, has been preserved, the latter is presented as one who has escaped the massacre and is there to tell the story. Thus, within the ritual itself the customary assignment of the role is legitimized.

The ritual of recruitment and induction of the altar boys in turn plays on the association. In Catalonia, until the 1900s, it was on Holy Innocents' Day that their ranks were replenished as follows: the newcomers were first immersed in the baptismal font before being dressed, for the first time, in the church, in their official garments.

"They purposely gave them clothing that was too big so that when they walked they would get caught up in their gowns and fall. The clergy and the faithful attended this ceremony. It was said that the altar boy who didn't fall would soon cast off his gown and abandon the choir."[45] Does the ritual not signify that one must pass through this symbolic death in order to be considered suitable, following the model of the Holy Innocents?

On December 28 an identical action recreates the story, from the medieval altar boys who incarnate the Innocents by falling onto the stone floor of the cathedral, to the *tirassous* of Corpus Christi in Aix, dragging themselves on the floor in their white shirts as Herod threatens them with his sword, to the Catalan *escolanets* tumbling about, hampered by their oversized cassocks. And it is this status as innocent victim that forms, everywhere, the basis of the altar boys' rights. In Rouen, where the choir can be followed since 1365, thanks to the deliberations of the chapter, the little bishop, elected on December 27 at the end of the service of Saint John, before giving his benediction to the crowd, had to withdraw to the altar of the Holy Innocents and, from there, was entrusted with "the special mission of ensuring that, in keeping with the prescribed rule, no one penetrated under arms into the cathedral choir; the chapter gave him the right to confiscate the spurs of any offenders."[46] This is the first step toward the antagonism that interests us: Herod's little victims had total power over the men under arms in the church, then, outside of its walls, they pursued the *Jews*, represented as armats, and finally killed them every year come Easter. They thereby reaffirm the strength of the bond with the innocents of holy history, massacred by the undisciplined soldiery. This occurs, as we have seen, through the reminder of the episode—a word or gesture suffice—but also, in ways that vary here and there throughout Europe, by stories and rituals that revive and explain the necessity of this solemn revenge.

A Parisian calendar of the late Middle Ages—reconstructed based on a breviary and a book of hours—shows us this recreation in all its strength. First we learn that on the date of December 6, for Saint Nicholas's Day, a festival of altar boys outfitted as clergymen took place, in every way in keeping with what we know. On the twenty-eighth of the same month, the "Innocents" were played, and again it was a matter of a theatrical representation of the massacre by these same altar boys. Finally, still in Paris, this day was marked by a solemn

Mass celebrated in the church of the Holy Innocents. Here are the details added by the calendar's commentator:

> The church venerated them by the name of the Holy Innocents (Bethleem natale S. S. infantium et lactantium quis ub Herode, pro Christo passi sunt). In Paris their church, sometimes called "of the fields" (*in campellis*) was called in the popular language Holy Innocent Church, in the singular, because in it was displayed the tomb of the child martyr Richard, whom, it was asserted, the Jews had crucified in Pontoise in 1179, an atrocious slander that allowed for the confiscation of their possessions and the free enlargement of the house of the Holy Innocents.[47]

Thus, at the end of the fourteenth century in Paris, the Holy Innocents had already ceased to be the Hebrew infants slaughtered by Herod and were instead Christian children killed by the Jews. A boy, as marked by the shift to the singular *Holy Innocent*, anchors the devotion in a concrete and intimate reality. Buried in the church of the "Holy Innocent," the young Parisian victim Richard de Pontoise, a figure of holy innocence, links the altar boys' festival to his memory, as well as the group of altar boys to the Jews, whose special adversaries they now become, after having been the special victims.

It suffices, now, to go back to the ritual crimes to see this "detail" emerge: in the case of Saint Dominguito de Val, sanctified and venerated in Saragossa, the hagiographer relates that he was crucified by the Jews when he was a very "young altar boy." The images representing him are carefully titled "The Altar Boy Martyr Saint Dominguito de Val and His Cult." France, too, has its martyred altar boy in the person of the little chorister of the city of Puy who became hateful to the Jews because of the angelic sounds he produced. With him, and by the manner in which the event was reconstructed at the dawn of the fourteenth century, we are close to being faced with an etiological story that bases the rights of altar boys on the Jews. Killed by a Jew around Christmas time, his body was never found. On Palm Sunday, however, he suddenly resuscitated as the procession passed; singing, he told the story of his death and of "his miraculous return to life." The Jew was denounced and punished. A local cult was instituted by the canons of the city, which commemorated the event every year on Palm Sunday. The Jews were banished from the area and "in 1325 Charles the Fair granted the altar boys of Saint Basilique the

8. From Paul Lacroix, *Moeurs, usages et costumes du Moyen Age et à l'époque de la Renaissance*, Bibliophile Jacob, 3d ed., (Paris: Firmin-Didot, 1873), p. 469. Engraving based on the *Livre de Cabale* of Abraham le Juif; see illustration 12b.

privilege of deciding the fate of any Jew who dared set foot in the city again."[48]

We recognize of course, in this news item, the legend of the young cleric killed by a Jew for having sung Gaude Maria, which appears in many European collections of the *Miracles of the Virgin*.[49] By making this child a local altar boy, through whose mouth the Virgin calls for the "destruction of all heresies," one establishes noble reasons for avenging him and pursuing his assassins. A half-century later, in his *Chroniques*, a citizen of Puy, Etienne Médicis, evoked the right of the cathedral's altar boys and the "historical event" in the old prose of the church of Notre Dame:

Digna fuit expulsio
Judeorum a Podio
Non intrent quia captio
Clericulis est data.

[Well deserved was the expulsion
Of the Jews from Puy
May they not enter, for their capture
Is in the hands of the altar boys.][50]

Soon this privilege was adopted by other acolytes wherever there were Jews. Thus in Provence, in Carpentras, in the days of the ghettos: "The altar boys of the Saint-Siffrein cathedral could freely invade the synagogue on Holy Innocents' Day and create a kind of uproar. It is true that, on that day, they were allowed to do as much in the Catholic churches. But, with respect to the Jews, they also enjoyed the privilege of removing their hats by force if they refused to uncover their heads upon the passing of the cross. Finally a deal was struck, and the alleged right of the clerics was bought back by the Jewish community, in exchange for an annual payment of seven florins—which didn't stop the youth from continuing to bully the Jews and shouting after them in the street *Capo!* throwing stones at them until they removed their hats."[51] Because he contests—for good reason—the legitimacy of this altar boys' right, Armand Lunel qualifies it as an "alleged" right, but it was quite real and lasted quite a long time in Provence, up until the end of the eighteenth century and even beyond. The altar boys maintained the right to perform "the Jew hunt." We know that a Jew had to stand aside before the cross or the Holy Sacrament in a gesture of humility when he happened to accidentally cross its path. Hence the acolytes were on the lookout for Jews, to ensure that the rule was respected. An ordinance of August 12, 1645, by Archbishop of Avignon Pinelly "gives the force of law to the custom," specifying that, in such circumstances, "in the event they are caught by the said altar boys following the cross, they will be obliged to contribute to the said altar boys *juxta solitum,* without nonetheless the said altar boys being able to enter into a Jewish shop or home, where the said Jews may have taken refuge."[52] Yet the pursuers transgressed these boundaries to the extent that many complaints were registered against them in the months that followed this ordinance, necessitating the intervention of the archbishop's vicar in the face of the "excesses that the altar boys daily committed against the Jews and Jewesses of this city." But, once the custom took root, it was difficult to censor it; efforts would be made during the entire century to come to put an end to abuses that grew increasingly intolerable. In 1746 the archbishop of Guyon de Crochons had to intervene, but in vain, and in 1765 his successor, Mauzi, was forced to note that despite numerous protests by the previous archbishops, "It often happens during funerary convoys and processions that when the altar boys, clerics, and cross-bearers of the various chapters and parishes of our city notice a Jew or Jewess, they quit their place in pursuit. Upon reaching them, they threaten and insult them and even pull off their hats to force them to give them some money."[53]

Abolished with the French Revolution, which also liberated Jews from the servitude to which they were subject, the practice actually persisted until about 1850, according to Provençal sources. Régis de La Colombière, Frédéric Mistral, and Armand Lunel all mention it. These witnesses bring us the very living reality of an ancient customary law—initially reserved for altar children and the best Christians, then extended to all children, and especially to boys—which authorized the youth of Provence and beyond, as we saw at the outset of this study, to position themselves at the exit of the synagogue or the school and to insult the Israelites "for no reason."

The memory of the terror the altar boys produced marked the Jewish memory to such an extent that at the beginning of this century the mothers of Comtat still threatened naughty children with The Big Black One. This priest was a strange bogeyman who seized little Jews who had crossed the boundaries of the ghetto, dressed them in red "to make them into altar boys," locked them in a church coffer, and fed them dry bread.[54]

The step from innocents to Holy Innocents on the part of altar boys and young Christians was a step in which the Jews were instrumental; when the pious little boy who played the role of victim in the "ritual murders" wasn't an altar boy, he could at least identify with those boys intercepted at the end of the Mass, when they had just received the host, or who were kidnapped while their parents were at the Tenebrae service. This was how the intricate mechanism of the myth operated, prompting the large symbolic clusters we have brought together, creating a bond between the altar boy institution, the accusations of ritual murder, and the sanctifications of innocents that have left so many historians perplexed.

The current and recent ethnological work on the ritual functions of children and altar boys at Easter is in agreement with religious history while shedding a more attentive light on real relationships, on the experience of the rituals. It is by going back and forth between the extremes spanning a long stretch of time that our approach to the phenomenon was gradually elaborated. Only the placing in perspective of elements that until now have been treated separately enabled us to express their inventive logic. Ethnological interpretation can be like those optical games in which two plates have to be superimposed in order to "clearly" read the blurry image on each of them. From the very real rights and privileges granted children as the purely mythical victims of the Jews, to the symbolic battle they still lead by ritually "killing Jews" at Easter, the same coherent model is at work. Here it is still incontestably a "savage mind," demarcating the respective statuses of children and Jews, that provides Christian societies with their grounds. In light of the latter, it appears that the Kingdom of Childhood is not a kingdom of pure "innocence," for, as the number of occasions to celebrate children has grown since the Middle Ages, the *Christian* qualities, in their natural virulence, have been exalted, which they have been given the opportunity to test at two strategic moments of the year: Easter and Christmas. Much could be said about the latter festival and about the period from December 6 to January 6 when Christian children are glorified. If we look at it closely, the relationship that unites them to the Jews is present in each of these otherwise complex celebrations. However, let us simply place certain essential markers.

Christ's Little Soldiers

In the middle of this period, Saint Steven's Day, December 26, celebrated not long ago in the region of Sault by offering children an *estienet*—a little man made of bread with anise eyes, baked by the godmother for her godchild—was also the date chosen to celebrate the Holy Innocents on the other side of the Pyrenees. On this day, in effect, Steven, a neophyte who sought out Jews to argue with them, was seized and stoned to death. The first deacon, whom iconography likes to represent as a child in the face of the cruel Jews who are stoning him, is also the champion of young Christians.[55] If we consider in turn the starting date, December 6, which is often when the children's bishop is elected—separate from the celebration of the Holy Innocents that initially justified it—a surprising correspondence arises. For the most popular miracle of the saint of this day, Bishop Nicholas—established, precisely, in the thirteenth century—was undoubtedly the resurrection of the three children who were killed and placed in a salt tub like little pigs. By making them "bishops" or "Saint Nicholases" on this day, we consecrate the little victims of the cannibal butcher, who was a Jew in his manner of treating children.[56] As for the Epiphany that brings an end to this period and is chosen in Catalonia and on the Balearic Islands for the presentation of the *Degollació*, we know it is a day of celebration for little Catalonians. The Magi Kings, the first to have recognized the kingdom of Christ, arrive bearing gifts, and the children of the various sections of Barcelona await them at the gates of the city with "drums and trumpets." In Majorca, a city of many glass artisans, the *trompetas* are usually made of this translucent and breakable matter. Once the kings are greeted, these instruments become weapons:

> After school, the boys head out in gangs to the Jewish quarters to break their trumpets over the heads of *xuetas* children. This tradition brought about violent riotous scenes for which the intervention of the authorities became necessary. Though they were forced to take coercive measures on many occasions, these measures were insufficient to quash the excesses of children who were acting with the complicity of their parents.[57]

Why, during these joyful days when children are celebrated in the image of the newborn Christ, is aggression against the Jews an obligatory counterpoint to every ritual?

The reason is because Christ's entry into the world and his infancy are placed under the sign of flowing blood. First, the great massacre of the Innocents marks the advent of Christianity. Then, the infant Jesus, bodily wounded, began the long Passion that would lead him to his last Passover. This first outpouring of blood, which has been debated since the Middle Ages, was none other than the circumcision.[58] Until the dawn of the nineteenth century, it was celebrated on January 1, while his baptism—which he received, as we know, at the age of thirty—was commemorated six days later. Despite the warnings of liturgists who insisted on seeing the Epiphany as only a "reminder" of the event, the closeness of the two rituals created a strong symbolic coherence: between the birth of Christ and his Christian "baptism" the circumcision occurred, which is understood to signify erasure. The succession of ceremonies concretizes the opposition, bringing into conflict the carnal Synagogue and the spiritual Church. The antagonism between the bloody sacrifice of the ancient Law and the Christian sacrament—baptism, then Eucharist—marks the very body of the one who introduces the break.[59] Was he not subjected to the two rituals?

Thus the "circumcision," which we have seen is the first stage, in ritual murder, of the little martyrs' "Passion," is a repetition of that of Christ. This at least is what is depicted by Medieval iconography, in accordance with the teachings of the Church. An examination of representations of the "Lord's Circumcision" between the thirteenth and fifteenth centuries is, from this point of view, entirely in keeping with what we have shown regarding the Christians' interpretation of the ceremony: the accent is placed on the knife, while Jews with hooked profiles hover around the operator. Sometimes, as in the case in a Savoyard painted mural in which the scene leads to a "massacre of the innocents," the newborn Christ is "laid on the white cloth of a small alter."[60] Meanwhile Christmas hymns, such as this Provençal *Cantinella in Natali Domini* from the fifteenth century, linger over the details of the operation, which Mary is forced to attend, thus reinforcing the pathos of the scene:

Quant fom circumsit
nom li van pausar,
Salvador del mont
Lo van appelar.
E cant fom talhat
Et annet saunar,
la maïre o vi,
comenset plorar.
Quant l'enfant senti
la peyra talhar
Gran peni li dona
e va fort cridar,
la carn si separa
lo sanc va rayar
So son las estrenas
que nos volc donar.

[When he was circumcised
He was given a name,

Savior of the World,
He was called.
And when he was cut
He began to bleed,
His mother seeing this,
Began to cry.
When the child felt,
The stone cutting him
He was in great pain
And began crying loudly.
The flesh detached,
The blood gushed out
Here is the New Year's gift
He wishes to give us.][61]

We should add that the little piece of detached flesh was the object of intense devotion in the Middle Ages. In his *Journal*, the Bourgeois de Paris noted that in 1421 the Queen of France sent the "silver jewel" to her daughter in England, who was on the verge of giving birth. Like the royal family, churches in France, Spain, and Italy prided themselves on possessing "the circumcision of Our Lord" among their treasures."[62] A metonymy of the divine body, the foreskin alleged to help women in labor was venerated in the image of Christ in swaddling clothes, which since the twelfth century was especially exalted. With the rise in manger and nativity scenes the adoration of this innocent figure took further root: the Italian Bambino, the Spanish Jesulino, the French Petit Jésus would transfer to the winter cycle and its parade of festivals the emotion until then inspired by Easter alone, so much so that one of the vocations of the great theatrical Passions was to return to the adult Christ the devotion of the people, who were too inclined to reduce him to the child. Yet this devotion persisted, with evidence of it recurring throughout the centuries. The seventeenth century liked to represent the baby Jesus sleeping on the instruments of his torture or carrying his cross on his shoulder. The nineteenth century, in turn, developing the cult of the *Preziosissimo sangue*, would revive the adoration of the wounded child given as a model to Christians.[63]

This association is already present in the treatment to which the Jews were alleged to subject young Christians. The confessions elicited from the accused reveal that the children were crucified "in memory of Christ." It also explains ritual murder's placement on the calendar: the altar boy from the city of Puy who was assassinated on Christmas Day was resuscitated on Palm Sunday. In the thirteenth century, in Germany, an affair known as the "crime of Fulda" served as a prelude to a wave of persecution and expulsion of the Jews: "In this year 1235," say the *annales* of Erfurt on December 28, "the crusaders slaughtered thirty-four Jews of both sexes, because on Christmas Day two of these Jews had perfidiously assassinated five sons of a carpenter living outside the ramparts while their parents were at church, had collected their blood in sacks rendered watertight with wax, and had set fire to the home as they departed."[64] On Christmas the crimes with which Jews were charged took on the aspect of a new massacre of children, as suggested by these retaliations that avenge Holy Innocents' Day. Christmas was also the day on which many Christians chose to go "smash some Jew." Thus, in the novel by Zalman Shneour, an invaluable testimony to relations between Orthodox Christians and Jews in White Russia at the end of the nineteenth century, one of the characters, a forest ranger, lies in wait to "avenge Jesus." His anger is fueled by the conviction that on this holy night the Jews celebrate *nitl*, a parody of the Christian Christmas in which they gather around their rabbi and rejoice in having killed Christ.[65]

These correspondences between Easter and Christmas find other means of expression, decipherable upon examination of details that are now obscure, such as the practice in some regions of France of referring to the period that includes Christmas and the Epiphany as the "blood weeks," or the habit, during Christmas collections, of singing those excerpts from the Passion featuring Judas and the Jews, while at Easter the sermons of the Tenebrae often celebrate the martyrdom of Steven, who is made into a Christ-like figure. We know that the liturgy of Christmas, which came after that of Easter, used the latter as its model, but the formal analogy also reflects a homology of meaning. While the similar prohibitions pertaining to the two holidays are well know, few of them have been carefully studied by ethnologists. One example is the slaughtering of animals. Holy Friday and December 25 are among the days when no blood may be shed: the birth and death of Christ prohibit the reenactment of gestures that cause it to flow. While the relationship to his death is clear, if implicit, the same cannot be said for Christmas, which is a joyful celebration in the Christian world, calling for the appearance of the pig on the holiday table. Nonetheless an analogy is developed with respect to this period, which is otherwise "good for killing pigs." In Italy slaughtering ceases on Holy Innocents' Day, the reason for which is generally given as follows: "If the pig were killed on that day, all births would fail, in memory of the children of Bethlehem sacrificed to the anger of Herod out of hatred for Jesus." Indeed, an adage with respect to the Innocents affirms that on this day "Porcino macellato, bambini macellati, A piglet killed is a child killed."[66]

In Catalonia, where the prohibition is also respected for the Nativity and December 28, it extends even further. According to Joan Amades, the elders "refrained from drawing the blood of an animal on the first of the year, since the first of the year was when Jesus was circumcised and when his blood flowed for the first time." In each case the detour by way of the animal—the piglet in particular—refers to the child and to Christ united in innocence. This bond is also the basis for the aptitude of altar boys and young Christians for fighting Jews in their own name and in that of Christ, in whose army they serve.

An examination of the great popular movements that marked the Middle Ages will reveal children to be privileged mediators. In times of epidemic and war, the two common scourges, they were the ones elected and delegated to solicit divine indulgence. In Paris, in 1412, a delegation of two hundred barefoot, candle-bearing children formed a procession. In 1449 a young boy was carried in great pomp to Notre Dame in the guise of the "Holy Innocent."[67] But, from the popes' first calls to holy wars, children all over Europe mobilized. We are familiar with the tragic outcome of many of these so-called shepherd crusades. To begin with, there were the thousands of twelve-year-olds—whom the chroniclers thus frequently called innocents—who, in France, at the prompting of a little visionary shepherd by the predestined name of Steven, and in Italy, in the steps of a young miraculously healed seer named Nicolas, took to the road in 1212.[68]

In 1320 a new call was launched, and the "forty thousand children" who mobilized were given a "holy" objective, that of chasing the Jews from France. In so doing, they were merely exercising their given right, but their violence overstepped the bounds of legitimacy initially granted them. As their criminal extortions grew, they were the ones being pursued: in Villeneuve-sur-Garonne five hundred of them would be locked up and burned alive in a dungeon. The Jew Baruch appearing in Pamiers before the bishop Fournier gave a long and realistic account of this horrific episode, revealing the constant reversal of popular opinion in the face of the shepherds. Thus, he described the entry into Toulouse of twenty-four cartloads of them, taken prisoner in the course of the massacre of Jews in Castelsarrazin:

The shepherds who were in the last carts began calling for help, complaining of being taken prisoners like this; they had wanted to avenge the death of Christ, and now they were going to prison. Some of the Toulousian crowd broke the ropes binding them in the carts. Once untied, they jumped from their carts and began shouting with the crowds: "To death, to death, kill all the Jews!" Whereupon they scattered throughout the Jewish quarter and massacred those who would not be instantly baptized.[69]

At the same time, peaceful crowds of children on pilgrimage to Mont Saint-Michel were called to the sanctuary by voices and apparitions. Those referred to as the "children of Saint-Michel" flocked from all over Europe to the new gathering site: there they prayed and implored the new mediator. They delegated to the warrior archangel, under whose protection they placed themselves, the mission assumed at one time by the bellicose shepherds. In 1458, with this "mystical delirium" coming to an end, the moment arrived for the chroniclers to account for it. This central question then emerged: "Everyone was wondering," we read in the chronicle of Lübeck, "what was meant by these voyages: were they the work of God or a temptation of the devil?"[70]

CHAPTER SEVEN

The Little Jew

Jueu, n.m. Jew . . . mischievous boy (Empordà); gesture of mockery or insult and particularly that of sticking out one's tongue (Majorca, Minorca); boys' game on nights of the full moon: one of them stands in the moonlight and the others in shadow. They try to pass into the light while avoiding being touched. "Jew! I'm in your house!" they shout when they succeed (Muro de Mallorca); Penjar jueus ("Hang the Jews"), to hang canvasses and paintings, commemorating the Passion, that constitute the backdrop of the sepulchre of Holy Thursday (Llofriu).

— ALCOVER AND MOLL, *Diccionari català*

The antagonism between Jews and boys seems clearly established and illustrated. In the nocturnal processions of Catalonia the armats—those Roman Jewish soldiers—take their places behind the mystery of the dead Christ, at which the children, dressed as angels, take the lead. Yet it is possible to be transformed from an "angel" into a "Jew," as revealed by the custom in several places in Catalonia of having the somewhat older boys play "Jews" in procession. Upon his first encounter with what he takes to be a singular novelty, Joan Amades ponders the matter and furnishes the following explanation:

As the procession of the armats is very long and takes place without any light in their path, someone thought of introducing boys dressed as torch-bearing Jews—*à la galatea*—with the idea that the kids of Jerusalem must have followed the troop of soldiers to the holy sepulchre. With this idea in mind, *el Jueus petits*, the little Jews, were created and mixed in with the armats in order to light their way. The innovation was sometimes aborted, but certain villages adopted it and the practice has been maintained.[1]

In Cerveno, in northern Italy, where the Passion is performed for the festival of Santa Croce, we find the boys dressed "as Jews" and armed with the infamous rattles, *raganelle* and *taccole*, the *ragazzi* put into service on Holy Friday during the Tenebrae. We do not know how this group of *bambini-giudei*, as they are called, was formed; the observer notes very briefly that "it constituted a novelty that, it seems, was not appreciated by everyone."[2] In both cases the "change" affected the same age group in the same way: the boys we saw fiercely fighting the Jews were called on to incarnate them, and we even find in the hands of these "little Jews" the instrument of their symbolic killing. This reversal, which we suspect constitutes neither an absolute innovation nor a local particularity, invites us to reconsider the very identity of the actors along with the ritual and its forms.

Not long ago, in the Sardininan hamlet of Sanluri, on Holy Thursday, children took their places around an enormous tree trunk called *su trunci de is martorius*, the "trunk of martyrs," placed purposely in the chapel of Saint Sebastian. Armed with olive tree sticks and knotty branches, they waited for the racket of rattles to erupt in the choir. Upon this signal boys and youths struck the trunk repeatedly until, "panting and dripping with sweat, they were finally chased from the church by the sextons; but no sooner were they out the door than they met up with the kids outside, who continued their racket using the rattles. Finally, they dispersed into the streets, spreading the sound of their deafening commotion everywhere." And one of the last parish priests recording these facts adds, "Considering the extreme and excessive ardor with which the boys 'flagellated Christ' (which is to say the trunk), it became necessary to prohibit this curious custom." From then on in Sanluri, on Holy Thursday, a bloody Christ, sculpted in wood, was merely transported from church to church to the sanctuary in which he was deposited. But the procession was followed by the boys, who forcefully shook their Tenebrae instruments, constrasting sharply with the crowd of grief-stricken faithful escorting Christ, "chanting meditatively, deaf to the clamor of the rattles, as if to mark the distance between these pagan killers and believing Christians."[3] And, by all appearances, in this instance the boys were situated on the side of the former.

This "flagellation of Christ," acted out symbolically by a segment of the boys, amid the commotion produced by the others, expands and explains the ritual itself, demonstrating, in a sense, its effects. Even if it is not explicitly stated, in this case, that the actors are playing Jews, their position in the procession, once the commotion has been transported and continued outside the church, confirms their role as the "killers" of Christ, about which the local priests were not mistaken. This is also the opinion of an abbot from the Ardennes who, not without humor, describes the form the ritual took in 1928: "It was a deafening racket. All the instruments went off at once in a horrible cacophony. Men and women fled while schoolboys, their tongues between their teeth—the better to thump, grind, and turn about—produced their devilish music for the pleasure of the Good Lord."[4]

In the Normandy Bocage two antagonistic groups appear on the scene: sometimes the children who "do the Tenebrae" are expelled with the active help of the vergers—the "tramp-chasers"—while sometimes they force the faithful to leave the church with their racket.[5] When a brief drama compliments the reading of the liturgical text, we progress even further in our understanding of the roles. In Italy, in the region of Irpinia, on Holy Thursday,

> when during the service the Jews are named, numerous boys appear dressed in white, armed with spears, hammers, and nails. The orator states that Jesus Christ was bound and crucified, and then other boys appear, also dressed in white shirts, dragging the bound Jesus. When the preacher says that the sky darkened and the earth trembled, the lights are turned out and a brief but loud clamor is heard. The 'Jews' disappear and the lights are restored.[6]

A fine sequence in which the vision of the boys as Jews alternates with the commotion of the Tenebrae during which they disappear. What is demonstrated here, nonetheless, had to be explicated elsewhere. Geneviève Massignon, investigating the instruments of the Tenebrae in Corsica, notes that "armed with sticks, the children bang on the church benches, or else, placing two fingers in their mouths, whistle as loud as they can. They represent the Jews chasing Christ." And they themselves, commenting on their actions, assert that they are "playing the Jews."[7]

How are we to understand this alternation? Knowing that commonly the Tenebrae commotion—that which is tolerated and commented upon in the liturgy—is supposed to reproduce the cosmic tumult that accompanied the death of Christ, the earthquake and eclipse that revealed to men, by a visible revolt of nature, the divinity of the one who had just been put to death like a mere human, should we take it that in the image of this chaos the "Tenebrae charivari" authorizes a certain confusion? Such a seemingly radical contradiction between "killing the Jews" and "playing the Jews" compels us to pursue our study of the roles devolved to young boys during the Holy Week. The areas of Catalan and Lorraine invite such a pursuit, for there we find numerous interventions on the part of the boys over the course a cycle of which this commotion is only the climax. Situating it within the dense network of gestures and expressions should allow us to better define the true "nature" of the boys, amid the shifting roles we might initially imagine would cloud their identities.

Judas Week

For Easter, in addition to the complex representation of the Passion, which sometimes mobilizes an entire commune, large and small children, often under the aegis of the priest or nuns, perform particular episodes in the life of Christ that were long played by the clerics themselves. The liturgy since the High Middle Ages has acknowledged the "foot washing" ceremony, at which even today the pope bows before twelve of his prelates. In many parishes custom had it that it should be poor people who enjoyed the benefits as a sign of humility. They were washed and fed—the Last Supper followed the ablution—and presented with a contribution. Next to them young clerics—the famous *minores*—were also called on to fulfill this function now devolved to the choirboys. In Catalonia these roles as "apostles" were highly desirable, for they included a singing part for which the priests chose the prettiest voices. The roles of Saint Peter and Saint John were the most coveted and were thus assigned as rewards to the best. No one, of course, wanted to play Judas. A lottery was organized for his selection, but the traitor was so reviled that the unlucky child only managed to escape his fate by paying another, who, on this condition alone, accepted to replace him.[8] As opposed to the Iberian games, in which the reviled role is cast onto an individual outside the group or the community—this age group is seen judging and punishing a straw dummy during the *función de Judas*—the testimonies gathered for northern and eastern France assign these same altar boys the role of Judas in person. What sense can we make of this shift of the role, fallen to normally accepted duty, financially negotiated, even sought after in the name of custom?

Until now nothing seemed to distinguish the Lorraine altar boy/rattlers from their Catalan homologues. We saw both of them busily preparing Judas's Fire, then striking the funeral pyre with sticks "to put Judas through the mill," and finally sprinkling pig blood "to show that Judas had been executed." All this gives us an idea of the distance they placed between themselves and the most Jewish of the apostles. Yet, as in Catalonia, sometimes the traitor was given a material reality and "walked around" before being punished in the manner familiar to us. In Bronderdorff it was still the custom in 1968 to "parade Judas" on Holy Saturday, and this role "was played by a rattler, his face blackened with soot, linked by a chain used for lambs that was passed around his waist; a spectacle that amused the adults and terrified the little ones."[9] Other Lorraine villages perpetuated this custom, and an altar boy always "played Judas." Furthermore, within their group the role usually fell to the leader of the altar boys, the one who held the money box during collections; according to witnesses, this function as treasurer designated him especially. Yet in our view it is not only from the temporary possession of the common purse that the boy drew his aptitude to "play Judas" but, more likely, from his function as head of the altar boys. We hold this view because of the evidence that it was around the Tenebrae service and its ritual—which we have seen was in their hands—that the hunt for Judas was dramatized. In the first third of the twentieth century the custom persisted in Lorraine, but, according to Van Gennep, "Only in the villages of la Seille did a chase take place after the Tenebrae service instead of a loud commotion, even in about 1930. They chased after a child who had to run around the altar three times. His friends tried to hit him and this Judas ran as fast as he could, down the main aisle of the nave to the church square, chased by the rattlers." In German-speaking Lorraine the same type of race determined who would play Judas and supports our idea that within the group of altar boys the role could be desirable; this was the case in Lixing, a commune near Sarreguemines, where "the boy who arrived first to church on Palm Sunday, after a triple race around the 'monument,' was nicknamed 'Judas.' He arrived on Saturday morning dressed as Judas, coiffed in a tall bonnet in the shape of a skittle, decorated with strips of painted paper. He was forced to undergo a trial by flame: the tallest and the strongest one took him by the head and feet and swung him over the pyre, from which the priest took the new fire; sometimes his trousers caught fire."[10] In Germany, the data from Lorraine devolve into variations that place the accent on the ritualization of the game. In all cases it was the altar boys who organized them: from Palm Sunday, when they elected their Judas, to the Tenebrae service, which dramatized his expulsion, to the fire of Holy Saturday, in which he was burned, they ensured the semantic unity of a week understandably qualified as Judaswoche, Judas week. But wasn't it really their week (illus. 21 and 22)?

Finally, if we compare the Catalan and, more broadly, the Iberian, regions and that of Lorraine, we are faced with two situations that at first glance seem like opposites: on the one hand, altar boys, the most Christian of the boys and among them their leader, take on the role of Judas as if fulfilling an honorific duty; on the other hand, we have boys who, because they "received Holy Communion" last year—and the detail is important—solicit the roles of apostle, an aspiration accompanied by the right to refuse that of Judas. Is the same distinction not brought into play when the Last Supper or the feet washing are represented, this time in the French High Alps? There, on Holy Thursday, twelve children sometimes play the disciples, around a table on which twelve little breads and twelve pitchers of wine are laid. It is specified that the young boys, whose feet are washed by the priest—assisted by his altar boys—are necessarily chosen from among "those who have not yet received first Holy Communion."[11]

These various positions, contrasted as they may seem, all designate a boundary, short of which or beyond which it is considered possible or impossible to play certain roles. There is a dividing line within the group of boys separating those who are in some sense "more Christian" than the others and who can, thereby, either claim the sacred role of apostle or confront, almost with impunity, the troubling role of the Jews and of Judas. How does the society produce this essential difference?

Fresh Meat and the Smell of a Christian

The baptism, they say half jokingly, makes the child's first horn fall off; the second sacrament, that of Holy Communion—one to two years after the baptism—makes the second fall, thus completing the passage to humanity. After the ceremony the parents or grandparents often comment to the child, "Ya te tumbo el otro cuerno. Ya eres completamente cristiano." The bishops are unable to delay Holy Communion until the age of seven, the age required for the child to become aware of his choice. This delay is unacceptable to the local people, who want their child to become a Christian as soon as possible.[12]

We should not attribute solely to the Mexican Indians of Tzinzuntzan the vision of such an inefficient baptism. The image of horns that fall, one by one, simply emphasizes an idea that has gradually revealed itself: that of a continuum, of a step-by-step process of acquisition of Christian qualities, as opposed to the often trumpeted idea of an immediate transformation by mere virtue of the ritual. The pagans and lepers in the exempla undergo quasi-miraculous transformations; it is they who, by healing instantly, provide the most spectacular examples. Yet doesn't placing the accent on metamorphosis already say something about the earlier state? In Christian societies, then, in which a progressive shortening of this prebaptismal time can be noted, what can be said of one who is situated in this state of waiting, an outsider to Christianity?

For Sicilians it is commonly believed that before the sacrament the little being, "quella carne di latte, this suckling meat," is "che un pezzo di carne buono a nulla, but a piece of flesh that is good for nothing." In Provençal it is called a *creatura*, a term that also encompasses women of ill repute and their progeny. The unbaptized child is thus lumped together with the natural child, if only temporarily, who is still qualified in Europe as a "left-side child," or even a "child of the devil."[13] A teacher from Toulouse, responding to a questionnaire at the end of the nineteenth century, suggests that the belief is widespread and exposes the real consequences: "When a child is born, one doesn't go to see it. So long as it isn't baptized, it belongs to the devil. The women who care for it refrain from kissing it. When it is baptized the entire neighborhood passes by, whether out of curiosity or interest. And each godmother attaches a pin to the cover of the crib, saying, "Diou te creysse, May God grow you [*sic*]."[14] In expressing the wish for growth only after the baptism has been performed, one points to the sacrament itself as the driving force of this growth. Until then one refrains from making such a wish as it would cause the growth of an imperfect or diabolical being. We know that witches are on the lookout for unbaptized children to inflict deformities on their maleable bodies. The child is therefore kept out of sight; one avoids exposing its swaddling clothes and garments, and special precautions are taken the day of the baptism on the way to the church. Once he becomes a Christian the change is invoked to remove him from the grip of this power. In Lucania, when one suspects a "fascination" or spell, one recites an incantation recalling that the victim is *carne battesata*, baptized flesh, and in certain cases this simple assertion triumphs over the charmer. We have seen how breeders, to ward off the evil eye that threatened both the child and the piglet, and playing on the analogy between the two, would have recourse to a baptism for the pig and a second baptism for the child, in addition to their fictive sale.

The first effect of the baptism is to modify the appearance of the baptized, for it seems the "piece of meat" is very ugly, as one would imagine a child of the devil might be. This is what we learn from a certain Jean Joufre of Tignac—suspected of heresy and questioned in 1320 by the inquisitor of Pamiers—who remembers the following: "Twenty years ago, it seems to me, I came to Ax and, in a house that now belongs to Master Raimond Macoul . . . we spoke among other things of having goddaughters. I was saying that it was a great grace to have goddaughters and to make little children Christians, for when little children were baptized they had prettier skin and a better face than before the baptism."[15] It is through smell that the ogres in fairy tales react to this same quality. Do they not exclaim gluttonously, when a child is hidden in their house, "It smells like fresh meat," but also, in langue d'oc and Italian variations, "It smells like Christian flesh," or, even, "It smells like baptized flesh?" When, in addition, as in a Serbian version, the cannibal is a Jew, the smell of the young Christian takes on further meaning: it not only gives an appetite to the ogre or sorcerer, who is deprived of piglets, as we have seen, since he doesn't know how to raise them, but constitutes a distinction "in nature" between the new Christian and the Jew and his stench.[16] By the grace and scent of the baptism the child separates himself from the Jew; for each "creature," then, the historical break is replayed. How was this original "conversion" demonstrated?

In Abruzzi, on returning from church and while reciting the following formula, the midwife passes the child to the godmother, who hands him in turn to the mother:

Ecche, cummare me
Tu mi tu sci dau pagane
I' te lu renne cristiane.

[Here, godmother
Here is the one you gave me a pagan.
I return him to you a Christian.]

In Le Mâconnais a very similar couplet is recited before departing for church: "On leaving the house, the grandmother made her recommendations to the godfather, saying: 'I give you a little Saracen, bring me back a little Christian.'" Regional variations abound. They refer, alternately, to the pagan, the Turk, the Saracen, and the Moor. The latter, notably in Catalonia, is supposed "to bring the children."[17] Among this grouping, which nonetheless sheds light on our subject, the Jew, one will note, is almost absent. Indeed, we have found mention of him only twice. In the French Pyrenees the ritual song is part of the so-called return from baptism chant. In it one narrates the ceremony and joyous march of the procession by the paths—"Les carreras" is the title of this chant—and finally the arrival before the home. There the godfather and godmother, in keeping with the custom, invite the parents to come out to the threshold and hand them the child, singing, under the porch roof:

Nous l'ats balhat
Coumo'n jusiou
Bous lo tournan
Enfant de Diou

[You gave him to us
Like a Jew
We return him to you
A child of God!]

Jean Poueigh, who noted this song in the twenties, doesn't comment on the word, but when Alphonse Lamarque de Plaisance transcribed an identical expression in 1845, in the former Bazadais, he was surprised by it: "Nous l'ats baillat comme un gigiou, bous lou tournen chrétien de Diou. Right from the first verses I was caught by the translation. I don't understand the word *gigiou*; does it perhaps mean Jew?" After investigating, it turns out that the "nice woman" who sang him the song didn't know either.[18] As marked by the verb *tornar* (in the Romance languages "to return" and "to change"), the restitution is inseparable from the transformation brought about by the baptism, which the women who "pass" the child from one to the next complete. This circulation is reminiscent of the cure for the child with a hernia and the song that accompanied it. Thus the right "change" is guaranteed. It acts against the change the devil and sorcerers attempt to impose on newborns when they "turn them" in front of the fire before they've been baptized.[19]

Let us follow this new "child of God," however, whom we might imagine, thus renewed, would no longer have any attachments to the "old," the Jew. This is when we find the Jew again. In the south of Germany, even if, in church, one takes care to pronounce the sacred formula, "The Jew is carried away by the baptismal waters," the belief persists that the child's first hairs, the fine, sparse hairs an infant sometimes has at birth, are "Jew hair." This belief echoes that regarding a tooth we encountered and that goes by the name "devil's tooth" or "pig's tooth."[20] Thus the Christian "is made" by abandoning a certain number of natural features; the reader will not be surprised that, to account for this change, comparable to a "moulting," the vast category of skin illnesses was seen as especially suited to signify the Jewishness one must shed. This is the case in Le Mâconnais and Le Morvan, where children's minor inflammations, dry skin, and peelings are grouped under the general name *Jew*, while in the Nivernais only the dryness, the most epidermal of these afflictions, bears the name *guèdre* (from *gué*: Jew). The latter, in the Messin area, is so associated with the Jew that the incantations aiming to make it "come out"—so that it won't "ruin the blood"—base their efficacity on this simple relationship. One calls to it in these terms: "I order you to come out . . . in the time that passed between the kiss of Judas the traitor and Jesus Our Lord's capture by the Jews." This elegant manner of inviting it to beat a hasty retreat may take a more vigorous turn:

> Active, itchy, or mealy patch,
> Whichever you may be
> I order you to reduce yourself.
> And just as the Jews
> Eat no pork
> So you will no longer eat
> Christian flesh.[21]

In other words, a twofold equivalency—from the dry skin to the Jew and from the flesh of the pig to Christian flesh—is the premise for analogical reasoning. Pronouncing the charm is enough to ensure its efficacity.

All these skin illnesses highlight—as we expected—an equivalent affinity regarding the leper and the measled pig. When the young Frédéric Mistral was carried to the baptismal fonts, his godmother, after giving him the customary gifts, vowed him to Saint Badilo, healer of childhood illnessess and in particular of the *rasqueta*. If milk crusts—*las rascas* in Provençal—generally pass for a sign of health and prosperity to the point that taking them off "would bring misfortune," their proliferation is something of a skin illness, associated here with tinea, which is called *rasca*. By extension, a *rasclet* is a dirty, mean, and stinking kid, while a *rascàs* is someone who is mean and stingy. Indeed, it is children who, during the ceremonies of Corpus Christi, in Aix, play lepers as well as the "Jews." Wearing shaggy wigs, they chase one another while combing each other's hair—or, rather, while threatening each other with combs—hence, perhaps, their name *rascassetos*. Still, in Provence, it is not surprising that in order to ward off evil one would impliment the dictum according to which "l'aigo de Pasco, aparo de la rasco" ("Easter water protects from 'tinea' "), while rubbing one's skin with a cloth soaked in the lustral water that baptized the children on Easter morning.[22] We should recall, finally, without delving into it, that in several French provinces milk crusts are called "bristles." With these skin illnesses the child is sent back to the heart of the semantic triangle Jew/leper/pig, of which he is made to occupy each corner. But, in addition to skin patches and milk crusts, additional light is shed on the entire gamut of eruptive childhood illnesses—which we have already discussed at length. The illnesses that affect the epidermus by coloring it and enflaming it, before the skin detaches in a true moulting, are also affected by the incantation specific to burns. "Fire against fire, change color like Judas the traitor when he betrayed Our Lord" is the order one gives, in the region of Gênes, to both infant erythema and to the dangerous erysipelas called *scròfola* (from *scrofa*, the sow).[23] These fires, we have seen, mark the excessive proximity of maternal blood. The pig furnished the model; now the Jew and the incestuous Judas occupy this place.

This also means that, for Christians, every woman, and not only the redheaded sorceress, is "Jewish," at least so long as blood flows out of her body. This homology is expressed in southern Europe during childbirth; Abbé Thiers condemned the belief according to which the woman became Jewish during the entire period between birth and the "godmother's Mass," which purified her and restored her Christian identity.[24] This gives us a better understanding of the ceremonies that, barely a few decades ago, surrounded the churching, which priests today qualify as "insulting" to women's dignity. Despite this rite of reintegration into the heart of the Church, in Catalonia a child runs the risk of being "made a Jew" forever if his mother chooses a Friday as the day of her first outing. To be born on this day, or to be carried in the left arm before his baptism, is enough for a little Catalan to remain a Jew definitively. Even after being baptized, in fact, every young child retains the mark of his origin. The posthumous status of small children is a case in point: three Jews, it is asserted in northern Germany, watch for their souls on the path to the sky and intercept them.[25] If, no matter what the fine baptismal phrases say, this ritual alone is not enough to break the Christian child away from his original Jewishness, what help is he provided, at least, to struggle against it?

The Great Battle

When probed, the beliefs relative to the performance of the ritual—which we know nonetheless to be an exorcism—remain silent, as does the liturgy. It is by looking to godparents and their roles as chaperons of infancy that we have seen the very gradual efficacity of the sacrament revealed.[26]

There are, among the songs beloved of Provençal nurses, tunes called *arris*, intended, it is said, to "awaken" the little ones. Pursuing their search in the region of Maillane, Montel and Lambert gathered many variations on these songs, including this one:

Ma Meirino
Papelino
M'a croumpà ni matino
De cinq sòu
M'a menat vers li jusiòu
Li jusiòu m'an pas vougut
M'a menat vers l'ase blu
L'ase blue m'a reguina
M'a jitat dins un valat . . .

[My godmother
Good Christian
Bought me matins
For five sous.
She took me to the Jews.
The Jews didn't want me.
She took me to the blue donkey.
The blue donkey kicked
And threw me in a ditch . . .

Various versions bring into play the godmother, the godfather, or both together, with their gifts, matins or bootees. These spiritual parents lead the child to the Jews—"to fight them," it is specified. As in the version cited, sometimes the latter refuse the confrontation. Were they perhaps dissuaded by the very nature of the objects offered? This is an idea the researchers didn't consider, focused as they were on the overtly aggressive dimension of the songs: "We cannot see what the meaning of this song might be, unless it is a matter of instilling in the child a profound horror of the cursed people. We gladly share the latter opinion; in the lands where Jews have always been numerous and powerful, it is the only one probable."[27] Let us stop a moment to consider these unusual weapons, the "matins" first of all. The langue d'oc term designates, metonymically, both the service—well known through another children's wake-up song, *Frère Jacques*—the book that goes with it, and the prayers in general. That the volume cannot be read matters little, in fact, when one considers the status accorded the written word in traditional societies and particularly those prayers that are carried about as much as they are recited. In Majorca, for instance, the day after the baptism, it was long customary to affix a tiny book of prayers, even a miniature Gospel, to the garment of the new Christian, in the guise of protection and as a sign of gratitude.[28] If, in the twentieth century, the tradition of giving a book was maintained only for Holy Communion, in the north of France the latter has generally come to take the form of a sumptuous cake: a "millefeuille" once baked by the godmother, now bought from the patissier. As for the bootees, in Provence it is traditional for the godmother to give her godson his first "boots," and for her to ritually put them on come Easter, in the church choir, before guiding his first steps to the foot of the altar. This is what is referred to as *donner les pieds*. We have found this ritual practice in Spain and Italy, always in the church and during Easter time. In certain cases, the child takes his first steps around the baptismal fonts. Sometimes a word from the dialect creates a semantic unity: in the region of Naples, the word *battente* is used with a double meaning, both "baptized" and he who "taps his feet," who walks, even who dances.[29]

Should these actual first steps be understood, then, as the start of a spiritual journey along the path cleared by the sacrament of the baptism? As we have already noted, only after this baptism may one express the wish for the child's growth, which is uttered by every visitor from Toulouse who comes to "see" the newly baptized child. In the central Pyrenees the godparents themselves oversee his progress in the following manner:

> The end of the first twelve months was the occasion for a very popular ceremony in the Gascon valleys: *et bouleng*. On this birthday the

godfather—*pairi*—and the godmother—*ménino*—brought their god-son a new garment and a certain number of breads called *ravailles*. After the meal the godmother formed a quadrilateral with super-imposed *ravailles*, and, holding one straight and high on top of the *mainatje*'s head, said to him:

Dieu te cresco

E que de oèi en un an

E-t-troboi auta gran.

"May God make you grow, and one year from today, may I find you this much taller." This wish, or, rather, this prayer, is spoken by the godmother as she measures the child by the yardstick of the *ravaille*, a long thin bread that represents the height to come.[30] In a culture in which counting, weighing, and measuring living beings are forbid-den—they are operations that halt development—only a ritual can pre-vent the dangers inherent in such gestures. Just as, when performed by therapists, they reestablish the movement toward growth in the body of the sick and therefore stagnant child, so, performed by godfathers and godmothers, they guarantee the child's health and flourishing.

We should note, however, that the effectiveness of the gesture is augmented by prayer, by the offering of a garment and by these cele-brated ravailles. This edible gift is worth considering a moment. We have encountered it—always given by godparents to godchildren—in other circumstances that are in no way coincidental: at Christmas and Easter. The baptism that makes one grow begins the cycle of these offerings. Through them the child who grows is associated with the bread that rises—the root *cresc* in the Romance languages gave the Sardininan noun *scrisce*, designating yeast. Following the calendar of these offerings, marking their starting and ending points, should indi-cate the time necessary for the fabrication of a Christian.

The Bread of Christ

The last ritual offering to have been maintained in the region of Sault, the *estienet*, which our interlocutors remember having nibbled with delight on the day of Saint Steven, when they solemnly proceeded to their godmothers' homes to take possession of it, hangs to this day, in Aveyron, on the decorated branches of the palms that are carried to the church to be blessed. The *nena*—which is its name—is one among many baked goods given by godparents to their godchildren. In Catalonia, Sardinia, and Portugal the *mona*, a round brioche trimmed with eggs, is proffered every Easter, while Christmas brings a multitude of small breads and cakes of various names and shapes. Let us put aside the inventory of these various shapes for a moment to focus on the patterns of giving.[31] Two groupings can be noted, one between Palm Sunday and Easter, the other around the Twelve Days. What, in each period, makes the particular offering of the godparents to the godchildren appropriate, and what meaning does each one bear?

At Christmas young Catalonians await Jesuset, setting garments by the chimney to cover him and a chair for the Virgin to warm herself. On the morning of December 25, they run through the streets shouting, "Jesús es nat! Jesús es nat!" before attending Christmas Mass. In Barcelona the churches are all decorated with garlands of ivy on which colorful hosts are hung: red, green, and white. The holy bread that is distributed on this day among the faithful is called *pa de Jesús*, of which the little children also get a piece. But the moment they await is when delicacies rain down inside the church itself: dried fruits, nuts, and, most of all, *neules*, the large unconsecrated hosts that hang over their heads. "They led the children to believe that these delicacies came from the 'baptism of Jesus,' which is why we use the expression *tirar bateig* to designate the custom of throwing sweets at the kids when a baptism is celebrated. It was also common, in these cases, to *tirar bateig* from the top of the choir."

Thus the Nativity makes the young Catalonians the first beneficiaries of a "baptism of Christ," which, as we have seen, spans this entire period. The circumcision, on January 1, is celebrated, in addition, as a "baptism of the little Jesus" in which the children get involved as participants. They officiate by performing the ritual on the little wax doll of the family manger. Until then, Jesuset was laid naked on the straw, but on this day he is dressed in beautiful garments reserved for this purpose and set in his cradle. Sometimes, as in Majorca, to show that a step has been taken via the sacrament, that he has grown, he is seated on a little chair, the duty falling to the youngest child of the house, the closest to him in age. From their godparents the children also receive cakes on this day along with red-tinted eggs, as at Easter. Again they consume the large colored hosts—provided by the church or found hung as decoration in the family manger. Finally, come dessert, the youngest child is enthroned "bishop," crowned with a paper miter made from the cone in which the hosts are held.[32] During this time the fact that the children ritually act out the baptism of Christ prohibits them from actually being baptized—a prohibition to be considered in the context of the one regarding slaughter during this same period. By not baptizing children on the day when their blood, or that of Christ, flowed, by avoiding causing blood to flow on the days when children and Christ himself are celebrated, one suggests a relationship whose significance we already know. But, still in Catalonia, the festival of the Epiphany will play it out fully. On January 6, offically proclaimed the Baptism of Christ, the young Christians take a new step, and Christ becomes their "general" (illus. 15). Once again, following the usual protocol, the large colored hosts and the delicacies sent by Jesuset fall especially for them in church choirs, where they fight for them bitterly, even though they'll be present on the family dinner table for dessert. Meanwhile the godparents comply with the pastry-giving tradition: "In Ripoll, they give a cake—*tortell*—to their godchildren, who receive it in their homes as at Easter with the mona, and the size of the cake varies according to the age of the child."[33]

In keeping with the logic of the first ritual—the one that opened this chapter—the cake that grows with the child over the years governs his development to come while keeping in step with his current size. And isn't this new vitality what the boys are expressing on this day, throughout Catalonia, by engaging in violent battles among gangs or neighborhoods? But if these obligatory twelfth night battles may be seen as an immediate test of the vitality and strength acquired and sustained thanks to the repeated gifts of cakes of growth, it is relevant to recall that on this same day, on the Balearic Islands, godparents offer not only the ritual cakes but also the famous glass trumpets, which the boys then break over the heads of the xuetas. How can we help but associate these pitched battles with the fighting among children, deliberately provoked in the churches on these holidays by the throwing of sweets, and, on a smaller scale, with the struggles that occur at each baptism, when the children are in conflict over the godparents? Van Gennep noted this analogy, even if he was unable to explain it.[34] By making the children fight, by measuring out their gifts—at the risk, in Provence, of being called *ladres* or *suco-barigoulo*, in other words, of passing for lepers or Jews—are the godparents not verifying the newfound pugnacity of their godchildren? As in the song, their gifts allow the young Christians to "fight the Jew"; in certain cases, they sometimes even lead them to him in the flesh.

It is more understandable, then, that the period between December 25 and January 6—which we have seen glorifies Christian children as victims of the Jews—should call for the protection of a renewed baptism at each of its holidays. The children are the active protagonists and beneficiaries of the sacrament, in the image of the infant Christ being celebrated, who honors them in return by distributing goodies to them, like their godparents. Thus, in line with individual baptisms but expanding by way of the "baptism of Christ" to the entire group of young Christians, we see the establishment of calendar-determined baptisms, in a strategy of defense and consolidation of the ritual by which the Christian is "made." For this the combined efforts of the Church, the family, and the godparents are necessary. Such being the case for the dangerous period of the Twelve Days, what can be said of the Easter cycle, when the young Christian must confront the "Jew" in yet other forms?

The custom of offering the mona at Easter is no doubt the one that has continued most strongly in Catalonia. In 1986 the pastry chefs who commercialized the cake long kneaded by the hands of the godparents enticed buyers in these terms: "Per a la recuperaciò de les nostres tradiciòns no obliden enguany la mona, For the safeguard of our traditions, don't forget to give the mona this year." Yet the sophisticated constructions they offered, the work of professionals, rivaled one another in audacity and innovation. The mona became a platform of nougat and biscuit, with an evolving cast of extraterrestrials inspired by popular films. The entire miniature world of Walt Disney was present, modeled in almond paste, gathered in a debauchery of glazed sugar, taking the form of trains, planes, or ships for the boys, sugar-coated fairylands for the girls. Meanwhile "chic" storefronts displayed the mona of yesteryear, "like homemade." Let us listen to this description by a Narbonnais woman whose Catalan grandmother, who had emigrated to France—and served as her godmother—gave her one every year:

> It was a round cake, a brioche in the form of a crown with hard-boiled eggs wrapped into the dough. I went to get it with my brother in the morning after the Mass, and we each had our own with one egg for every year. You didn't share with anyone. Everyone guardedly ate his own. And you always had to eat the eggs in the same direction. From left to right, in the direction of the hands of a clock, without skipping an egg!

Each year the children retravel those that have passed via their mona. Indeed, the gift is inscribed with a duration that sometimes inspires its very shape. In Sardinia, where we have found it by the name of *cozzula di l'obu*, the little children are first given a *pupate*, a dough baby with an egg planted in the stomach or mouth. The same in Calabria and Portugal, where the egg cake takes the same shape under various names: fish, birds, and lambs replace the little man; next come the crown and basket shapes, for the eggs add up as the child grows, and such forms allow for their accumulation until an age that varies little. In central Europe eggs and cake are given until the age of fourteen; on the occasion of this final gift a small ceremony takes place at which the godchildren thank their godparents, who in addition offer them a book or a piece of clothing.[35]

In Catalonia, confirmation makes this age limit meaningful:

> According to tradition, the mona is offered from ages one to twelve, the age at which one used to be confirmed and at which one ceased to receive the godparents' offering. From the day they were confirmed for the first time, which constituted a rite of passage from childhood to adolescence, they were considered to have become "men," as their grandparents explained to them after the overwhelming event.

This testimony verifies the sacred nature of the mona, the offering of which can give rise to a ceremony: at Christmas and Easter the child kneels before the godparents and recites the Pater or the Credo, sometimes undergoing a further "doctrinal test," to use the expression of the ethnographer Violant i Simorra, who mined his personal experience. "It was common for the godparents to subject their godchildren to a kind of examination, which enabled them to check the state of their knowledge in matters of religion based on simple information, without the answers being very difficult. If the child didn't perform to satisfaction or was unable to answer, the godparent didn't give him a present."[36]

This requirement makes the significance attached to the cake clear. Like confirmation, one must prepare to receive it, one must deserve it, and it is therefore possible that it will be denied. Just as the priest judges whether the children are ready to participate in the catechism ritual, the godparents, the first teachers in the subject, decide whether or not they can give the mona. We should note that in both cases the recitation of the Pater and the Credo constitutes the minimum to be demanded. Is the ritual offering of this pastry not a kind of Eucharist? The association that we encountered between the host and holy bread, as well as a number of calendar-specific pastries, would suffice to support this hypothesis. It seems more interesting to us to put one detail to the test: that of the egg, an obligatory element of the gift, that crowns the cake or accompanies it.

The Sign of Man

> The friends, relatives, and godmothers of the neighborhood brought
> me, as per the custom here, eggs, a piece of bread, a grain of salt, and a
> match, saying: Little one, may you be as good as bread, as wise as salt,
> as straight as a match; then, giving me the eggs: vaqui toun signe d'ome
> [here is your sign of man].
>
> —FRÉDÉRIC MISTRAL, *Mémoire et récits*

In Germanic Switzerland, on every Easter from birth to confirmation—in other words, at the moment one renews the baptismal vows—
children receive three eggs and three breads from their godparents. In
Hungary these are solemnly remitted to them on the threshhold of the
church. In Bulgaria, on Holy Thursday, colored eggs are added to the
usual gift of little round breads, the *kravai*. The latter are not associated
with Easter week alone, however. In Catalonia red-tinted eggs are
offered along with the ritual Christmas cake. While throughout all of
northern and central Europe a great spectrum of colors and ornamen-
tal motifs make the decoration of Easter eggs an artist's work, the simple red egg, a highly ritualized object, holds its own. In Romania it
bears a particular name, *merisoare*, derived from the berry that for a
long time lent it its blush; here, as elsewhere, it is connected by its redness to the homogeneous grouping of beliefs and legends that explain
the origin of such a color. The gist of the explanation received by the
young Catalans who received the mona is as follows: "Eggs had been
given to some Jewish children from Jerusalem to throw at Jesus when
he passed. But as soon as the eggs came into contact with their innocent
hands, they reddened with blood, and the children couldn't throw them
in the face of the Crucified one."[37] The eggs and their color are immediately linked to the blood of Christ in a manner that recalls other "miracles." The examination of some of these stories of origin will shed
light on such an association.

In Romania the legend of the red eggs is alive and well. Without
claiming to present it in its totality or oversimplify it, we shall note
that it is primarily organized around the Passion of Christ but attributes the reason for the eggs' color to the Nativity. Mary is the heroine
of these stories in which she is depicted as throwing eggs—tinted red
to celebrate the birth of her son—at the Jews pursuing her. Or else it
is the basket of eggs she brought to the foot of the cross in a call for
mercy that became tinted with the blood of Christ's wounds. Sometimes the miracle of the coloration of the eggs occurs following a

provocation by the Jews, in which case the analogy with the profaned hosts is glaring. Most often, the stories situate the episode after the death of Christ, as incredulous Jews denied his resurrection. One scene opens with Mary Magdalene passing through the market on Easter day, proclaiming to whoever would listen, "Jesus is resuscitated!" To which a mocking Jew who happened to be there with a basket of eggs for sale allegedly responded: "He'll be resuscitated when these eggs turn red!" And, of course, the eggs colored instantly. In another the Jews, thinking they were rid of Jesus once and for all, are depicted celebrating the event with a boiled rooster, served at the center of a crown of eggs, swimming in an abundant sauce—basically a holiday meal. In the course of the dinner one of them "remembered that the Lord had said he would resuscitate on the third day. The host burst out laughing, saying 'When this rooster we are eating resuscitates, and when all these nice white eggs turn red, then Christ will resuscitate from the dead!' Instantly the eggs changed color and the rooster stood up crowing, showering the guests with sauce." This spray of sauce is seen as both the origin of skin illnesses "that are claimed, absurdly, to affect Jews particularly" and that of the custom of coloring eggs red at Easter.[38] This last story situates the use of eggs on a metaphysical level. Like the host, the egg that reddens manifests the presence of the blood of Christ, whom the incredulous Jews called on to reveal himself. Also, like the host, the red eggs establish a split between Jews and Christians. By being given to children, they contribute to feeding those whose growth is entrusted to "spiritual" nourishment. Echoing the legend, in the image of the Virgin and her son, godmothers bake cakes in the form of a basket, which they fill with red eggs marked with little dough crosses. These are the Provençal *cavagnat* or the Italian and Corsican *canestrello*. In Romania, upon arranging the eggs in these same baskets of dough, they recall their origin by emphasizing that each egg represents a wound inflicted on Christ. The lexicon, in turn, establishes the equivalency we have just brought to light: in central Europe Easter eggs are still called *hostinets*.[39]

Now, in Christian Europe, the altar boys' Holy Week collections have long included the distribution of unconsecrated hosts in exchange for eggs, which are generously granted them. In lower Picardy the same word, *blandyu*, serves to designate both.[40] In Normandy the *nurol*—in low Latin, *nebula*, cloud, which also produced the Catalan *neule*—refers both to the host, to the ritual cake granted by godfathers to godsons, and to a gift of eggs. In addition, this shared eucharistic value of the bread and the egg results, throughout Europe, in many names for the cake that combines them. The Catalan mona is also called *cristina*; in Greece the ritual pastry is referred to as *christó psomon*, Christ's bread, in Sardinia *kokkòi de angùlla*. For young children of communion age, these are all paraphrases for the host, the "bread of God," of "Christ," or of the "Angels."[41]

Thus the egg or the bread, the egg and the bread, or the egg on the bread, which are offered to children for every birthday and every one of Christ's holidays—often supplemented by pastry hosts also colored red—form a kind of eucharistic ladder. The Church and the spiritual parents furnish the steps with the requisite solemnity; prayer and blessings accompany these gifts, whose consumption follows strict rules. Every child must eat his entire cake and can stuff himself with it, we are told, "without ever getting sick"; conversely, biting into it before it has been blessed can prompt his own death or that of the godparent. The term assigned to the offerings—*communion* or *confirmation* almost everywhere—makes these pastries, which form a bridge between two moments—from Christmas to Easter, from baptism to confirmation— nourishment par excellence. It is a food that protects, makes the Christian child grow, keeps the Jew away, prolongs the effects of the first sacrament while preparing for the reception of the second. These ritual gifts mark and, most especially, signify a period that might be considered an apprenticeship of the Christian. The baptism is thus the starting ritual of this period during which one attempts to progressively reduce "nature," which, as we have seen, takes on the twofold image of the pig and the Jew. Indeed, this representation suggests that the historical passage from Judaism to Christianity must be experienced in every Christian life. The "Jewishness" of the young neophyte is certainly not always the most apparent of these natural features—"devilry" is often required to express this cursed part, which is variously identified. In all cases it is inscribed within a greater conceptual system that constitues the very center of the Christian world vision. Earlier we saw how the tapping of the boys' abilities during Holy Week for "roles" as varied as angel, devil, apostle, and Jew invited us to follow the progression leading to the mastery of their identity as boy and Christian. A great producer of rituals, Christianity interacts with custom. Since the Middle Ages it has made a point of marking life's moments according to its own progression and stages. In our societies its language and ritual also enable us to explain how one becomes a man or a woman.

In Italy, Catalonia, and Languedoc pine nuts are a traditional food at Christmas and on Holy Friday. Children are told that if they divide them in two they will see the outline, on one half, of the hand of Jesus performing a blessing and, on the other, depending on the version, the hand of Malchus striking Christ, or that of Judas, or the latter's purse with thirty coins. And when the child, logically, asks how he can tell the difference between the hand of Jesus and that of Judas, one points to his right hand and says, "This is the hand of the little Jesus!"[42] If the body of every child is a battleground between good and evil, God and the devil, his soul is the entity at stake. Until the beginning of the nineteenth century the famous Corpus Christi of Aix dramatized this confrontation in the Joc de l'armeta, the "game of the little soul." The inner rift that every child, in the secret of his heart, could experience was represented in the following manner: the *armeta*, represented by a little child dressed in a long white shirt, clung to an angel who defended him against horned pitchfork-bearing devils. But all of Christian Europe, in fact, played out this representation of the soul by means of a children's game practiced to our day: "the game of the Devil and the Angel," still known as the "game of Colors."

As we consider the variations gathered by Roger Pinon, based on a Walloon study, we see the elements of the Christian cosmology fall into place. It includes its own spaces—the bridge over which souls transmigrate, the door or the threshold to Paradise, Paradise itself, Hell and its fire—and the characters that preside over them: the Holy Virgin, Saint Joseph, the Good Lord, but especially the Angel, the guardian angel Gabriel. In Hell reigns the Devil, and sometimes the *Jew*, always endowed with a physical attribute. One child plays the Devil, another the Angel or an associated character. The leader of the game is the third and main protagonist. Behind him stand the troop of children who play the Souls and who are also sometimes called Colors, for each one secretly has to chose a color, of which he informs only the "game leader." The Angel and the Devil approach one after the other and ask for a color. The child corresponding to this color then goes to Paradise or Hell. At the end of this first round a battle occurs between the two groups thus formed. On either side of a line that marks the boundary separating the two worlds—those of the Angel and the Devil—the Souls clasp hands and try to pull the subjects of the opposite side into their camp. But this isn't the end. Other trials await those who remain on the side of the Angel, who must watch the funny faces and contortions of the devils "without laughing," at the risk of becoming little devils in turn.[43]

In collective games Christian children throughout Europe embody this image of a "soul" that a mere laugh may "change," thereby experiencing the instant reversibility—via the comings and goings from one camp to the other in the course of the game's successive rounds—the oscillations and rifts demonstrated by the catechism. In the seventeenth century François Marchetti, an attentive observer, was disturbed to note that the masks and large white shirts of the Aix-en-Provence *tarassous*, the children who represented the Innocents massacred by Herod at the Corpus Christi games—and who were long played by altar boys—hid the worst scamps of the city. In the meantime the children of the Christian schools, blackened with soot and wearing tails and horns, were called on to mime the rage and fury of demons before the holy sacrament, in extremely violent games.[44] In underscoring the lack of correspondence between the children and their roles, Marchetti bemoans an absence of decency. More frequently, the Church put its priests on the alert against the dressing up of "little ones," whether "as angels" or "as devils," without giving any discernible reason. In addition to these recommendations, which appear throughout the synods, prohibitions abound from the civil powers. Both testify to a concern for order and measure—the excesses of youth are always being quashed—and to an implicit recognition of these customary roles devolved to a given group. Thus a decree of 1552 taken by a magistrate from Hainaut "prohibits young people and children from being on the streets in disguised dress on Innocents' Day, imitating the Innocents, pending a penalty of ten pounds, except for young children, who may be so attired in all honesty."[45] The nuances established between the age groups make manifest the notion of childhood that developed in European societies beginning in the thirteenth century and whose progression under the ancien régime has been sketched by Philippe Ariès.[46] Today simply questioning the actors reveals the precise limit they place on their participation: in Catalonia, one must be under seven to "play the Innocents."

If early childhood has appeared to us as an age of indetermination, an analysis of the rights and duties associated with the following stage will allow us to better grasp how this dual nature, to which until then one was passively subject, is henceforth actively assumed by the children themselves.

The nuns' chains became heaviest with the game of the cross. The boys had borrowed it from village performances of the Mysteries, those in which someone played Judas, who once hung himself for real from a fig tree in the person of the baker, and someone played Jesus, who was crucified I don't know how many years back in the person of a defrocked priest—a poor guy who inspired the village's pity after being attached to a large cross on the church square. The boys imitated the processions, the lamentations of Golgotha. I wanted to be neither Christ nor Judas. The coin had it, nonetheless, that I play Christ. And they tied me up. In the spirit of the game, or to see how things would turn out, they left me on the cross, leaning against the wall of Santa Maria di Gesù, surrounded by the vapors of the dumping ground. Once the smoke had cleared, I saw a flock of crows. They turned in the empty sky and rose up, their wings a metallic black. They were heading for the grottos where dead mules and dogs were thrown. They would come back to me and rip out my eyes and my flesh if I didn't manage to untie myself; at least that was what I thought. Liberated from the cross, I went to kick Sebastien, the real Judas of the game, and fled toward Sgricciolo, where my family then lived. I was seven years old and on my report card I was accepted into the first year of primary school.[47]

We should retain from this beautiful text the narrator's lack of desire to play any of the roles proposed, the impossibility, nevertheless, of evading the decisions of chance, and the idea that at the end of the ordeal a page of childhood was turned. Let's take a closer look at this seven-year-old threshold so often recalled. It is the indicator that will allow us to better define what changes in the child when "the age of reason" arrives.

In Cyprus, on Palm Sunday, as a prefiguration of the Passion, the death and resurrection of Lazarus is performed. The boys are the actors on this day, which is as important for them as Easter Sunday—here the cakes and red eggs are offered for Lazarus's day. But this celebration requires certain precautions. In Larnaca care is taken that the principal icon of the saint should remain in the church during the procession, "for, according to popular belief, all children under the age of seven would die if they crossed its path." These same children "must not visit the saint's tomb since, according to a legend, they would be stricken with fever and risk death." They are therefore kept away from the image and from the sepulchre of the one who, because he received the gift of passing from death to life, carries the reverse power. Here, too, only a ritual can ward off the danger, and it is the seven-year-old boys who perform it, playing Lazarus, dying and being resuscitated on this day.[48] In Catalonia the same age requirement applies to "playing the Innocents." According to common belief there, this age is accompanied by events that mark it as a distinct threshold: indeed, it is said that the image of death that hangs over every newborn and that progressively grows more distant over the course of the first years of his life reappears on the seventh birthday. On this birthday the mother who had knowledge of an innate gift when her child was born is authorized to divulge it. Until then she had to keep it secret at the risk that it would be lost. Other examples can be cited, such as the belief in Gironde that poorly baptized children revealed themselves to be *ganipautes*—werewolves—at the age of seven. In all cases, seven-year-old-children manifest, and sometimes act upon, what until then was just a potentiality of their being.[49]

If the age of reason is when exceptional situations are revealed, how does it affect ordinary life? The changes that occur also express themselves with regard to death. It is common knowledge among believers that a child is subject to divine jurisdiction only after the age of seven. Until then, it is his godparent who "assumes" his sins; as a corollary, the child who dies before this age has the power to redeem the sins of his spiritual parents.[50] There are many well-known rituals that have long marked the attainment of this age in our societies—the cutting of hair, the first trousers, the untying of the umbilical chord that has been preserved, and so on—but let's focus on Holy Communion, at the moment when it becomes a ritual specifically for seven year olds. It was Pius X who was responsible for this initiative. In 1910 he lowered the first Holy Communion to the "age of reason," which had been fixed since the Council of Béziers in 1246 at the age of seven, yet the councils had never taken a firm stand on this question, advising at most that it should coincide with the "years of discretion" that could be situated at about ten or eleven.[51] As we know, this controversial reform, aside from recognizing an age already strongly marked by custom, had the effect of splitting the ritual into two communions, the "first Holy Communion" and "confirmation," situated respectively at seven and about twelve years old. Thus the church itself sanctioned the entrance and exit from the group previously defined by custom, which, from then on, situated itself in reference to this ritual.

In Majorca, as in many Catalan regions, the Sunday after Easter was chosen for this celebration. From Holy Saturday on, the children are invited to play the *angels de Pasqua*, accompanying processions with their wings deployed; on this day, still called Angel Sunday, the class of seven year olds receives the host, the "bread of angels," for the first time.[52] But the age of seven, in the Catalan region, is also the age at which one proudly accedes to the role of the devil in the theater:

> Just as Judas was hanging himself, in the midst of the thunder and lightning, a trapdoor opened and all us little devils came out. We had red and black costumes with tails, little horns, and a pitchfork, and we did our "dance" amid the exploding firecrackers and the smoke that represented Hell. This was already a serious role.

After the role of devil came that of "little Jews," which was abandoned in turn on the threshold of adolescence. Thus the age of reason, in the church as in the theater, gave access to roles and functions that progressively shed light on the various facets of the young Christian. The pedagogy the Church brought to bear in its institutions was not in contradiction with the customary apprenticeship. At first glance, nonetheless, the altar boys, in fulfilling the functions assigned them, seem to be proposing a developmental model for the edification of Christians, which, passing by the roles of Innocents, angels, and apostles, leads them to that of Christ. But we have seen this same group, otherwise mandated to combat the enemies of the faith, in this case the Jews, "keep the custom" by paradoxically taking on the roles of the Jew and of Judas as well as the ritual and instrument of the Tenebrae. Are the altar boys, the best of the young Christians, not also the reddest of the boys?

Between Two Reds

The boys of the choir are all liars
A day will come, God will have them hung.
—Children's rondo

Chierici rossi they are called in Italian, but mostly they are referred to as *russulidi*, redheads, a generic term that associates them with the raucous gang of boys called *rojanilha* in Provençal and with an undisciplined troop of pigs. They are red from head to toe, like the bright red poppies used to make the dolls called "altar boys."

Let's complete the portrait of the young singers and Mass servers based on information provided us, for the ancient régime, by the archives of choir schools and music chapels. We find boys pledged to song from the age of seven until puberty. Initially sought far and wide and recruited with difficulty, they later began to crowd the doors of the chapels, where a careful selection occurred. They contributed to the prestige of the choir schools to such an extent that they circulated from one to the next, purchased but more often kidnapped with such frequency that the little singers could no longer leave their dwellings, where their teachers closely watched over them. Aside from a vocal and religious education, the chorists needed a suitable health regimen: private doctors, whose visits and the illnesses they detected were recorded in a register, bled them every month. They were prohibited from eating pork, which would harm the "purity" of their voices. Despite these precautions, and even as the ardor of their young blood was tempered—a blood whose movements one attempted to delay by its subjection to the surgeon's lancet—they remained red, dressed from head to toe in this color. Frock coats, stockings, bonnets, or hats—most often gifts of an attentive canon—were uniformly scarlet, at church as at home, even though the regulations stipulated wearing gray outside of services.[53]

Was it therefore not incumbent upon these "red boys" to play Judas or the Jews? In Germany, when an altar boy didn't play the role, it was entrusted to the sexton, who donned a "red jacket" before embracing the part. More often, the task fell to a red-headed boy of the parish.[54] Now, as we have seen, thoughout Christian Europe, *red hair* betrays Judas, in some sense fixing the redhead in a state that for other children, as we know, constituted only a moment, a stage. While altar boys were between the ages of seven and twelve—the age of change—they were mercilessly dismissed from the choir school when their voices broke, lost their silvery timber, their high notes, when they became the voice of a rattle, the voice of a Jew.[55] We can now assert that, even when it stigmatizes a natural feature—redness of the skin and hair that can't be erased—the identification with Judas in Christian culture, and along with Judas the leper, the Jew, the devil, and the pig, serves to conceptualize and express an age of life, a passing stage, like "left-handedness," that is tranformed as one grows or is forgotten. Thus, for a time, every child shares the redness of which the red-headed boy, the little Judas of the European tradition, is the model. But if one is more or less Jewish until Holy Communion, which marks the full assumption of the Christian identity by "whitening" the child's redness, the latter is necessarily a Jew or Judas until Easter.

From the first centuries of Christianity Easter was elected as the festival marking the association and break with Judaism. It was during the Easter period that neophytes were first baptized en masse, and to this day Easter Sunday preserves its character as a baptismal holiday with the ritual of renewing the holy water: when mothers accompanied by their little children aren't gathering around the fonts to partake of the new water's virtues in a kind of collective baptism, they make sure, throughout most of France, that they "evangelize" their little ones on Holy Thursday. For older children Easter was long the moment of the first Holy Communion, so much so that while *faire ses Paques* generally means to receive the Eucharist, in northern and eastern France the boys and girls who receive Holy Communion are referred to as "pâkets" and "pâketes." This deliberate coincidence between individual time and Christian collective time establishes an overlap between an age and a moment of the year, both conceived according to the same principles, subject to the same dualities. Just as, during the Twelve Days, children are prey to certain dangers that only a "repeated" baptism can exorcize, the same threats are equally present during the "Black Week." The devil, but especially Herod and Judas, whom Christ liberates from Hell or from the island where he was in chains, eye the young Christian to seize hold of his now vulnerable body and soul.[56] Thus the slightest misstep can tip him on the side of Judas.

In Catalonia vigilance begins on Palm Sunday. The first order of concern is the handling of the palm, which must sit straight up, for it is said that a palm falling forward betrays a child who has not confessed. Next one must be careful that it remain whole, at least until it has been blessed. According to the tradition, "Judas, the bad disciple, carried a palm that was missing its tip when he entered Jerusalem with the Lord and the other disciples." Carrying a damaged palm is thus considered to be a "bad omen." And this risk is run by the "middle" age group. Indeed, a strict hierarchy is established between the palms and their bearers. Little children are responsible for the elaborately braided, multitiered creations, laiden with pious sweets—sugar rosaries and dried fig chaplets—which, in order to be carried without hindrance all the way to the church, require the help and protection of the godparents who prepared them. The eldest carry branches of laurel and olive that, once stripped of their leaves, become effective weapons for the pitched battles in which they subsequently engage on the church square. The middle group is entrusted with the *palmón*, the true, fragile leaf of the palm, identical to the one held by the procession's farcical Judas. In Argentona twelve boys play the apostles. They parade in

9. Palm Sunday, in Ramó Puiggari, *Costumbres populares de Barcelona*,
Barcelona, 1860.

two rows, each proudly carrying his branch. "A little bit behind, alone,
walks Judas, holding the broken palm in one hand, in the other continually shaking the purse and jangling the money. While everyone else
walks with their heads bowed meditatively, Judas arrogantly holds his
head up high. Upon arriving at the monument, all genuflect and rever-
entially salute. Judas turns his back, makes a face, and thumbs his nose,
even gesturing with his foot as if to kick it." Later on this same Judas,
in the course of the Last Supper, brusquely rejects the piece of bread
Christ offers him or rushes to the table to grab the largest piece to
"filthily wipe up his plate."

We recognize here, in all these attitudes, the reverse of what "Christian civility" teaches children. Judas, the bad disciple, is set up as a neg-
ative model; "bad manners" are stigmatized with "What a Judas!,"
which, for young Catalans brought up on tales involving the character,
leaves little doubt as to the implied message. The following affords us
a glimpse of all the possible levels of association proposed:

Judas was redheaded, which is why one says: "redhead, with bad hair
like Judas." He had rheumy eyes—*lleganyós*—he was a stammerer—
farfallós—rowdy—*taboll*—he looked like a tall, lanky good-for-noth-
ing—*despenja-porcs*. He was weaned on an onion omelet, which is why
he was so ill inclined. And that is why one mustn't give onion omelettes
to little children, because it makes them mean. An omelet prepared this
way is called an "omelet on which Judas was weaned."[57]

Dirty, mean, with runny eyes—another effect of redness—awkward in speech, Judas was the image of the "poorly brought up" child. We should note the inclusion of a failed weaning in this avalanche of defects, not the slightest of which is difficult speech. When we learn that Judas was left-handed to boot, the portrait is complete. During Holy Week it is essentially with respect to table manners that children risk being identified with him: eating with one's hands, talking with one's mouth open, dipping one's bread in sauce, are all chastised with "What a Judas!" "What a Jew!" and children are warned of the effects of such behavior: *Fa jueu*, in other words "it makes you Jewish." And, as we have seen, the Judases of the Last Supper, illustrating the Gospels' enigmatic "He who has dipped his hand in the dish with me will betray me," put their bare feet on the table, gorge themselves on bread dripping with gravy, wipe their mouths with a corner of their clothing—in short, eat like pigs.

The boys admonished by their mothers sometimes defend themselves in fact by casting the blame—as one might expect—back on mothers. In Andalusia on Holy Saturday, after assembling their Judas in neighborhood groups, they walk him through the streets, singing:

¿Quén sería la madre
que parió a Judas?
¡E que hijos indignos
paren algunas!

[Who might be the mother that
Brought Judas into the world?
To what unworthy children
Do they not give birth!]

In the process they arrogantly cross the thresholds of homes, throwing stones and causing a ruckus.[58] The young Sardinians and young Italians are equally careful about their attire and, this week in particular, avoid making faces, sticking out their tongues, and spitting, "for that is what the Jews and Judas did."[59] The risk of slipping onto the wrong side thus culminates in these trials, which play on the potentials of an age in combination with a moment that lends itself to every type of reversal.

At the same time, Easter week offers an enactment of the childhood we outlined in our examination of theatrical roles. Organizing passages by a gradation—from angels to apostles by way of devils and "little Jews"—this enactment lays out the ideal succession for the ages of childhood, just as the Church guides each child to the threshold of the first great ritual, which is the eucharistic meal. Two timelines come together: the calendar is built around the course of the life of Christ, which establishes the scansions from Christmas, his birth—the festival of children and their "baptism"—until Easter, his death and resurrection—the death of the children and their symbolic rebirth. And the rituals that express this juncture must have an enhanced power of revelation for the actors in whom the change is incarnated. Participation in the Tenebrae commotion and the first Holy Communion—the latter sometimes giving access to the former, and vice versa—is the twofold goal associated with this moment, and while we have not yet completely grasped the bond uniting the ritual in which one "eats" Christ for the first time to that by which one "makes" or "kills" the Jew, we sense that by each of these necessary tests, with their highly ritual forms, childhood indeterminacy is dispelled. If Holy Communion, the only ritual offically "recognized" by the institution, often signals the end of regular churchgoing for the majority of boys, what is it that authorizes this break? Or, rather, what deeper change does it reflect?

The "Jewish Ill"

Let's go back one last time to this Tenebrae commotion, which has become the birthright of a group and an age that, while excluding children under seven, doesn't entirely lock them out, as other rituals do. On the contrary, its effects seem to extend to them, demonstrating the scope of the ritual's efficacity. As we know, a number of protection rituals concerning children occur during Holy Week, while its high points are designated as the moment for them to enter new stages, whether by wearing new garments or by taking their first steps during the services of Holy Thursday or Saturday. We have also emphasized the extent to which these peripheral rituals, viewed as a whole, suggest a coherent reading: they connect the child's physical development to the construction of his Christian identity. By sharpening our focus on the proceedings, we can further refine our analysis, grasp the instant, at the very heart of the services, when the ritual takes effect. In Roussillon, for instance, one awaits the moment of "killing the Jews" to rid children of their swaddling clothes and have them take a few steps.[60] In Sicily the "Jews" actively participate in the Thursday and Friday ceremonies and are killed on Saturday; we have seen how comically they fall at the announcement of the resurrection. At the moment when *fanno la cascata*, when they are taking their tumbles, the mothers grab their youngest under the arms and raise them in the air as the rattles sound, shouting, "Cresci grande, che tu possa crescere subito, Grow big, may you suddenly grow"). This is called *fare i crisciranni*.[61] The ritual thus aims to achieve instantaneously what the gifts and vigilant care of the parents and godparents produce progressively. And it is at the moment when "the Jews die" that the gesture and expression become efficacious. The conjunction between the action on the one hand—the shaking of rattles—and the performing of a curative or preventive ritual appears more clearly still in the following case: according to Valeri Serri i Boldù, a Catalan ethnographer from Urgell, "On Holy Thursday the women make a point of attending as many services as possible with their young children. In Borges the presence of children is equally notable. Essentially it is believed that attendance will preserve them from hernias [*trencadura*], while in Saint-Martin de Maldà mothers put their little girls on the ground at the moment when one "kills the Jews" [*maten Jueus*], convinced that this will shield them from "the disease of hysteria." We have found this gesture and belief in Roussillon as well.[62] In all cases—whether it makes them walk or grow, protects boys from hernias, which as we have shown to be an illness associated with growth and sexual identity, or girls from hysteria, an analogous malady—the ritual ensures a change, marks a stage. But what we have just read into its margins must be resituated at the heart of the lived, experienced ritual. Indeed, the boys prepare for it by a long progressive approach, passing through it by degrees, following a trajectory for which Holy Week offers the guiding thread.

Palm Sunday, when the children play the "Hebrews" come to welcome Christ, constitutes the first act of this initiation (illus. 16 and 17). From this day forward the boys in Catalonia get organized. While the little ones gather the *fais*, the leafy branches they exhibit in the streets in imitation of their elders, the seven- or eight-year-olds polish their "weapons." They are the ones who carry the *massa*, the mallet that serves to produce the commotion to which one accedes by a trial. The boys who have already been inducted stud their mallets with nails, unbeknownst to the new boys. Within the group, specifies Amades, drawing on his own experience in Barcelona, the expression *claus a la massa* was like a battle cry, a sign of rallying and recognition, to the point that those who didn't have one were struck on the back with a well-studded hammer. Thus initiated, the neophyte had only to plant the nails he'd been lacking before baptizing his weapon, since, as we may recall, "every year, before beginning to *picar* [bang] with the hammer, one dipped it in the holy water basin" and those who were christening one "dipped it, stirring it well as if they were baptizing it."[63]

By performing the Christian gestures on this object, the boys reinforce the bond uniting them to their instrument and to their Church. Yet, as we observed, the mention of this weapon almost always evokes comparison with another object: "You don't lend a rattle, it's like a knife"—according to the carpenter of the village of Catllar—"It's sacred, you see? Everyone had his own and was very protective of it. I remember, when I was little, my father showed me his, which he had kept, but I wasn't allowed to touch it." A former altar boy and a chorister at the church, he was also the village purveyor: "I've made my share of rattles for the local children. Over a hundred maybe. The *patriques-patraques* had to be all alike, or else!" But then, afterward, with their knives, each one engraved the marks that personalized them, especially their initials. Particular to this age group and to the ritual, the specificity of the instrument persisted even as other musical means entered into competition with it. In 1956, in the valley of Barèges, two objects were used as much to announce the service as to contribute to the noise: a type of friction drum referred to locally as a *toulouhou* and wooden rattles. The toulouhou, often made "expressly" for the child by a man in the house—father, grandfather, paternal uncle—had a limited life span: that of the young boy's participation in the ritual, even if its usage was sometimes extended. In 1956 all the boys in the village—little ones under the age of seven included—participated in the racket. The older boys—the twelve- or thirteen-year-olds—fabricated the toulouhou, which were also found in the hands of youth during the carnival and charivaris. The rattles, on the other hand, were made to last, and their use was strictly limited. They were brought out only during Holy Week and were kept at home from year to year, passed down from generation to generation. Dated and engraved with the initials of those who crafted them, they combined numbers and letters with religious motifs—mainly crosses—affording them the status of "popular" art objects that now are exhibited in museums.[64]

Aside from these marks, their conservation in the manner of other souvenirs—such as baptismal robes and first communion armlets—is enough to connect the use of these objects to the group of recognized rituals by which the Christian is "made." Just as the future communicants participate in a three-day "retreat," the rattlers are subject to a period of marginalization, but while the former prepare themselves under the guidance of the priest, the latter experience the separation among themselves, without any higher authority. It leads them to the doors of this kindgom of shadows, to which they are admitted by the voice of the rattles.

The young Catalans gather together beginning on Holy Thursday, temporarily invading the streets. At the same time, these rattle- and mallet-bearing boys suspend solidarity with their homes, whose inhabitants they ritually attack. They demand, as if by right, the food they collect throughout Holy Week, announcing themselves from afar by their sonorous signal in the tradition of medieval lepers, whose instrument and means of existence they briefly borrow. Indeed, these collections serve not only to amass provisions in view of a collective meal on Easter Monday, but directly feed the gang of rattlers in places such as Frioul, where they count on them as their source of food. The rattle-bearing boys form a temporary troop, which, for three days, organizes itself apart from their respective homes, collecting and preparing common meals at improvised dwellings. Their ritual activities begin at the service of Holy Thursday with *lis turbis*, the Tenebrae, where they create *la batinade* in order, they say, to represent the Jews who beat Our Lord, and continues on Friday outside the church. At the end of the procession that leads the crowd to the site of the crucifixion, they shake their rattles again at the passing of Christ.[65] In many communes they "sang the Passion" whose subsequent progression they accompanied, ever equipped with their instruments, clustered behind the man dressed in red who carries the cross. Further east, within this same region, in the area of Trieste, another activity specific to their group extends their ritual functions, inscribing them explicitly in the relationship to Christ suggested by their three-day retreat. Here they construct "sepulchres," which they exhibit in public, submitting them to the judgment of passersby from whom they beg while chanting. In so doing, they assemble a modest sum intended to provide for everyone's needs as well as for the purchase of the *titola*, the Easter pastry with red eggs encrusted in dough. These displays were prohibited beginning in the early nineteenth century and disappeared with varying degrees of rapidity depending on the local level of tolerance. Competition played a role in the creation of these ephemeral masterpieces, which were produced in great secrecy. The miniature sepulchres were created in the image of certain mangers, in wood or cardboard crates. In 1940 they could still be seen in the streets of Trieste:

A little altar was set up, with the steps leading up to it topped by a kind of tabernacle and a cross cut out of white cardboard which imitated marble, all on a painted cardboard and gold paper background with little candelabras, even, and burning candles. The front part of the altar, a piece of glass, allowed one to see the body of Christ in the tomb, crudely sculpted in wood, resting between vases of cut-paper flowers, and particularly the wooden soldiers, at the foot of the steps, who stood guard on both sides.[66]

When they are not their creators and owners, the boys may nonetheless have a role to play in the "monuments" created by each church and convent. This is the case in Palermo where, according to Fulco di Verdura, "a centuries-old custom consisted in entrusting a sepulchre key to a little boy who became its guardian until Holy Saturday." Recording in his *Memoirs* this tradition, which was still active during his childhood, he relates how he was chosen by the mother superior of a neighboring convent and had to be present on the morning of Holy Thursday at the chapel square: "I was squeezing a white silk purse in my hand containing thirty coins, the price of Judas's betrayal. My mission was to deposit this sum in a dish that was to be solemnly presented to me by the verger. After which, kneeling before the high altar, I was blessed by a *monsignore*, who hung a ribbon of moire around my neck, strung from which was the silver key."[67] This official duty, the purchase of which was also a buying back—the key is exchanged for "thirty coins"—while ratifying the religious authority's recognition of the customary role played by young boys during the three days, is also something of a test. Fulco di Verdura never forgot the nightly terror he felt when he groped for the precious key, which was safe on its silk cushion. But, more commonly, according to our interlocutors, their group collectively "stood guard" around a sepulchre, watching over it every night into the wee hours, taking the opportunity to explore the most secret and obscure recesses of the church, reviving the games of terror the altar boys had already experienced. Some also admit to having smoked their first cigarettes there. The next day, drunk with fatigue, they nonetheless waited at the church doors, opened by day to the familiar crowd of the faithful, for the moment when the signal for the commotion would sound, at which point they swarmed the sanctuaries, taking possession of them before reemerging just as abruptly in disorder and confusion and transporting their racket to the next church. For this racket was performed repeatedly.

In Italy and Sardinia the boys created their commotion in various places and on various occasions: at the church, during the Tenebrae service and during the processions of Holy Friday and Saturday as well. In Catalonia and on the Balearic Islands they also fill the services from Thursday to Saturday with a staggering finale at the moment of the hallelujah. We saw our actors in Conflent repeat their performance on Sunday morning as the statues of the Jews were being toppled. This extension from Thursday to Saturday, sometimes even until Easter Sunday, of an action previously defined by its punctuality and brevity, invites commentary. By being repeated throughout these three days the boys' ritual commotion constructs its own moment while inscribing itself in the duration of the successive events being celebrated. Is it not at the moment when the faithful repeat the great founding passage of Christianity that the boys, by incarnating Judas and the Jews, and through the voice of the rattles, enact their own passage?

From Darkness to Light

When we look at it today, at the end of a long history that terminates with our witnesses and the final participants, the Tenebrae commotion presents itself as a complex ritual that surpasses its luturgical meaning. A male ritual, it nonetheless founds an identity that is not merely sexual, as one might be led to believe by the exclusion of girls. If the girls cannot "kill the Jews," according to the logic whose progression we have followed—since by the blood of menstruation and childbirth they periodically reconnect with an unshakable Jewishness, they are forever red and only intermittently Christians—this means that the Tenebrae ritual "makes the man" and "makes the Christian" (the latter two being indissociable) in the image of the baptism it completes and in conjuction with communion.

It is now clear that the boys come to both rituals as "Jews." Already, the reception and ingestion of the host situated those who prepared for it, and particularly the young Christian boy, on the verge of profanation, a profanation the Jew was long charged with putting into action. The implicit analogy is maintained in the sticking out of one's tongue, which, in Catalonia, "makes you Jewish"—an act of derision by which one stigmatizes the other. We have also found it at the moment of communion: "At catechism, the priest explained to us: 'You must put it like this,' so we did that [mimicking gesture], and he got angry: 'No! I'm telling you not to stick out your tongues!' We laughed! There were some who did it on purpose to get him mad. He threatened them: 'You won't receive communion.' " Echoing this testimony, a contemporary Rouergue memorialist, Monsignor Calmels, remembers his discomfort as the event approached: "How to stick out my tongue in such a way that it would be a suitable plateau for the holy host?" It is thus as close as possible to the central mystery of Christianity that the danger becomes palpable, to the point of marking every gesture and object. The prelate, a former altar boy, has not forgotten what the priest revealed to him as mystery: "He took me all the way to Carminade to show me how small hosts were made out of a big one. All the scraps were for me, which prompted me to say to my friends: 'I'm coming from the priest's' —'What were you doing there? —I was eating the *edges of the Good Lord*!' Did they understand me? Since I found this an appealing expression, I repeated it to my parents."[68] While we have seen these "edges of the Good Lord" given to children everywhere, it was appropriate to know what division was established here. It passed, of course, between the consecrated host and the one that remained simple unleavened bread, left to those who were either not of an age nor of a state to receive communion. In Wallonia one could buy such broken pieces from the makers of *nûles*, referred to as *pan d'Juif*, Jew bread.[69] Thus, the same name identifies these pieces and those to whom it is granted by custom.

To take communion is thus, by acceding to the "bread of Christ," to die a Jew in order to be reborn a Christian. The significance for our interlocutors of the talk of risking death—even beyond the sanction incurred by those who "bit" the host—the images of real fainting that mark the memories of first communion, the extreme emotion of those who feared it, teach us that on this solemn day something necessarily comes to an end. The abandonment of the "little Jew" whom everyone carries within himself is marked, this same year or the following, by Holy Communion. The neophyte, the only Jew who can be completely converted by the host, then reiterates, *in his own voice*, the baptismal vows. This is what is suggested by Ramón Sender, the Spanish novelist, when he writes of his character, the young, zealous altar boy we have already encountered, "Paco emerged from the Holy Week as from a convalescence." This metaphor of evil and illness accompanied us throughout, and it seems that it was particularly called upon to express not only the Jewishness of the children of Israel but also that of Christians, who had to go all the way to ritual death in order to fully "emerge from it."

PART THREE

𝕮𝖍𝖗𝖎𝖘𝖙𝖎𝖆𝖓 𝕱𝖑𝖊𝖘𝖍

CHAPTER EIGHT

The Return of the Pig

I a plus religioun en liò
Li crestian manjon de coudolo
E li jusiòu de saussissot.

—FRÉDÉRIC MISTRAL, *Dictionnaire provençal français*, s.v. "Candolo"
(unleavened bread)

e shall begin this chapter with an anecdote that brings us back to the heart of our subject. It is attributed to the young Karl Marx, whose parents had converted to Christianity, but without renouncing their origins. The young boy therefore often visited his close Jewish relatives.

> On the eve of Easter Karl would make his way to the ghetto of Trier. The Jewish Passover preceded the Christian Easter. The members of his Uncle Jacob's house would be busy baking *matʒa* and preparing the stuffed fish for the Seder . . . in Brueckengasse [outside the ghetto] they were coloring eggs and roasting a piglet. Karl used to bring some *matʒa* home and eat it with thin slices of Paschal pork. "We all have the same God," his aunts would say indulgently. "Sacrilege!" Henrietta [his mother] would storm indignantly, trembling in expectation of God's wrath.[1]

Thus adherence to one religion or another is clearly marked during Easter. The emblematic matzo and fish on the one side, pork and red eggs on the other, stand in contrast to one another, the latter, in particular, marking the end of a seven-week period of privation.

Beginning Ash Wednesday, the start of lent, the pig is "placed in quarantine," to use the common expression, eliminated from diets, kept out of sight. Placed under the sign of ash—at the service one was marked on the forehead by the priest with the gray dust produced by the cremation of last year's palms—the start of Lent took effect at midnight with the domestic ritual of meticulously scouring the pots and pans. All culinary receptacles were rubbed with ash, all fresh provisions of meat were wrapped in it: the hams were sewn into their "shroud" and covered for forty days, the sausages were taken down and packed into the depths of kneading troughs, the *pastiera* and *mait* of the slaughters, which in the Sault region were stored in the attic where they served as grain chests. The pots of fat covered with an oiled paper were sealed; on the empty shelf sat only the liter of oil, purchased from the grocer, that would have to be measured out for as long as the reign of cod, red herring, and herb soup would last. Such is the image many times sketched of this time of austerity, broken here and there by foods and dishes whose presence followed rules that should be defined.

Let's take the example of bread and cakes. Religious legends noted by ethnographers speak of a belief in a tangible presence of Christ in the bread; original myths of Christian bread bring into play the metaphor of the "rising Christ," of Christ ferment, dear to allegory. One of these stories, recorded in the Abruzzis, situates the miracle at a moment when, chased by the Pharisees, *i farisei*, in other words, the Jews, the holy family arrived at the doorstep of a home where a woman was kneading; the Virgin asked her to hide her child in the dough. Once the Jews had passed, this dough began to rise and overflow the kneading trough. " "Benedetta quelle massa che di venerdi s'ammassa, Blessed be the dough kneaded on Fridays," said the Virgin, before setting off again. And, indeed, the woman began to shape her breads without being able to deplete the rising mass. And all the neighborhood women were called in and rushed to take a little of this dough to make *lu scrisce*, the leaven. The story ends as follows: "This was the origin of the use of leaven to make dough rise."[2]

Consequently, in most areas risen pastries disappear from tables come Lent. Yet, in Catalonia, *bunyols*, puffed-up cakes, are consumed in abundance, "good Christians" going so far as to eliminate everything else from their diets during Holy Week, when they "fast" on water and these doughnuts or fritters. Joan Amades resorted to the local explanation to make sense of this anomalous practice: "It seems that fritters constitute a ritual dish in the face of the unleavened bread of the Jews; that is why they are made at home as an act of domestic liturgy. They necessarily include yeast in opposition to the Jewish bread that does not contain any. A dictum from Empordà clearly states:

Qui no fa bunyóls
per la Setmana Santa
Es que es jeu.

[He who does not make fritters
For the holy week
Is a Jew.][3]

We can detect in this example the specific application of the principle that underlies the alimentary habits of Christians in this period of fasting and abstinence. In Catalonia it is the proximity of the neighboring Jews that calls for the choice of puffed-up doughnuts. But even when the choice of a dish is not as clearly justified, or when the Jews are not as concretely present, we might nonetheless imagine that, at a time when pork is being banished from their diets, Christians might feel obliged to increase the signs of their difference in order to distinguish themselves from the Jews, with whom they temporarily share this prohibition. Lent and Holy Week—which reinforces taboos and prescriptions—therefore seems a particularly appropriate observation point to question those foods that, in the absence of pork, still "make Christians" over.

And, first of all, fish. Lent is a time of fish eating, par excellence, and yet, on closer inspection, things are not always quite so clear. Let's listen to one of our interlocutors from Conflent: "Here the tradition of Holy Friday, the typical dish, is conger with chickpeas. Conger salted like cod. In the past there were also eels, but now you can't find them easily. And on Fridays, all year long and during Lent, it was cod with white beans. But I've never seen conger eaten in my life except on that day with chickpeas!"

This comment is confirmed by a Barcelona custom: until the beginning of the century, early in the morning of Holy Friday, a large fish market called the "conger fair" was held in the city. Indeed, conger, consumed here fresh, dominated the fishmongers' stalls. Yet, in this same Catalonia, cod dominated Lent, becoming mixed up with this period to such an extent that this time of year, often represented in the form of an old lady with seven legs—one for each week—was called, in Barcelona itself, *la bacallanera* (from *bacallà*, "cod"). A large cod, to which seven little ones were attached, embodied La Caresma here, and, during these days, this fish was "in every sauce," according to cooks. Yet they kept it off their Holy Thursday and Friday menus, when conger, eel, or *gall* (John Dory) or *clavell* (a type of skate) were chosen instead; the latter made their appearance on Thursday evenings at the "holy supper," seen as a commemoration of the Last Supper. Even today the fish market in Perpignan offers early morning buyers several cases of live eels. "We eat them on Thursday night. But it's more and more difficult to find them, so we make do with conger. It's the same thing, it's like a fat eel. Conger is a *good* fish." A glance at Catalan stories enables us to understand this epithet and this choice: the conger, referred as the "eel of the sea," offered its long-limbed body to stuff the hole that had opened in the hull of Noah's arc, saving its precious cargo. The "goodness" of the conger situates it next to John Dory and skate, which bear on their bodies, in their heads, the imprint of the hand of the Lord, the face of the Mother of God, even the sketch of the instruments of the Passion. While they are not the only ones to bear these marks, which, in the system of dualist classification that governs these stories, distinguish them as "Christian fish" as opposed to "diabolical" or "Jewish" species, it is by choosing them—in place of cod— on the days most strongly linked to Christ's destiny that their nature is fully affirmed. As for the specific elimination of cod from the diet, partly justified by the desire to mark the day of Holy Friday more strongly within the days of abstinence, the rigorousness of its application calls for further investigation. On the Catalan coast the fishermen, extending the interdiction to all of Lent, say they would "rather die of hunger" than eat cod on these days.[4] Where does this rejection come from? Very quickly, upon inquiring here and there, the true face of the cod appears: "It has an ugly head, if you saw it you'd be too disgusted to eat it!" is the answer one gets from fishmongers upon expressing surprise that certain fish, including cod, are presented in their stalls beheaded. "In many places people believe that cod has a human head and that the merchants cut it off before putting it up for sale," according to Rolland.[5] For young Catalans cod represents the anthropomorphic figure of La Caresma, an ugly, dried out, wrinkled old woman with whom they are threatened as with a bogeyman, while in Portugal it is openly referred to as a "face painted with two devils." Hence, it is already situated in contrast to the "Christian" species; it is marked like them, but with a false face, with a double mask that makes it an infernal creature. In many Portuguese communes, finally, it is the Jew who hides himself in the guise of the cursed fish, and in the indictment compiled against *bacalhau* at the end of Lent, on the Saturday when elsewhere one burns the "Red Jew," the cod is called *Judas traidor*. Confused with the traitor for which it serves as a substitute, it is judged and hanged, burned, or drowned.[6]

Such justifications make its banishment from Christian tables more understandable, and its consumption, where it is maintained or increased during the Holy Week, takes on added meaning. For the foods that "make Christians" are not necessarily "Christian" themselves, and "abstinence" sometimes entails "eating Jew" through interposed meats. It is not unrelated that beyond the resemblances one hastens to detect between certain "bad" species and the Jews, it is the most emblematic of the foods of Lent—and among them the fish and their flesh—that lend themselves to these games of similarities and differences. But from this exemplary case we can infer an enlargement and systematization of the process. All the foods of "abstinence" would thus be implicated, and in the first place the leguminous plants, the consumption of which, forming a pair with our fishes, would be inscribed in the same game of opposition. The hypothesis is easily verifiable: cod and beans on the one side, conger and chickpeas on the other.

Already, in Catalonia, chickpeas are called *cigróns de fra Pere*, peas of Saint Peter, a name that doubly associates them with the fish they accompany on Holy Friday and throughout the week, when they are eaten "in an act of popular liturgy"—the donkey who carried Christ upon his entry into Jerusalem is alleged to have grazed a tuft of this plant that grew on the doorstep of the Temple.[7] It is therefore beginning on Palm Sunday that they appear on the Catalan table. The same was true in the Cevennes, where the entry of Christ into Jerusalem was celebrated with a pig's knuckle and chickpeas, a relatively rich preparation that contrasts with the acidic vinaigrette accompanying them on other days. Obligatory on Holy Friday—at lunch in a salad, at dinner in a soup—their presence also harks back to a legendary episode in the life of Christ:

> It seems that the Good Lord crossed over a field of chickpeas and that the chickpeas began growing to hide him from the Jews who were chasing him. To pay them back, he said that chickpeas would always be wet. And it's true, even in the middle of summer, even if there's not a drop

of water, if you run your hand over the leaves of the chickpeas in a drought, they produce water. That's why on Holy Friday chickpeas are planted in the driest spot: in the fields where there is no source, in the *traversiers* [terraces] where there is no water. I remember my mother every year saying on Holy Thursday: 'Tomorrow, we have to sow the chickpeas *au secòla*,' dry, in the dry parts. Since then we eat them every Friday of the year, on Palm Sunday with the pig's *garron* [knuckle] and on Holy Friday with salt cod.

Here chickpeas are wed to the Christian calendar while lentils and white beans are reserved for ordinary days. But things change once we reach Narbonne, the land of the white bean, where chickpeas are nonetheless still prized. The competition grows stronger in Catalonia and in Spain, where their joint presence further reveals the values associated with each one. The oral tradition brings the two vegetables into confrontation, each one bragging of its qualities—delicacy, taste—and asserting its superiority over the other, but the dispute can be understood only if one looks at the words that designate them and at the ritual practices in which they play a role come Easter.[8] In Castilian the white bean is often called *habichuela*, from *haba*, fava, but the most common name for it is *judía*, Jewess, local variations of which include *judión* (fat Jew) and *judía careta* (Jewess's mask). Catalan possesses several terms without it necessarily being possible to distinguish between the generic and the specific: *fesol, mongete, jueu* are sometimes used. The epithet *Jew—judiòu, jueu*, etc.—also applies to a small bean; this is the case in Provence and in the Catalan regions, where a *fesol jueu*, Jew bean, is found.[9] The quasi-explicit association between the bean and the Jew, in the Iberian world, is the basis of Coromina's somewhat tongue-in-cheek commentary on the word *judía*:

> The semantic explanation is not clear. Could it be because when they are cooked, unlike chickpeas, which remain on the bottom, the beans rise to the surface of the water, in the image of the Jew refusing baptism? Or is it because the name was first applied to a variety of bean characterized by a yellow spot, like the one the Jews had to wear to distinguish themselves in the Middle Ages? Or is it a question of the horned form of the bean's pedicel, reminiscent of the two-pointed hairstyle the Provençaux forced Jews to wear in the Middle Ages?"[10]

The two analogies—form and color—may enter into the equation; they are the ones retained in Provence in the designation of a little yellow escargot as a "Jew." But it is the status of this strange animal—neither masculine nor feminine, neither fish nor flesh, neither living nor dead—as much as its appearance that prompts the association.[11]

In Catalonia the Jewishness of the bean led linguists in the past, aligning themselves with the Castilian model, to make the substantive *fesol* a Jew in their own manner. They saw it as a contraction of the Latin *fariseus*, Pharisee, a term by which the Jew was also designated locally, thereby flying in the face of the most elementary laws of philology, as shown by Alcover and Moll in bringing the Catalan word back to its original *phaseolus*.[12] It should be noted that the ethnographic etymologists base themselves on the custom we discussed earlier with respect to young boys, that of *matar jueus* during the Tenebrae services. In the region where the ceremonial commotion of the rattles and bludgeons is supposed "to kill the Jews," the action, still called *matar els fassos*, or *picar els fassos*, beat the beans, sometimes expands to include the assembly of faithful. Beans are distributed to all those who attend the Tenebrae service, along with sticks. "People spread the beans on the ground and hit them to make them jump, an action in which one saw the Jews attempting to escape the Christians."[13] On this same Holy Friday the women head toward the dark churches, their pockets filled with chickpeas for the purpose of saying the Prière aux mille noms de Jésus. As they run through the litany they pose one chickpea by their side for every ten "Jesuses" spoken.[14]

With beans beaten and killed in the image of the Jews, with chickpeas serving as rosary beads and sanctified by the name of Christ, daily words and gestures take on meaning at the foot of the altar. Every worshiper, in his manner, contributes to this *remotivation*—to borrow a term from linguists—of a food product that, swept up in the ritual period, also participates in this redefinition of beings and things prompted by the Passion. In a distant echo of the Middle Ages when it was prescribed to keep one's distance from Jews and from their table, the elimination of a certain number of elements considered "Jewish" or their special treatment on these "saints'" days speaks of the Christians' heightened attention to everything that made them Christian, and first of all their food. And it is clear that those areas where Jews were present possessed a more heightened consciousness of this necessity, which was always sharpened during Lent. In Catalonia the onion, among other things, was suspected of "Jewishness" and avoided, since Judas, as we recall, was "weaned on an onion omelet." Also avoided were lentils, the favorite dish of "old women and Jews"—both reputed to sort them "with their noses"—acidic oranges and vinegar—which one eliminates from seasoning so as not to be confused "with the enemies of Christ, who offered him some mockingly."[15] We have seen, furthermore, how closely children's manners were watched throughout the Holy Week, out of fear that they might behave "like Judases." What now remains to be considered are the Christian ways of fasting.

The forty days of abstinence have been cut down to two days a week, Wednesdays and Fridays, fairly recently—we were able to measure the rapidity of the change through our elderly informers—in most practicing families. Emphasis is placed, nonetheless, on Holy Week. In Catalonia, where Lent is often strictly observed, this fast—from the day after Palm Sunday to the Easter vigil—is called *dejuni dels sis dies*, the six-day fast. It was during this period, in Empordà, that the puffed doughnuts without which "one is not a good Christian" were consumed in abundance, and sometimes exclusively. Some of our female interlocutors from the Conflent plain remember that their mothers fasted completely on Holy Thursdays and Fridays, consuming only a soup or a dish of "herbs"—mostly spinach or white beets. After making a "wish," they themselves sometimes observed the so-called forty-hour fast, which corresponds to the time Christ spent in the sepulchre. Many devout Catalan women, and primarily those who took part in the Holy Friday processions, respected this limited fast, encouraged by the Church, which, already for several centuries, contrary to common belief, had come out against overly rigorous fasting at Lent. Beyond the hateful coincidence between the Jewish Passover and the Christian Easter, which we know was initially resolved by reducing the Christian holiday and displacing it every time it fell at the same time as the Jewish one, it is the very practice of fasting—apt to recall a specifically Jewish behavior—that is questioned; the Church, after having followed the lead of Judaism in this area for a time, made an effort to distinguish itself from it.[16] While the alternation between "fat" and abstinence governs Christian food, it is mainly characterized by the former. This category includes both fat and meat—that of the pig especially—situating those who maintain a prohibition against it, even provisionally, on the side of the Jews. This split is illustrated in the original myth of the *escudella*, a meat and vegetable stew that, for Catalans, is the holiday dish par excellence: "The legend says that the cooking pot, stock, and escudella were created by Jews. It says that the Jews, with a deeply anchored sense of thrift, wished to find a type of cooking that was easy, quick, and that didn't require them to devote attention that would have taken them away from work and business, a type of cooking that would also be economical and nourishing." A competition was launched and the Jews invented the "meatless soup," so that, even today, a bouillon consumed alone or made without meat is called *brou jueu*. The Christians, for their part, are alleged to have introduced the ingredients that "make" the escudella: many cuts of pork, the ear, the knuckle, the *saborell*, a ham bone that adds smell and unctuousness, black blood sausage, lard, and finally the balls of *pilota*, the "stuffing," without which the dish would be incomplete.[17] In its varied presence the pig is the animal "of thirty-six tastes," the animal that serves as the basis for Christian cooking and allows one to qualify the economical—Jewish—cooking as "bland" and "meatless" by contrast; it is this cooking that is reintroduced every year from Lent until the break at Easter (illus. 23, 24, 25, 26).

This "Jewishness" of fasting and Lent, which makes explicit the oppositions in the culinary domain, is further expressed through the use of another code, that of sounds and noises. We have encountered several examples of the equivalency between silence and the privation of meat with regard to the expression "fast of the bell," which in several regions of France and Spain refers to Lent. Children's songs add an interesting nuance to the illustration of the difference between the two periods:

> Lent comes in with a wooden bowl,
> Easter goes out with a basin of tin.

Meanwhile, little children are told—as in the High Alps—that the bells went to Rome to bring back "permission to eat meat," even to "bring them back sausages."[18] The name of *campana carnissera*, meat bell, is in keeping with this logic; this was the name given to the bell of la Seu in Barcelona in 1845, a bell that, as an exception, due to a shortage of fish that year, by ringing a particular sound authorized parishioners to eat "flesh" during Lent. As we have seen, the return of the bells prompts a resumption of the commotion by which "one kills the Jews" and signals the end of culinary abstinence: "Quand toquen Alleluia, ja es pot menjar xulla, When hallelujah sounds, we can eat meat," says the adage. In Majorca this means that everyone instantly sets about pummeling everything in sight. The artisans set about striking with the instruments of their profession—blacksmiths' and carpenters' hammers, hidden during the week "so as not to resemble the Jews who crucified Our Lord," echo on anvils and workbenches—youth shoot rifles in the air, boys shake their wooden rattles, and, finally, the young children, provided with clay bells for the occasion, ring them until they break. At each bang or shot, at each broken bell, the cry is heard: "One less Jew! One less Jew!"[19]

The first chime breaks the silence and brings an end to Lent by abolishing the ascendancy of cod. When the pig returns, the Jews are heard one last time, through the objects that represent them: the disharmonious voice of the rattle—still called "Jew"—the muffled clink of the clay bells, the hollow sound of the wooden tongues of clappers retreat before the clear resonance of the Christian bells. Acoustically disqualified, Lent is relegated to silence because ultimately fish are first and foremost silent creatures.

In particular, carp, which, on Jewish tables, commonly celebrates the Sabbath and Passover to such an extent that "Jewish-style carp" appears as a "local" specialty in the cookbooks of many regions and countries of Europe. Among Christians it was one of the most widely consumed fish during Lent until the nineteenth century, which brought fish from the sea to French tables, bestowing on saltwater creatures the place that belongs to them today. Until then carp enjoyed a paradoxical position: a Lenten fish, it was long at the bottom of the hierarchy of species. Among the features noted to describe it, the most remarkable is no doubt that it is "Jewish." It is born of and proliferates in the mud—reproducing itself up to six times a year, we are told—its longevity and mutism are legendary, and, most of all, "it smells bad." This smell, becoming a "slimy taste," must be combated by preparations that dress it both on the outside—it is served on a bed of spices—and on the inside—Christian stuffings, in the variety of their ingredients, rival those of the Jews. But where Jews were very present, as in the pontifical court of Avignon, for example, or in Alsace, chopped pork and lard were included, except, of course, during Lent. Moreover, it is through the choice of a particular morsel, the tongue—considered the only part worthy of being eaten at noble and bourgeois tables—that the carp redeems itself. The organ in question, as one might suspect, has never been abundant enough to provide for the tables of Christian gourmets; the term improperly designates the very meaty palate of the fish, and it was for this fleshy "tongue" that sophisticated recipes were invented between the fourteenth and nineteenth centuries.[20] It becomes possible to understand this unusual distinction when we place carp in relation to its homologue of the sea, cod, whose equally paradoxical position we have noted. In Catalonia, a story explains its name, *baccallà*, in the following manner: cod was for a time the king of fish, which filled it with pride. It thereby made itself intolerable to God by its arrogant banter. *Tu, calla!*, You, hush! he told them, or else *Va callar!* Will you be quiet! which became *baccallà*, the name that designates it. As a result, it also came to be called on occasion *tall mut*, quiet morsel. And it is always forced into silence by being reduced to this tongueless head—the first gesture of fishermen when they take cods out of the water is to cut out their tongues—and, later, to this decapitated body, to this formless shape hung above the fishmongers' stalls.[21] It now becomes clearer how cod and carp, one without a tongue and the other reduced to this organ, could become emblematic of abstinence and Lent and that the Jewishness of the latter could also be expressed by silent fish, which are sometimes said to "speak on Easter day."

Thus the characters of the "Old Woman," the "Jew," and the "Cod" appear as interchangeable representatives of Lent, of which each one, taken in isolation, possesses every feature: old age, deafness, dumbness, and stench are ultimately their common lot, but it is mainly Jewish "oldness" in contrast with "young" Christianity that is newly interpreted here. An entire springtime theater dramatized this passage. The Caresma, which Italian Alp masks carved in wood represented not with a toothless mouth but with one that was clasped shut, provisionally victorious over "Carnival," was in turn replaced by the fresh "Lady Easter," surrounded by a court of dashing butchers who awaited her advent to bleed the first pigs in her honor.[22] But these seasonal games could also take the form of ritual battles between fishmongers and butchers on the morning of Holy Saturday. This was the case in Catalonia and in Italy, where fish merchants, always defeated, sometimes revolted against the real Jews. In Rome, where their stalls were situated near the Sant Angelo Church in Pescheria, one of the boundaries of the ghetto, their profession was among those that most hounded these close neighbors—themselves great lovers of fish—whose market was contiguous to their own. Furthermore, between the sixteenth and eighteenth centuries their corporation was among the organizers of the *giudiate*, the grotesque performances that ridiculed the Jews: a *vecchiaccio*, wishing to marry a maiden, repeats his attempts at marriage, which necessarily fail, so that at the end of the play the old man dies after having made his will.[23]

Yet just as the role the Jew is made to play here cannot be reduced, in our view, to mere seasonal dramaturgy, his presence next to the Old Lady and the Cod are not enough to make him a simple allegory of the period. His presence makes current the old game of passage from one period to another. From the perspective of the New Law, the death of the one who incarnates the Old Law naturally takes place at the moment when spring is reborn and, on the same day every year, that establishes the advent of Christianity by resuscitating Christ and resuming consumption of the pig. Christians as a group, who for a time became "Jews" again, also have to experience this passage. This is the paradox of Lent and of Holy Week: while exalting the Christian values attached to silence and fasting, they "Judaize" those who practice them. Which is why, in the absence of the pig, so as not to run the risk of being fully associated with the Jews, Christians must *speak* their difference for want of embodying it. They therefore work at restoring its relevance via linguistic even more than culinary operations.

With the return of the pig, equilibrium is reestablished. Throughout Christian Europe it signals the resumption of meat eating in ways that, while varied, nonetheless have an obligatory quality. We have already noted, in many provinces, how as soon as the bells ring one "breaks Lent" with a piece of sausage—even if it is still "fresh." But it is on Sunday, the day of Christ's resurrection, that this flesh is authorized to appear at tables in a more widespread and solemn fashion.

Preparations are already underway throughout Holy Week. The songs sung by Catalan youth during their collections, the *goigs dels ous,* the canticles of the eggs, solicit the generosity of donors with an urgent and precise appeal:

> Mestressa si teniu ous
> guardan los per als de casa
> que nos altres bé prendrem
> botifarra i cansalade.

> [Mistress if you have some eggs
> Keep them for yourself.
> We would rather have
> Blood sausage and salted cutlets.]

The latter morsels are particularly coveted by these beggars, who employ great ingenuity to procure them well in advance of the time when they may be eaten. Conversely, it is on Saturday night that the youth, circulating from house to house, intoning the *góigs de bótifarres,* the blood pork canticles, demand the ritual pork gift. They enumerate the best morsels: the blood sausage and the breast, the *sacsonera* and the *culera*—the fat sausages and the largest blood sausages, respectively— the cutlets and filets (*llomillo*), and promise to "unsalt" them. Beyond breaking Lent, the youth reconnect with the Christmas pig on this night when, anticipating official authorization, they eat and drink abundantly, for charcuterie and salted meat make you thirsty.[24]

The domestic ceremony, a complimentary inauguration of a new cycle of the pig, is quite different. In Catalonia it can only begin with the benediction of the Church, after the priest, accompanied by his acolytes, has toured the homes for the *salpasser* ceremony. In Vallespir each mistress of the house prepares for this with a large dish of salt prominently placed on a table that has been transformed—by the white embroidered tablecloth, religious images, and candelabras—into a minidomestic altar. The priest blesses the salt and the altar boys are given eggs and sausage. This salt, according to one of our interlocutors, was "reserved for the salting of pork to come." Thus, the ritual that reestablishes the relationship with "new salt," as opposed to the Lenten brine, calls for a restocking of salted meat. And this task is embarked upon without further ado in this Pyrenean valley with the killing of a pig that very day.

The Easter *Porquet*

From our first investigations into the region of Sault, although the ethnographic literature emphasized the image of December slaughters, which linked the death of the animal with winter just about everywhere—so much so that one identifies the other in medieval illustrations of the months—this other pig emerged. "Here, we brought in three; the one we sold, the one we killed in the winter, and the third, smaller one we fattened for Easter. The big one we killed at Christmas or at carnival and with the other, about a hundred-kilo pig, we made mostly sausages and saved only the hams. We ate this *porquet de Pasca* fresh for the most part. We grilled it and made lots of sausages."

Its presence in Catalonia is so connected to the holiday that in Urgell the long, thin, smooth intestine that was filled with chopped meat was called *xoricet de Pasqua*.

To see this new face of the pig emerge we needed to listen again to the testimonies of our first interlocutors and to reread the ethnographers with a different eye. Both always spoke of this "Easter pig" but merely gave the practical reason for it—"It was to tide us over"—a reason that was immediately invalidated, for, unlike the winter pig whose consumption had to last as long as possible, that of the "Easter

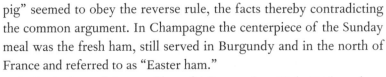

pig" seemed to obey the reverse rule, the facts thereby contradicting the common argument. In Champagne the centerpiece of the Sunday meal was the fresh ham, still served in Burgundy and in the north of France and referred to as "Easter ham."

In Paris the well-known "ham fair" started on Holy Friday when, beginning in the fourteenth century, the habit was formed of stocking up for Sunday, while in Bresse Louhannaise after the *cochonnailles*—cooked meats including pâté and headcheese as appetizers—the ham was solemnly brought to the table, decorated and flowered.[25] In Rome, according to a nineteenth-century witness, beginning on Holy Thursday, "the shops of candle makers, charcutiers, and pig merchants are decorated and illuminated in fantastic fashion. In their center sits an image of the Virgin and Child surrounded by flowers and burning candles." Furthermore, in Sicily, in Trapani, a priest blessed the knives of the *macellai* (pig slaughterers) who gathered on the morning of Holy Saturday before the church of Saint-Roch.[26]

If the unsalting of the winter pig is not enough to launch a new cycle, if just about everywhere the Easter holiday takes the form of a new "pig festival" for which a young animal is slaughtered, is it not because a relationship is being posited between the "return" to the Sunday table of this fresh meat and the event that gathers the Christians around it: the resurrection of Christ? Just as the birth of the Savior at Christmas brings an end to the fast of Advent, broken upon leaving Midnight Mass with abundant pork preparations, the Easter vigil sometimes ends with a meal consumed as soon as the long nocturnal service is over. Christianity in the East has even given this ceremony a special spark in which the relationship can be glimpsed. The ethnologist Edith Durham, an observer of the Balkans of her childhood, retained a strong image of this anticipated moment:

> Very good it was, too, when stuck with sweet herbs and roasted under an iron cover on the hearth. I remember eating hot suckling-pig, smothered in cream, at one o'clock in the morning to celebrate the dawn of Easter Day at Sophia Petrovna's school at Cetinje, with all the girls and many of the members of the Russian Legation. We had just come from the chapel after crying triumphantly "Christ is risen." All save myself had abstained from flesh and fat many days. And they fell on that pig![27]

The coincidence is not accidental; it invites us to uncover in the custom the echo of distant prescriptions, prescriptions that, beginning in the first centuries, were formulated by the Church in these terms:

The Christians would not imitate the Jews on the subject of abstinence from [certain] foods but would even eat pork, the Lord having said that what enters the mouth does not sully the man but [rather] what exits the mouth, as if coming from the heart; that they would not be attached to the letter [of the law] but would conduct themselves according to [its] spirit and [its] elevated meaning, for the carnal synagogue of the Jews execrates pork but is possessed by unkindness in keeping with the prophetic word: they gorged themselves on pork and left the scraps for their little ones.[28]

The founding break is thus repeated every year at Easter. The medieval English custom prescribed serving, in the church, at the end of the ritual game of ball, which brought priests and young clerics into competition, a collation including bacon that chroniclers report was purposely eaten in this place and on this day out of hatred for the Jews.[29] In the eighteenth century, songs from Burgundy invite the repetition, at each Christian holiday, of a meal whose function was to reinforce Christian identity:

> While the Jewish law
> Prohibits lard as heretical
> The same is not so in Christian lands.
> Let us eat fresh pork, Let us eat!
> The more we enjoy the piglet
> The better Catholics we become.

One of these hymns ends with a resounding exhortation proposing the Christian table—overflowing with bacon, blood sausages, and andouilles—as the antidote to "cagot" food. The injunction "Let us eat fresh pork" highlights the necessity that the meat be "young" in all cases.[30] Hence the massive pig slaughterings at Easter and the Church's recognition of a ritual meal, of which certain French provinces still maintain a written trace: the old liturgies include a special oration for the benediction of the ham and the bacon that were destined for the Easter meal after they had passed through the sanctuary.[31]

The Blood of the Lamb

Yet there is some discordancy here, at least in appearance. It is manifested in a seventeenth-century Provençal dialogue. A priest, Marchetti, after having assembled the *Usages et coutumes des Marseillais*, proposed to "explain" them in two works: one, devoted to the secular customs, was never completed; the other, dealing with "sacred customs," appeared in 1683. The author investigates the alimentary traditions of his countrymen that follow the calendar of Christian holidays. The ritual of breaking Lent, our starting point, is examined at length. Through the mouths of two interlocutors engaged in conversation—Polihore, a young and curious stranger who plays at incredulity, and Philopatris, the local wise man and spokesman for the author—Marchetti reveals to the outside observer the hidden logic of the practice:

> POLIHORE: I know [your people] pride themselves on breaking Lent by eating eggs with a slice of piglet flesh cooked on the fire. One can see that this is to build up an appetite in order to better enjoy the wine afterward. For you emerge mortified from Lent.

> PHILOPATRIS: We would seek out the most delectable morsels, more delicate ones than that, if we were as sensual as your teasing makes us out to be. What we do with the pig is only to distinguish ourselves from the Jews and show by the consumption of this meat, prohibited to all those of their Nation, that no longer being under the yoke of their law, we also no longer wish to take any part in their Easter. It seems most likely that this custom was introduced among us during a sojourn of the Jews long ago in Marseilles, during which time our citizens, so as not to meld their Easter with that of this people, knowing that piglet flesh was prohibited to them and that abstinence from this meat was something of the characteristic of Judaism, chose to eat some on this day, the better to demonstrate that the Easter they were celebrating had nothing in common with theirs.

Until then we remain within the bounds of this differential marking, which we have demonstrated several times and for other foods. There is no question that in Provence—as in Catalonia—the force of the argument grows with the very real presence of the Jews, especially since this proximity induced yet another practice that is in contradiction with the one just explained, as revealed by Marchetti, who is very knowledgeable in matters of the Church:

> POLIHORE: How can you say that? After having assured me yourself that your Bishop and your clergy ate a roasted lamb together on this day, that this lamb was served to all those present at the table and that, instead of giving the scraps to the poor, they were thrown into the fire? In your opinion, is this not Judaizing?

Philopatris, experienced in the dialectic of Christian commentary, which, for centuries, developed the art of dealing with "resemblances" to the Jews in a certain manner (of which we have encountered many illustrations), contrasts the Hebrew lamb with the entirely "spiritual" lamb of the Christians and, in conclusion, justifies the custom of burning the leftovers in these terms:

> It was to eliminate any occasion for the poor to fall into error, in believing that they had celebrated Easter like the Jews and that they would have been bound like them to this legal ceremony. And it was for this reason that the manducation of the lamb occurred only at the common table of the Cathedral and not in the private homes of the city where the people, being ill-adept at such types of discernment, would have been in too great a danger of Judaizing.[32]

Thus the priest sees this custom as an illustration of the equivalency posited between Christ and the lamb, between the lamb and the Eucharist, denying the consumption of pork—a common meat for the people—any sacred, or even metaphysical, dimension. Running counter to this distinction, however, is the medieval custom we have already mentioned, that of consuming the meat of the pig in church, *among clerics*. In this case, should we also attribute to the ecclesiastics the fear of Judaizing that Marchetti attributes to the Provençal people? Conversely, what can we make of the "spiritual" lamb of the Christians, eaten so prosaically at Easter in so many regions and Mediterranean countries, where, in the form of a leg of mutton, it constitutes a beloved Sunday dinner? Should we not, since the two meats take center stage by turns and together, examine more concretely and more broadly the way in which the division between them occurs?

In support of Marchetti's thesis, we should first recall that at the very beginning of Christianity the consumption of lamb was indeed the object of a debate. In the second century one still abstained at Easter from eating the animal, which was considered, in keeping with the Gospels, "to have already been sacrificed." Eight centuries later, when the Christian world divided, we find the Greek Church accusing the Latin Church of offering "a lamb on the altar with the Body of Our Lord" at Easter.[33] For Orthodox Christians the real lamb eaten on this day is the *amnos*, the piece of raised dough detached by their pope from the *phosphora*, the offering breads that the women continue to knead and that are used for communion. Explicitly elected the "eucharistic" animal by Christianity, the lamb is thus as high and close to the sacred as possible. Does the consumption of its flesh at Easter, in areas where it is cited as a dominant custom, preserve traces of this position?

On the Balearic Islands the resurrection of Christ is celebrated on Holy Saturday by a solemn procession in which the young children, dressed as angels—the same ones who are preparing to make their first Holy Communion the following Sunday—play the principal roles. In the morning the participants begin by gathering for a meal. Together they break the fast with a lunch, "esmorzar de freginat, de freixura i sang," a meal composed of rare lamb meat. The *freginat* is the flesh cut from the neck of the animal, the part still called the "cut of the knife"; the *freixura* (lamb's fry) is composed of the liver, the heart, the spleen, and the lungs. The throat and giblets are prepared in a sauce to which the blood collected in the course of the slaughter is added, but this is often cooked separately in the form of a *sanqueta*, a biscuit that is flipped in the pan like an omelette. The meal is associated with the religious ceremony that follows it to such an extent that in Calella and Fugueres it is called Processò de sang i fetge, "procession of blood and liver." Yet, in reading Amades attentively, we discover that this bloody part now taken from a lamb was more often—and is sometimes still— taken from a young goat for one simple reason: the xuetas, converted Jews, had a great aversion to this young animal, which they considered a diabolical creature and therefore banished from their diets. This banishment in turned induced a predilection on the part of the Christians, who consumed this meat abundantly at Easter along with the pig. In Majorca this meal of giblets and blood of lamb or kid—eaten at home as well—inaugurates a festive period that includes a large proportion of pork: freshly grilled and prepared meats follow one after the next. Here, again, the pig is killed at Easter and the preachers of Lent are remunerated with sausages.[34]

In Cáceres, a Spanish village of the Estremadura famous for its "lamb fair" on Holy Saturday, the facts are more complicated: custom has it that lambs are bought by young boys, to whom they are also sometimes given. The boys arrive at the fairgrounds equipped with bread and salt in order to coax the animal, which they decorate with colored ribbons and pompoms. They then walk it, thus adorned, through the streets of the city, parading it until evening, before returning with it to their homes to live among the family until the day of the local festival, Santísima Virgen de la Montaña, the second Sunday after Easter. Only then is the lamb put to death, after which a dish is prepared that is now famous within the local cuisine; the *frite de cordero* is eaten outdoors, near the sanctuary, where joyous groups gather to honor the Virgin. But, more often still, "in some villages of this province, the life of the animal referred to as the *cordero pascual* (the Paschal lamb) continued until the period of the *matanzas*, the pig slaughter. It was then bled the day of the festival, at the same time as the pig. Its flesh supplied the meal or was mixed with the pig's." This seems to have been the use to which it was truly destined in the north of the upper Estremadura, after it was "fattened."[35] What more general ideas can we draw from these culinary variations?

First the proximity of the Jews or those qualified as such—xuetas here, Marranos there—incites the Christians to play one meat against the other and banishes lamb from their tables for a longer period, whereas returning to it implies preparing it in a manner breaking radically with that of the Jews. Such is the function of the "bloody part"— blood and giblets—which serves to nuance the "white meat" classification generally applied to lamb. In the Cévennes and the Languedocian plain, in the region of Sault where the animal is still killed at home, the *sanqueta* is eaten for breakfast on Holy Saturday. At Easter, the charcutiers of Fenouillèdes exhibit the "lamb's fry" in their windows. Hung from hooks by the trachea, they drip over white plates filled with coagulated blood which the merchant turns over with a nimble gesture onto glossy paper for those who "had some put aside," for during these days demand exceeds supply. Other manners of handling it confirm the difference. In regions where one cannot conceive of Easter holiday without a lamb, it sometimes seems as if killing the animal and immediately consuming it would be inconceivable. A waiting period is established, its consumption is postponed, even coupled with that of pork. Indeed, at the end of its fattening period the lamb is treated in the manner of the pig: their slaughters are simultaneous, they are served at the same meal, their fleshes mix together to the point of confusion—take, for instance, the Calabrian custom of killing a lamb at Easter and using its blood to make blood sausage, which is stuffed into pig intestines reserved for the occasion. Similarly, in Friuli, the paschal lamb is served on a bit of fresh pig breast and liver.[36]

It seems, then, that these individual cases reveal a common manner of operating, the exception confirming the implicit rule: at Easter the meat of the Christian lamb is subject to a treatment that, bringing it back to its carnal nature, reverses the position theologians assigned it on the scale of the sacred. Hence it rejoins the pig, with which it is confused in more than one respect, this displacement necessarily throwing into question the unequivocal division—between the spiritual and the carnal—of which Marchetti hypothesized.

From another perspective, all the regions where custom calls for a second pig at Easter—those equally numerous regions where a roasted milk pig covered in cream is served after the evening service—suggest that the "Paschal piglet" occupies a place to be redefined within this system. We know that in the north of France, in Germany, and in a large part of eastern Europe, it constitutes "a particularly Christian dish." Thus the "milk" pig, as well as any pig, for which the "fresh ham" eaten at Easter is certainly the metonymical equivalent, presents itself as a substitute for the lamb. It occupies the place—and thus assumes the function—of the animal Christianity designated to incarnate "the lamb of God." Is it not the pig, rather than the animal said nonetheless to be "innocent," that Christians place at the heart of this network of analogies? By making it similar to their children—those young victims sacrificed at Easter on the model of Christ and in his image—they reveal its aptitude to signify not Christianity and Christians in body, not the mystical body of Christ, but his human body, his flesh and blood.

A custom has been preserved in northern and eastern Europe of which we possess several descriptions and mentions: the blessing of foods consumed for Easter lunch. We have already commented upon these blessings of the Church with respect to the pig alone, which, in southern Europe, often constitutes the holiday meat. It is also interesting to find such blessings in countries where its association with ritual foods—such as red eggs—calls for further investigation.

In Hungary Margit Gari highlights the preeminence of pork within an array of foods whose abundance is recalled by a young peasant girl deprived of meat: "There was ham, sausages, pork jelly, and eggs, especially eggs knotted into handkerchiefs. When our mother came home with the pork jelly and hams that had been blessed, we could finally eat, the fast was over!"[37] Another testimony, this time from a Polish immigrant, contributes additional details as to the presentation of these ceremonial foods and further enlarges the ritual assortment: "At the center of the basket was the lamb of white sugar—it could also be made out of dough or butter, but I never saw any like that. I only saw the molds. Around the lamb we placed colored eggs, very ordinary bread, salt, sausage, horseradish. Those are the obligatory foods to which you could add what you wanted. . . . But it isn't Easter unless there's a large ham, all sorts of sausages, and colored eggs."[38]

In Romania and Slovenia the custom of "carrying the basket" is very much alive. Here, on Palm Sunday, the children take up the task with a care and respect that are quite legitimate when one considers the significance attached to each of the elements involved:

> The smoked ham is the Body of Christ. The lamb is the Lamb of God. The white bread is the sepulchre. A large nut or a raisin cake kneaded into the shape of a crown represents the crown of thorns. A rosary of little sausages depicts the bonds that chained Christ, a few radish roots the nails that attached him to the cross. Oranges represent the sponges soaked in vinegar with which he was humiliated, and, finally, the five red-tinted eggs equal the five wounds of Our Lord. All these things are covered with a fine white handkerchief embroidered with the image of the lamb, representing the shroud in which Christ's body was wrapped. Once these baskets were blessed, they were returned to the house and placed behind the family crucifix, where they had to remain until the Sunday of the Resurrection.[39]

In northeastern Italy, where there is a clear Slavic influence, each house delegates one of its members to present himself at the holy place with a large basket covered in an immaculate cloth. Here, again, a gloss makes the details explicit:

> Bread, ham, sausage, nut and honey pastries, colored eggs, radish rind, black radish juice. The ham symbolizes the body of Jesus Christ, the radish skins, cut in the shape of a spiral, the chains with which he was bound; the *ciambelle* (circular cakes) the crown of thorns, the eggs the drops of his blood scattered in the garden of Gethsemane and on Golgotha, the sausages his wounds, the black radish juice the gall and vinegar with which he was soaked.[40]

The inventory of foods and objects collected in these "Easter baskets," the significance attached to each of them, sheds an unprecedented light on the nature of the customary division that living Christianity creates between two animals, between two types of flesh. Even though the content of the basket, with its fruits, vegetables, and pastries related to the instruments of the Passion, is based around the central figure of the lamb, the latter is never present as only a meat. Its image, sculpted in sugar, dough, or butter, or embroidered on a fine white cloth, becomes a representation. An allegorical figure, the "lamb of God" refers only to itself here. As for the pig, it is present "in flesh and bones" in various forms, all of which nonetheless evoke the person of Christ at the moment of his Passion—the moment that depicts him as a man par excellence and, particularly, as a mutilated and suffering body. The sausages make the wounds and blood visible, while the ham, everywhere and plainly designated as the "body of Christ," confers a palpable materiality to the divine incarnation. The flesh and blood of the pig become the very substance of Christ, while the lamb is at most the envelope: is this not the meaning of the handkerchief embroidered with its effigy, whose Romanian gloss specifies that it represents the shroud? Thus adorned, the ham is placed in the tomb in the sepulchre of bread in the image of the host itself—the body of Christ—and of Christ who is liturgically deposed during these days.[41]

In this context there is every reason to believe that the pig—served in Russia whole on this day, "a red egg between its jaws"—participates in the customary Eucharist, which, beginning with varied pastry forms, we have seen grow with red eggs. In Catalonia, in fact, the ritual cakes, the monas, are also prepared by charcutiers, who garnish them with ham and *chorizo*, a spicy sausage, before exhibiting them in their windows. Here the pork occupies the place of the eggs, while in Mediterranean Europe they are combined in other ritual pastries. In Cyprus the *pasces* are stuffed with pork; in Teruel the *rosca de Pascua* is a crown garnished inside and out with slices of sausage. The pork is so much a part of the cake that one sometimes even refers to the children's Holy Week search for pieces of pork and sausage as *rosca de Pascua*.[42]

At this point the pertinence of the combination—bread, eggs, pig— seems certain. The Church also had to adopt it: "In the region of Provins many churches had a field called the Easter bread field, because the wheat harvested there was used to make the loaves that, along with the eggs gathered during Lent and the pigs killed during Holy Week, constituted the makings of the meal that took place in the church itself. And this collation was called the *festival of the wafer*," in other words, of the host, in several communes of Montois.[43] Thus the place devolved to the ham within the larger picture is in turn illuminated.

In the region of Sault, as we saw at the start of this chapter, the hams are buried in ash for forty days—the period of Lent—only to be exhumed the Saturday of Easter, when they are considered "fresh," since, according to custom, a slice is placed on the grill. Is the pig not thereby following a journey identical to that of Christ? The potential audacity of this comparison falls away upon reading a text emanating from the Church or, at least, from one of its clerics attentive to translating theological thought into concrete language. One medieval exemplum, the substance of which we have commented upon—a boy witnessing the sacrament of the Eucharist sees the miracle of the change in species and his Christian brothers eating "a little child" before his eyes—continues in these terms:

> Similarly this sacrament protects from temptation, as a castle full of weapons and food allows one to resist one's enemies, for therein is housed the strength for combat, therein is found bread and wine, in other words the Body and Blood of Christ, therein is found the flesh taken from the larder of the Holy Virgin, cooked in the salt of the Passion on the gibbet of the Cross."[44]

To account, in one demonstrative act, for the mysteries of transubstantiation and incarnation by conjoining the images of a "Body of Christ" as a child and a pig is thus neither arbitrary nor blasphemous. The familiar concepts of the "cooking" and "salting" of the divine body by the Passion, used by theologians, are spelled out, in keeping with the logic, by a predicator concerned with making things visible to his audience. When the idea is captured in imagery, it tends in the same direction:

> In Worms, in Saint-Martin's Church, is a curious painting about five-feet square. God the Father is on top in a corner, from which he seems to be speaking to the Virgin Mary, who is kneeling in the middle of the painting. She is holding the little baby Jesus by the feet and placing him, head first, into the mill's hopper; the twelve apostles are setting the mill in motion by turning a crank. They are assisted by the four animals of Ezekiel who are working on another side. The pope is kneeling and collecting the hosts that fall ready-made into a golden vessel. He presents one to a cardinal, which the cardinal gives to a bishop, the bishop to a priest, the priest to the people.[45]

The mill, transforming not grain but flesh, functions as a chopping machine; after being reduced to "sausage meat," the body of Christ emerges in the form of disks or, rather, hosts.

Our journey has taken us from a fast-breaking ritual celebrated with pork just as the bells were announcing the resurrection of Christ and led us to ponder the coincidence between the cycle of the pig and the destiny of Christ. At the end of this journey the parallel has become clear: Christ is incarnated in the "larder" of the Virgin just as the pig in the salting tub is buried during Lent. Both are placed in the sepulchre until Easter day. By killing the pig on Holy Thursday and eating it on Sunday, one merely recreates the time and duration of Easter and the three days that pass between the death and return to life of Christ, a killing and consumption that, in whatever manner or moment of the year they take place, refer to Christ. This affinity governs the slaughter of the pig and, in return, explains its *absolute interdiction* during the two key moments of Christ's destiny: Christmas and Holy Friday.[46] Although the prohibition is extended to all animals, it is the pig in particular that it targets. But while the slaughter of the animal coincides with the rhythms of the destiny of Christ, thus emphasizing the carnal reality of the divine being, the analogy is constantly marking its own limits; the pig is not Christ; there is never any question of confusing its slaughter with a repeated killing of Jesus. On the other hand, it is enough for these gestures to be displaced in time for their coincidence to become possible. The change in place of an isolated episode of the Passion can cause the relationship to become more sweeping, more complete, especially when a novelist brings it out, as Pirandello did in his *Novelle per un anno: Il signore della Nave.* In Agrigente, in fact, the flagellation of Christ is celebrated on September 10, and this day, which marks the resumption of slaughters, is itself the occasion for a massive pig slaughter. Pirandello brings to life the great gathering of men and animals that this celebration occasions at the edges and at the heart of the little square before Saint Nicolas Church, a country church that serves as the setting for the event. From morning on the pilgrims arrive there, the families settle in for the day, which begins with the fair. Once purchased, the pigs are placed in the expert hands of the slaughterers, the *macellai*, who slit their throats and cut them up in front of the church. They are cooked on the spot and a banquet takes place without delay, after which a procession is formed behind the statue of a dead Christ. Pirandello ends by questioning the nature of the emotion that then overcomes the faithful followers. Are they crying for Christ bleeding on his black cross or for the pig who has just been killed and eaten? Their Christ or their pig?[47]

For it is this very Christian pig that we have seen emerge in the exempla, where it is found at the sides of believers, denouncing the sacrilegious Jew. It falls to its knees before a trough where the profaners have thrown a host, uncovers the chalices that have been stolen and concealed, discovers the remains of the young martyrs sacrificed in hatred of Christ; by giving its body and heart in the place of their own, it saves Christians selected for death. Thus "sacrificed," in the image of Christ offering himself for humanity, we find it again—perhaps not surprisingly—lying at the feet of the stations of the Cross in Galician and

Portuguese churches, or represented in places one would expect to be occupied, as is the case elsewhere, by a lamb: it supports the cross when the latter marks a tomb and designates to the world, from the roofs of sacred buildings and sanctuaries, that one is before a house of God.[48]

Does it not, like Christ, have a message to transmit to us, a *testament* to bequeath? In the eschatological expectation that in Catalonia is believed will be signified by the fall of Orion's belt—three stars that survey the progress of humanity and that are called *Els Ulls de Nostre Senyor*, The Eyes of Our Lord and, also, *Els Ulls de Porc*, The Eyes of the Pig—what role does this pig play? The old people of Barcelona insist that these eyes observe men in order to take account of them and of their actions on Judgment Day.[49] Like Christ, the pig appears as a divine arbiter of posthumous destinies, and it is no doubt in this light that we must also read the initially enigmatic but necessary gestures that, everywhere, accompany its slaughter.

CHAPTER NINE

Blood and Soul

A light fog, something damp in the air, a gray, cold dawn, "un temps de cochon," pig weather . . . in short. The vast uncluttered farmyard, with the large main door open, appears barer, larger. The men have had a nip to drink. They emerge from the kitchen, one of them opens the pig hold, the pig rushes out, all dazed; the others dash forward, lasso its hind leg, down it in the middle of the courtyard. It has only time to squeal before the slaughterer knocks it out and silences it. In the past this regulation measure didn't exist and its cries echoed louder and stronger throughout the village. In Minot the cow slaughterer is the one who taught the pig slaughterer how to brain the animal. In the meantime the women hover around the kitchen door pretending to hide their faces in their hands, plugging up their ears.

—YVONNE VERDIER, *Façons de dire, façons de faire*

The day of the slaughter and distribution arrives. The pig then fits the image of the animal that is divided up and parceled out with great care among families, among those who consume it, and also among the moments—immediate or deferred—of its consumption. The very varied relationships to the living animal are set out, and even amplified, when its flesh is divided up, when it is transformed, when each of its distinct products is classified and distributed. It is our view that this death, these preparations, and this cooking revolve around the same analogical axis of which each slaughter still provides evidence. For the similarity to us is pushed when the animal is opened up. It is our mirror: its intestines, blood, and particular bones reveal a common origin.

But this humanity, which in the end is seen as Christian, is necessarily qualified, divided. The vertebra is "Jewish," as are the "intestines," which are filled with blood to make blood sausages. And in medieval Passions and iconography it is by the image of his guts escaping from his punctured belly that one signifies the exit of the soul of the most Jewish of the Jews: Judas, burned at Easter after the blood of the freshly killed pig was sprinkled around the fire "to show that he is really dead."[1] Yet, what reveals itself at Easter time to be Jewish blood is above all, let us recall, "female" blood. The secret analogy, initially legible in these fabulous births by which the sheer force of desire caused sterile women to conceive piglets, was based on the postulated equality between the physiology of women and that of sows. The exploration of an illness emblematic of the child and the pig—measles and its animal double, erysipelas or diamond skin disease—makes explicit in the domain of pathology the nature of this blood bond that, uniting mothers to their progeny, designates their common origin: menstrual blood marks both, definitively or temporarily—and according to varying degrees that go from red birth marks to leprosy. The raising of the pig by women, establishing it as an infant basking in the feminine aura, connects it even more to the food-providing mother. And this attachment is strongly affirmed on the day of the slaughter: all the animal's blood automatically goes to the women.

The Women's Share

"I am the bleeder of the pigs." This is how the last *sannaire* of a village in the Lauragais region presented himself. "It's passed down from father to son in the family. We are the "*saigneurs* of the village," he laughs (playing on the words *seigneur*, lord, and *saigner*, to bleed). The man speaking is tall, strong, and redheaded. He is also a castrator—from *sanaire* to *sannaire* is an easy step—and this twofold expertise magnifies to the highest degree the features that we have brought to light among our red men. Unlike in the Pyrenean Audoises where, in recent years, the master of the house "did his pig"—killed it himself—while, under the authority of the eldest female, the women produced the blood sausages, here the responsibility for the two operations is delegated to "professionals": the bleeder "bleeds, cuts up, prepares and salts," a village woman who always works with him "collects the blood, cleans the tripes, and makes the blood sausages." In the Lauragais region she's the *boudinière*, but we have found this same role in French-speaking Switzerland, where it falls to the *tripière*, in Catalonia to the *apañaora*, the *botifarrera* (from *botifarra*, blood sausage), or the *mandoguera*. This last designation is derived from the name of the largest blood sausage, made from the large intestine—the *mandongo*—whose forgotten root is the Frankish *mauka*, belly. We find it again, still in Catalonia, in a similar form, *mocadera*, and in Cantal. There, the *mangounière* is also a midwife, a wedding chef, and prepares the dead for burial.[2]

Thus from the bleeding of the pig to the cooking of the blood sausages an autonomous sequence is described, governing the actions of the bleeder and of the woman who "takes the blood." Her first concern is the success of the bleeding. "When the blood doesn't come as it should, the sausages aren't good," states the boudinière from Aude, who is instantly corrected by the bleeder: "It's because you didn't turn it well." And, upon the tasting of the first blood sausage or, much later, of the first sausage, one recalls the way the blood flowed. As the bleeder explains to us, "everything is in the cut of the knife." It has to strike just right, so as to produce a slow and continuous flow. Among the failures feared are "splaying the shoulder of the pig" and "piercing the trachea": "The bleeding isn't complete and the meat stays red and doesn't keep." The animal has to be "bled white," and for that the bleeder makes a distinction between "the bloods." Even when there is no apparent change, the woman who "turns the blood" knows: "Toward the end, I sense it's clearer, it doesn't clot as quickly. In the beginning, I have to stir without stopping because the first blood curdles instantly. After, I can go more slowly, there's no risk." Thus the blood circulates from the man to the woman, their movements in synch with the agony of the pig. Together, it is said, "they make the blood." Collecting it, "taking" it, is therefore not the simple, picturesque gesture fixed for centuries by the sculpted, then painted representations of the months of the year; it's work that involves a certain treatment of the blood and that not all women are suited to perform.

First, of course, women of menstrual age and pregnant women are excluded. We know the power of the former—who can prevent sauces from "taking"—and the vulnerability of the latter. But, more generally, girls and young women are kept away from the bleeding: "Once I prepared the blood. I wasn't sick or anything. But then, when I felt it clotting around my hand, I felt like vomiting—it completely sickened me. After, I told my mother-in-law to continue. I didn't want to do it anymore." When the woman doesn't have the strength to turn the blood, it's the blood that "turns" her. Only women past menopause, because they are no longer at risk, "prepare the blood" by stirring it with a wide movement. The one who collects the blood, in fact, sometimes "beats" it with a little whisk in order to separate the whitish filaments formed by the fibrin. But it is with the naked hand, forearm plunged up to the elbow in the frothy liquid, that I, personally, have always seen it done: the hand, fingers splayed, is the instrument that holds the "sponge, "the tow." This contact with the matter that "catches around one's fingers like a spider's web" constitutes the sometimes insuperable test. "You have to be strong," because "taking the blood" means not being "taken" by it. This language of force is still present in the verb *parer*, both to prepare and to parry. *Parer le sanc* is both to collect it and, in keeping with the primary meaning of the verb in French and in langue d'oc, to act against it, extracting from it the power that makes it clot and congeal like rennet, pacifying it, making it inert. And the woman whose blood is immobile is specifically designated to master this blood that is so sensitive to the feminine mood. "If you pity the pig, it holds back its blood." This belief governs behavior and justifies the distancing of all women who are too moved by its cry. The power of blood passes through women and pigs, and it should be noted that in Languedoc and Catalonia it is the feminine noun, whether singular, *parar la sanc*, or plural, *las sancs*, that designate this outpouring: blood that flows is always feminine, while the blood one speaks of generally, is, in certain places, masculine: *lo sang*. Also masculine are the values attached to "good blood," the kind transmitted by lineage, along with all the qualities that make up families and houses. Which is why, when one of our interlocutors specifies of the pig merchants that *avián la sanc!* "they had the blood," it was an entirely feminine redness he was ascribing to them. Indeed, ones says of a menstruating woman that she *a les sangs*.[3] This affinity between the blood that flows, in particular that of the pig being bled, and the blood of menstruating women is powerfully expressed in a Majorcan couplet the boys sing about the girls:

Com sa lluna fa mudances
Ses allotes fan matances
I no conviden ningú.[4]

[Like the moon has its quarters
The girls do the pig
And invite no one.]

If having one's period is having "one's moons" or "killing the pig," one would expect that the similarity between the two moments would be expressed in the other direction: menstruation is often called the "bad week," during which one is having one's "bad days." In the Basque mountains, the month of December, the month when the most pigs are killed, is also called the "bad month."[5] And this blood of the pig has an effect on women when they are having their periods or are pregnant: the sight of the flowing blood, the bloody flesh, brings with it the risk of an increased loss of blood, but touching the organs that contain blood—the spleen especially—brings on hemorrhaging and provokes miscarriages, when the child to be born isn't marked with red spots that cannot be erased.[6] This is how the distancing of young women on the day of the slaughter and, reciprocally, the role played by postmenopausal women, are explained. Why then is the latter "baptized" with a splash of blood, and why is this showering so necessary?

Our female interlocutor from the Aude, the boudinière who, for ten years, "did" sixty pigs every season, was "plastered" by the bleeder for each one. The custom is essential: no woman responsible for collecting the blood escapes it; not even, the bleeder tells us smiling, the nun of the neighboring convent where he goes every year to kill the pigs and whose immaculate winged cornet he aims for "on purpose." In upper Aragon the custom extends to little girls: when they come too close the slaughterer points his bloody knife at them and spangles their white smocks with red. Is this "baptism" in blood not precisely the mark of a fertile femininity, established ritually, in the case of little girls, or restored with every slaughter? If the women who collect the blood and make the blood sausages are always the oldest in the house, if the boudinière assumes her duties only at the age when she "has nothing more to fear," it is nonetheless necessary for the bleeder to symbolically reintroduce her into the cycle of blood by this measured spraying that makes her suitable for preparing the "women's share."

As soon as the pig is bled, after it has been scraped and washed, it is hung upside down and cut open. The strict division of tasks is then rigorously established. In order to prepare the "men's share"—the portion that goes to the salting tub—one must separate from the women and from the blood.[7] In return, when the time comes to "make the blood sausages," the women send the men off to the cafés. Let's stay with the women in order to understand the meaning of this separation (illus. 27).

In Catalonia any man who breaks the rule and enters the room, kitchen, bakehouse, or washhouse where women are working is greeted with a very particular form of mockery: "Cuckold! cuckold!" Should he approach the table, the hairy extremity of the pig's tail, *el rabillo*, is hung from his lower back. Its feigned discovery triggers hilarity and the jeering strikes the buffoon all the more as it is considered that the caudal appendice must neither be seen, touched, nor eaten by men. In Galicia this part, which the women keep within reach when they cook the blood sausages, is sometimes designated by the explicit term of *cega-maridos*, husband blinders.[8] In the Audois plain and in the region of Sault, where we were first present to witness this day, one of the jokes consisted in hiding the tip of the tail in a blood sausage that, as if by chance, was served to the man of the house at mealtime. "Holding the tail" at the moment of the slaughter is a task that falls to the youngest boy, who on this day is the object of ritual teasing: the bleeder—in solidarity with the women—asks him for his knife to scrape the pig and lets it slip into the anus of the dead animal, where it disappears. In order to recuperate it, the boy must plead his case with the women who will later wash the guts. Thus the pig's tail is used to ridicule these two opposing moments in men's lives. Ultimately confiscated by the women who cook the blood, the sight of it exposes any man who enters the room where the blood sausages are being prepared to jokes about his cuckoldry. And this "blindness" brings us back to the question of feminine power.

Is it not the women's presence and the blood of the pig they are handling that would "blind" the men, and particularly the most virile among them? Yet it is precisely with respect to the inverse risk—that to which the men, by their presence, would subject the cooking blood sausages—that this relationship is specified in other places. In Poitou, Angoumois, Saintonge, and Limousin the belief that men "make the blood pop out of the intestines" if they watch them cook explains the interdiction: no man may witness the operation. A corollary to this banishment is the "mocking" custom of a "blood sausage baptism"— often noted and commented upon—intended to ward off the feared rupture. The procedure is quite uniform: for each blood sausage, just as it is being placed in the cauldron, one utters "the name of a cuckold"— and, adds the narrator, "the list was long! The women compiled an inventory of all the men who wore horns in the village and all those from the neighboring farms." Which is why, in some places, a single "blood sausage sponsor" was elected—the most cuckold of the commune—and "his name is spoken gently and distinctly like a kind of incantation, in the name of . . . in the name of . . . swinging the blood sausages by the hook that holds them together against the lip of the cauldron."[9] Just as femininity is a factor by the salting tub, which women are forbidden to approach if they are of menstrual age, is virility not being evaluated before the cooking sausages? The most threatened and most threatening person is the grown man, the "husband," who is granted a power—the man of the house is said to "judge the blood sausages"—that now turns against him. To "cuckolds," in other words, to those whose virility is deficient, devolves a powerlessness that makes them suitable sponsors for the blood sausages: it prevents them from bursting.

There are two possibilities when it comes to the blood sausages: either the man is already blind, or he becomes so. What mustn't he see? And what are the women concocting around these smoking vats, hovering over bowels filled with blood, a blood that is prey to forces that need to be tamed?

Women at Work

In the warm room the normally talkative women are silent. All eyes converge on the large copper pot, the surface of which is beginning to wrinkle. But the tension that is making their bodies stiff as they stand in a circle reflects not just the state of anticipation: each one participates in the cooking, which, in order to be successful, requires their active presence. In western France the official cook recalled the operation's guiding principles before it even began: during the entire process each woman had to be careful not to let slip "the slightest improper remark." She herself must "exercise restraint," in other words, "abstain from going where no one could have gone in her place."[10] Elements for understanding the Saintonge cooks were first furnished us in Scandinavia, where studies on the preparation of blood sausages were conducted in 1917, 1944, and 1973. There, at the heart of the numerous directives governing this preparation, we found the precept expressed more directly.[11] Once assured that no man would bother them—since there, too, a man's presence would cause the blood sausages to burst—the cooks observe a silence as one of them taps each sausage on the edge of the vessel or against the mantle of the chimney and drops it into the pot. From that moment on, all the women must "hold their breath and squeeze their lips and buttocks" without stopping, so that the blood sausages don't "fart." The only speech allowed is the "prayer of the blood sausages," an incantation—sung softly rather than spoken—addressed to each sausage and also intended to ward off bursting. Let us join Nils-Arvid Bringeus—who attempted to bring order to the corpus assembled by researchers

from Denmark, Norway, and Sweden—and examine some of these
unusual orations:

> Be hard as a stake
> Solid as a vulva
> Hold together
> And don't burst.

A first metaphorical axis suggests an analogy between the blood
sausages and the male sex organ. In addition to "stakes," we find
"sticks," "horns," "pipes," and "posts," objects that, according to
Bringeus, refer clearly to the penis without naming it. The female sex
organ, for its part, is designated in crude and direct fashion and often
identified with that of the speaker. Progressing beyond the usual
explanation—that of women working among themselves and without
men, a situation that would authorize playfulness and linguistic
obscenity—Bringeus invites us to take their words at face value. If the
female sexual organ is invoked so directly, and, notably, its resistance
and solidity, it is because it is directly concerned: the cooking of blood
sausages is a *birthing*. Just as, during the delivery, one expects the
vagina to hold together, so the guts must "hold" during the cooking.[12]
This reading is confirmed and further illustrated in our area. First, in
Languedoc and in the eastern Pyrenees, the *mangonièra*, or boudinière,
is frequently a midwife, or at least a "helper." An equivalent aptitude
is thus required for "making babies" and "making blood sausages."
Each of these moments necessitates the distancing of the men and
constitutes a threat to their virility. Like the husbands whose wives
cook the blood sausages, those whose wives are giving birth mustn't
enter the room, at the risk of mockery and teasing whose meaning is
clear.[13] The analogy is extended when, comparing the Scandinavian
region with the methods and expressions of southern Europe, this
cooking of the blood sausages is recognized not only as a birthing, as
Bringeus chose to show, but as all the states that women "pass
through"—from conception to gestation to birthing—as they conduct the delicate operation. A rereading from this perspective of the
silence and corporeal rigidity that has been noted everywhere invites
comparison with the posture recommended, in Europe since the sixteenth century, by works on fertilization: the woman is advised to
squeeze her fists, jaws, and vagina in an all-over bodily tension during
the sexual act. The Scandinavian blood sausage prayers, upon close
inspection, are distinctly evocative of this moment. Upon striking the

blood sausage against the wall, for instance, the mistress of the Scandinavian home says:

> Hold like a rod
> And not like the skin of a cunt
> They held together
> My mother told me so.[14]

As the expression "they held together" suggests, the prayers bring about the conjunction of the sexes. For, by virtue of their words, the women hold this power or at least appropriate more than just the solidity and force of the male instrument of procreation. Its "skin," that of the scrotum, becomes the model of a resistance they adopt for this "important work." The women must "hold" like men, but without men. Does the cuckoldry that threatens those who venture into the room where blood sausages are cooking not first make them, by antiphrasis, into *couillons* (both testicles and dimwits)? Baptizing the blood sausages under the sponsorship of a "cuckold" or reciting the prayer by which the cooks take on the force of men thus come down to the same thing. Moreover, a similar gesture—gently striking the blood sausage three times against the pot, the wall, or the chimney mantle—manifests the common reference to the baptism of children. Bringeus already noted the similarity in his Nordic area. In the second half of the eighteenth century, according to a customary Swedish ritual, the godmother, holding the newborn by the head and feet, tapped it three times against the door of the church or the house "to protect it from boils," those swellings of the skin that also threaten the blood sausages as they cook.[15] The ritual is the same for both. We have already seen that "baptisms" for piglets, and second baptisms for sick or bewitched children, constituted effective remedies.

But the "blood sausage baptism" does not apply to completed beings: they are baptized before being cooked, and are thus like "children" in the process of growing. Is the feared "bursting," which the advance baptism averts, not therefore something of a premature delivery? An elaboration of our investigation into the pieces of the pig—organs or parts—accused of "making the blood sausages pop" will add to this correspondence.

In Catalonia, in the Pallars Sobirà, after splitting the pig, the bleeder removes from the belly, on either side of the opening, a strip of whitish flesh with a very delicate taste—the "streaky bacon"—which is instantly eaten. "They say that this piece doesn't keep and that if the slightest particle of it were left on the meat that is added to the blood sausages they would burst."[16] The Catalan *xuia arrebentadora*—bursting bacon—is also called *rosta llevadora*, "birthing bacon." As soon as it is detached by the bleeder, the *rosta* is given to the cooks, who prepare it and eat it among themselves before beginning their preparation of the blood sausages. The equivalency postulated earlier between "bursting" and "miscarrying" is as if reflected and redoubled in the Catalan name and in the use that women make of this morsel.

The spleen further affirms the role played by certain parts of the pig in this preparation process that associates the cooks of the blood with pregnant women. In Galicia the *paxarela* is accused of provoking miscarriages and is considered responsible for the red marks on newborns. Thus pregnant women are kept away from the slaughter and from all the operations that follow: they must particularly avoid seeing or touching the spleen. In Castile a large violet birthmark on the face bears the name *melsa*—spleen—while saying that a girl's "spleen hurts" clearly means she's pregnant. The langue d'oc *melsa* is included within the same semantic field, designating both the organ and the whimsical mood of a capricious girl. In Latvia, when it is eaten, the spleen is given to young girls, for it has the virtue of making their hair grow.[17] But usually the spleen is not eaten by humans; according to the common argument, its reputation is everywhere tainted with the same defect, that of "making the blood sausages burst." Common practice confirms this rejection: the spleen is given to the cat, whose share it becomes. If we return to the Scandinavian investigation into the cooking of blood sausages, an equally complex reality comes to light, emphasizing the positions and uses of the organ that appear contradictory and that can only be understood by looking at everything we now know. From Denmark to Norway the spleen is in principle thrown away: it makes the blood sausages burst and is considered unfit for consumption; its name is taboo. However by the name of "herdsman," "guardian," "patron," "saver of blood sausages," it is sometimes placed in the pot, where it cooks next to them, or else is placed in a visible spot on the chimney near the hearth, its presence then forestalling the fatal bursting. Another part of the pig is used in the same ways and enjoys the same powers: the bloody triangular piece the bleeder cuts from the throat, from the spot where he planted the knife. Although considered inedible, this morsel, which acts as a "saver of blood sausages," is given, cooked, to the animals of the house.[18]

Thus we find a remarkable correspondence between the Spanish and Scandinavian domains. Behind the seeming diversity of the parts considered dangerous, a coherence is revealed: it is always from the perspective of blood that their use or exclusion is justified, but in neither cases is this use or exclusion complete.[19] Disconnected from its name, designated by metaphor or periphrasis, or unmentioned by virtue of a principle that appears to unify arguments and practices from Catalonia to Norway, the spleen constitutes both the disturbing and regulating element of the system, but in it are first objectified the powers attributed to women's blood. While some are kept away from the pig precisely "because of their blood," the women responsible for preparing and cooking the pig's blood are introduced into the fertile cycle upon being "baptized" with a stream of it. Similarly, this part must always be symbolically manipulated, as it is a part that, in the body of the animal, retains the force of the blood, the capacity for dissolving it, or, on the contrary, of making it congeal, of making it *like flesh*.

After chasing away the men and appropriating their procreative power, after baptizing these budding beings, the women entrap the "saver of the blood sausages." But their task is not complete—far from it. It is, in fact, during the cooking time that the perils to which these blood children and their worried cooks are exposed are fully revealed.

The Witch's Kitchen

In Bavaria, if the water begins to boil during the cooking of blood sausages, an old broom handle must immediately be burned to scare off the witches.[20] The belief that boiling convenes evil forces is widespread. It spans the centuries and regions with nuances and subtleties that a list of "superstitions" collected in the Comtat Venaissin at the end of the eighteenth century renders perfectly. Of the housewife whose soup spills it is said that "her house fills with demons."[21] This eruption of the infernal, this reversal of the domestic order, are thus risks women confront and assume when cooking the blood sausages according to a technique that, hovering about an unstable limit, threatens to "spill over" in a manner whose forms and nature we shall now identify.

Wherever they work—washrooms, oven rooms, a former unused kitchen that has since become the "women's workshop"—it is in the midst of a thick fog, amid the insipid odor of guts, fat, and blood carried by the steam of the water being heated, that the women move into action. Several vats are going at the same time: the largest, which in langue d'oc receives a feminine augmentative, the *pairòla*, the "cauldroness," is first filled with the mixture to be cooked before being stuffed into the intestines. A woman bearing a long fat stick—in the

Audois Pyrenees it is called the *remena*, which is also used for making buckwheat and corn soup—turns the mixture of fat and "bloody meats" with a continuous movement so that it doesn't solidify. Meanwhile, the others chop the "herbs" into small pieces: spinach and white-beets in eastern Languedoc, but also wild greens and "blood plants" (artemesia, nettles, red poppies . . .), the same ones that were mixed into the animals' gruel and that they also consumed in springtime health treatments and at critical moments in their physiological cycles. Every house has its "secret."

Midway through the cooking, the content of the vat is colored green by the herbs and later will tend toward brown, when the blood is added, after the mixture has been removed from the fire and cooled. Poured in uncooked, the blood clarifies the sauce, which must continue to be turned: the remena keeps stirring and homogenizing the mixture. Pouring five liters of blood necessarily entails some splattering, and it is up to the women to mutually "baptize" one another, united by laughter. Sometimes a man stops behind the closed door, knocks, and asks, "What are you up to in there?" Of course he receives no reply. Sheltered from the eyes of men, this is the moment for the women to perform their divination. In Germany they examine the spleen, in the folds of which they count the deaths to come. In Scandinavia they examine its thickness: if it is even, it announces an early and hard winter, while irregularity indicates pleasant weather, a mild season. In Corsica "the liver of the animal reveals who will next be pregnant in the house where the sacrifice occurred or in the vicinity." In Calabria the pig's kidney is cut lengthwise in two and put up to boil in the vat, then removed and checked to see whether its two halves match up. If so, the pregnant woman on whose behalf the oracle was consulted will give birth to a boy. The same prediction may result from cleaning the guts and separating them from the epiploon, the membrane that binds and covers them with a fine white web, which is compared, by the name of "fringe," to the hair of a newborn: gathered into a "ball," the fringe indicates that a boy is on the way. Interrogating the internal organs of the pig is an art long practiced by women, but now lost. In the region of Sault our oldest female interlocutors spoke of women whom they called "gut readers" without being able to tell us precisely of what their reading consisted.[22] And we have seen how the cooking of the blood sausages is still accompanied by magical discourse, with unorthodox prayers and conjurations being exchanged by the women, sheltered from the men, whom they threaten with "blindness." Is there not something witchlike about these blood cooks? In our Pyrenean region it falls to the oldest woman to fabricate from the caecum, the "blind" intestine—taking infinite precautions since it breaks easily—a large blood sausage referred to locally as the *breisha* or *maramauca*: the witch, the nightmare. Dropped into the water first, like the *melsat*, no doubt, the "saver of the blood sausages," it protects from the feared bursting and in particular from the gaze of witches, whom it casts back from the depths of the caldron.[23]

To deflect the "evil eye," in fact, doors and windows are closed; the room, lit only by the hall light, is immersed in darkness. In Franche-Comté the grandmother is appointed to watch over the cooking sausages, to make sure the "witches" stay out. Aside from the meanness ascribed to them, prompting them to make the blood sausages burst out of sheer spite—for they don't know how to "prepare the pig" themselves, which is a fundamental difference—their covetousness and gluttony also prompt them to steal the blood sausages during the cooking process or to send their emissaries. In Wallonia, where Christmas is celebrated by eating the blood sausage made from the pig killed the day before, undesirable visitors taking advantage of the Midnight Mass sometimes beat the members of the house to their feasts. There the sorcerer, the *macré*, has the power to *fénn'aler les tripes* (make blood sausages disappear). All he needs to do is spread a white sheet near the dwelling at midnight:

> Soon you could see the blood sausages exiting the chimney and descending the wall. The sorcerer grabbed the first blood sausage and threw it far behind him, shouting *vola t' pourt* (here's your share). He was speaking to the devil. The other blood sausages were divided up among those present. The next day we found the pot empty. The water in which they had been cooked was filled with soot.[24]

But, more commonly, the cooking of the blood sausages attracts a multitude of hungry little beings around the cauldrons who descend the chimneys and clamp on to the chimney hooks. Every peasant society of Europe knows of and names these characters—we'll call them gnomes or elves to simplify things when discussing them globally, reserving their vernacular names for particular cases. These creatures, over the course of the Twelve Days between Christmas and Epiphany, manifest their presence noisily and ostentatiously on the approaches to homes. If they manage to get inside, they dirty them, urinating in the pots, sprinkling ashes and soot in the cauldrons, or, even more viciously, attacking the cooks and their blood sausages, women and their children.

In Cyprus, Greece, and on the islands of the Aegean sea their arrival also coincides with the slaughter of the Christmas pig. Beginning on Christmas eve the women prepare sausages and blood sausages; from the large glittering vats wafts the pleasant smell of meats cooking in a stock of wine and herbs in preparation for being stuffed into the intestines. On this day tradition has it that one eats thin pancakes with bacon, the *pittès*. But no sooner has the pig been bled than *kalikandjarai*, attracted by the blood, rush in to lick up the splatterings from the court-yard. They try, moreover, to steal the intestines from the women, devouring them instantly if they are successful. They also attack the skins put out to dry and pull out the bristles, with which they are said to make their bonnets. They are constantly bothering the cooks with their whining. To prevent them from descending from the roofs, where they act up, threatening at any moment to spoil the contents of the cauldron by sliding down the chimney, the women throw pancakes and blood sausages for them to fight over. On this same occasion the *mazzarelo* of Friouli and the Venitian *sanguanelo* arrive at homes where a bit of pork is reserved for them, a "liver sausage." In Lithuania on so-called sausage festival day, the *kaukai* are given blood sausages, "pig intestines stuffed with flour and blood," while in Germany a plate of "slaughter soup" goes to them.[25] All, on this day, receive a gift of pork. Are they not coming to collect their share? The Walloon *macré* unabashedly take it; the cooks of the Audois Pyrenees prepare a *breisha* or *maramauca*, a type of blood sausage specifically for the spirits. But who are these spirits? And what authorizes them to exercise this right?

Blood and Milk

Let's start with the Cyprian gnomes. Endowed with speech, they directly accuse the cooks, "their mothers," of not having baptized them and thus of making them kalikandjarai. The status of the dead child without a baptism or a similar status—aborted children, stillborns, even children killed at birth by their mothers—characterizes all these elves, from the Mediterranean to northernmost Europe.[26] Though each has its particularities, a certain number of features and behaviors are common to all. First, all are feared by women—by new mothers especially—who are afraid of potentially fatal attacks on themselves and their infants. Many stories present one of these elves, disguised as a human, attempting to trick a midwife, asking her in the middle of the night to visit a woman in confinement in order to secretly exchange the newborn once inside the house.[27] In Cyprus, where Christmas is also a celebration of the Virgin and her birthing, *koumouliès*—the ritual pancakes brought to the bedside of women who have just delivered—are offered to Mary and exchanged among the neighboring women.[28] On the day when they make the blood sausages, the cooks also participate in this nativity. Placed entirely under the sign of birth, the period of the Twelve Days—at each celebration of which we have seen that the "baptism of Christ" is acted out, even though there is a prohibition against baptism—releases the kalikandjarai. Not having been freed by this baptismal sacrament—the first to "whiten" the Christian from the maternal redness—a blood bond, that of their birth and of their violent death, attaches them to women in childbirth and, consequently, to the blood cooks. They are visibly marked by this redness; their clothing—red bonnets, red jackets and shoes and, even little slippers—exhibits it on the surface, but they are also deeply impregnated by it. In Lorraine the word *sôtré* or *sutrêt* is used both for our creature and for menstrual blood, while the Venetian sanguanelo, with its red hair and bloodshot eyes, carries a same wealth of meaning.[29]

Some are still represented with a pig snout and bristles or, simply, as piglets, by virtue of the equally widespread belief that aborted children sacrificed by criminal mothers appear in this form.[30] This close bond to women's blood and to the pig, one equaling the other, allows us to understand the urgent attraction they feel both for the confined women and for the freshly bled animals. Throughout their liberation during the period of the Twelve Days, these "innocent" children, who arrive with the wild hunting party that travels the winter sky night after night behind Herod, mutate into ferocious meat eaters. Except for during this moment, they preserve an infant status in death, because of which they naturally tend toward milky foods and grain porridges. Fixed in this state and at this age, they nonetheless grow older, as signified by the long bushy beards and sharp claws with which they are sometimes presented. When they are not irresistibly drawn to blood, they return to their favorite foods, for which they are insatiable: the sanguanelo accepts only polenta and milk, the *maʒarol* likes ricotta cheese—a fresh cheese from lambs—the little *sarrasin* from Ariège pancakes and millet porridge, which is also served to their childlike mother the fairy. And all, when they have gained entry into human homes, eat bountifully without growing or getting fat, demanding their food with loud cries for, with the exception of the talkative kalikandjarai and the Scandinavian *yping*, they express themselves most often in this manner. One might speculate that, being neither baptized nor weaned, they are unable to acquire speech, which their minimal use of language seems to confirm.[31] Some stammer a few words, but most limit themselves to the cooing of newborns, when they aren't mimicking the inflections of the human voice as a means of trickery, for they are great imitators. Indeed, their power lies in their ability to adopt the appearance and take the place of small children. And they use this power, seconded by fairies, witches, and devils, who exchange the healthy infant for a sickly, malicious, whimpering creature, sometimes without anyone's noticing.

In all cases this evil deed is possible because the child has not been baptized. It is still a "piece of flesh," a "Moor," a "Sarrasin," even a "piglet" or a "child of the devil." All our little ghosts eventually cross one or another of these known figures. Even the "little Jew" is among them. In several German provinces, the *Jüdel* or *Jüdchen* is the soul of a dead child that hasn't been baptized. Associated with "nightmares," it haunts the sleep of newborns and crushes them in their cribs. Extensive contact with it also provokes "red spots" on their bodies and skin diseases, including measles. It is warded off, in fact, by placing a scarlet piece of fabric at the head of the crib. Like the kalikandjarai, which are also said in the north of Greece and as far as Albania to be the "souls of Jews," it seeks blood and attaches itself to women in labor.[32] The substitution effected by the *lutons*, *sôtrés*, or *mazarols* is therefore inscribed in the logic of the change that baptism is alleged to produce, even if it reverses the principle. By postulating a similarity of nature between the changers and the "changed," it makes the question of their recognition even more critical. Except when, like the kalikandjarai, they appear in noisy gangs and show themselves bare-faced, that is, at their most animal and diabolical, the "changelings"—children of fairies and all the elves or goblins put in the place of the child of the house—are not differentiated from the latter.

This similarity is further expanded in the ambiguous roles played by the children themselves on the occasion of the holidays that mark the Twelve Days' cycle. We have already seen the young boys between seven and twelve called upon to "play the innocents," Herod's young victims; we find them circulating in groups from house to house, taking up collections beginning at Advent. These rounds, in the Landes, Chalosse, or Béarn, take such a particular turn that they have attracted the attention of ethnographers and inspired various interpretations.[33] Dressed in rags, the young children travel a circuit that includes only the homes where a child was born since the previous Christmas. If the donors aren't generous enough, the *pique-hoù*, as they are called, produce an unusual litany of threats. Terrible predictions are made about the newborn: he will become "black as the chimney hook," will remain small, "no bigger than a shoe," or will be "twisted like a pig's tail." In their curses the children go so far as to call for the death of the infant. *Crèba, crèba, crèba,* "Die!" they cry, like an evil spell, pointing in the direction of the windows with the skewers they carry to steal sausages and blood sausages. The form these rounds take, the choice of only homes where a newborn is found, the threats made to this newborn (is it not a matter of "changing" him into a demonical being?), the "game" of the actors, their forced reception into the home, each of these details is illuminated when we consider the "descents" the kalikandjarai make upon homes, where they, like the pique-hoù, are assured of finding freshly bled pigs and newborn children. In the Landes ritual the young boys who play the role of creatures from the beyond—in some instances, they cease performing these collections upon their first communion—also loudly demand their share of the pig and, particularly, the "tripes" and "blood sausages." The meaning to be ascribed to this detail, so seemingly banal it has been neglected by ethnographers, becomes clear on the occasion of collections whose only reason for being is the presence of a slaughtered pig, quite a few of which are killed in the days before Christmas.

It is thus as recognition of their right to this portion—in which the infant and the blood sausages are construed as equivalent objects—that the children are made to act out, in the time and space assigned to the visits of the dead children, their attack against the newborn or their kidnapping of the piglet. But if we look at it closely, the boys play a more complex role. In Chalosse it is by the repeated cry of *Ahum! Ahum!* that the pique-hoù announce their presence, skewer in hand. Now these "children's cries," on the eve of Christmas, in the region of the Pyrenean torrent of Oloron, would have the power to stop the witches on the verge of casting a spell on a newborn or kidnapping it.[34] A broadening of our perspective confirms this new meaning. In northern Italy, in the provinces of Treviso and Belluno, the rounds of the boys, equipped with these same skewers, but also with chimney hooks and stools, take the form of a "witch charivari," when the instruments are not involved in silent rituals—sometimes limited to a simple gesture like that of unhooking the chimney hook or knocking over the stool—intended to ward off their evil deeds. In the Genovese countryside, the first Thursday of January, when the dangerous period of the Twelve Days is over, masked boys parade through the village streets,

announcing their presence by crying *I fanciullin, i fanciullin!* "The little children!" There they are welcomed into homes and, like the dead,
are given a portion of chestnuts they silently accept. Before the troop
withdraws, the "company chief" takes the chain of the chimney hook,
unhooked since the day before in order to prevent the witches "from
shaking it" during the night, and walks around the kitchen or the house
three times, dragging it behind him. This is said to ward off the witches
or prevent them from entering.[35]

The ritual that follows the collection sheds light on the young boys'
action: they too work to defend these precious and vulnerable possessions we have seen them attack. By standing in for the visitors from
beyond, they keep them away. The reason they can play such a dangerous role is because they are protected, by their baptism, from total identification with the beings they incarnate. Separated from their diabolical origin by the sacrament, the new Christians become the agents, then
the actors, of rituals explicitly destined to combat both the young vindictive dead and the witches who are connected to them. In eighteenth-
century Scotland this quality was effective the day of the baptism. Just
home from church, the newly baptized child was passed around the
chimney hook three times. This gesture was intended "to increase the
resistance of the pots in which liquids are boiled or foods cooked," but
it also had the power to "ward off the evil spells of witches and bad
spirits on newborns."[36] All this forms a cohesive whole, and the
Scottish ritual, by bringing us back to cooking and fear of bursting,
which a single "baptismal" gesture applied to the blood sausages and to
the children already conjured, only highlights through these chain
reactions the circular relationship uniting children and their avatars—
blood sausages and gnomes, the culinary recipients, and, more broadly,
the objects of the fire—with women, cooks, midwives, and witches.

Let us further consider the form of the ritual and its instrument. We
have already noted, with respect to the Twelve Days, the presence of
skewers, stools, and chimney hooks, which as an exception have been
removed from the hearths, and the manner in which the boys used
them in their rounds as offensive and defensive weapons. But it is in the
hands of women that the efficacity expected of such objects when
applied to fragile infants is fully revealed. Such is the case of the passage around the chimney hook, the same gesture witches perform to
"change" newborns: either they turn them around the hearth's chain
"three times," as they confessed before judges, or they "vow them by
sorcery to the devil" by making them "crawl by themselves to the

chimney hook," transformed into black little clawed creatures. Triple rotation around a skewer produces a similar effect, and we know that midwives, of sinister repute, changed newborns by "passing them through the fire" under the pretext of warming them, the customary birth practice.[37] This is why gnomes and the unfortunate children who died without baptism hover around chimneys in expectation of the change or the hoped for exchange, on the very site and against the objects likely to make them effective. How, then, can we distinguish the "real" children from these imitators, who borrow the formers' appearance and take their places in the home, when a simple gesture—the gesture of a woman or of a witch—suffices for the transformation? How can we be sure that these blood sausages, over which invisible powers have rights, belong entirely to the human and domestic universe? Into the blood sausages, the *nenòts*, as the mangonièra of Cantal calls them when she presents "her children" to those gathered after their cooking, the women themselves inserted the "sorceress" and the "nightmare," similar in every way, which slipped out of their hands. Since they render suspect everything they do, it is now up to them to dissipate doubt, to make the distinction. And it is perhaps with this task, which ultimately qualifies them as women, that the secret of our cooks is revealed to us.

Pancakes and Blood Sausages

We have seen beings from the beyond emerge from the chimney, either because an involuntary boiling over of the vats triggers their liberation or because, when the time comes, the house is open to their presence. Although tolerated during the period of the Twelve Days, the ploy of the little gnomes, using the chimney hook as a ladder by which they mount and descend, sullying everything they touch in their passage, must come to an end. Until then, the women came to terms with them. In Greece and on the islands of the Aegean sea they fed them pancakes and sausages, while keeping them at a respectful distance from the pig meat, which they never let out of their sight. Thus much surveillance is required around the fire, where the flavorful meats are turned. When, attracted by the smell, the kalikandjarai get too close, they receive a burning skewer instead of the anticipated morsel.[38] Day after day, everyone mobilizes to contain them, unable to distance them in any lasting way. They are threatened with "baptism" for, despite their recriminations, they are considered unable to receive it, having become diabolical creatures. The men throw burning bits of straw at them, women in labor place scissors and knives under their beds, housewives put sieves on their doorsteps "so they can keep themselves busy counting the holes," and this goes on until the women, by the appropriate ritual that takes place the eve of the Epiphany, obtain their departure. That evening, in Cyprus, they secretly knead the dough necessary for the fabrication of *lalaggoudkia* or *xerotania*, the wheat pancakes, for the last time. Throughout this first operation they mustn't open their mouths, no words must pass their lips. When midnight strikes, they rise without a word and, still silent, begin cooking the pancakes. They then go out into the courtyards and vigorously thrust three pancakes up to the roof, stating in a loud and clear voice:

> Little slice of sausage, little slice of sausage,
> Black-handled knife,
> Piece of pancake.
> Eat and leave
> For the old priest is coming
> With his sprinkler and his stick (illus. 28).[39]

Only at this moment do the kalikandjarai disappear. Does this mean that the pancakes and the stuffed intestines, reversing the force of attraction they habitually exercise over the kalikandjarai, now make them flee? How is such a change possible?

Moving from rituals to stories that present "fantastical creatures" gravitating around the cooks will allow us to map out the cluster of relationships that, from food to words, constitutes the operative mechanism. In western Europe they depict a single stratagem imagined by a woman to make the undesirable quest reveal itself, with the understanding that its identity is always uncertain. A young mother stricken with doubt as to the nature of her child, which has become whiny and insatiable, and suspecting that a fairy has substituted her little one during her absence—it is usually specified that the infant wasn't baptized or that its mother had omitted to "cross" the child before going out—consults a neighbor who suggests that she boil a pot full of water, milk, and porridge, but also nut shells, "without laughing or speaking," which she carefully does. In Gascony the *hadet*—the fairy's child—instantly cries out, "The milk is rising!" or, "The milk is vanishing, the milk is boiling!" and faints. Its real mother sometimes has time to run and put the stolen child back in place.[40]

It is thus around words and food—the two being indissociable—that the singular bond attaching these alien children to women is bound and unbound. In the stories the manner in which the women apply themselves to performing each gesture, their meditative silent bearing, is the same as that of the Cypriot women performing the annual nocturnal ritual that delivers them from the pesky kalikandjarai. But, in every European country where we encounter them, the stories emphasize the efficient culinary technique, boiling, and its instrument, the cauldron. We know that boiling attracts "evil forces" and this is indeed what happens: the elf speaks, its mother dashes in. Women know and use this property; because they master the mechanism they capture its force. Overflowing, which is feared at other moments, is necessary here for the usual order of things, domestic peace, to be reestablished. Only a ritual can bring about this positive reversal.

But, in the case that interests us, that of the elves, the effective technique is combined with specific ingredients that also serve to identify them. Given that porridge is classically the dish that is cooked at the boiling point, it is not surprising that it should appear in the majority of the stories involving these strange infants. It is their favorite dish, the one that is especially prepared for them. Yet alongside the porridge stories appear variations that, at first glance, seem highly enigmatic, in which pork makes an appearance and is served to the suspicious child. It is now that the gift of meat given the kalikandjarai and the young collectors of the Twelve Days takes on full meaning. In several German, Danish, and Swedish provinces a changeling took the place of the child of the house. Following the model of the "porridge and cauldron" stories, but this time without recourse to outside advice, its mother prepared sausages or blood sausages as a test, even "a fat milk pig roasted in its skin," which caused the *wechselbalg* of Oldenbourg to exclaim, before disappearing, "Old as I am, I have never seen such a big sausage." A Danish story goes even farther. The mother of an unbaptized child, intrigued by the change perceived in her infant, which suddenly began to whimper discontentedly, and being a "shrewd woman," killed her pig alone and in secret. With it she made a "black blood sausage," a single blood sausage that condensed the entire animal—blood, skin, hair, bones, and flesh combined—into its intestines (thereby implementing the belief that "a good pig must be able to fit entirely inside its guts") and presents it to the changeling. Struck dumb initially, he literally bursts:

A blood sausage with skin
A blood sausage with hair
A blood sausage with eyes
A blood sausage with bones inside

Three times I saw a young forest
Grow on Lake Tiis
And never have I seen such a blood sausage
The devil won't stay here much longer!

And he disappears "forever."[41]

The parallel between the Cypriot ritual in which the kalikandjarai are offered pancakes and pork and the stories that revolve around these two elements is remarkable. Seeing the porridge and the blood sausages, the elves, children of the fairy and the devil, speak. As we have emphasized, with the exception of the Greek kalikandjarai and the Scandinavian yping, who say what they are and what they want during the period of the Twelve Days, these beings remain silent. But we now know, from having heard them, that this silence is not mutism. To break it the women take advantage of a property of boiling that is well known to them: what makes the blood sausages burst makes the elves and the changelings "burst." All that is shown by the beliefs relative to these very old and very crafty characters is that they are subject to a pact of silence to which they in turn subject humans, who accept their services and companionship. Respect for this contract is the condition under which they are kept in the home that welcomes them as "domestic genies," zealously performing productive tasks. They always act without speaking, in order, they say, not to betray the "secret" of their art—that of welding and boilermaking for some, of dairy production and fermentation for others.[42] Humans, for their part, know that one should never ask them questions; this interdiction applies particularly to their age—which we have heard them state at emotional moments—and to their identity. Simply saying to the fairy, "You are *fada*" (which means, in langue d'oc, both a "fairy" and "crazy") makes her faint immediately, just as all our gnomes disappear once the fatal words have been pronounced. Is it not perhaps the case that speaking causes boiling?

The Words That Kill

In Germany one says that "talking too much while cooking the blood sausages makes them burst," but in Scandinavia simply talking provokes an instantaneous rupture. Recall the cooks watching their cauldron, their mouths sealed, buttocks squeezed tight, holding their breath. But unlike blood sausages that merely burst, the kalikandjarai, the elves, and the changelings speak. What do they say? The kalikandjarai say "pancake," "sausage"; the Danish elf repeats "a blood sausage" over and over like a litany; the *hadet* says "The milk is boiling," "The milk is pouring," and all the gnomes are surprised, finally, before "so many little boiling pots." To speak is thus also to designate, to identify by naming the objects that are presented to them and the processes they undergo. Is it not because they speak these words that they burst? As for the women who trigger speech, silently bringing their pots to boil, are they not prompting the utterance of what they themselves keep silent? The prohibition against speech while cooking blood sausages also extends to a prohibition against naming them. This too takes effect as soon as the blood begins to spurt—perhaps even well before, if we consider that the word *pig* is not mentioned anywhere. In Scandinavia you can't say "bleed the pig" but only "take the red" or "sweat it." In Denmark, where "to sweat" is used as a euphemism for "to bleed," the word *sweat* is prohibited throughout the preparation of the blood, while in Denmark the blood sausages can be called "sweat sausage." The fact that the English word *sausage* can mean both sausage and blood sausage is a confusion that no doubt results from a similar prohibition. As for the spleen, the organ reputed to make blood sausages burst, many periphrastic creations already noted—"saver of sausages," "herdsman," or "patron"—help to circumvent its mention; in Gascony and Languedoc it becomes "sacristan" and "belly tongue."[43] Finally, the boiling point itself, which must be avoided, is lexically taboo. Yvonne Verdier noted it already with regard to laundry.[44] Generally, the terms of substitution used by the washerwomen who create steam are used as well in the culinary domain. When a kettle is on the fire, one avoids letting it boil because it makes the water "heavy" and, if need be, it is preferable to say that it is "simmering," "humming," "jumping," or "popping."

Making the blood sausages boil or talking while cooking them both make them burst. Women know this and keep quiet during this delicate phase of the cooking. But, more than a causal relationship, a similarity is posited between two operations that, consequently, must always be separate. Witches alone not only talk without stopping, but repeat "boil and bubble" to their cauldrons.[45] Herein lies the difference, and it is an essential one, even if the cooks employ the equivalency to make these visitors from the beyond speak and to send them back—these visitors who come to fight them for their children of flesh and blood. By offering them blood sausages to name, a boiling to designate, they catch them in the trap of words they themselves silence, knowing their powers. And this speech makes them "burst," finally differentiating them from the real blood sausages, the real children, both of which are baptized and thus have nothing to fear.

Children Changed, Children Exchanged

Once cooked and ready, blood sausages can be looked at, measured, counted, named—all things until then forbidden. As soon as they are removed from the cauldron, a basket lined with fresh straw or white linen awaits them. In Cantal, greased by the mangonièra with a piece of lard to make them shine, the *nenòts*, the babies, are presented for all to see. In Poitou a toast is held in their honor, the master of the house is congratulated—who, as we have seen, had nothing to do with the process—kidding his wife who "made a big one." Then comes the moment for distribution, gift giving and consumption, which is always a solemn and collective affair, for these bitterly defended children already no longer belong to their mother. Saved from the covetousness of the dead children, and from witches, they circulate among the living and are exchanged among homes according to rules that should now be elucidated.

First, in several regions of France, everyone "goes to the blood," to the house that killed the pig. In Aunis and Saintonge the "blood sausage soup" is consumed among neighbors, after each guest has "given it a turn" with a large wooden spoon. Everyone takes some home in a pot, with which guests come prepared. The poor are also included in this distribution. In Languedoc one receives not soup but the *présent* or gift: the mesentery, the "caul," divided up into so many shares. Each person will wrap up the blood sausages along with a little backbone, liver, and streaky bacon. Protected by this bonnet, which completes the analogy between the blood sausage and the coddled child, the gift goes to relatives unable to accept the invitation and neighbors. Its composition and volume vary as a function of generosity and customs, but blood sausage is always and everywhere at its heart. Indeed, it suffices all by itself; it is central to the rule expressed by our interlocutors: "Lo tripon se dona e se torna, Blood sausage is given and returned." To kill the pig is to share the bloody portion, which often lends its name to the festival—*sangonée* and *boudinée* in central France, *tripée* in Picardy—and to commit to accepting it in return. Yet, just as Lévi-Strauss taught us to read behind the prohibition against incest the law of exogamy, should we not understand these obligatory gifts as the inseparable underside of a taboo that is sometimes distinctly formulated: one does not consume the bodily fluid that humanizes the animal, *one does not eat its blood*.

Thus, the first effect of the custom is to reaffirm the necessary disjunction between the house and the creature that had become something of its child. The steps that, throughout its rearing, maintained a sufficient distance from the pig and those that, on the day of the slaughter, turned it suddenly into a savage beast—in the region of Sault the youths prick it in the dark so that once the sty is opened it emerges furious and ready for a "good fight"—culminate and take on meaning in this gesture of separating out the blood. But, from one end of Europe to the other, this separation takes varied forms. Spilling blood on the ground, giving it as a gift, watering it down are so many ways of separating oneself from it. Mixing it, dividing it up, and classifying it are all ways of distinguishing those who must first and foremost be protected from this contact, which, as we have shown, is openly associated with a cannibal act.

In the Pont-l'Abbé region, at the edge of Brittany, the blood is "let go"; when Pierre Jakez Hélias tried to find out why, he received only two replies: "Either the *erc'h*, which is the supreme expression of distaste, or the stone-faced affirmation that collecting the blood "is not a thing to do."[46] In some villages of Switzerland, upper Provence, and Venezia it is never eaten. This absolute rejection of blood may seem extraordinary, especially since letting it fall to the ground is the central gesture of the Jewish slaughter. But isn't it required in almost all places, at least for part of the blood? In Languedoc, along with the little spray that marks the women, the earth drinks another splash at the foot of the sannaire. Elsewhere, a division seems to be established between the blood one abandons and that which is reserved for the cooks. This is the case in French-speaking Switzerland, where only one to two liters are kept for the fabrication of blood sausages and pies, and in Scotland, where the part of the blood that is not cooked feeds the dunghill.[47] This partial rejection is justified, when almost all the blood is collected, by the diversity of the treatments it then undergoes. In Sardinia and northern Italy the gustative and social effects of its cooking are particularly apparent. Two kinds of blood sausages are made on the island. First the *primadzu*, the "first blood," simply salted or peppered, fills the small intestine. Immediately roasted on a flame between two wooden sticks, it is eaten only by the men "because its taste is too strong." With the rest the women then make the *sanguinacci*. One of the rare blood sausages that openly mentions blood in its name, it actually contains only a small quantity of it, usually cut with milk. But generally a variety of spices are added (cinnamon, nutmeg, clove), dried or crystallized fruits (walnuts, pine nuts, grapes, almonds, orange, and lemon peels), chocolate, or honey. The entire concoction sits overnight so that the blood becomes impregnated with these rich flavors. Stuffed into the large intestine and cooked in the vat, the *sanguinacci* are then offered to the family. But one part of the mix, poured directly into an earthenware bowl or frying pan, becomes the *torta,* which the women and children, who appreciate it "for its sweetness," eat together.[48] Next to this fruity and sugary predilection, equally present in the north of Europe, often combined with milk or with a grain, there is the tarter predilection for plants, foremost among which is wild spinach, present in Italy, Sardinia, and in the south of France. Almost everywhere in our areas of research we found "herbs" and greens mixed with blood: young nettles, sorrel, dandelion, but also "the green of white beets," to cite only the best recognized. As plants of "feminine flow," which the breeders used for the pig's green diet, they reveal their principle at the heart of these mixtures: to rein in the movements of coursing blood, soften its force even after death. In addition, the women, the progenitors of pigs and blood sausage, are the ones who are initially distanced from the consumption of blood, when they don't abstain from it on their own. Many cooks "don't care for them" and, furthermore, "you have to give so many of the blood sausages away there's never enough." They make it a duty, however, to "taste" those offered by their neighbors. In the region of Sault the first blood sausages, still warm, are brought to the café where "those who held the pig" play cards while waiting for the *triponada.* The distance placed between the blood and the house increases further when we reach Catalonia: the *botifarra,* the black blood sausage, as strongly spiced as the Sardinian *primadẓu,* is a male meat. Its consumption on all occasions—hunting, conscription, carnival, the day of the patron saint—seals the male fraternity. Sometimes men even make the blood sausages in the street, outside their doors. The traveler and artist Gaston Vuillier sketched the scene in Ibiza in 1888, but it is equally familiar to the residents of Barcelona in the early part of the century. This reversal appears as the flip side of a distancing; here lies the middle ground between the absolute exclusion of blood and that of women. It is usually enough to open the consumption of blood sausages to the outdoors and to the greatest number to ward off the risk of cannibalism, as confirmed by a news story related in the sixteenth century by a doctor, Laurent Joubert, who sees it as proof "that blood sausages are not worth keeping":

A Montpelier woman long ago gave the example, as they say. She died suffocated for having eaten blood sausages that had been kept, thinking thereby to economize by not giving any to anyone and not eating any other meat so long as they lasted. Barely had she finished them than she died, seemingly poisoned.[49]

Thus was created the rule that stipulates both the giving of the blood and its immediate and complete—and therefore collective—consumption. Not only must one separate oneself from *its* blood, one must also accept that it belongs neither to those who "took" it and cooked it nor to those to whom one offered it and who must "give it back." For a portion that is always reserved goes elsewhere and launches another circulation, other exchanges.

The Soul of the Pig

In Spain people invite one another to the meal following the slaughter as follows: "Tomorrow we will bury the pig" or "We're having the death," "Come to the funeral." In Catalonia at every killing of a pig— the calendar for which overlaps with that of carnival, to such an extent that the animal incarnates the period—the "pig's funeral" is sung in the course of an evening filled with games; a mask declaims the will and testament by which the pig itself determines the dividing up and distribution of its body. Like the game that long accompanied it, the tradition is very old. The first *Testamentum porcelli* is a fourteenth-century Roman schoolboy's parody, noted in passing by Saint Jerome. But very quickly the testament developed quasi-autonomously as a literary genre. The clerics had no monopoly on it, and the late nineteenth century renewed the fashion. An 1896 text from Ariège speaks of a pig who made his will before a notary *foro l'batemo*, after the baptism:

> Doni l'pus brave cambajon
> Al capelan, nòstre ritor
> Pel cas que dedins ma carcassa
> Da'ama s'escaisse qualqua traça . . .
> Me soven qu m'agan apres.

"I give the nicest ham to our priest, in the event some trace of my soul is left in my carcass, according to the teachings I've received." And he ends by saying " "Senti ja que l'esprit s'envola, I feel my spirit is flying away."[50] If the pig is endowed with a soul, of which Pliny the Elder spoke (*Natural History*, book 8, 77), its slaughter, cutting up, and cooking must manifest this unusual property. "Come make the soul of the pig," "Come eat the pig's soul," they say in the French Vexin, the Norman Bocages, and in Champagne. But where is this carnal soul? How can it be "made," and what portion of the work, in this collective operation, falls to each of the participants of the slaughter?

In the region of Santander *sacar al alma*, to remove the soul, is the usual expression to designate the killing of the pig, but it also refers to the particular technique used by the slaughterers for opening up the animal and the professional butchers' manner of first removing a "piece of the belly"—particularly the band of fat circumscribed by the two rows of teats, which involves a double incision on either side of them. A relationship is furthermore established between this "soul" and the intestines that will house the blood: *sacar el alma, el vientre,* or *el mondongo*—the ensemble of guts prepared by the *mondonguera*—are equivalent expressions there.[51] The soul is thus caught in the belly, the tripes, and the blood sausages, for it is none other than the blood prepared by the cooks. In addition to the blood sausages, the "soup of the slaughter," the porridges and the "blood cakes" offered to visitors also constitute the portions to be eaten together. First, on this occasion, from the north to the south of Europe, a portion of the blood is poured into the dough. From the Swedish *paltbröd* to the Estonian "blood bread" made of rye flour, by way of the lower Breton *fars gwad*—the blood cake—and the Galician *filhoa*, the entire spectrum of baked goods from breads to pancakes or thick crêpes is colored by the blood of the pig.[52] The "black flan" of the island of Ushant is a porridge that, wherever it constitutes the ordinary food, is on that day enriched with blood. The Venitian *polenta* and the Languedocian *millas*, today made with corn, are given the same name, because of the dark coloration caused by this addition. In addition to the blood sausages filled with a mixture of flour and blood, the porridge mixed with blood sometimes becomes a blood sausage, as in Ariège and Gascony, where the balls of corn or millet formed by hand and cooked in plain salted water are known by the name of *micas*, but also in some places by the more singular name of *tripon de mil*, "millet blood sausage," or else *armòtas*. These two names can only be understood in relation to the blood of the pig, which enters into their composition at every slaughter before being thrown into the blood sausage stew. The armòtas, prepared in this way, constitute the gift.[53] Now the word *armòta*, or *armeta*, first designates the souls in purgatory. In the Spanish domain, on the days when these souls are expected—Christmas and All Saint's Day—

breads and cakes are kneaded called *còcas* and *tortas d'almas* (soul cakes) that are sometimes consumed at the cemetery, on the tombs, after being blessed at the service for the dead.[54] Vats full of porridge are also prepared by virtue of the relationship everywhere connecting grain production to the dead. In the Pyrenean Audois and the Ariège, where the custom is followed, it is the common belief that for each grain of millet eaten on that day a soul is freed from purgatory.[55] As for the *armettes*, they have the property of "marking" with red the white linen folded in wardrobes; in the Languedoc regions the *armari* is one of the sites where they manifest themselves.[56] As for the blood-red coloration that sometimes spontaneously tinges the porridge, as well as the bread and the hosts, it was long interpreted as a sign by the cooks, who saw it as a trace of suffering souls.[57]

These blood stews, these red stocks, are not simply marks, signs, or the food of souls, they are their very substance, as revealed by the dead without souls, the dead without baptisms, the incomplete dead. In Sardinia the *súrbile* materializes as soon as the pig is bled and haunts the houses as long as the slaughtering season lasts. Once on site it goes in search of a newborn—a baptized newborn in this case—whose blood it sucks and later spits out into the ashes of the hearth where, mixing with the gray ash, it forms a *pagnotta*, a crude pancake that signals its arrival.[58] And the elves, changelings, and kalikandjarai, who pounce on the stews and blood and are fed with pancakes and blood sausages, sometimes bear the name of a grain—the "little buckwheat" of Ariège—or sometimes that of the blood with which it is permeated— the Venitian and Friouli *sanguinelo*. Now, in these Alpine provinces, *sanguinela* is the name of the blood millet, a gramineae that is connected to a childhood tradition familiar to us. Already noted by Mattiole in the sixteenth century, the game that consisted of "stuffing blades in one's nose to make it bleed" persists in Toscani and gave its name to the plant.[59] This *sanguinela* long served in the fabrication of the traditional stew, next to other millets now fallen into disuse, including, again in northern Italy, the Turkish sorghum. And just as the blood millet is incarnated in the *sanguinelo*, sorghum also has its elf. Dressed entirely in red, the *gambaretol* kidnaps little children in this same region and hides them in its habitat, the depths of the reddened fields.[60] This return to our gnomes only reinforces the substantial link established between blood and grains, a link the stories depicting them brought into play as alternatives: a porridge or a blood sausage were in effect granted them. Nonetheless, the affinity uniting two products at first glance so distant ultimately revealed itself in their common effect: to cause the little dead ones, who had come to beg and steal a little of this mixture of soul, blood, and flour on the day the animals die, to burst.

This is the "soul of the pig." It remains to be discovered what becomes of it, what is done with it now by those who captured it by taking the blood, who better materialized it with the porridge, ultimately eating it collectively. In Catalonia all this is made explicit on December 21, for Saint Thomas's Day, which brings an end to the fast of Advent and opens the cycle of winter slaughters. On that day, in every home, a major cleaning occurs and a full oven prepares the Christmas banquets. Both in the city and the country the fair for fattened pigs and prepared pork begins. In Barcelona a fourteenth-century regulation allowed pigs to enter by the Porta Ferrissa "two days before Saint Thomas's Day and until Christmas," a custom that was maintained until the end of the nineteenth century. In upper Pallars these slaughters are presented as a natural deadline, for once Saint Thomas's Day is over, the pig being fattened loses weight, shrinks. Which is to say that it follows the opposite direction of the daylight, which decreases until this date—the exact moment of the solstice—then begins growing by a *pan de nas* or *de la boca al nas*, by the distance that separates the nose from the mouth, according to the proverb. On this exceptional day boys throughout Europe play a complex ceremonial role. In Austria and Germany the *Swine-thommes*, the Pork Thomas, is the moment when the "pigsty listener," a boy delegated by the group, questions the pig. The night before the slaughter the grunting of the "Pork Thomas"—ever more humanized by its imminent death—takes on the value of an oracle. Its response to knocks on its door reflect the number of years until one will be married, the attributes and flaws of the future spouse, the children to come. In Wallonia and England the youngest children, rejecting their "elders" in the streets and occupying the houses, are already asserting the rights and temporary power granted them during the cycle of the Twelve Days. In Worcestershire, Saint Thomas's Day inaugurates their rounds of collections.[61] In the Catalan region, let us recall, they make their noses bleed with the stalk of the *mil-en-grana*, a wild gramineae we recognize as millet, called *herbeta de Sant Tomàs*, while reciting a rhymed incantation in which the expression "Sang a terra, sang als nas, Blood on the ground, blood in the nose," is repeated, making sure the blood drips in the center of a little cross of straw. In addition, on this same day they let themselves fall to the floor several times to the cry of "Sant Thomàs cau!" (Saint

Thomas is falling!) an enigmatic gesture for the ethnographer who recorded it but, in our view, meaningful when viewed in relation to the other "games" combining nose bleeds and the mimicking of epileptic crises that constitute the trials by which the boys, in unison with the pig, enact their own changes, their own passage. Let us return nonetheless to the details of the ritual such as it was observed at the beginning of the century in upper Vallespir:

> The boys await the twelve noon bells to climb on a bench, a chair or any other place from which they can easily jump. At the first bell, they fall to the floor, crying, joyously, "Sant Tomàs cau, Sant Tomàs cau!" Then they perch again, falling three times more with great delight. In the past practically everyone did it; now the children have become the sole repositories of the custom.[62]

The gesture takes on new light when compared to the belief that follows, noted in the form of a legend in Palma de Majorca, where it was also practiced:

> You know that among all the fasts commanded by the Church there is that of Saint Thomas's Day: "ses tempores de Sant Tomàs." It is said that those who do not observe this fast will suffer a great deal at the hour of death. The story is told that souls, when they leave this life, must pass over a high mountain, the *serra*. This passage is so difficult for the poor "little soul" that it cries:
> "Jo caic! Jo caic!" [I'm falling, I'm falling!]
> And the good Jesus responds:
> "Use it! Use it!"
> The soul asks:
> "What must I use?"
> "The fast of Saint Thomas's Day, if you observed it."

Indeed, if the soul did not observe it, it falls immediately into hell. On the other hand, if it fasted the tempores properly, it passes over the serra as easily as a star and ends up in the sky.

This story explains at least two expressions common in Majorca: "Ses tempores de Sant Tomàs, de la serra no cauràs, si dejunades les has, The day of Saint Thomas, you will not drop from the serra, if you fasted the tempores," and, even more elliptically: "Cling to the tempores of Saint Thomas's Day!"[63] On this day of the year, when everyone gathers, a new element weaves ever more tightly the customary relationship between the boys, their blood, and the pig. Now transferred to the collectivity as a whole, whose participation Amades recalls, the gesture and the expression take on their full weight. By fasting as the pig fasts on the eve of its death, then by sharing, for them and with them, this "animated" blood, the living help the passing souls liberate themselves, as one sun replaces the other, on Saint Thomas's Day. But the ritual long performed by all cannot be dissociated from the more secret gesture of the boys' custom: it is also because these boys let a little of their own souls flow—their *blood on the ground*—on this day when the pigs are bled, a minute effusion mimicking that of the bleeder, that the souls can rise up.

Whereas Jewish culture, basing itself on the openly articulated belief that "the soul is in the blood," abandons the blood of animals at the moment of the bleeding—it must flow to the ground before being covered—Christianity almost everywhere chooses to consume it following a preparation and a cooking that, by "making the blood," make the soul. This major reversal is the point at which Christianity's desire for rupture is most radically expressed: to return to the pig was first to return to blood, even if this reconciliation occurred progressively. In the same manner, Islam rejected both the blood and the flesh of the pig, while medieval heresies usually associated a questioning of the eucharistic dogma with vegetarianism, of which several Provençal communities still bear the trace; they do not consume animal blood. "Arma, arma, orca, orca, Our soul is but blood," affirm the last Cathars, who abstain from all meat in the Ariège mountains, where the pig is the meat par excellence.[64]

A natural continuation of all that has preceded, the distinction "by blood" came to classify Christians, by opposition to the Jews and also among them. In Portugal certain pork butchers in the region of Belmonte still carry a blood sausage called *botifarro de marrano*, "Marrano blood sausage." With neither the meat, the fat, nor especially the blood of the pig, but with the appearance of a "real blood sausage" thanks to the red spices used to color it, it was, let us recall, prepared in the past by Jews converted by force, the Marranos, ever suspected of crypto-Judaism. At each inspection of an inquisition officer, they produced this blood sausage as proof of their fidelity to the Catholic faith. In Majorca, another land of conversos, local society maintained a strong hierarchy, reinforced by the daily contact between Christians and Jews. As a compliment to the xuetas, who were classified, as we may recall, into two porcine groups ("high ears" and "low ears"), the island's

Christian community produced *cavallers*, nobles who couldn't claim an old lineage—and we know the extent to which in Catholic Spain *limpieza de sangre*, purity of blood, was the criteria for a faultless Christian belonging. The alleged descendants of these "old Christians" were therefore called *butifarras*, blood sausages, for the blood of the pig, prepared and cooked, was what made them different.[65]

It will not be surprising then that this food should possess virtues, for Christians, that make it an antidote to "bad blood," whose effects are familiar to us. In Bavaria and Franconia, the fresh blood sausage eaten on an empty stomach with millet porridge protects from red sicknesses, especially from Saint Anthony's Fire, erysipelas, malignant fevers, and all afflictions that are manifested on the surface of the body by "spots" but infect it more secretly, such as the disease referred to as the "black Jewess." Among the animals given a little blood sausage to eat, epizootic diseases cannot propagate and fecundity increases. Which is why, after the collective meal bringing together the family and its close neighbors, nothing that touched the blood sausages is wasted. Each guest takes home a little stock from the cooking and even the straw that served as a bed. Scattered in the fields in tiny drops, attached to the trunks of fruit trees, they fertilize and protect them.[66]

Like the blood of the baptized, the blood of the pig is that metaphysical bodily fluid that the alimentary rituals of Easter have already revealed. But, for this quality to be manifested, the part of the animal that is mixed up with the most Jewish part must be dealt with. It therefore falls to women—Jewesses by "nature," by their blood—to convert this part, for every slaughter and for every pig, into a Christian part and to accede, themselves, by this correct knowledge of cooking, to an incontestable Christianity.

CHAPTER TEN

The Bone That Sings

A little further on, over there, was a concrete bed, and the bones that hadn't burned for example, the big foot bones, we ... there was a box with two handles and we took them there, where others had the job of crushing them. This bone dust was very fine. Then we put it in bags and when we had enough bags, we went all the way to the Ner, where there was a bridge, and we emptied them into the Ner. It all disappeared with the water, it floated away.

—SIMON SREBNIK, in Claude Lanzmann, *Shoah*

There is another part, a bone this time, presented in myths explicitly as a mark of the pig's Jewishness. We find it first in Lorraine, on the Easter table, where the resurrection of Christ is celebrated by reuniting with a divided pig:

For Easter dinner in the country, the housewife placed in the pot, along with the dried cabbage, the first vertebra of the pig that had been killed for Christmas. This *corrosse* or *Jew* had been prepared in the same fashion as the *wolf's share* [the piece of pork that is given to the wolf] preserved in ash and wrapped in thick paper. In addition, it was customary to fatten a little pig for Easter, the *grèhhlat*, which furnished the grilled meats, the *hatrés* ... for the two days of the holiday.[1]

In addition to the piglet, which is related by name to the infant—in the patois of Metz *grèhheler* means to cry like a newborn—a bone of the old pig, a vertebra more precisely, kept specifically for this purpose and eaten at the same time, introduces something of a discordance on this day when, as we have shown, the pig is Christian and makes one Christian. What is the meaning of this presence?

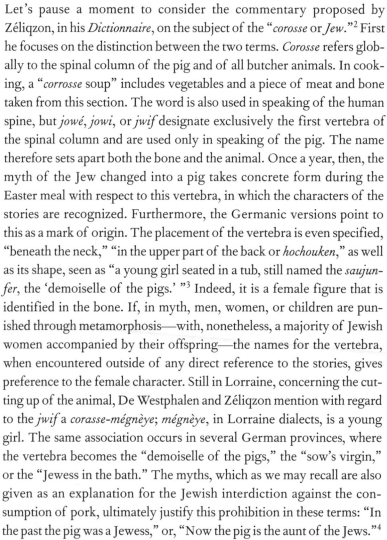

The Jewess in the Tub

Let's pause a moment to consider the commentary proposed by Zéliqzon, in his *Dictionnaire*, on the subject of the *"corosse* or *Jew."*[2] First he focuses on the distinction between the two terms. *Corosse* refers globally to the spinal column of the pig and of all butcher animals. In cooking, a *"corrosse* soup" includes vegetables and a piece of meat and bone taken from this section. The word is also used in speaking of the human spine, but *jowé, jowi,* or *jwif* designate exclusively the first vertebra of the spinal column and are used only in speaking of the pig. The name therefore sets apart both the bone and the animal. Once a year, then, the myth of the Jew changed into a pig takes concrete form during the Easter meal with respect to this vertebra, in which the characters of the stories are recognized. Furthermore, the Germanic versions point to this as a mark of origin. The placement of the vertebra is even specified, "beneath the neck," "in the upper part of the back or *hochouken,*" as well as its shape, seen as "a young girl seated in a tub, still named the *saujunfer,* the 'demoiselle of the pigs.' "[3] Indeed, it is a female figure that is identified in the bone. If, in myth, men, women, or children are punished through metamorphosis—with, nonetheless, a majority of Jewish women accompanied by their offspring—the names for the vertebra, when encountered outside of any direct reference to the stories, gives preference to the female character. Still in Lorraine, concerning the cutting up of the animal, De Westphalen and Zéliqzon mention with regard to the *jwif* a *corasse-mégnèye; mégnèye,* in Lorraine dialects, is a young girl. The same association occurs in several German provinces, where the vertebra becomes the "demoiselle of the pigs," the "sow's virgin," or the "Jewess in the bath." The myths, which as we may recall are also given as an explanation for the Jewish interdiction against the consumption of pork, ultimately justify this prohibition in these terms: "In the past the pig was a Jewess," or, "Now the pig is the aunt of the Jews."[4]

From the "Sow of the Jews," illustrated in the iconography, to the "Jewess of the pigs," all manners of filiation have been covered in both directions; what remained was to give this Jewishness an irreducible character, to make it concrete by placing a "Jewess" in the most secret recess of the porcine body. And what do we see in the vertebra, making it even more Jewish still? A young girl in a tub, purifying herself at the end of her period, according to the ritual, thus a woman of menstrual age. Plunged halfway in the water, she allows only her human torso to be seen, for, like Melusina who bleeds and whose lower body takes on the form of a snake during the Sabbath, the menstruating Jewess is in a state of metamorphosis.[5] Thus the vertebra, the "Jewess," is above all a permanent trace that nothing can undermine, indisputable evidence of the state of origin, the equivalent of a birthmark, which our tales of metamorphosis take care to extend to the entire porcine species: "Since then all pigs have a bone in their spine that shows a Jewess in a tub and which is called the *saüludi*."[6]

It remains for us to examine what ultimately becomes of this bone. Some versions of the myth note the reactions triggered by its discovery on a guest's plate: mockery of the one to whom it falls to eat the "Jewess," or envy, for entirely positive qualities are also connected with the bone, causing it be "avidly sought after at meals." Only Germanic ethnography furnishes the elements to allow us to sketch a picture of its properties and uses: there the vertebra is considered a talisman, the wearing of which protects from back strain, fractures, rheumatism, and from all sorts of "back problems" in general. It is equally active when placed in the stable or in the chimney of the home: there it preserves livestock from epizootic diseases and from evil spells and keeps away storms and hail. But its preferred place is in the attic, where it is hung for a time before being hid among the seed to ensure an abundant harvest. Soon it appears that other pig bones, other parts, even, on the condition that they are ossified and baptized "Jew" or "Jewess," are used in the same manner, invested with the same powers. This is the case for a "little bone" found in the ear, also called the "Jew's bone" or the "head of death," but, more commonly, for the bones that touch the vertebra, whether they are situated on its axis or come into contact with it—those of the head that rest on it, the ribs that are articulated from it, the spinal column, in whole or in part—join it in the attic. Set aside the day of the slaughter and salted together, they await carnival to be eaten. In upper Palatinate and Hesse the "Jewess in the bath" and its train of bones are stuffed into grain sacks by the sower himself, after being allocated to him at the meal of Fat Tuesday. The "Jew" or "Jewess," seed at the heart of seeds, bring fertility to the grains, the earth, and the livestock.[7] Just as, beginning with blood sausages, we had to broaden our focus to the various blood-based preparations in order for the significance attached to its cooking and consumption to be revealed, so the Jewish vertebra now invites us to look at the spectrum of these bones and their ritual uses.

Already, by a series of semantic shifts—from the "Jewish" vertebra, to this little ear bone called the "Jew's bone" or "head of death," and to the head itself—the German arena invited us to consider this part, which, throughout Europe, is always treated in a special manner. In Venezia, it is separated from the body as soon as the bleeding is done and removed from the site of the slaughter as quickly as possible, "so that the soul of the pig doesn't leave with the blood." The next day, cooked at great length in a stew, it becomes the ritual dish of the festival; all these bones, broken or sawed, must by gnawed by the guests "to the last."[8] Other moments of the year furnish occasions to make explicit the significance of this bony, bloody part that is also called the "head of death" in the Swiss valley of Blenio. There it is associated with the collective wine pressing. Once a year, at the start of winter, it brings together the inhabitants of those villages that have maintained the custom. First a wine obtained by setting apart a bit of the harvest of every proprietor is put up for auction in order to celebrate Masses for the dead. Next to this *vin di mört*, the *testa d'mort* or *salam da testa*, head sausage—so-called because it is the dismembered, finely chopped head of the pig that is stuffed into the largest intestine—is shared among those who helped in the pressing, in the course of a meal that takes place by turns at the homes of all those who participated in the work.[9] In Latvia the pigs are preferably killed in autumn, on which day wheat flour blood sausages, "blood bread," and "blood crepes" are eaten, but the head is reserved for the festival of the patron saint of pigs, *Tenis*, Saint Anthony, in whose honor it is divided up on January 17.[10] Throughout southern Europe this saint of pigs prompts the accumulation in sanctuaries of feet, heads, and ears, but also of bundles of blood sausages that one has blessed in order to offer them to the souls of purgatory.

Thus, like the blood cooked and eaten for the souls, the bone has a role to play in this metaphysical division, and if we look at it closely, their association is constant. It takes effect the day of the killing. Already, in the Norman Bocages, "to make the soul of the pig" is to eat the blood sausages and the blood porridge together, along with *ossailles*, a plate of bones. We find the same custom in the center of France, where a "bone soup" serves as the primary dish, sometimes combined with a "bouillon de boudine," a soup made from the water in which the blood sausages cooked. Further, in French-speaking Switzerland, where people invite one another to *faire fracache* on the day of the slaughter, the term *fracache*, which designates both the pig's spinal column and the first vertebra in particular, is still used to name the tripes and the blood sausage.[11] Finally, from the Metz region to our region of Languedoc, a "piece of spine" is added to the blood sausages in making up the gifts. But the bond is further woven with the blind intestine, the caecum, into which one sometimes pours the largest of the blood sausages—*galabar, breisha, maramauca*—in the Audois Pyrenees. Elsewhere it serves as an envelope to a curious sausage, the *cap del monde*, the edge of the world, which is filled "with tiny ossicles," held together after cooking by a little meat and fatty skin. In the Rouergue, near Rodez, it is a "bone situated between the two shoulders" that is chopped into tiny pieces and stuffed.[12] We end up with a strange condensation of the pig in the form of a "blood sausage," in the image of the one that, "with hair, blood, bone and skin inside," so surprised the Danish changeling. But even though our "edge of the world" can be found in the Cevennes under related names—*sound of the world, bottomless sack, end of the world*—the center of France, the Lyons region, holds other surprises in store. In the latter region the word today refers merely to the envelope of a large sausage, known to all by the name of "Jesus." This appendage, then, is ideally where the transformation of the Jewish part into a Christian part takes place, the passage from bone to flesh—from "Jew" to "Jesus"—including some movements back and forth, oscillations of which the lexicon and the ever ritualized consumption of this initially enigmatic morsel bear witness. In Minot and Burgundy this large irregularly shaped sausage goes by the name of *judru*.[13]

Thus the vertebra divided and the ossicles enclosed in this pocket-like intestine echo the "Jewess" and the bones that, stuffed in the bottom of large grain sacks, fertilize the grain, guaranteeing germination and with it the return of life. For them to be fully efficacious, they must also be eaten for carnival or Easter, when the pig returns, when Christ is resuscitated. And these rituals of connection concern both the community of the living in its relationship to time—the cyclical time of the pig reborn as its successor—and to the dead, whose return is also specified on the calendar.

At the end of our preceding chapters the Easter slaughter of a piglet established a first association, the "old" pig and the "young" pig, salted meat and fresh meat incarnating the disjointed and perfectly antagonistic figures of the Jew and the Christian, such as they appeared to us throughout this book. From this point of view "Jewish oldness" seemed entirely contained in this vertebra, which is salted and hidden in the ash of Lent, while the roasted piglet and its avatars—sausage, fresh ham, the lamb—are situated on the side of the New Law. The Lorraine meal, in which one followed the next, completed this passage. Yet the ritual presence, in this festival of renewal and resurrection, of the "Jewish bone," whose properties and usages we now know, invites us to replace it in turn within the eschatological horizon in which blood took on meaning, that of the final destination of souls.

Pig for the Dead

Saint Anthony, who we may recall was a swineherd before becoming a hermit, is the object of very lively devotion.[14] Beginning in the eleventh century the Antonins popularized the figure of the hermit with a piglet, even embodying the image by making this breeding their specialty. Their pigs enjoyed the privilege of going about the streets of cities, whereas the pigs of ordinary individuals were kept separately; a little bell on their neck or ear and the emblematic tau, a mark the monks also bore on their chests, was their sign. These pigs furnished meat for the poor and the sick, who were collected and cared for in asylums and quarantine stations that the Antonins founded wherever they settled, for this merciful order developed a reputation for treating the black plague, then leprosy, and, more generally, the various inflammations and diseases of the skin, both human and animal, collected under the name "Saint Anthony's fire."[15]

The saint's festival is mixed up just about everywhere with the festival of the pig, which is never killed on this day and is honored in various fashions. Until the end of the nineteenth century, in Barcelona, the young swineherds arrived from the surrounding areas to take part in races, at the outcome of which the one whose animal was the best competitor was declared king. But this anointing also served as a reminder of the humble origins of Anthony, whose trials and miracles were enacted at the same time.[16] In Majorca, where the most beautiful animal of the island was chosen, "everyone was bent on caring for his pig so that it would be elected, for it was thought that one would thereby obtain special favors from the saint." In the Terra Alta when a sow was sick, one promised a little one to Saint Anthony if he cured it. As soon as the piglet was weaned, the "vow" was kept by bringing it to the priest, who announced from the pulpit "that a piglet had been given to the church." From that moment on the animal, endowed with a little bell, became collective property. Everyone fed it, and it traveled about freely until the priest had it auctioned for the benefit of the church.[17]

In Galicia many rural communes perpetuate the tradition of Saint Anthony's pig. The animal lives from public alms until January 17, when it is put up for auction, after having been walked through town by a beggar who plays the role of the hermit. The money from the auction serves in part to finance the festival that brings all the animals the protection of the saint, to whom the feet, head, and ears of the pigs killed in early winter are also offered. Often these gifts go to the poor of the parish, among whom a little of the money collected is divided up. Finally, the rest of it pays for Masses for the souls in purgatory. Galicia thus offers the most complete picture of this redistribution of the sums derived from the pig, traded well above its value: the community of the living celebrate it, whereas it belongs to the poor and the dead by right. While in some villages a formal distinction is established, it only underlines the necessary presence of the third partner: the community of the dead. Thus, in Betanzas, in about 1810, two collective pigs were being raised. One to provide expenses—common meals, maintenance of the site of worship—in honor of Saint Anthony, the other, *o porco das ánimas*, whose sale at auction paid for masses for the invisible society of souls.[18]

From "Saint Anthony's piglet" to the "souls' pig," the status of the pig as a symbol of the saint as well as its function as mediator between the dead and the living are affirmed. The legendary life of the hermit furnishes both justification for and an illustration of these qualities; it is the myth that founds the festival, based on three stories of inception.

A first collection, well represented in the south of the Italian peninsula, casts the future saint as a creature of diabolical origins. Offered to a sterile mother consumed with desire for a child, at the age of seven the boy had to be returned to hell to perform his service. But the young Anthony, who had become a Christian through baptism, confronted the ordeal with courageous determination. Various versions depict him as a porter in hell or even a stoker for the devil:

> His task consisted in stoking the fire beneath the cauldrons containing the souls. While he was attending to the fire, he heard a voice: "Anthony! I am your mother's father, don't cook me!" Instantly he seized the burning log and threw it at the devils who were passing. The latter ordered him to resume his work at a different cauldron. And again a voice rose up: "Anthony! I am your father's mother, don't cook me!" So this time Anthony again removed the logs from beneath the cauldron and threw them at the devils who, exasperated, made him move on to yet another vat. But Anthony, filled with compassion for the pleas of the souls, even

those outside his family, rebelled against the devils, who chased him from hell. He returned to earth where he became a saint.[19]

We recognize here a tale well known for its episode of a young boy's service in hell. In this first set of legends, passing through the fire appears as an initiation trial that makes the saint a metaphysical liberator, an intercessor between hell and the celestial heights, thus a familiar to the intermediary site: purgatory.

But while the Abruzzi stories give preference to Anthony's actions among the damned, the versions collected in Sardinia or northern Italy highlight the piglet while displacing the fire from beneath the vats, where the souls are cooking, to a hidden location. Here is a summary of one story from Frioul: Saint Anthony, accompanied by his pig, out of pity for humankind, which is living on a cold earth and unable to cook food, decides to go down to hell. The devils, who recognize him, refuse to allow him entry but crack open the door of their domain enough for the pig to pass. Once inside, the piglet wreaks havoc by turning over boiling cauldrons and knocking over the various instruments that serve for cooking in the underworld, so much so that the demons beg Anthony to intervene and bring the chaos to an end; the saint grants them this on the condition that they allow him to sit by the fire. He takes advantage of the occasion to catch the fire on the end of his stick and to bring it to men for use in cooking and reheating the world. In certain variations it is the pig who brings back the spark on the end of its burning tail; in Sardinia the pig also endeavors to destroy the diabolical arsenal destined "to punish the imprisoned souls."[20]

The piglet is able to play this role because Saint Anthony has granted it favors that henceforth link the destiny of its species with that of the miracle worker. A third set of stories focuses on the encounter that brought them together. In Catalonia the entrance to Barcelona is cited as the location of the healing of a sickly piglet. Having been called upon by the city's governor to liberate his daughter from the demons inhabiting her, Anthony was on his way there:

> It was then that a sow presented itself to him carrying a piglet in its mouth because it couldn't walk, its members being deformed and missing a leg. The animal deposited its little one at the feet of the saint, who blessed it; instantly the healed piglet began joyously frisking about. From that day on the grateful sow never left the saint and followed him everywhere he went. It is even said that when the saint died the animal went to his funeral.[21]

Narrated as early as 1534 in the *Antonianae historiae*, published in Lyons, it is said the episode "justifies" the presence of the pig at the feet of the saint; the Catalans recognize the mother, the Italians the baby, one or the other having become the hermit's inseparable companion, his second and his double.[22]

But the saint's mark on the animal is fully revealed when one situates the two of them in their relationship to the dead. Saint Anthony's entire life was a perpetual struggle against demons: the exorcising saint was persecuted by "evil forces," devils and the dead, who break loose particularly on the day of his festival. In some instances it's the pig they're after. An object of desire for demons and souls in damnation, the creature who shares Saint Anthony's destiny can also be "inhabited." Its transitive quality is thus verified. In the home it is sometimes the equivalent, sometimes the receptacle of the suffering soul.[23] Thus the cooking of the pig soup is the occasion for unusual evenings. In Pallars Sobirá, on the southern side of the Catalan Pyrenees, while the large cauldron simmers on the fire and as the evening progresses, women sit up reciting the litanies of the service for the dead: "A l'ànima dels defunts de la familia, a Sant Antoni, a les ànimas del Purgatori . . . " "intentions" (prayers intended for the souls of the dead) of exorcistic value confirming our belief that with every pig and every slaughter the question of the metaphysical destination of the deceased in the family arises.[24]

Open, in the experience of every house, to the terrestrial wanderings of restless spirits, just as in the legend it is mischievously acquainted with the infernal landscape, at the festival the pig, through the mediation of the saint, of brothers, and of the Church, belongs to the dead, or at least a piece of it is reserved for them. In addition to the head, whose central position we have already highlighted, included are the ears, the feet, or a piece of sausage, such as the Andorran *bringuera*, echoing the custom in the Baronnies, where, if one cuts up meat on a forbidden day, a "sausage" must go to the work of purgatory.[25] But equivalencies and associations limit this possible variety: the ears often stand in for the head, which is sometimes reduced, as in Capcir, to the crown of the skull; in Catalonia the head and feet can be offered together at the auction of Saint Anthony and, in the vast majority of cases, the offering of feet is the minimum required. In La Maçana and Andorra, moreover, we have noted the emotion they inspire in the crowd when the sacristan raises them high, and the passion of bidders who are ready to pay a high price for them, suggesting an importance yet to be explained (illus. 29). The priest, when questioned, confirmed our first impression: "Today, for the auctions, people give a little of everything! Cakes, wine, sausages, or the *bringuera.* Even blood sausages! But it's because there aren't enough pigs any more to have a sufficient number of feet. There aren't many houses anymore that kill a pig. In the past you gave only the feet, and sometimes the head. I've seen entire heads and ears here. But especially, and always, the feet." Enlarging the scope of our focus verified this primary importance. In Brittany Saint Anthony is the object of similar veneration. In the parishes, on his saint's day, he is brought bacon, cabbage, ears, heads, and other pieces of the animal. But the observer who related the "strange old custom" notes "a large number of pigs' feet . . . more than eight dozen," he emphasizes, leading him to specify that locally the custom of offering these foodstuffs as gifts to be sold at auction for the benefit of the church council was called the "pigs' foot fair."[26]

Upon closer inspection, the presence of these feet instantly establishes a relationship with the dead. Evidence of this was articulated by the most varied sources, the testimonies all the more valuable for being scattered. In the region of Sault, in the seventeenth century, they went to the poor or to the *oeuvre du purgatoire*, still by intermediary of the Parish council.[27] Even while certain convents, such as that of the Capucins of Palermo, were entrusted with the dead of the local nobility until the beginning of the century, caring for their bodies—the bones—and souls, it happened occasionally, especially on the eve of large festivals, that monasteries were solicited by individuals "to pray for the dead" in exchange for pigs' feet, or else that they received the latter as dues from a professional group. In the Landes, in Gascony, between the eleventh and fifteenth centuries, butchers were also known to give convents, on Christmas eve, *pees de porcz*. In the fourteenth century the leper hospitals, aside from gifts in kind from slaughtered animals, received the *inglotz* of pigs, their feet. This information sheds light on a particular clause of a seventeenth-century testator from Gévaudan who, among other arrangements, had his wife give "a pig's foot" to the church every year.[28]

Offered to the poor and to beggars, to certain religious representatives and to lepers—individuals whose positions as mediators are familiar to us—these pigs' feet thus seem destined to pass between two worlds, a quality that is manifested on Saint Anthony's Day but that the treatment of each pig repeats for every house. First, generally speaking, the very human character of the animal emerges the day of its slaughter: it is "washed," "shaved," and a vigil is kept by its body. In many places, in fact, the meal that gathers participants to the festivities is called a "funeral." While the men occupy themselves with "tidying" it, their tongues are moving full speed, and the discussion, making even those who participate in it and those around them at that moment smile, pursues its ritual course, which we caught in passing, in Munès, in the region of Sault: "Come on, got to get it clean." "Right, get him to the sky to ready our place." "Oh! you, I don't know if we'll see you up there one day!" [laughter] "Come on, scrape this foot for me, it has to be pretty to go see Saint Peter in paradise." And the conversation some-times reaches the point of personification: "What will the others say when they see him coming?" "They won't recognize him anymore, all clean-shaven and well shod!" "To shod" the pig means to scrape the skin with an old piece of scythe and pop off the hoof with the tip of a knife. An unshodding, in reality, but one that, by converting the hoof into a foot, "shods" the pig, treats its feet in the reverse manner of those of the dead, who are sent into the other world endowed with shoes indispensable for their journey; placed on their feet or simply deposited in their coffin, they serve to ward off their return.

The pig is then taken away on a stretcher, the same one that serves for the transportation of bodies, and placed beneath a shelter where it drips and cools, head down, until the next day. During the vigil the youth play their "nocturnal games"; they displace the pig, making people think it has disappeared, steal the loins, and eat them at the inn. They operate most often masked, one of them sometimes even carry-ing a *careta* made of the skin detached from a pig's head before his face. They play at ghosts.[29] Their task is facilitated by the fact that they are exercising a right recognized to the dead—that of taking what already belongs to them. The fillets of the hanging animal are partly detached and set on a small horizontal stick: a single stroke of the knife suffices to detach them completely. But thefts and displacements take yet other forms:

> Once the youth went to a house near the washhouse where two pigs had been killed that very day. Not to make trouble! You know they're hung head down. They said: "We'll go there and turn them around." And they did. And suddenly the sister-in-law heard some noise. She came out, "Mes, que vesi!" "Chut, calha-te! Tira nos la lampa!" "But what do I see. Shut up, turn off the light!" Back in the dark the youth continued to go about their business. The next day the owner went to check on his

pigs: "And do you know what he saw when he arrived? The pigs were praying! All neat with their hooves folded!"

The posture arranged by the youth can be the rule elsewhere. A meticulous ethnographer of the area of Urgell, Valeri Serra i Boldù, notes: "When it's nice and clean, they amputate the head and the feet and set them up against a kind of bench in a particular position, kneeling, as if the animal had prostrated itself of its own accord." Thus the animal is really praying, in dialogue with the living who, at the end of the meal that brings them together around this singular defunct, chant its will and testament to a tune in which the priest in this region of Catalonia recognizes "the litany sung at funerals throughout the diocese of Solsonà," every couplet ending with a "Jesus Christ, *audi nos*" sung by the entire assembly.[30]

If, upon stealing the fillets to eat them together, the youth are exercising a legitimate right, the stealing of feet, which is also practiced, is singled out by an implicit clause:

> That year, at one house, they wanted to act mean. They had killed a pig at the Margots' and, so that the youth wouldn't go there, they had stored it at the home of a neighboring woman, well locked up. They succeeded in getting in at night with master keys and they got it! They cut off the ears and the two feet! The next day, when she saw that, she was furious! She'd have killed them if she could! . . . And then, the day of carnival, she received a package with the two ears and the two feet! They had salted them! . . . Imagine her surprise upon opening the package.

The feet must be returned in order for their particular circuit to be complete; by making this gesture, the youth of Bessède-de-Sault are merely applying the precept noted in Urgell:

> Roba els porcs
> i dona els peus
> per amor de Deu.

> [Steal the pigs
> But give the feet
> For the love of God.]

For, even if they aren't given to the Church or to the poor, even if they aren't put up at auction, as in the region of Sault today, they must be shared for Fat Tuesday in order to ensure the ascension of souls:

Per carnaval, els pès dels porcs montan al cap, For carnival the feet of the pig rise to the head, in other words, to the summit, up high, to the highest height.[31]

And even while the pig is still alive these feet "walk," "circulate," physically repeat the passage. Like the ambulant poor, like the dead who are still near, the former pigs of the Antonins or the collective pig still pledged, here and there, to Saint Anthony, wander freely. Unlike the pigs who are locked up or led in flocks to the woods, they stroll through the village, walk into homes, and all their wanderings become meaningful: they are observed and commented upon, considered, as we have seen, propitiatory and oracular. Did the legend not include them from the outset, since, to the sow who deposited its paralyzed or crippled piglet at his feet, Saint Anthony returned a nimble, boisterous being? A miraculous healing, of which each domestic pig may bear the trace: in Sicily, when the satiated animal lies in the sun, the boys approach, scratch its ear, and ask: "Toni, Toni, which is the foot of Saint Anthony?" The pig stretches one leg to scratch itself where it tickles and the boys deduce that that's the foot.[32]

Chosen by the saint and endowed by him, the pig is thus the creature who travels from one world to the other. Its feet are the means and the metonymic symbol of this circulation, which must never stop. But, within the foot itself, a tinier, more secret bone further establishes the ritual and relaunches the circulation of meaning.

The Voice of the Dead

Bonjour, ma grand-mère mérine,
I vous apporte dau boudin-boudine
De notre truie courtine.
Et un petit ous dou pé
Mais si vous vlez poué
Y ou retournerai.

[Good day, my grandmother and godmother
I've brought you some blood sausage
From our farmyard sow
And a little bone from the foot
But if you don't want any
I'll go home.]

    —LITTLE RED RIDING HOOD, Vendeen oral version recorded by
      Geneviève Massignon

In Andorra the feet acquired at the auction—the *encants*—are eaten as a family in the *escudella* of Fat Tuesday: "A pig never has enough feet, if you wanted to please everyone! At home, my father's the one who eats them. 'As long as I'm alive,' he says, 'I'll be the one to eat the pig's feet!' " If the foot automatically goes to the oldest—in La Maçana the village elder had precedence over the sacristan and directed the *encants* until his death at the age of ninety-four—the latter will gladly sacrifice the last bones to the children. "We had fun counting them. We put them in a circle or made the hoof shape on the plate by arranging them from largest to smallest. It took time!" When the impatient women clear the table, the children keep the foot, have it put aside for the evening meal, when "they'll finish it." In any case the bones will be *rouségués*, gnawed, to the last. And then? "Never, never must they be given to the dogs! They're blessed. These feet were blessed in church by the priest. You mustn't throw them out. My grandmother gathered them up and put them in the fire. Sometimes, we kept one, a little bone." Today in Andorra the cycle of a pig's foot usually ends in this way but, in this same place, perhaps in another age, and elsewhere not long ago, this little bone sparked another ritual.

Let's listen to the ethnographers who were able to glimpse this initially surprising practice, which is disappearing along with the slaughters: "When we eat the pigs' feet, the children ask for the bones of the phalanx, pierce them in the middle, put a string through them, and move them left and right, so that they produce a fairly loud, rough sound."[33] In Franche-Comté the instrument is called *frelon, frode, frondo,* or *brodo.* We find it in Moselle by the names of *bruyat, ʒondat,* and *ʒoneu,* "from *ʒonner*: to produce a whirring sound like that of a top, to buzz." De Westphalen, for the Metz region, gives a drawing of it and explains it as an ethnographer and a doctor: "To make a *bruyat* you take a bone from the metacarpus or from the metatarsus of a pig's foot and pierce it in the middle using a metal rod reddened by fire. . . . You make the bone spin, which produces a muffled sound becoming less and less resonant from one player to the next."[34]

From Eastern Lorraine and Franche-Comté a continuous and homogeneous terrain is mapped out extending south, into the Swiss Jura and Mettemberg, where the invaluable *Glossaire des patois de la Suisse romande* mentions an *och'vira,* "turning bone," made from a pig's tibia. The uniformity of these first attestations highlight the specific link uniting the object and the consumption of the pig's feet. It is in these same terms that the practice is noted in Venezia:

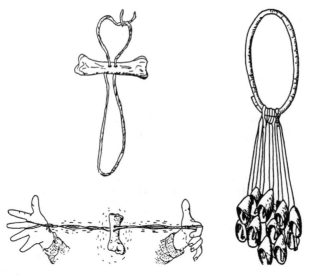

10. Rhombus made of a porcine metatarsus; multiple rhombus made of the nails and ossicles of a pig, based on J. Amades, *Customari* (Barcelona, 1956).

> The bones, including those of the head minus the jaw—which are used for a different purpose—broken or sawed into pieces, enter into the composition of a stock, and are chewed in the days that follow. . . . The metatarsus of the pig left on the plates of children and adults can be used, after a hole has been pierced in them, to make rhombuses (*rombi-rotella*). The use of a pierced bone for the fabrication of this type of rhombus was widespread in Polesine until recently and is still current in many localities, with the name *frullo, frulla, frull, frombolo*.[35]

The object is thus identified, situated within a grouping—the rhombuses—the presence of which in antique and primitive societies excited the curiosity of Italian ethnologists and brought us, for half a century, an infinitely precise series of studies. These studies, from Piedmont to Sicily, confirm the presence of this vibrating, rotating instrument; it can be made of stone, wood, horn, cardboard, pits, and, lastly, of bone.

Rhombuses allow their dead to be heard via their buzzing without our being able to determine, solely by looking at the Italian studies, the meaning of the gesture that allows one to hear these voices. It is here that a work that attempts to bring out the meaning merely from considering the object and its lexicon, rich as it may be, reaches its limits. To expand the horizon, it is first appropriate to plunge further into the details of practices, as some Italian ethnographers intuited when they emphasized that all the rhombuses do not carry the same ritual requirement. Studying the region of Mantua, Giovanni Tassoni specifies:

> Unlike the Sicilian boys' *lapuni* (made of wood like the *konos* used by the Greeks for certain religious rituals), the *fürlen* is cut from a small pig bone, the perforated center of which has a string running through it, which, maneuvered by turning and pulling, makes it vibrate while producing a hum similar to that of a bumble bee. . . . It should be classified among the most archaic and unusual types because it is constructed *exclusively* with the phalanx of a pig's hind hoof. It is the boys themselves, between the ages of eight and twelve, who make this rhombus, with its characteristic sound. The game is seasonal, situated during the period when the pig is slaughtered (from December to February), and fell into obscurity during the Second World War.

And Cleto Corrain reports for Venezia:

> It would be interesting to be able to measure the area of diffusion of the fixing of a pig bone to the end of the string of the most typical *rombo-tavoletta* (rhombus made with a small plank), which I had an opportunity to observe in Ceneselli (upper Polesine), for it could be associated, it seems to me, with a strange name for this instrument, "death," that was widespread about eighty years ago in the region of lower Polesine, as emerged from the trustworthy testimony of an old priest, Dom Bassiano Paiato.[36]

Thus the importance of this little pig bone is confirmed when viewed in the context of the society that produces it and the period assigned for its use. Far from blending into a general category that would evoke a single meaning, the Venetian rhombus brings together the two spheres that interest us: the pig on the one hand, death on the other. Some of its properties as a musical instrument will be called up to further tighten the bond. We know, for instance, that the pig inhabited by the dead *rondine* (revolves around itself grunting); sound and movement are always conjoined in the descriptions provided in Languedoc, but, along with the grunting of the animal, this same root, in other Romance languages, designates the rhombus: *rundún* in the province of Santander and *rumbón* in that of Murcia are among its names, while the company of the dead, in Corsica, can be recognized by the grunting of a troop of pigs who *rôde* in the brush.[37]

This sound and motor affinity, which establishes a double metaphor between the souls, the animal, and the instrument made of a tiny piece of its skeleton, is activated—as is often the case—in an effort toward repulsion. The buzzing of the turning bone called *frullo*, in the region of Modena, allows young swineherds to keep the pigs away from cultivated fields, to chase wild boar as well as the "malicious beings" that threaten the herd and its guardian.[38] In Catalonia it is the nails of the pigs—which elsewhere children slip onto the tips of their fingers like claws on the day of the slaughter, after having sucked out the fat—that serve to produce a complex instrument: each nail forms the body of a bell whose clapper is a bone from the porcine foot. Collected by the dozen and fixed to a ring, we find them in the hands of children and women who, upon leaving the village at night, "chase away fear" by shaking this multiple rhombus.[39]

After a pig's foot has been consumed, there remain the bone and horn, which, upon turning, allow the dead to be heard. But if the boys must play at signaling to the spirits, it is best that the latter not come too close to the living, and, here again, the rhombus traces something of a boundary in the air, a physical and sonorous circle that surrounds its player, keeping the alerted souls at a healthy distance. But this bone, *animated* by a powerful movement that gives it voice, seems to acquire new value if we stop to consider the final gestures in which it is involved.

In Andorra none of the foot must go to the dogs; an elder makes sure of this, and "a little bone is preserved"; in Venezia, as soon as the children are given the nails, "they rush to throw them in the pigsty, so that the pig doesn't lose its property" or they stuff them under the pigpen or throw them on the roof, out of dogs' reach, to protect the piglet to come from bewitchment, the evil eye, or an early death. Thus a bony remnant must be preserved. This is the rule, which is stated every year with respect to every pig, the scope of which turns out to be widespread and essential. This at least is what a vast cycle of tales and ballads throughout Europe illustrates, describing all the passages between the destiny of pigs and that of humans.[40]

They all begin with a devouring jealousy: a girl envies her sister, who is so pretty and so sought after; elder siblings are angry at their younger brother, the only one to have discovered the magic flower; a stepmother detests the little boy born of a first marriage. One day the hatred explodes: the pretty one is thrown in the water, the younger brother is stoned and summarily stashed in a distant meadow, the little boy's throat is slit by the mean wife. The deaths are violent, the murderers are not even suspected, and silence falls on the unresolved enigma of the disappearance. Some time later everything unfolds in a kind of miracle. In the Scandinavian and Scottish ballads it is usually a minstrel who fishes out the body of the beautiful girl; in the tales of southern Europe an animal digging in the earth finds an anonymous bone, a little finger, or a collection of bones that an innocent party—a shepherd or the younger sister of the defunct—instantly seizes. With the drowned girl the musician makes a bagpipe or a strange kind of harp: the sternum becomes the frame, the blond hair makes the strings, attached to and harmonized by the ossicles and phalanx. The one who discovers and grabs up the bones may suddenly find a bird forming in his hands, but, usually, he carves a whistle or a flute with his herdsman's knife. Sometimes merely bringing the raw bone to his lips is sufficient for the miracle to occur. Whether simple or complex, these instruments have the same property; no sooner has the harp been strummed, the bagpipe brought to one's lips, the bird set free, the whistle, the flute, or the bone touched, than they begin to hum an accusatory couplet in which the victim speaks in the first person. In the region of Sault the old storytellers like to tell the tale in which the bone whistle sings:

> Whistle, whistle, O shepherd,
> T'was my brothers killed me,
> For the rose of Pimperlé
> Which I had found.

The crime is revealed, the assassins named and sometimes punished. Most often these words are a prelude to a more complex reversal: the assassinated girl or child whose bones sang—whether all the bones of their bodies or a single bone—returns to life.

Yet another thread may be woven into this tapestry, emphasizing the qualities of the protagonists and giving certain episodes an even more dramatic luster by translating the story into another language, that of the slaughter and cooking of the pig. Several versions of the murderous stepmother are permeated by this correspondence. We see her cut the boy's throat, collect his blood, knead cakes, and concoct a blood fricassee of hands and feet for her husband. In Cantal a simple juxtaposition powerfully establishes the full equivalency. In order to seduce the widow, the "witch," adopting the appearance of an honest neighbor, "one fine day," which happens to be the day when the little boy mysteriously disappears, prepares a *batilhon*, a pig's foot, for him. After enjoying this delicacy, he gives the ossicles, as per custom, to the little sister to play with. It is while "she is amusing herself with all these little bones in the courtyard" that the Holy Virgin suggests she assemble them to make a bird, which, barely out of her fingers, takes flight singing:

Ma mairastra
Pica, pasta
M'a fait bolhir
Mon papá m'a manjat
Ma sòreta m'a massat
Più, più, più, più
Encara ieu soi viu!

[My stepmother
Larded, kneaded
Boiled me
Roasted me
My father ate me
My little sister put me back together
Tweet, tweet, tweet, tweet
I'm still alive!][41]

Here the bone obviously acquires its power from the culinary treatment it receives, culminating in the boiling cauldron, which, as we know, releases words. The Breton and Nevers versions, in fact, situate the miracle of the talking bone at the moment when the little sister, who is charged with watching over the cooking, stokes the flame: "Little fire, my sister, little fire, you are boiling my blood," cries a voice in the chimney. "Little sister, you're hurting me, foot aches, arm aches." In the chants and stories that do not include the cooking of blood and the cannibalistic meal, the pig's snout occasionally comes into play. Often it's a swineherd who discovers the prophetic bone or else the bouquet of roses that grew over the child's body: with it he carves a flute that, to our ears, brings to mind the whistle the castrator used to charm the pigs. Sometimes a sow scours the meadow and brings the bone to light; sometimes its breath is enough to animate the "singing bone." "And afterwards, a shepherdess was in the fields watching pigs, and one of her pigs found the little girl's pinky. 'Pig, my little pig,' the pinky said when the pig found it, 'breathe here.' "[42]

This porcine presence beside the child is no longer surprising to us. Their places are interchangeable: medieval Irish legends have a cut-up and cooked pig as their hero, a single bone of which is kept and whose entire skeleton is recreated and returned to life. Similarly Saint Nicolas, in the most famous of his miracles, resuscitates three little children placed in the salting tub by a pig butcher. A Picardi version sheds light on the context of these interchanges; the culinary torture of the little girl put to death is replaced by her "live" crucifixion in the back cellar of the house. The storytellers, who sometimes speak of "passions" and "martyrdom," are thereby picking up the thread of ritual murder stories: the Jews are accused of the same bloody preparations, attempts are sometimes made to substitute porcine flesh for that of the boy, a sow at times discovers the body of the tortured Christian whose sweet voice is heard. But in the stories the convergence is pushed to the most minute detail, that of the final remains, through which the story establishes a bridge with the ritual. Is the boy's posthumous destiny not the perfectly symmetrical reflection of that of the pig? The latter is dismembered and its last bone, in the form of a rhombus that cuts through the air, is made to sing by the boys, the very bone that will later be preserved, even buried. Opposite him the young female victim of the stories is either stashed away or eaten, yet a bone is nonetheless preserved and animated by a breath that gives it voice. "Ossicle," "pinky," even "last bone of the pinky," as in the Nevers version—this fragment alone is worth all the bones, the entire body and life itself. Now, every living being possesses a little bone, a "pinky"; is this the "bone that sings"?

Little Finger and "Little Jew"

Judas, spit me out
The Good Lord will punish you.
The knife, the scissor
Will cut your little finger.

—Walloon rhyme

In Swabia, when a child's pinky is bleeding, he is told, "Look at your soul flowing" or "The soul is running." If his nose is bleeding, he is told not to go to bed with "his head at the bottom," for, if a drop happened to fall on the ground, his soul would escape with it.[43] In children's beliefs the pinky, still called "the finger of the heart," commands the nose's bleeding: if you bite the little finger opposite the nostril from which blood is flowing, it stops. Children's finger theater always shows four fingers acting and the littlest one speaking or crying when pinched hard. In rhymed and sung couplets in which the fingers are shown preparing and sharing a feast—usually a hare in Languedoc—the "pinky" must demand its share. It does so with the voice of a bird:

"Tweet! Tweet! or "Cui, cui! I a pares per ieu? Is there nothing for me?"
And it is told, still being pinched: "Vej'aqui un osset. Vai majar al can-
tónnet, Here's a little bone. Go eat it by the chimney."[44] Every child
knows, furthermore, that the gesture of adults approaching their pinky
to their ear indicates the feared "my pinky told me." Some know how
to silence the scandalmongers from a distance: when their left ear whistles or rings, a sign that someone is "speaking ill" of them, they bite the
tip of their pinky hard and the ill-intentioned gossip simultaneously
bites his tongue.[45] This twofold connection between the pinky and
blood and the pinky and speech—words that sing a morbid secret—
explains its persistent presence during situations in which one passes
from one world to the next. The bloody pinky brings together two
facets of this great passage: the blood, a fleeing bodily fluid, flows out
with life and instantly hardens—the volatile soul has often been seen in
it; the bones whiten over time, constituting the final resting place of the
body and the speaking image of death. Which is why the incredulous
woman sees a pinky appear, as proof of the incarnation of Christ, in the
bread of communion that she kneaded with her own hands. Children
who make a pact seal it, in sixteenth-century Rouen, "by the faith of my
pinky," an expression that youth in nineteenth-century Provence
accompany by a gesture, hooking the pinkies of their right hands "like
two interlocking rings."[46] The man who sells his soul to the devil sometimes abandons a finger, along with several drops of blood that can
become an ingredient for evil deeds and spells: as a sign and tool of the
witches' power, a child's pinky floats on their brew in *Macbeth*.

This is the first placement of our little "bone that sings," but, if we
listen to the children who continue to pass along these experiences and
these bodily words, there is another, more secret placement one both
experiences and discovers upon banging one's elbow, specifically the
funny bone, referred to as the *petit juif*, the little Jew. The diagnosis
"he banged his *petit juif*" is based on the belief in the presence of a
very sensitive ossicle that in Paris, Switzerland, Alsace, and Gascony
is called the "little Jew" and in Provence simply *juiou*, the "Jew." The
twinge that occurs when it is banged hard is described as follows: "The
little Jew creates an electric shock and pins and needles that run
through your fingers." Indeed, the pain irradiates the entire forearm
right to the end of the pinky, which has been innervated, with the others, by the cubital nerve. The Alsatian dialectical terms designating
the ossicle interpret the sensation and explain its origin. Next to
Placken—suffering—and its compounds, *Narrenpläckel*, "suffering of

the crazy," *Judenpläckel*, "suffering of the Jew," figures a "pins and needle sack." Within this abundant grouping—a dozen terms for the lower Rhine alone—we find our singing and talking bone in the word *Musikantenknochen*, "musicians' bone," and even a *Telephonpläckel*, "telephone pain," the banging of which naturally indicates that "news" is on its way.[47] But the generic term known to all remains *der klein Jud*, "the little Jew," which awakens its alter ego, a pinky gifted with similar powers.

We now need to understand the enigmatic Jewishness attached to this ossicle. Those who use the expression offer a first explanation that is fairly recurrent and invokes the social necessity of "locking elbows," of closing ranks, a "gesture" attributed to the Jews throughout their history. More direct is the mechanical justification: when you bang your elbow your fingers close reflexively. The Christian thus finds himself with a hooked hand—a Jewish hand. And, since the pinky is the first finger affected, this naturally explains, in the eyes of the linguist who questions its name, why it is sometimes called the "little Jew."[48] In Germany an illness of the tip of the finger and the last phalanx is called *Judsche, Judin*, "the Jewess." As far as the elbow goes, the name is part of a cluster of designations that are familiar to us: it is all the more "Jewish" because it possesses certain anatomical and functional characteristics of its own. First, children have delicate articulations: violently pulling the arm you are holding in your hand—a gesture familiar to women who "pull" a child who refuses to budge—causes a painful and poorly explained blockage that disappears at about the age of five. The head of the cubitus, furthermore, is a cartilage whose ossification is only fully completed when one stops growing, at about the age of twenty. Before that the olecranon exists as a small "extra" bone that is mobile and detachable.[49] Now everything that disappears from or is transformed in a child's body—the infant's fine hair and scaly skin at birth—is called "Jewish," for these traces of an earlier state are erased, as we have seen, by the baptism, when Christian growth begins, the growth that will be completed by Holy Communion and the Tenebrae ritual on the threshold of adolescence. The "elbow bone" is thus the ultimate Jewish part; it reminds us of its existence by a shooting pain and never fully disappears. Situated in the body of every child, all of whom are "little Jews" for a time, it is the mark of the passage each one must experience, just as the Jewish vertebra in the body of the pig is the evidence and sign of the original metamorphosis that created the species. This symbolic bone was even acknowledged by the former German anatomists, who spoke of the "Jewish ossicle" native to Christians. Among the latter, moreover, it was only the good, true followers who felt with special force the "suffering of the Jew." In French-speaking Catholic Switzerland, where it is sometimes referred to as the *òs dla ràj*, the "bone of rage," initiation to this pain occurs among young boys as follows: "Show me your arm, I want to show you where the Germans don't have a bone." If one produces one's arm upon this request, one gets punched between the forearm and upper arm, eliciting a cry and thereby offering proof that one is neither "a German" nor a Lutheran.[50]

If this hidden painful bone designates Christians, it must therefore be missing in others. Symmetrical and reversed, the defective bone forms a reflection of itself. In fairy tales the "Devil's daughter," who is dismembered and incompletely reconstituted by her human pretender, is recognized by her sisters thanks to her missing pinky. Similarly, the Devil limps when he circulates on earth, as does the Jew with whom he is occasionally identified. In the Walloon game of Angel and Devil, in which the two compete for souls with the archangels and the Virgin, it is their feet that first qualify them, with one remarkable precision in an Austrian variation: the Jew has a twisted metatarsus, "Jud mit'n krumpn Haksn."[51] Passing from one world to the other thus implies the abandonment of or defect in a bone. This in fact is what happens to ghosts when they have had contact with the living, but an entire marginal species is inherently marked by the sign of the missing bone. Portuguese witches make up for it by concocting a rib out of willow, while in central Europe this same wood is used to sculpt the missing ossicle that identifies the children born during the period of the Twelve Days— thus destined to be exasperating elves. This defect signals one's belonging to the world of the dead, commonly transformed into a diabolical world, and distinguishes those who travel to and from the beyond.[52]

In the stories the hidden bone, furtively stashed away by the jealous brother or abandoned by the criminal stepmother, is the bone that is found; since death here is the language of initiation, after a series of trials, including being cooked, the hero usually returns to life when all his bones have been reassembled. His immediate resurrection is foreshadowed by the ritual circumstances of his temporary or, rather, *passing* death. It is also illuminated by everything that the boys do, in conjunction with the pig, on the day of the slaughter, when they let a little of their souls flow to the ground before giving voice to bony rhombuses. But another outcome is nearly as frequent: it confers on the young victim the status of a very particular ghost, that of the newborn child killed or abandoned by his parents. In Sweden the yping, or dead child, in the form of a bird, attracts the attention of nocturnal passersby and won't rest until it has led them to the scene of the crime. There a voice can be heard denouncing the murderous parents, until a charitable hand performs the gestures of appeasement: *burying* the bones. This is what happens at the end of the stories: the "bone that sings" points to the site of the body; the latter is exhumed and "reburied in the cemetery." In certain tales about the murderous stepmother in which the role of the younger sister is developed, the latter merely gathers up the bones; following the advice of the Virgin or an old woman, she washes or places them in a "sacred handkerchief" before interring them. Sometimes, in stories in which a pig uncovers the pinky of the dead little girl, the latter, reviving at the breath of the animal, expresses a final wish: "Boar of my father's house. Take me back slowly." Which the swineherd does. And the body is buried with the ritual consideration it is due.[53]

Thus the question of the funerary ritual, which alone is able to preserve the bones, the ossicle, is also at the heart of our stories in which the voice of suffering children's souls are heard. How, then, can we help but recognize in this grouping of words and gestures a knowledge and an operation that bring the metaphysical destiny into play for everyone?

Judgment Day

A little bone resists the flame.
It serves according to the cabala
As seed for resurrection.

—JEAN FOLLAIN, "Futur passé," *Ordre terrestre*

In the bodies of Christians and their pigs we have found two bones around which the complex network of these observances and exemplary stories revolve. A foot has the pig walking toward the Church, in the steps of Anthony, its tutelary saint; a vertebra connects it to its prior Jewish state. As for Christians, they have a pinky gifted with knowledge and speech that is joined to the Jewish point at the tip of their elbow. For these bones are always connected, one awakening the other or taking its place. They are connected to other parts of the skeleton—the head and the spinal column. For the souls one offers that of pigs, while that of the young martyrs found in tales can also speak and sing a song. They maintain a constant affinity with the most volatile vital bodily fluid: the pinky is both blood and bone, the vertebra of the pig, the young girl in her tub, is a figure of Melusinian purification, and the bone that sings can spatter with blood the murderer who brings it to his mouth. Thus the chosen bone evokes the whole of which it is the final remnant. What is more, the body reassumes its shape from it, whether immediately by the effect of the miracle or at the end of time after resting in the earth. If, as the Church teaches, each of us must be saved by a part of himself, however minute, this article of faith invites us to examine whether a trace of our ossicle can be found among Jews.

When, in 1690, Glückel of Hameln, who had become a widow, began writing her memoirs, she addressed herself first to her children. This Jewess from Hamburg, whose long life would end in Metz some twenty-five years later, applied the same enthusiasm to managing the business of precious stones inherited from her husband and the successive marriages of her eight children. But this brainy woman was also a woman with heart, steeped in love and piety, who, although she denied it, had a knowledge, a working morality to transmit. Her story is filled with exempla drawn from the common stock of oral tradition, itself legitimized, as she wrote repeatedly, by "the writings of our wise men." While pondering divine mercy and man's capacity "to face the judgment that awaits us all in the world to come," she continues in these terms:

> In the writings of our sages we find answers to everything. Thus it is told that Rabbi Yochanan, who was a great talmudist, lost nine sons in his lifetime. He was left with only one, a three-year-old child. Then, one day, a servant responsible for washing clothes put a vat of water to boil on the fire. Watching the steam rise, the child wanted to see what was happening in the vat. He climbed up on a stool, lost his footing, and fell into the boiling water. Hearing his cries, his father tried to pull him out, but all he could grasp was a finger, whereas the child had already entirely disappeared in the boiling water. He began hitting his head against the walls, then hastened to his students shouting: "Cry for my vanished star! This finger is all that remains of my child whom I raised in the love of God!" From then on, he wore the child's bone as a pendant around his neck, in memory of him. When a stranger or a colleague came to visit, he showed them this bone with great humility, as if he were showing them his son.[54]

Because he wants to present it on Judgment Day before the Eternal One the unhappy father never takes the bone from around his neck. Indeed, according to Jewish belief, at least one bone is required. Thus the worst malediction among religious Jews is expressed as follows:

"That death may overtake him in such a way that not the slightest remain can be found of him, not the slightest ossicle."[55] Around this germinative bone the two religions thus form the major lines of their eschatology. Supported rather late—first by the Pharisee doctors—the teaching in this domain is put to the test in Talmudic dialogues.

> Adrien asked Rabbi Josué Ben Hananya: "By what will the human being be pulled into the beyond by the Holy One?" "By a bone and by the spinal column called *luz*," he responds. "How do you know?" "Bring me a bone and I'll show you how it's done." Once the bone was furnished, they tried to pulverize it in a mill, without success. They wanted to burn it in a fire, in vain. They put it in water; it wouldn't dissolve. They placed it on an anvil and pummeled it with blows of the hammer. The anvil split and the hammer broke without any portion of the bone having given way.[56]

This unbreakable kernel is also called "almond bone," for around it the body will be reformed on the Judgment Day. *Luz*, furthermore, is also the name of the *City of Immortality* situated at the summit of the hollow trunk of an almond tree, inside of which the traveler must pass.[57] For their part, the Christians immediately exalted this theme of the resurrection of the body and also based themselves on the text of Ezekiel's vision (37:2–14), in which the prophet sees Yahweh breathe spirit, replace sinews, and make flesh grow on the dry bones scattered in the valley. If Christian teaching does not openly include the luz, the almond bone, one need only listen to stories and services centered around holy relics consecrated by the churches to hear the same discourse on the bony kernel that will restore life. Both religions therefore require burial and perform second funerals after decomposition. The skeleton—or a part of it—is unearthed, washed, and preserved. The Jews of the diaspora choose, to our day, to return to the land of Israel; Christians, sometimes until the twentieth century, deposited these funerary remains in the sacred walls of a chapel, a convent, or an ossuary, with highly varied procedures that fuel the variation in time and space of Christian death in Europe.[58] For our purposes, we should simply retain this common divide: within antique societies, whose evolutions, hesitations, and backtracking with regard to the treatment of the body are familiar to us, the Jewish *and* Christian identities based themselves on burial followed by the preservation of bone matter. They opposed both the integral preservation of the body, embalmed according to Egyptian custom, and cremation, which remained, until the fourth century, the dominant

Roman fashion. Only certain saints present—spontaneously, since they were discovered as if they had never died or were already resuscitated—a state of conservation and pleasant odor that owe nothing to the artifice of "mummy makers." But it is burning the body that constitutes the worst barbarity and is thus the most severe punishment in this world and in the other; Gehenna and hell support this point as well. Hence the pagan determination to break, burn, and disperse the bodies of martyrs. That of Saint John was subject to this fate, which is recalled, according to Guiart Desmoulins (end of the thirteenth century), by the *bonefires* lit on the eve of his saint's day and the descriptions of infernal vats heated by the bones of the damned.[59]

Which is why, for their part, the Christians made punishment by fire the most severe of retributions and most serious of trials. It is inflicted on those who are suspect. The Jew, the heretic, or the witch end up in a fire that is expected to reveal their true nature. A single example will suffice to illustrate the stubborn minutia of this metaphysical violence. The year is 1691. Several autos-da-fé have already been inflicted on the Majorcan conversos. Their attempts to take to the sea have been in vain and the Inquisition has decided to eradicate the Mosaic faith with one last fire. The trial then begins of those referred to from this period on as the xuetas. The account of the Jesuit Garou is entirely built according to the symbolic code whose principle we have just outlined. After the auto-da-fé, in the church of the Dominicans, twenty-one conversos were burned, fourteen in person and seven in effigy. The latter were not represented by crude mannequins: on each silhouette care was taken to draw in their bones. Similarly, the condemned were unearthed posthumously, if necessary, to inflict the same punishment upon them. One of the rabbis, Rafael Valls, died, according to the Jesuit father, like a real Judas, like a pig, losing his entrails; all, far from presenting the serenity of Christian martyrs, had faces deformed by a diabolical grimace. But the punishment, executed before an enormous crowd, was only complete upon the cremation of the bodies and the scattering of the ashes. To maintain the memory of this solemn act, the Dominicans hung in their cloister the faces of their victims representing the fifteen lineages of xuetas. At the start of the nineteenth century, these images were still visited by the two communities. The Christians showed their children "the mean people who tortured little Jesus" and the xuetas furtively attempted to save their ancestors from metaphysical misfortune by drawing little ossicles on these portraits in the shape of a cross, reestablishing their right to resurrection by this gesture and sign.[60]

On this shared knowledge and these shared customs the Christians thus built their difference. First they singled out a Jewish bone in their body, which they designated by referring to the belief of their neighbors—in lower Alsace, the names of the "little Jew" are for the most part mixed with Yiddish. They asserted that this bone faded away, as the native imprint must fade in every man, while suggesting that on the day of resurrection, the end linking up with the beginning, this part would become original again, would give birth to the blessed body while the Jews would burn in hell. And this punishment, to which Christian eschatology condemns them, was long inflicted by the Church on this earth, especially since by virtue of the shared belief cremation destroys any hope of resurrection for them. Conversely, the passage through fire makes the best Christians. Several companions of Christ—Saint John, Saint Peter, Saint Andrew—voluntarily subjected themselves to this ordeal. The only oral tradition in all of Europe relates that they had themselves burned to atone for a sin. But a bone—or their heart—resisted the flame, testifying to their purity. A young girl who found it, swallowed it, became pregnant, and gave birth to a child who was none other than the saint "reborn." Saint Anthony, the daring explorer of the underworld, is also among these "renewed" Christians.[61] In addition, the recluse appears as the mythical initiator of the Christian burial. Sensing the approach of death, he recommends to his two companions:

> If you have some wish to please me, do not allow my remains to be transported to Egypt and my body to be embalmed, a ritual I have many times condemned. You will lay me in the earth, and will take care to hide from all eyes my paltry remains: may no one but you know the site of my burial. I have sweet confidence that on resurrection day the Lord will return to me this flesh become incorruptible.[62]

This, according to Athanasius, was the hermit's testament, the legendary commentary of which says that the pig, his faithful companion, performed the ritual, paying Anthony the honor of being buried "like a Christian." Later this body reduced to a bone was found and brought back to Egypt under Constantine, at the end of a quest that expanded and confirmed the virtues of the little bone: guided by the archangel Gabriel, Theophilus the bishop and twelve monks retraced the path of the saint and crossed through hell again, where the passage of the distinguished relic awakened the liberated souls.[63]

Saint Anthony, his life, his legend, and his saint's day thus bring together the entire network of these behaviors and beliefs. A promethean *trickster*, he converted the fire of hell, which abolished all hope of rebirth, into a domestic fire, the power of which nonetheless has to be watched when it roars beneath the cauldrons. Master of the pig, he accompanies its pedestrian peregrinations on earth and toward the beyond; he is the model for all patron saints of piglets and humble swineherds who, following their vagabond animal, pass from the midst of the forest into the other world.[64] And, most of all, he is the guarantor of the annual return of the pig: in the Catalan will and testament the sow vows to be buried in the pigsty, and we have seen children burying a bit of bone and horn there. This gesture is now clear: from each pig it is necessary to set aside the seed of its successor. This principle is equally valid for Christians, who, it is taught, are like pigs, "since they have the same foot and the same number of bones," but, when it comes to humans, this gesture can only prepare one's final destination.[65] The festival that occurs around each pig always articulates—with rituals, words, and objects that are varied yet equivalent within the Christian world—the moment of the returning pig and the metaphysical time during which souls wait and advance, at the end of which the bodies will join together by virtue of the little bone that has been preserved.

The Time of Sacrifice

Today, in the homes still active in the region of Sault, two animals are predestined for a remarkable death every year: the lamb that is kept in the stable all winter to be slaughtered at Easter and the pig that is killed at the end of January. Until 1914 a cow was also slaughtered at the home from time to time, but only on major festive occasions—a marriage, for instance—was it divided and immediately consumed. Nonetheless, in some villages the custom was maintained of bleeding cattle from the jugular vein, collecting their blood in large frying pans, and cooking the *sanquette* over the fire, but this took place for only one occasion: the local festivals, days devoted to the patron saint of the village, and large family gatherings. Many took place in winter, close to Christmas. Slaughtering these domestic animals, dividing them up, consuming them together thus implies an inscription in that moment of the year, in the cycle of gatherings, in the holiday calendar. Blood never flows without a ceremony.

Some have criticized the facile use of the word *sacrifice*—and rightfully so—its application whenever an animal in Europe is put to death following the forms set by custom. But even while avoiding it, it is nonetheless necessary to be aware of the debate that the use of this term as well as its rejection denote. The dilemma is simple: when these gestures are referred to as "sacrifices," it designates primarily a certain barbarity, a dark and ineradicable depth. The teacher who, as a young woman, was a horrified witness to the bleeding of cows saw it as an indication of a primitiveness to be confronted. The bishop, for his part, sometimes recommended that priests not attend pig slaughters and meals, even if they couldn't avoid the "present" of chops and blood sausages, of bone and blood. Today's animal defenders attack the refusal to knock out the pig, refusing to accept the notion that its cry and its blood must be uttered and flow at the same time.

Conversely, the automatic rejection of any sacrificial reference denotes a cognizance of the founding change Christianity promoted. Next to the scribes, it was the sacrificers that the Gospels showed to be eager in their pursuit of Christ. Even if he rejects, in principle, the idea of a selective impurity of beings created by God—"Do not ye yet understand, that whatsoever entereth in at the mouth goeth into the belly, and is cast out into the draught? But those things which proceed out of the mouth come forth from the heart; and they defile man" (Mathew 15:17–20), teaches Jesus—Saint Paul asks believers to abstain from meats that have been cut up on idolatrous alters: "For if the sprinkling of defiled persons with the blood of goats and bulls and with the ashes of a heifer sanctifies for the purification of the flesh, how much more shall the blood of Christ, who through the eternal Spirit offered himself without blemish to God, purify your conscience from dead works to serve the living God." Thus the sacrifice took place "once for all," it seals the New Covenant (Hebrews 9:13–14, 10:10). The Mass is its sublimated spiritual expression. Consequently, it would be ill founded or, in any case, illusory, to recognize sacrifice where Christianity prevails. The real flesh and blood of animals offered to the divinity and eaten no longer constitute the path to the sacred, as Henri Hubert and Marcel Mauss would say. However, whether one uses the word or rejects it, the "carnal" sacrifice therefore exists only outside of or prior to our world; it can only survive as a remnant.

What remains of these contrasted but convergent positions at the end of our journey? Let us first note that we have carefully avoided the word *sacrifice* itself; we have been wary of presumptions that are particularly weighty since the first model, proposed by Hubert and Mauss, gives too large a place to the Christian conception as clearly expressed by Saint Paul. In it we see blood—that of animals replaced by that of Christ—open the doors to the tabernacle, lead to the saint of saints, delineating, *as if in space,* the profane and the sacred. This boundary is crossed by the human sacrificer and the sacrificed animal with the same step. Yet haven't the anthropologists of Vedic India, ancient Greece, and black Africa recently shown that, less than a rite of passage, the bloody sacrifice could be common cookery, one that makes it "licit and pious to eat meat" (Marcel Detienne) on the condition that a portion is sent up to the gods?[1] The sharing is everything, a sharing that involves cutting up and distributing but also, and especially, makes apparent each individual's place and role: the nature of men and women, old and young, as well as the local power structure. A closed universe of differences inscribes itself on the opened body, its body parts and fluids— the blood instantly separated out—and gives the invisible a gift of its predetermined share. Nothing about the pig escapes this first "domestic" definition of *sacrifice*. It is thus possible to resume use of the word.

Furthermore, we see that the choice of the victim itself is not indifferent, the sacrifice necessary manifests its position within the species that are killed and eaten. Here the singularity of the pig stands out through the unique manner in which it is reared, through the concomitant multiplicity of analogies that are attentive to its complexion, interpret its being, try to shape its strange nature. "In the pig everything is good," says the adage; it contains "thirty-six tastes" adds another, meaning that the entire spectrum of meats and their flavors are found in it. We now know the source of this attribute: everything must be shared, thus everything from the sacrificial animal is not only food but food for the anthropologist's thought; this exhaustiveness—everything concentrated in one—setting it apart before placing it center stage, when the time for the slaughter arrives.

But the selection of the pig, the constant reference to its meat, which here is the *gras*, the "meat," par excellence, implies the consideration of a dimension that has been denied. It is not *despite* Christianity that these gestures are perpetuated to our day, but rather *within it*, in relation to what founds it. The Jews did not sacrifice pigs, which they forbid themselves from eating. The Christians ate pork, but not without subjecting themselves to fastidious rules by which it came to occupy the sacrificial place in every home. The game of mirrors did not stop with this inversion; the comprehension, the full mastery, of the other, his reduction to a particular nature had to fill the void left by the prohibition: "How can they not eat pork?" Thus the Jew was fated to an eternal resemblance to the animal he called unclean. An ostentatious display of distance that, for Christians, is the equivalent of a confession and reveals a secret, because incestuous, appetite.

Based on this, the pig is a creature divided. It incarnates the sins of lechery and gluttony; demons take up residence within it. At the same time, it is Christian flesh, endowed with a soul of blood, called upon to appear at the meals of Christmas and Easter, and sometimes dedicated to the Church and to the indigent dead. But this duality is always shifting. The pig represents passage, no longer in space but *in time*. It leads not from the profane to the sacred but from Jewish oldness, from which it originates, according to the myth, to young Christianity, which chose it as a tangible mark of the New Law. One Hungarian story relates that the pig rubbed itself against Christ's cross. No witness was able to say on which side its body had touched it. The Jews thus concluded that it was doubly inedible.[2] To this we could add that the Christians instituted its sacrifice in order that its cursed part would be purified, to make it entirely their own.

The participants in the ritual accompany this ever renewed transformation with the powers inherent to them. We have seen women, Jewesses so long as their blood flows, handle the most dangerous portion come the proper age, producing new Christians out of Jewish blood. We then saw the boys take the lead as warriors, killing the Jew within by subjecting themselves to the bloody death of pigs and hunting and cutting up a Judas who resembles them. And this is key. Christians can only repeat the passage from the faith of Israel to that of Christ. When present, the Jews are caught up in the total logic of this reading, which the flames of anti-Semitism revive and intensify and the customs of liturgy and domestic sacrifice reiterate in the calm facts of the slaughter and division or the theatrical exaltation of the Passion.

NOTES

Introduction

1. See "Carnival, essai d'ethnologie culinaire," in *Aspects des collectivités rurales en pays de Sault* (Toulouse, 1972), pp. 31–65, and "Le testament du cochon," *Via Domitia*, vol. 2 (Toulouse, 1979), 14:121–156, written with Daniel Fabre in homage to Jean Séguy.

2. This exploration was initially supposed to constitute a chapter, "Apprivoiser le sauvage, encore et toujours," part of which, reformulated, furnished material for the article "Le partage du *ferum*, un rite de chasse au sanglier," *Etudes rurales* (July-December 1982), pp. 377–400.

3. Some of these stories are translated in the appendix of "L'enfant, le four et le cochon," *Le Monde alpin et rhodanien* (1982), no. 1–4, pp. 155–179.

4. For more details, see "Juifs et chrétiens autour du cochon," *Recherches et Travaux de l'Institut d'ethnologie de Neuchâtel* (1986), no. 6, pp. 59–83. Marvin Harris, in *Pigs, Wars, and Witches: The Riddles of Culture* (New York, 1974), develops the health and ecological thesis, vigorously discussed by Marshall Sahlins, "Culture, protéines, profit," *Libre* (1979), no 5, pp. 105–128 (first appearing in the *New York Review of Books*, 1978). Paul Diener and Eugene Robkin, in a widely debated article based on a hypothesis by James George Frazer, invite us to return to a more political explanation in "Ecology, Evolution, and the Search for Cultural Origins: The Question of Islamic Pig Prohibition," *Current Anthropology* (1978), 19(3):493–540. Mary Douglas has laid out her interpretation in *Purity and Danger* (1966); she returned to and developed it in a chapter of *Natural Symbols: Explorations in Cosmology* (New York, 1970) entitled "The Bog Irish," pp. 59–76.

5. An example of these precocious illustrations is presented in the work of Henri Stern, *Le Calendrier de 354* (Paris, 1953).

6. Jack Goody cites this example regarding the state expansion of writing in medieval England in *The Logic of Writing and the Organization of Society* (Cambridge, 1987).

7. Historians of food have added a greater nuance to our understanding of the place of pork, have contrasted the various social strata, regional productions and traditions, periods of greater or lesser extravagance, but have confirmed its presence almost everywhere and always. The reference work remains that by Jean-Jacques Hémardinquer, "Faut-il 'démythifier' le pork familial d'Ancien Régime?" *Annales E.S.C.*, 25th year (November-December, 1970), no. 6, pp. 1745–1766.

8. The langue d'oc terms are transcribed according to a standardized spelling that I use when I quote my informers. When I cite texts, on the other hand, I use the variant spellings of the authors.

9. I have had the occasion to explicate the method followed here in a text written with Daniel Fabre, "L'ethnologie du symbolique en France: situation et perspectives," in *Ethnologies en miroir, Actes du colloque "Ethnologie française-Mitteleuropäische Volkskunde,"* Bad-Homburg, December 12–15, 1984, under the direction of Isac Chiva and Utz Jeggle (Paris, 1987), pp. 123–138. One can also read our contribution "Identification d'un rite, la cure de la hernie" in Gérard Althabe, Daniel Fabre, and Gérard Lencluc, eds., *Vers une ethnologie du présent* (Paris, 1992), pp. 59–73.

1. The Red Men

1. Archives départementales de l'Hérault, C 616.

2. Many examples of these accumulated debts were found among the judgments of the justice of the peace of Belcaire (Archives départementales de l'Aude, 4 U 4, 49).

3. Henri Maders, *Caux, mon village en Bittérois* (n.p.,n.d.), p. 23.

4. Archives départementales de l'Hérault, U 508 Z, 94 items.

5. The expression is in Achille Mir, *Glossaire des comparaisons populaires du Narbonnais* (Montpellier, 1882), p. 98; and Jacques Boisgontier, *Atlas linguistique et ethnographique du Languedoc oriental*, 3 vols. (Paris, 1981–1986), map 493.

6. Antoine Sylvère, *Toinou* (Paris, 1979), pp. 216–220.

7. H. Maders, *Caux, mon village en Bittérois*, p. 73; Achille Millien and Paul Delarue, *Recueil de chants populaires du Nivernais* (Paris-Nevers, 1934), p. 36, on the nicknames of merchants in about 1880.

8. Anonymous, *Contes picards* (Paris-Geneva, 1978 [1883]), p. 20.

9. Charles Beauquier, *Faune et flore populaires de la Franche-Comté* (Paris, 1910), pp. 162–163. On representations of the otter, see Eugène Rolland, *Faune populaire de la France. Noms vulgaires, dictons, proverbes, légendes, contes et superstitions*, 11 vols. (Paris, 1967 [1877–1915]), 1:54–55; 7:126–130.

10. The text is quoted from Jacques Le Goff, *La Bourse et la Vie* (Paris, 1986), p. 103, who elsewhere analyzes the analogy established in the Middle Ages between the merchant, the usurer, and the Jew (pp. 35–49).

11. The word *ladre*, as we shall see further along, means "measled" for the pig, "leprous" for humans, and "greedy."—Trans.

12. We gathered three testimonies regarding the pig tongue examiner, two from the south of Cévennes (the region of Vallerauge and the French Saint-Etienne-Vallée), one from a man from Aveyronne (Naucelles) who had married in Mazuby, in the region of Sault.

13. Jean Séguy, *Atlas linguistique et ethnographique de la Bourgogne* (hereafter *ALG*), 6 vols. (Paris, 1975–1984), map 1405; see also J.-M. Fontan, *Nouveau guide pratique pour l'élevage du porc* (Tarbes, 1905), pp. 93–94. Etienne Louis Raynaud, *Les Usages locaux dans la haute vallée de l'Aude* (Toulouse, 1914), p. 312, n. 8. Similarly, Victor and Sylvain Fons, *Usages Locaux de la Haute-Garonne* (Toulouse, 1910), p. 511.

14. In France, because of regulations on the profession, the texts are numerous after 1378; Frédéric Godefroy, *Dictionnaire de l'ancienne langue française* (Paris, 1889–1896), s.v. See also Nicolas Delamarre, *Traité de la police* (1705), vol. 2, book 5, title 21 ff.; and Legrand d'Aussy, *Histoire de la vie privée des Français* (Paris, 1815 [1782]), 1:316–317. Examples are given in F. Ménard, "Le métier de langueyeur à Angers il y a deux cents ans," *Mémoires de l'Académie des sciences et belles-lettres d'Angers* (1965), series 8, 9:42–44; *Société d'études folkloriques du Centre-Ouest* (July-August), p. 310. The practice is confirmed for Catalonia by Agustín Miquel, *Libro de los secretos de agricultura* (Barcelona, 1762; [1617, Catalan ed.]), p. 477; and for Switzerland by Saloz de Moudon, *Mémoire sur la ladrerie des porcs* (Lausanne, 1810), p. 7.

15. The langue d'oc lexicon of the *langueyeur* and of the ills detected by him has been established in the work of Pierre Nauton, *Atlas linguistique et ethnographique du Massif central* (hereafter *ALMC*), 4 vols. (Paris, 1957–1963), map 528; and Frédéric Mistral, *Lou tresor dóu Felibrige, Dictionnaire provençal-français*, 2 vols. (Aix-en-Provence, 1878), s.v.

16. L.-V. Collaine, *Moyens de conserver la santé des cochons* (Metz, 1839), p. 19. Célestin Bailly, in *Art d'élever, de multiplier et d'engraisser les porcs* (Paris, 1848), proposes an equivalency between *dents de lait* and wolf's teeth, p. 10.

17. The destruction of infested pigs was common in Angers in 1768 (Ménard, "Le métier de langueyeur," p. 44) but the local Pyrenean custom was far more flexible and accepted the consumption of the meat provided it was well cooked and salted. The inventory of terms designating this flesh and its usages in Gascogny has been compiled by Jean-Louis Fossat, *La Formation du vocabulaire gascon de la boucherie* (Toulouse, 1971), pp. 98–101.

18. For leprosy, we have used the works of Henri Marcel Fay, *Histoire de la lèpre en France: lèpreux et cagots du Sud-Ouest* (Paris, 1910); Edouard

Jeanselme, "Comment l'Europe du Moyen Age se protégea des lépreux," *Revue de la Société française d'histoire de la médecine* (1931), 25:1–55; Jean Imbert, *Les Hôpitaux en droit canonique* (Paris, 1947), which details, along with the telling marks, the social condition of lepers, and the ritual of *separatio*, known since the early fifteenth century. For a synthesis, see Saul Nathaniel Brody, *The Disease of the Soul: Leprosy in Medieval Literature* (London, 1974); and François Bériac, *Histoire des lépreux au Moyen Age* (Paris, 1988); see also François Bériac, *Des lépreux aux cagots* (Bordeaux, 1991).

19. Guillame Bouchet, *Les Serées* (Paris, 1873–1882 [1584–1598]), 36th *serée*; Plutarch debates this question in his *Table Talk*, vol. 9, second section. The interdictions that separate the *lepreux* and *les cagots* from the pig are described in Fay, *Histoire de la lèpre en France*, pp. 111, 234–235, 343, 372–374.

20. On this confusion see Fay, *Histoire de la lèpre en France*, pp. 28–29; and Francisque Michel, *Histoire des races maudites de la France et de l'Espagne* (Paris, 1847), which sketched a portrait of lepers and *cagots* based on medical and literary texts; 1:245–258 and 366–371. We will return to this question in part 2.

21. Léon Cladel, *Le Bouscassié* (Paris, 1869), p. 118.

22. These practices are already advocated in *Les Agronomes latins* (Paris, 1874), Columelle, 7:10. The techniques are described in Séguy, *ALG*, map 423; Nauton, *ALMC*, map 527; and Pierre Gardette and Paulette Durdilly, *Atlas linguistique et ethnographique du Lyonnais* (hereafter *ALL*), 5 vols. (Paris, 1950–1976), map 325.

23. Albert Goursaud, *La Société rurale traditionnelle en Limousin* (Paris, 1976), 1:268. Similar descriptions are furnished by J. B. Saulières, "Le langueyeur," *Bulletin de la Société d'éthnographie en Limousin* (September 1965), no. 12, p. 152, which comments on the scene that gave rise to the postcard that everyone locates in his or her own region; see, for example, Calelhou, *Souvenirs d'enfance* (Rodez, 1977), p. 46–49.

24. Mistral, *Lou tresor*, s.v. "Languejaïre," "Lengueja."

25. J. Gourdon, *Traité de la castration des animaux domestiques* (Paris, 1860), pp. 312–337. See also Séguy, *ALG*, map 1143; Nauton, *ALMC*, map 436; Denis Chevallier, *L'Homme, le Porc, l'Abeille et le Chien* (Paris, 1987), p. 151.

26. See Jakob Jud and Karl Jaberg, *Sprach und Sachatlas italiens und der Südschweiz*, 6 vols. (Zofingen, 1928–1940), map 1098; Geneviève Massignon and Brigitte Hériot, *Atlas linguistique et ethnographique de l'Ouest (Poitou, Aunis, Saintonge, Angoumois*, 3 vols. (Paris, 1971–1983), map 483; Nauton, *ALMC*, map 435. Gourdon, *Traité de la castration*, details these techniques, as does Ziedonis Ligers, "Le castrage des animaux domestiques en Bessin," *A.T.P.* (1959), no. 3–4, pp. 281–285.

27. On "Sanar" see Xavier Ravier, *Atlas linguistique et ethnographique du Languedoc occidental*, 4 vols. (Paris, 1978–1993), map 398; "Aranjar" and "Crestar," Séguy, *ALG*, map 1383; "Habiller," "Rhabiller," Gardette and Durdilly, *ALL*, map 323.

28. Pierre de Marca, *Histoire de Béarn* (Paris, 1640); and *L'Emigration des Pyrénéens vers l'Espagne* (Pau, 1972) are our sources.

29. Cited by Norbert Rosapelly, *Au pays de Bigorre: us, coutumes et légendes* (Tarbes, 1892), p. 55.

30. Carlo Levi, *Le Christ s'est arrêté à Eboli* (Paris, 1948), pp. 174–177.

31. Taken from *Folklore de Champagne* (1981), p. 35; and Colette Dondaine, *Atlas linguistique et ethnographique de la Franche-Comté*, 3 vols. (Paris, 1972–1984), map 771.

32. We are borrowing our examples from José Figueira Valverde and Casto Sampedro y Folgar, *Cancaniero musical de Galicia* (Pontevedra, 1941), 1:204. We have analyzed the assocation between the flute and the castrator in "Le charme de la syrinx," *L'Homme* (1983), 23(3):5–39.

33. Pierre Letuaire, *Notes et dessins de la vie toulonnaise, 1796–1884* (Marseilles, 1976), pp. 121–122.

34. On this musical surgery, see M. Justin-Godart, "L'opération de la taille," *Revue d'histoire de la médecine* (1954), 11:27–35; and the pieces for harpsichord and bass viol by Marin Marais (1656–1728) intended to accompany the extraction of stones.

35. Simin Palay, *Dictionnaire du béarnais et du gascon modernes* (Paris, 1980), s.v. "Pihurlet," "Pihet"; Longus, *La Pastorale de Daphnis et Chloé* in *Romans grecs et latins* (Paris, 1980), book 3, chapter 28; Pliny the Elder, *Natural History*, book 8. For the hunting panpipe, see Jean Aymard, *Les Chasses romaines, des origines à la fin du siècle des Antonins* (Paris, 1951), p. 336.

36. For confirmation, see also Pierre Charié, *Le Folklore du Bas-Vivarais* (Paris, 1964), p. 322; on "redness," see Levi, *Le Christ s'est arrêté à Eboli*, pp. 174–177.

37. Yvonne Verdier, *Façons de dire, façons de faire: La laveuse, la couturière, la cuisinière* (Paris, 1979), p. 48, highlighted the relationship between redness and women's periods.

38. Edward Hoffmann-Krayer and Hanns Bächtold-Staübli, *Handwörterbuch der deutschen Aberglauben*, 10 vols. (Berlin-Leipzig, 1968 [1927–1942]), s.v. "Kastration." On the castrator-sorcerer, see Robert Hertz, *Sociologie religieuse et folklore* (Paris, 1970), p. 186. A Mayennais *chatrou* is at the heart of one of the main scandals related by Jeanne Favret-Saada and Josée Contreras in *Corps pour corps: Enquête sur la sorcellerie dans le Bocage* (Paris, 1981), pp. 235–244. Jules Lecoeur, in *Esquisses du bocage normand* (Saint-Pierre de Salerne, 1979 [1883–1891]), devotes several pages to *langueyeurs-affranchisseurs*, "healers and sorcerers"; 2:91–97.

39. Still called *sposàr el por\,iel* in Feltrino according to Angela Nardo Cibele, *Zoologia popolare veneta* (Bologna, 1966 [1887]), p. 123.

40. Arnold Van Gennep noted these names and compiled the map for the Ardèche and Savoy, in *Manuel de folklore français contemporain*, 8

vols. (Paris, 1943–1988), 1:268–271. On the *bacialé*, see Edoardo Ballone, *Cultura della cascina: Mediatori di donne e di bestiame nel Piemonte contadino* (Milan, 1979).

41. Juan de Luna, *Segunda parte de Lazarillo de Tormes* (Madrid, 1847 [1620]).

42. Jehan de Brie, *Le Bon Berger* (Paris, 1979), p. 163. The sketches by Denis Bonnet are in the collection of the Bibliothèque Inguimbertine of Carpentras. See, on this painter, *Rencontres: Denis Bonnet (1788–1877)* (Carpentras, 1969). Nine of these works are reproduced as an insert in *Etudes rurales* (1980), no. 78–80, p. 29.

2. Children's Stories

1. We are using the following versions of the pig-prince: Gian Francesco Straparole, *Les Facétieuses Nuits* (Paris, 1857 [Lyons, 1560]), 2d night, fable 1, noted by Aarne-Thompson in T. 433; Giuseppe Pitré, *Fiabe, novelle i raconti Siciliani* (Palermo, 1978 [1888]), 2:531–539; Geneviève Massignon, *Contes corses* (Aix-en-Provence, 1963), tales 11 and 42; Charles Joisten, *Contes folkloriques des Hautes-Alpes* (Paris, 1955), pp. 44–47; Ion Creanga, *Contes populaires de Roumanie* (Paris, 1931), p. 3–20.

2. Ambroise Paré, *Des monstres, des prodiges, des voyages* (Paris, 1964 [1573]), p. 190; and Laurent Joubert, *Erreurs populaires au fait de médecine et régime de santé* (Avignon, 1578), p. 235.

3. In M. Vidal, "Livre de raison d'un notaire albigeois," *Bulletin de la Société littéraire et scientifique du Tarn* (1928), pp. 85–86.

4. Paul Sébillot, *Le Folklore de France*, 4 vols. (Paris, 1968), 3:148–149.

5. Our work continues in the direction of the fertile analysis by Yvonne Verdier, *Façons de dire, façons de faire: La laveuse, la couturière, la cuisinière* (Paris, 1979), pp. 40–56; Karl Jaberg, "The Birthmark in Folk Belief, Language, Literature, and Fashion," *Romance Philology* (1957), 10(4):307–343, is fundamental. See also Giuseppe Pitré, *Medicina popolare siciliana* (Palermo, 1978), pp. 116–119.

6. Miguel de Cervantes, *Don Quijote de la Mancha*; A. Hock, *Croyances et remèdes populaires du pays de Liège* (Liège, 1888), pp. 90–91.

7. Gabriel García Márquez, *One Hundred Years of Solitude*; Joubert, *Erreurs populaires*, pp. 224–225.

8. See Frédéric Mistral, *Lou tresor dóu Felibrige, Dictionnaire provençal-français*, 2 vols. (Aix-en-Provence, 1878), s.v. "Roujan," "Garri"; Louis Alibert, *Dictionnaire occitan-français* (Toulouse, 1966), s.v. "Noiridor"; Jean Séguy, in *Etymologica (Mélanges W. von Wartburt)* (Tübingen, 1958), established the origin of the "langue d'oc *tésu(n)*, piglet; pig," pp. 699–705.

9. Joan Amades, *Folklore de Catalunya. Costums i creences* (Barcelona, 1969), pp. 39–41.

10. Antoine Fueldez, *Observations curieuses touchant la petite vérole* (Lyons, 1645), p. 96 ff.

11. On this cure through red, see Jean de Rostany, *Traité sur les erreurs vul-gaires de la médecine* (Lyons, 1689), p. 476; Manuel Alvar, *Atlas lingüístico y etnográfico de Andalucía* (Grenade, 1961), map 295; Léon de Galtier, a doctor in Saint-Affrique, in his *Traité de la rougeole* (Paris, 1645), recommends a poppy syrup.

12. Simon Tissot, *Avis au peuple sur sa santé*, 2 vols. (Paris, 1770); P. Scoutteten, *Rougeole et scarlatine* (Metz, 1868). Theories and controversies were highly homogeneous until the mid-nineteenth century, at which point a break was established between levels of discourse, scholarly and popular.

13. To use Anthelme Richerand's expression, *Les Erreurs populaires rela-tives à la médecine* (Paris, 1812), pp. 16–23.

14. Luis de Hoyos Saínz, *Folklore de embarazo* (Madrid, 1953), pp. 3–7. The relationship between styes and unsatisfied desires is noted by the Mediterranean ethnographers: Amades, *Folklore de Catalunya*, p. 20; Pitré, *Medicina popolare siciliana*, pp. 278–279.

15. Jesús Taboada, "La matanza del cerdo en Galicia," *Revista de dialec-tología y tradiciones populares* (1969), 25:89–105. We will return to the spleen in chapter 8.

16. See Paré, *Des monstres*, p. 184; and Joubert, *Erreurs populaires*, pp. 156–161.

17. On the red poppy, Eugène Rolland, *Flore populaire, ou histoire naturelle des plantes dans leurs rapports avec la linguistique et le folklore*, 11 vols. (Paris, 1967 [1877–1915]), 1:162–179, is very rich. Pitré, *Medecina popolare siciliana*, p. 1131, details the opposition between children and women of menstrual age. The Majorcan poems are in Gabriel Janer Manila, *Sexe i cultura a Mallorca: el cançoner* (Palma de Mallorca, 1979), pp. 133–134. For an overall view of langue d'oc terminology, see Jean-Claude Bouvier and Claude Martel, *Atlas linguis-tique et ethnographique de la Provence*, 2 vols. (Paris, 1975–1979), map 244; and Jean Séguy, *Atlas linguistique et ethnographique de la Gascogne*, 6 vols. (Paris, 1954–1973), map 191.

18. On eye sicknesses, see Joubert, *Erreurs populaires*, p. 304; and Mistral, *Lou tresor*, s.v. "Mau d'uei."

19. Robert Jalby, *Le Folklore du Languedoc* (Paris, 1971), p. 289.

20. L. V. Collaine, *Moyens de conserver la santé des cochons* (Metz, 1839), p. 19.

21. Nicole Roure, "La sorcellerie en Roussillon," *C.E.R.C.A.* (1964), no. 26–28, provides beautiful incantations against *enaiguament*.

22. Rolland, *Flore populaire*, 5:226–247.

23. Adrienne Durand-Tullou, "L'élevage du porc dans le Gard au début du XXe siècle," in *Le Porc domestique* (Paris, 1976), pp. 89–99; Georges Rocal, *Le Vieux Périgord* (Toulouse, 1927), pp. 142–143.

24. Barthélemi Amilha, *Tableu de la bida del parfet crestia* (Toulouse, 1673), p. 225; the Romanian ritual is in Paul-Henri Stahl, "Soi-même et les autres:

quelques exemples balkaniques," in *L'Identité*, Claude Lévi-Strauss, general editor (Paris, 1977), pp. 287–303. One cannot help but compare these rituals with the buying back of the newborn in Jewish culture: Patricia Hidiroglou, "Pidyon ha-ben. Le rachat du premier-né dans la tradition juive." *L'Homme* (1988), no. 105, pp. 64–75.

25. Ramón Violant i Simorra, "Costums de la cria i de la mantança del porc al Pallars Sobirà," in *Obra oberta* (Barcelona, 1981), 3:9.

26. Jean Audiau, *La Pastourelle dans la poésie occitane du Moyen Age* (Paris, 1923), pp. 128–134.

27. The langue d'oc, Catalan, and Spanish versions of *La Porcheronne* are presented by Jean-Maris Petit and Jean Tena, *Romancero occitan* (Montpellier, 1969), pp. 57–70. Our version of reference is in Damase Arbaud, *Chants populaires de la Provence* (1862), 1:91. Arnold Van Gennep studied this theme in "Une version méconnue de *La Porcheronne*," *Mercure de France* (January 1947), no. 1001, pp. 84–98. See, on the genre, Michel Zink, *La Pastourelle* (Paris, 1972), pp. 50 and 70.

28. Verdier, *Façons de dire*, pp. 236–245, analyzed the symbolism attached to these objects.

29. Paul Sébillot, *Le Folklore de France*, 4 vols. (Paris, 1968 [1906]) 3:100–101. Edward Hoffmann-Krayer and Hanns Bächtold-Staübli, *Handwörterbuch der deutschen Aberglauben*, 10 vols. (Berlin-Leipzig, 1968 [1927–1942]), s.v. "Schwein," p. 1484.

30. H. Mouly, *Mas espingadas* (Rodez, 1945), pp. 109–113; Daniel Fabre and Jacques Lacroix, *La Tradition orale du conte occitan* (Paris, 1973–1974), 1:135–136.

31. See Freddy Sarg, "Comment on élève et on tue le cochon en Alsace Bossue," *Revue des sciences sociales de la France de l'Est* (1980), no. 9, p. 294; and Charles Forot and Michel Carlat, *Le Feu sous la cendre. Le paysan vivarois et sa maison* (Saint-Félicien, 1980), 2:995; on the *rospaliaire*, see Pierre Charrié, *Le Folklore du bas Vivarais* (Paris, 1964), p. 322.

32. Ambroise Paré, *Textes choisis* (Paris, 1953), p. 90 and the note, pp. 219–220, by Marcel Sendrail; see also Etienne Thévet, *Les Erreurs et Abus ordinaires commis au fait de la chirurgie* (Poitiers, 1603), p. 50; Tissot, *Avis au peuple sur sa santé*, 2:153–154; Richerand, *Les Erreurs populaires*, pp. 156–157; Alfred Franklin, *La Vie privée d'autrefois: Variétés chirurgicales* (Paris, 1894), pp. 200–203.

33. The file on the Latapies was reconstituted based on several sources: in the archives of the Société royale de médecine, Académie de médecine, box 179, dr. 30, nine items relate the affair after inquiry to the bishop of Saint-Papoul, but two legal files are preserved in the departmental archives of Hérault (C. 4723) and of Aude (B. 2563). It seems that the preceding years posed problems, since, in 1692, we find a surgeon who brings one of his clients to court seeking "payment of eighteen pounds for the costs, troubles, and

times employed in cutting and operating on a small child, in order to cure him of a hernia" (Archives départementales de l'Aude, B 2728).

34. Quoted by Franklin, *La Vie privée*, pp. 200–203; on the Neopolitan *norcini*, see also Bernard Mojon, *Mémoire sur les effects de la castration dans le corps humain* (Montpellier, 1804).

35. Quoted by G. Pinot, *Etude médico-légale de la castration* (Lyons, 1890), pp. 56–57.

36. In Michel Bozon and Anne-Marie Thiesse, *La Plaine et la Route* (Royaumont, 1982), p. 53.

37. Gaston Vuillier, "Chez les magiciens et les sorciers de la Corrèze," *Le Tour du monde* (1899), pp. 505–518.

38. We have developed this analysis in "Identification d'un rite, la cure de la hernie," in Gérard Althabe, Daniel Fabre, Gérard Lenclud, eds., *Vers une ethnologie du présent* (Paris, 1992), pp. 59–73.

39. On this bibliography, we refer readers to our study cited above; Alfonso M. Di Nola devoted a fine work to the ritual and its history based on a contemporary area in southern Italy in *L'arco di rovo: Impotenze e agressivita in due rituali del sud* (Turin, 1983).

40. Julio Caro Baroja, *La estación de amor* (Madrid, 1979), chapter 27.

41. R. Violant i Simorra, "Costums de la cria," p. 8.

42. André Chamson, *Le Chiffre de nos jours* (Paris, 1954), pp. 254–257.

43. Séguy, *ALG*, map 1322 and commentary.

44. Charles Galtier, *Le Trésor des jeux provenéçaux* (Arles, 1952), pp. 25–26 and 102.

45. The autobiographical description of this blood game reappears on several occasions in Catalan ethnographic work as a fundamental feature of children's customs: Joan Amades, *Folklore de Catalunya. Cançoner* (Barcelona, 1951), p. 38; Joan Amades, *Costumari català. El curs de l'any*, 5 vols. (Barcelona, 1950), 1:16; Amades, *Folklore de Catalunya*, p. 1181, which we are translating here. See also Antoni Griera, *Atlas lingüístic de Catalunya*, 8 vols. (Barcelona, 1942–1968), 8:255, s.v. "Herbeta de Sant Tomàs," and Mistral, *Lou tresor*, s.v. "Tintin-terro." Blood-evoking expressions have been noted for the Abruzzis by Gennaro Finamore, *Tradizioni populari abruzzesi* (Palermo, 1894), p. 136; and Antonio de Nino, *Usi abruzzesi* (Florence, 1879), p. 137.

46. Given by Rolland, *Flore populaire*, 9:45.

47. Nicolas Stanislas Des Etangs, "Liste des noms populaires des plantes de l'Aube et des environs de Provins," *Mémoires de la société d'agriculture, des sciences, arts et belles-lettres de l'Aube* (1844), no. 91–92, p. 184.

48. Aimé Courtois, *L'Ancien Idiome audomarois* (Saint-Omer, 1856), pp. 46–49.

49. For the Abruzzi, G. Finamore, *Tradizioni populari abruzzesi*, p. 173; see also Marcel de Genermont, *Physiologie du Bourbonnais* (sl., 1835), pp. 165–166.

50. In Paul Delarue, *Recueil de chants populaires du Nivernais* (Paris, 1934), p. 43. On milfoil and the bloodroot plants in Nivernais, see Jean Drouillet, *Folklore du Nivernais et du Morvan* (La Charité-sur-Loire, 1959), vols. 4 and 5; on the meaning of the word *envorne*, see Hippolyte F. Jabert, *Glossaire du Centre, 1864–1869*, s.v. "Envornement."

51. On this theme, Wilhelm Fliess, *Les Relations entre le nez et les organes génitaux féminins présentés selon leurs significations biologiques* (Paris, 1977 [1897]), paved the way for Bruno Bettelheim's study, *Symbolic Wounds: Puberty Rites and the Envious Male* (Glencoe, Ill., 1954).

52. Emile Guillaumin, *La Vie d'un simple* (Paris, 1977), pp. 74 and 315.

53. Arnold Van Gennep, *Manuel de folklore français contemporain*, 8 vols. (Paris, 1943–1988), 1:193–194, noted this ritual rubbing but did not see the connection with the offering of the pig in return, which one must therefore read in Henri Le Carguet, "Le mousse d'Audiern, II," *Revue des traditions populaires* (1900), 15:99–104.

54. Rafael Ginard Bauça, *Cançoner popular de Mallorca* (Palma de Mallorca, 1967), p. 134.

55. The tale is in Pitré, *Fiabe, novelle i raconti*, 2(84):324; and in Sebastiano Lo Nigro, *Raconti populari siciliani* (Florence, 1958), p. 298.

56. Simin Palay, *Petite bite et bite bitante* (Pau, 1961), pp. 165–167; on the forbidden and euphemisms, see Eugène Rolland, *Faune populaire de la France. Noms vulgaires, dictons, proverbes, légendes, contes et superstitions*, 13 vols. (Paris, 1967 [1877–1915]), 4:213–256; Charles Beauquier, *Faune et flore populaires de la Franche-Comté* (Paris, 1910), 1:157–170.

57. Ernesto de Martino, *Italie du Sud et magie* (Paris, 1963), p. 50.

58. Edmund Leach, *L'Unité de l'homme et autres essais* (Paris, 1980), whose reflections expand on those of Claude Lévi-Strauss regarding the naming of animals in *La Pensée sauvage* (Paris, 1962), pp. 270–277.

59. On this personage, Séguy, *ALG*, maps 1275 and 1488.

3. The Circle of Metamorphoses

1. The story we are citing appears in two version in Jacob and Wilhelm Grimm, *Kinder-und Hausmärchen* (Stuttgart, 1980), accompanied by commentaries. Rich parallels are proposed in Johannes Bolte and Georg Polivka, *Ammerkungen zu den "Kinderund Hausmärchen" der Brüder Grimm* (Leipzig, 1913), 1:202–204.

2. On T. 327, see Paul Delarue, *Le Conte populaire français* (Paris, 1957), pp. 306–329; Charles Joisten, *Contes populaires du Dauphiné* (Grenoble, 1971), 1:303–306; and Delarue, ibid., pp. 313–314, for Nervais versions of the Millien-Delarue manuscript.

3. Geneviève Massignon, *Contes de l'Ouest* (Paris, 1954), pp. 231–232. On the use of the culinary code of the pig in "sacrificial" meals, see Yvonne Verdier, "Le petit chaperon rouge dans la tradition orale," *Le Débat* (1980), no 3, pp.

31–61. We attributed meaning to this fiery punishment, which also assumes the appearance of a trial, in "L'enfant, le four et le cochon," *Le Monde alpin et rhodanien* (1982), pp. 155–178. We will return to this question in chapter 9.

4. Jean-François Bladé, *Contes de Gascogne* (Paris, 1883), 2:152–165.

5. The work of Oskar Dähnhardt, *Natursagen* (Leipzig, 1909), is a tome to which only the collection of Joan Amades for Catalonia can be compared. A few isolated versions can be found in Ireland, in Provence, and in Béarn, where they respond to the question "Why don't Jews eat pork?" We provide them as an appendix to our article, "L'enfant, le four et le cochon."

6. This version is in René Basset, *Mille et un contes, récits et légendes arabes* (Paris, 1927), 3:159; see also Fabre-Vassas, "L'enfant, le four et le cochon," for the medieval versions. Among the most interesting, we should note Karl Bartsch, "Les Evangiles de l'enfance, versifiés en ancien occitan," *Denkmäler der provenzalischen literatur* (Stuttgart, 1856), pp. 301–303; and the English version of the *Evangiles de l'enfance* (thirteenth century) based on the Egerton manuscript (British Museum, no. 2781). Jean-Claude Schmitt procured images for us of the two scenes illustrating the Bodleian manuscript (Ms. Selden supra 38, fo. 22, vo., and fo. 23). He also pointed out pavement tiles from the early fourteenth century, no doubt from Trinch Church (Hertfordshire), representing the same scenes, and reproduced in G. E. Eames, *Medieval Tiles: A Handbook* (London, 1968). We thank him for this information and many other equally valuable details.

4. The Jew's Sow

1. Testimony of Jacques Boisgontier, who furnished us with valuable information on the Jewish community in the region of Bordeaux.

2. We are quoting, in order, Martial-Blaise de Régis de la Colombière, *Les Cris populaires de Marseille* (Marseilles, 1980 [1868]), pp. 155–156; Frédéric Mistral, *Lou tresor dóu Felibrige, Dictionnaire provençal-français*, 2 vols. (Aix-en-Provence, 1878), p. 132; Armand Lunel, *Juifs de Languedoc, de la Provence et des Etats français du pape* (Paris, 1975), p. 132; and Armand Lunel, *Niccolo Peccavi, ou l'affaire Dreyfus à Carpentras* (Paris, 1976 [1926]), p. 60. See also Albert Schweitzer, *Souvenirs de mon enfance* (Paris, 1984 [1924, German]), p. 20; Augusto Segre, *Memorie di vita ebraica (1918–1960)* (Rome, 1979), p. 87; Primo Levi, *Il sistema periodico* (Turin, 1975), pp. 4–5; Joan Amades, *Tradició des jueus a Catalunya* (Barcelona, 1933), p. 3; Guillaume Apollinaire, "Anecdotiques" (1911), in *Oeuvres complètes* (Paris, 1966), 2:306, in which a "donkey's ear" is identified as "the oldest sign of anti-Semitism."

3. Ladislas Reymont, *Les Paysans* (Lausanne, 1981 [1904]). It is in the first chapter of his work, *Campagnes insolites: paysannerie polonaise et mythes européens* (Lagrasse, 1986), that Ludwik Stomma, basing himself on the work of Jan Stanislaw Bystron (*Megalomania Naradowa*), which appeared in 1923,

constructs an image of the *Other* in which the Jew, the foreigner within, is not dissociated from other stigmatized groups. It seems to us rather that the traits that define the Jew with remarkable consistency—in Poland as in the other countries of Europe—also individualize him.

4. The primary reference work remains Isaiah Shachar, *The Judensau: A Medieval Anti-Jewish Motif and Its History* (London, 1974); Bernhardt Blumenkranz, in *Le Juif médiéval au miroir de l'art chrétien* (Paris, 1966), p. 67, also comments on these images.

5. Adolphe de Chesnel, *Dictionnaire des superstitions* (Paris, 1856), p. 225.

6. Goths and Arabs who took refuge, under the last Merovingians, at the foot of the Pyrenees, are referred to by the injurious name of *cagots*, that is, *canes gothi*, dogs of Goths (Francisque Michel, *Histoire des races maudites* [Paris, 1847], 1:284). This name is still given today to a race or a caste from which others remain separate. This insulting name given to people whose faith is suspect could have easily passed into the current meaning of *cagot* (hypocrite). But this etymology, for which there is no intermediary, has against it the ancient form *cagotus*, which is unrelated. Adapted from *Littré*.—Trans.

7. See Henri Marcel Fay, *Histoire de la lèpre en France* (Paris, 1910), p. 644; Michel, *Histoire des races maudites*, 1:178 and 2:117–181; Simin Palay, *Dictionnaire du béarnais et du gascon modernes* (Paris, 1980), s.v. "Aurelha" and "Eschaurelha"; Waldemar Deonna, "Un châtiment domestique: tirer l'oreille," *Nos anciens et leurs oeuvres* (Geneva, 1914), pp. 129–137.

8. It is also said that the *agotes* of Navarre are descendants of the same Gehazi; see Michel, *Histoire des races maudites*, 2:211. On the custom of cutting thieves' ears in Bordeaux and in Bayonne in the fourteenth and fifteenth centuries, see ibid., p. 295. For an example of this penalty, see Marie-Laure Le Bail, "Le droit et l'image: sur un cas d'essorillage," *Médiévales* (1985), no. 9, pp. 103–117.

9. Jean Duvernoy, *Le Registre d'inquisition de Jacques Fournier* (Paris, 1978), 1:164, 175, and 179.

10. Quoted by Michel, *Histoire des races maudites*, 2:95; see also J.-M. Guardia, *La Ladrerie du porc dans l'Antiquité* (Paris, 1866), pp. 15–16. Let us recall that the word *escrouelles* comes from *scrofa* (sow), from which "scrofula," "scrofulous" are also derived.

11. Saul Nathaniel Brody, *The Disease of the Soul* (London, 1974), p. 34.

12. Etienne Goytheneche, "L'elevage des porcs en basse Navarre au XIVe siècle," in *XVIIIe Congrès de la Fédération historique du Sud-Ouest* (Salies-du-Béarn, 1966), pp. 11–22.

13. Thomas Brown (Paris, 1753 [1646]) borrows extensively from Laurent Joubert, *Erreurs populaires au fait de médecine et régime de santé* (Avignon, 1578), 4:48–56. Moses Maimonides, *The Guide for the Perplexed*, insists on this necessity of salt, which is even one of the signs of opposition to the "idolaters."

14. Reproduced in Freddy Raphaël and Robert Weyl, *Juifs en Alsace: société, culture, histoire* (Toulouse, 1977), p. 36.

15. Quoted by Edouard Jeanselme, "Comment l"Europe du Moyen Age se protéga des lépreux," *Revue de la Société française d'histoire de la médecine* (1931), 25:29. On the policing of meat under the Ancien Regime in the Gascon region, see Jean-Louis Fossat, *Le Vocabulaire gascon de la boucherie* (Toulouse, 1971), pp. 84–85, 98–100, and 103; The ordinance of 1333 is in Jean Ramière de Fortanier, *Les Chartes de coutume du Lauragais* (Paris, 1939), pp. 241 and 315–317.

16. S. N. Brody, *The Disease of the Soul*, reviews this knowledge and etiology.

17. L.-V. Collaine, *Moyens de conserver la santé des cochons* (Metz, 1839), p. 19.

18. María Cátedra Tomás relates this feature in "Qué es ser vaqueiro de alzada," in *Expresiones actuales de la cultura del pueblo* (Madrid, 1976), pp. 155–182; this cursed group of the Asturias has already been noted by Michel, *Histoire des races maudites*, 2:33–45, and ibid. for the quotations related to the *agotes* (2:211) and the lepers (1:13).

19. On the relationship between the sun and redness, see Hans Niedermeier, "Die Rothaarigen, in Volkskundlicher Sicht," *Bayerisches Jahrbuch für Volkskunde* (1963), pp. 76–106.

20. Quoted by Michel, *Histoire des races maudites*, 1:18.

21. Reprinted in Guardia, *La Ladrerie*, p. 7.

22. Michel, *Histoire des races maudites*, 2:127.

23. On the mystery of the antichrist, see Jacques Chocheyras, *Le Théâtre religieux en Savoie au XVIe siècle* (Geneva, 1971), pp. 20–27 and 181–224 (quoted on p. 185). Jean Céard, *La Nature et les Prodiges au XVIe siècle* (Geneva, 1977), mentions a sheet by Sébastien Brant and an engraving by Dürer (1496) representing a sow with two bodies, a wonder alleged to announce the domination of men "with piglet's hearts" (pp. 78–79). In 1574, in Strasbourg, a Jewess, this time, gave birth to two piglets in which were recognized the figure "of the only messiah that the Jews deserved"; see Raphaël and Weyl, *Juifs en Alsace*, p. 36.

24. See René Basset, "Les tâches dans la Lune," *Revue des traditions populaires* (1902), 17:322–330; Niedermeier, "Die Rothaarigen," p. 85; Jacques André, *Etude sur les termes de couleur dans la langue latine* (Paris, 1959), remains fundamental. Ruth Mellinkoff, "Judas's Red Hair and the Jews," *Journal of Jewish Art* (1982), 9:31–46, highlights the recurrence of red-headed Judases in the painting of the Middle Ages and the Renaissance; see also Michel Pastoureau, "Tous les gauchers sont roux," *Le Genre humain* (1988), pp. 343–354, for the relationship between Judas, left-handedness, and redheadedness.

25. We are summarizing based on Jacques de Voragine (1265), *La Légende dorée* (Paris, 1942), 1:94–98.

26. These version are collected by José Romeu Figueras, "La légende de Judas Iscarioth dans le théâtre catalan et provençal," *Actes et mémoires du 1er Congrès international de langue et littérature du Midi de la France* (Avignon, 1957), pp. 69–106.

27. Gustave Cohen, *Histoire de la mise en scène dans le théâtre religieux français du Moyen Age* (Paris, 1951), p. 146.

28. These accounts are in Oskar Dähnhardt, *Natursagen* (Leipzig, 1909), 1:176 and 200; Joan Amades, *Folklore de Catalunya. Rondallistica* (Barcelona, 1950), no. 1194, p. 1229; Eugène Rolland, *Flore populaire, ou histoire naturelle des plantes dans leurs rapports avec la linguistique et le folklore*, 11 vols. (Paris, 1967 [1877–1915]), 4:79, 6:262, and 11:175 for *Peziza auricula Judae*.

29. The couplet was noted by Camille de Mensignac, *Coutumes, usages et chansons populaires de la Gironde* (Marseilles, 1982 [1886]), pp. 120–121; the expression relating to the elder tree is in Rolland, *Flore populaire*, 4:79; Roger Vaultier, *Le Folklore pendant la guerre de Cent Ans d'après les lettres de rémission du Trésor des chartes* (Paris, 1965), cites a letter from 1367, p. 67.

30. *Xuetas* are descendants of fifteenth-century Jewish converts to Christianity. See further in the chapter—Trans. The insult was still noted in 1977 by Eva and Juan F. Laub, *El mito triunfante: Estudio antropológico-social de los chuetas mallorquines* (Palma di Majorca, 1987), pp. 253 and 262. Kenneth Moore, *Los de la calle: Un estudio sobre los chuetas* (Madrid, 1987), noted this same ritual aggressiveness (p. 36).

31. Michel de Montaigne in *Oeuvres complètes* (Paris, 1967), p. 493; Félix and Thomas Platter, *Notes de voyage de deux étudiants bâlois (1552–1559 and 1595–1599)* (Marseilles, 1979), p. 85; see also Jacques Gutwirth, *Vie juive traditionnelle. Ethnologie d'un communauté hassidique* (Paris, 1970), p. 235–238.

32. Anton Giulio Bragaglia, *Storia del teatro populare romano* (Rome, 1958), pp. 246–265. On the *giudiata*, Paolo Toschi, *Le origini del teatro italiano* (Turin, 1955), pp. 333–340; examples of this are given by Martine Boiteux, "Les juifs dans le carnaval de la Rome moderne, XVe–XVIIIe siècle," *Mélanges de l'Ecole française de Rome* (1976), 88(2):745–787.

33. Michel, *Histoire des races maudites*, 1:369, devotes a chapter to the examination of "various opinions relative to the origin of *cagots* and the etymology of names that have been given to them." Unable to base themselves on a certain etymology, the historians who examined the question after him remained highly cautious.

34. M. Cátedra Tomás, "Qué es ser vaqueiro," p. 159.

35. René Moulinas, *Les Juifs du pape en France: Les communautés d'Avignon et du Comtat Venaissin aux XVII et XVIIIe siècles* (Toulouse, 1981), p. 116; Christian Jouhaud, *Mazarinades. La fronde des mots*, (Paris, 1985), pp. 41–62, analyzes these texts. We thank him for having shared the original parts of this work.

36. Lunel, *Niccolo Peccavi*, p. 35; Moulinas, *Les Juifs du pape en France*, pp. 210–212; Mistral, *Lou tresor*, s.v. "Cavo."

37. Bragaglia, *Storia del teatro*, pp. 67 and 71; and Toschi, *Le origini del teatro italiano*, p. 336.

38. For the text and its illustration, see G. Grégoire with commentary by Roux-Alphéran, *Explication des jeux de la Fête-Dieu à Aix* (Aix, 1851).

39. Lunel, *Juifs du Languedoc*, p. 134. On the equivalency between sheering and castration, see Daniel Fabre, "L'ours, la vierge et le taureau," *Textures mythiques, Ethnologie française* (1993), 23(1):7–19. Edmund Leach, *L'Unité de l'homme et autres essais* (Paris, 1980), pp. 321–361. Edmund Leach, "Anthropological Aspects of Language: Animal Categories and Verbal Abuse," in Eric H. Lenneberg, ed., *New Directions in the Study of Language* (Cambridge, Mass., 1964).

40. J. Duvernoy, *Le Registre d'inquisition*, 1:2238 and 2233. Riccardo di Segni, in *Le unghie di Adamo: Studi di antropologia ebraica* (Naples, 1981), pp. 122–171, highlights the relationship between the finger and the penis, the nail to be cut and the foreskin to be slit, within Jewish culture.

41. Joubert, *Erreurs populaires*, p. 205.

42. Jacques Basnage, *Histoire des juifs* (Amsterdam, 1710), 3:237.

43. Baruch Braunstein, *The Chuetes of Majorca: Conversos and the Inquisition of Majorca* (New York, 1936; 1972); see also Michel, *Histoire des races maudites*, 2:33–45; and Angela Selke, *Vida y muerte de los chuetas de Mallorca* (Madrid, 1972).

44. Cecil Roth, "The Religion of the Marranos," *The Jewish Quarterly Review* (1931), 22:19; and Cecil Roth, *A History of the Marranos* (New York, 1974 [1932]). See also the review *Douro Litoral*, which regularly devoted articles to the Portuguese Marranos.

45. Platter and Platter, *Notes de voyage*, p. 196 and p. 108.

46. Noted by Laub and Laub, pp. 299 and 391.

47. See Christian Anatole, "L'anti-marranisme en Provence (fin XVIe-début XVIIIe)," in *Les Juifs, object de connaissance* (Toulouse, 1984), pp. 93–105.

48. We are speaking of Arturo Farinelli, *Marrano, storia di un vituperio* (Geneva, 1925), and Joan Corominas, *Diccionario crítico etimológico de la lengua castellana*, 4 vols. (Berne, 1954), vol. 4, s.v. "Xueta."

49. Braunstein, *The Chuetes of Majorca*; Roth, *History of the Marranos*, p. 19, n. 73.

50. Noted by Moore, *Los de la calle*, p. 148; and Laub and Laub, *El mito triunfante*, pp. 299 and 409–411. We will return to this relationship in our final chapter; Rafael Ginard Bauça, *Cançoner popular de Mallorca* (Palma di Majorca, 1967), 2:391–394, provides satirical couplets addressed to the Jews of Majorca that refer to pig meat.

51. See, on the first point, Marie-Laure Le Bail, "Images de la mort: le châtiment du parricide," in *Le Corps, nature, culture et surnaturel* (Paris, 1985), pp.

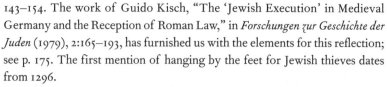
143–154. The work of Guido Kisch, "The 'Jewish Execution' in Medieval Germany and the Reception of Roman Law," in *Forschungen zur Geschichte der Juden* (1979), 2:165–193, has furnished us with the elements for this reflection; see p. 175. The first mention of hanging by the feet for Jewish thieves dates from 1296.

52. We are summarizing based on Jean Vartier, *Les Procès d'animaux du Moyen Age à nos jours* (Paris, 1970), pp. 35–55. For a synthesis of these little-studied trials, see Edward Payson Evans, *The Criminal Prosecution and Capital Punishment of Animals: The Lost History of Europe's Animal Trials* (London, 1987 [1906]).

53. Kisch, "The 'Jewish Execution,' " p. 180.

54. Quoted by Shachar, *The Judensau*, p. 76, nn. 55–56. The German text (p. 14) is accompanied by a seventeenth-century engraving (plate 4) illustrating the scene. Carol Iangu analyzes this in "Le serment *More judaico* in Rumania," in *Revue des études juives* (1976), pp. 125:169–176.

55. Kisch, "The 'Jewish Execution,' " p. 185.

56. Quoted by Robert Badinter in his preface to the Abbé Grégoire (1789), *Essai sur la régénération des juifs* (Paris, 1988), p. 9; see also Daniel Feuerwerker, "L'abolition du péage corporel en France," *Annales E. S. C.* (1962), no. 5, pp. 857–872. Eugène de Chambure, in his *Glossaire du Morvan* (Marseilles, 1978), s.v. "Jui," p. 478, gives the tarifs applied to Jews who wanted to cross the Loire in 1438. They appears on a certificate of merchandise taxed at tolls as follows; "A single Jew owes XIJ d.; the pregnant Jewess IXd.; a regular Jewesse Xj d.; a Jew child vj d.; item a dead Jew v d.; a dead Jewesse XXX d."

57. Leopold von Sacher-Masoch, *A Kolomea, contes juifs et petits-russiens* (Paris, 1879), pp. 205–221; see also Carol Iancu, *Les Juifs en Roumanie, 1866–1919. De l'exclusion à l'émancipation* (Aix-en-Provence, 1978), pp. 139–140.

5. Red Easter

1. The bibliography on the question is extensive and varied. For a chronology and geography, one should consult J. Jacobs and H. L. Strack, "Blood Accusation," in *The Jewish Encyclopedia* (New York 1903), 3:260–267, and Léon Poliakov, *Histoire de l'antisémitisme* (Paris, 1981 [1955]), 1:231–366, which records the best-known medieval cases; see R. P. C. Hsia, *The Myth of Ritual Murder* (New Haven, 1988), for a recent historical perspective based on seventeenth-century German examples, and especially the very well documented articles of Gavin I. Langmuir, now collected in *Toward a Definition of Antisemitism* (Berkeley, 1990). A good anthology of the interpretations, accompanied by a bibliography, was edited by Alan Dundes, *The Blood Libel Legend: A Casebook in Anti-Semitic Folklore* (Madison, 1991).

2. André Vauchez, *La Sainteté en Occident aux derniers siècles du Moyen Age* (Rome, 1981), deals with this in the chapters "*Sancti* and *beati*" (pp. 99–111)

and "La sainteté populaire" (pp. 173–183); see also Etienne Delaruelle, *La piété poulaire au Moyen Age* (Turin, 1975), pp. 787–790.

3. R. P. Baudot and Chaussin, *Vie des saints et des bienheureux* (Paris, 1941), 3:532–535, March 24; the history of this worship, which was abrogated only in 1965, is retraced in *Biblioteca Sanctorum* (Rome, 1968), 11:1184–1188.

4. R. P. Baudot and Chaussin, *Vie des saints*, 3:533.

5. *Acta Sanctorum*, 3:495.

6. In André Monniot (a notorious anti-Semite), *Le Crime rituel chez les juifs* (Paris, 1914), p. 170.

7. On these reliquaries and their worship, see Eugène Vacandard, "La question du meurtre rituel chez les juifs," in *Etudes de critique et d'histoire religieuse*, 3d series (Paris, 1912), pp. 351–352.

8. Isidore Loeb, "Le saint enfant de la Guardia," *Revue des études juives* (1887), 15:203–232, followed by "Le folklore juif dans la chronique du Schebet Ihuda d'Ibn Verga,"ibid. (1896), 24(47):1–29.

9. Francisque Michel published the "Ballade anglo-normade sur le meurtre commis par les juifs sur un enfant de Lincoln," *Mémoires et dissertations de la Société des antiquaires de France* (Paris 1834), 10:358–392. Robert Chambers, *The Book of Days* (London, 1967), 1:446–448, recalls the main English accusations and gives the Scottish ballad, noted by Jamieson, that we summarize. The stories of martyrdom of other children are in Baudot and Chaussin, *Vie des saints*, s.v. William (of Norwich), March 24; Werner (of Bacherach), April 19; André (of Rinn), July 12; Huges (of Lincoln), July 27; on William, see also d'Augustus Jessop and James Montague Rhodes, *The Life and Miracles of St. William of Norwich* (Cambridge, 1896).

10. Isaiah Shachar, *The Judensau: A Medieval Anti-Jewish Motif and Its History* (London, 1974), p. 93.

11. For a synthesis, see *Dictionnaire de théologie catholique* (Paris, 1937), s.v. p. 277. Sophie Brouquet, in "Alimentation et hygiène alimentaire dans l'Occident du haut Moyen Age, d'après les pénitentiels," master's thesis, University of Toulouse-Le Mirail, 1978; and Cleto Corrain, in *Documenti etnografici nei sinodi francesi* (Rovigo, 1976), pp. 23–26, give several examples of this tolerance.

12. Norman Cohn, in *Démonolâtrie et sorcellerie au Moyen Age* (Paris, 1982 [1975]), pp. 17–33, analyzed the emergence and the continuity of this "stereotype."

13. Michel de Montaigne, *Oeuvres complètes* (Paris, 1967), p. 493.

14. For an analysis of these rules, see Joëlle Bahloul, *Le Culte de la table dressée: Rites et traditions de la table juive algérienne* (Paris, 1983).

15. René Moulinas, *Les Juifs du pape en France* (Toulouse, 1981), p. 138 and n. 45, p. 511.

16. On the status of blood professions in medieval society, see Jacques Le Goff, *Pour un autre Moyen Age: Temps, travail et culture en Occident* (Paris,

1977), p. 93. Noélie Vialles, in *Le Sang et la Chair* (Paris, 1987), sheds light on this avoidance with respect to modern slaughterhouses.

17. The ritual is analyzed by Riccardo di Segni, *Le unghie di Adamo* (Naples, 1981), pp. 26–41.

18. See Jacques Frey, *Sur le procédé juif d'abattage des animaux de boucherie, étude historique et critique* (Paris, 1945), p. 178. Today, the C.N.D.A. (Collectif national de défense animale) condemns "ritual slaughter" by the same token as the "massacre of dolphins, bullfighting," etc.; Régine Mihal-Friedman, *L'Image et son juif: Le juif dans le cinéma nazi* (Paris, 1983), p. 109 (the sequence on slaughter is in *The Eternal Jew*).

19. Hans Peter Richtel, *Mon ami Frédéric* (Paris, 1979), pp. 61–62.

20. Cited by Noël Coulet, "Juif intouchable et interdits alimentaires," in "Exclus et systèmes d'exclusion dans la littérature et la civilisation médiévales," *Senefiance* (Aix-en-Provence, 1978), no. 5, p. 220, n. 19.

21. According to Jacques de Voragine (1265), *La Légende dorée* (Paris, 1942), 1:180–187. The nail of the mohel is also the mark of purity of the one who performs the *periah*, according to the myths that see it as the remainder of the garment of light that covered Adam before the fall: R. Di Segni, *Le unghie di Adamo*, pp. 71 and 122; and Robert Graves and Raphaël Patai, *Mythes hébreux* (Paris, 1987), pp. 91–97.

22. Frey, *Sur le procédé juif*, p. 178.

23. Joan Amades, *Costumari català. El curs de l'any*, 5 vols. (Barcelona, 1950), 2:801, reproduces the image.

24. Armand Lunel, *Nicolo Peccavi, ou l'affaire Dreyfus à Carpentras* (Paris, 1976), pp. 197–198 and 233.

25. The argument of a Jewish plot is put forward in the affair of Niño de la Guardia (Loeb, "Le saint enfant de la Guardia," pp. 203–232), sometimes in association with lepers; see Jean Duvernoy, *Le Registre d'inquisition de Jacques Fournier* (Paris, 1978), 1:639. Carlo Ginzburg, *Storia notturna, una decifrazione del sabba* (Turin, 1989), established the pertinence of the sequence Jews/lepers/sorceresses by following the thread of the plot. This analysis relieves us of the obligation of a demonstration, which, on this point, would seem redundant; on the Jewish doctor and his "magic," see Julio Caro Baroja, *Vidas mágicas e Inquisición* (Madrid, 1967), 1:59–65 and 2:133. The work by Joshua Trachtenberg, *The Devil and the Jews: The Medieval Conception of the Jew and His Relation to Modern Antisemitism* (New Haven, 1945), is fundamental, particularly the chapters entitled "The Blood Accusation," "Host and Image Desecration," and "Ritual Murder," even if the figure of the "diabolical Jew" that emerges remains too general.

26. Trachtenberg, *The Devil and the Jews*, p. 145.

27. Jacques Basnage, *Histoire des juifs* (Amsterdam, 1710), 3:420.

28. Basnage, *Histoire des juifs*, pp. 410–420, and Trachtenberg, *The Devil and the Jews*, pp. 50–52, summarizes this list; Yosef Hayim Yerushalmi, *De la cour*

d'Espagne au ghetto italien. Isaac Cardoso et le marranisme au XVIIe siècle (Paris, 1987), pp. 109–119, comments on one of these works, refuted in its time by Fernando Cardoso, a Marrano doctor of Portugese origin who returned to Judaism and is the author of *Las excelencias de los Hebreos* (ibid., pp. 329–453). The bad smell of the Jews is parallel to and the reverse of the "good smell" of the Christians healed of their leprosy by the blood of Christ, associated with the baptismal chrism and with the balm that is its main ingredient: see Jean-Pierre Albert, *Odeurs de sainteté: La mythologie chrétienne des aromates* (Paris, 1990).

29. We are citing the work of Jacques Le Goff, "Le juif dans les *exempla* médiévaux: le cas de l'*Alphabetum narrationum*," in *Pour Léon Poliakov: Le racisme, mythes et sciences* (Brussels, 1981), p. 216.

30. Trachtenberg, *The Devil and the Jews*, p. 50.

31. On this theme and its evolution between the high Middle Ages and the thirteenth century, see Bernhardt Blumenkranz, *Le Juif médiéval au miroir de l'art chrétien*, Paris, 1966, pp. 50–60 and 104–110.

32. The story is narrated by Jacques de Voragine, *La Légende dorée*, 1:219–228 and 3:242–255; the iconography is in Louis Réau, *Iconographie des saints* (Paris, 1958), 1:341–343. A fine collection of frescoes from the thirteenth century is visible in Rome in the SS Quattro Coronati Basilico where it decorates the walls of the chapel dedicated to Saint Sylvester.

33. Trachtenberg, *The Devil and the Jews*, p. 50.

34. One of the champions of this polemic is Guillaume de Bourges (1235), whose *Livre des guerres du Seigneur* (Paris, 1981), ed. and trans. Gilbert Dahan, is particularly virulent; see also Bernard Neunheuser, *L'Eucharistie au Moyen Age et à l'époque moderne* (Paris, 1966), who situates the eucharistic theology; and Rolande Foreville, Histoire des conciles oecuméniques (Paris, 1965), for the doctrine of the dogma of transubstantiation; finally, for a synthesis, see Miri Rubin, *Corpus Christi* (Cambridge, 1991). Origène's commentary on "the letter that kills" is quoted by Bernhardt Blumenkranz, *Juifs et chrétiens dans le monde occidental (430–1096)* (Paris, 1960), pp. 55–60.

35. Duvernoy, *Le Registre d'inquisition*, 1:639.

36. The apiarian miracles taken from the *Dialogus Miraculorum* by Césaire de Heisterbach (early thirteenth century) are in Philippe Marchenay, *L'Homme et l'Abeille* (Paris, 1979), pp. 137 and 143. Frédéric Tubach, *Index exemplorum: A Handbook of Medieval Religious Tales* (Helsinki, 1969), furnished us with abundant materials (nos. 2644, 2647, 2668, 2687, pp. 207–212). Similarly John Alexander Herbert, *Catalogue of Romances in the Department of Manuscripts in the British Museum* (London, 1910), vol. 3, chapter 32, "De eukaristia et ejus virtitibus," pp. 51–55. Stories of host profanations are equally well represented in Spanish anthologies, the model for which is *Espéculo de los leges* (late thirteenth century); see Rameline E. Marsan, *Itinéraire espagnol du conte médiéval (VIIIe–XVe siècle)* (Paris, 1974), pp. 309–317.

37. On this usage, see Trachtenberg, *The Devil and the Jews*, p. 115–116; François Marchetti, *Explication des usages et coutumes des Marseillais* (Marseilles, 1682), pp. 447–448; and Jules Corblet, *Histoire dogmatique, liturgique et archéologique du sacrament de l'eucharistie*, 2 vols. (Paris, 1885), 1:340–341 and 395.

38. Summarized in Tubach, *Index exemplorum*, no. 2687, p. 211, and reproduced in Herbert, *Catalogue of Romances*, no. 369; see also Marsan, *Itinéraire espagnol*, p. 312.

39. Le Goff, "Le juif," sees in this, along with the birth of anti-Semitism, an indication of the increase in power and authority of the clerics.

40. The earliest known version is that of Grégoire de Tours in the sixth century, "De puero judaeo valde memorandum miracolum," followed by that of *Mariale magnum*, compiled between 1187 and 1246. Vincent de Beauvais's *Speculum historiale* returns to it. For the Spanish versions, see Marsan, *Itinéraire espagnol*, pp. 88–93 and 546–548. The complete text is in *Vierge et Merveille: les miracles de Notre-Dame*, ed. Pierre Kunstmann (Paris, 1981), pp. 56–63. Gilbert Dahan, "Les juifs dans les Miracles de Gautier de Coincy," *Archives juives* (1980), pp. 41–68, comments on the "hateful anti-Judaism" that motivates their author.

41. In Le Goff, "Le juif," p. 211.

42. We are summarizing and quoting from Giuseppe Sergiacomi, *Il miracolo eucaristico de Offida* (Ascoli, 1967). See also Giuseppe Panza, *Il rito giudaico della profanazione dell'ostia e il ciclo della "Passione" in Abruzzo* (Naples, 1916).

43. Paul Perdrizet, *Le Calendrier parisien à la fin du moyen Age* (Gap, 1933), p. 159.

44. Quoted by Mania Lifschitz Golden, *Les Juifs dans la littérature française du Moyen Age* (New York, 1935), pp. 89–91; and Léon Petit de Julleville, *Les Mystères* (Paris, 1880), 2:103. On the iconography and the bibliography of this miracle, see Gérard de Tervarent, "Les tapisseries du Ronceray et leurs sources d'inspiration," *Gazette des Beaux-Arts*, 10:79–99; Pierre Francastel, "Un Mystère parisien illustré par Paolo Uccello: le miracle de l'hostie d'Urbino," *Revue archéologique* (1952), pp. 180–191; Corblet, *Histoire dogmatique*, 1:447 and 2:542.

45. Basnage, *Histoire des juifs*, 3:237.

46. *La Dispute de Barcelone*, transcribed by Nachmanides, is translated and presented by Eric Smilevitch and Luc Ferrier (Lagrasse, 1984). Alain Boureau, in a forthcoming article, draws a relationship between the form taken by the disputes at the turn of the 1240s and the autos-da-fé of talmudists during the same period. Gilbert Dahan, *Les Intellectuels chrétiens et les Juifs au Moyen Age* (Paris, 1990), shows how much the controversy fed Christian literature of the thirteenth century. On the comparison of the Jew to the heretic, see Ginzburg, *Storia notturna*, pp. 36–60. Let us recall that the

origin of the genre of the dispute has been situated in the discussion that Helen, mother of Constantine, is alleged to have had with the Jews (Jacques de Voragine, *La Légende dorée*, 1:219–228 and 2:242–255).

47. We can follow this sign throughout the councils. See Foreville, *Histoire des conciles*, p. 381; Charles-Joseph Hefele, *Histoire des conciles d'après les documents originaux*, 4 vols. (Paris, 1907–1959), 3:1453 and 1698. On the Italian *sciamanno*, the best sources are Emmanuel Rodocanachi, *Le Saint-Siège et le Juifs* (Paris, 1891), pp. 162 and 185; and Attilio Milano, *Storia degli Ebrei in Italia* (Turin, 1963), pp. 46, 96 and chapter 7, pp. 585–588. As emphasized by Michel Pastoureau, *Figures et couleurs: Etudes sur la symbolique et la sensibilité médiévales* (Paris, 1986), the story of this sign has yet to be told, the only synthetical work to date being that of Ulysse Robert, *Les Signes d'infamie au Moyen Age* (Nogent-le-Rotrou, 1889).

48. For additional details on the schism, we refer the reader to our article, "L'azyme des juifs et l'hostie des chrétiens," in *Le Ferment divin*, Dominique Fournier and Salvatore d'Onofrio, general editors (Paris, 1991), pp. 189–206.

49. In Alfred Cioni, *Bibliografia delle Sacre Rappresentazioni* (Florence, 1961), p. 53.

50. Tubach, *Index exemplorum*, no. 2647, pp. 210–211; see also Marsan, *Itinéraire espagnol*, pp. 307–314.

51. Trachtenberg, *The Devil and the Jews*, p. 114.

52. The text is in J. T. Welter, ed., *Tabula exemplorum secundum ordinem alphabeti* (Toulouse, 1927), a late thirteenth-century compilation, p. 59, no. 219: "Item nota de puero, qui vidit fratrem comedentem puerum, dum assumeret Corpus Christi in missa et fugit et abscondit se et inventus dixit quod de cetero non iret ad fratrem illum, quia pueros comedebat": Tubach offers a summary under no. 1001, "Christ, eating of, confuses child." The example is already in Guibert de Nogent (ca. 1125). That of the Jew is in Tubach, *Index exemplorum*, no. 1042, p. 84, "Christians eating bloody child: A Jew sees Christians at Mass each eating a bloody child." But, of course, in all these cases, as St. Thomas Aquinas reminds us in his *Summa theologica* (question 75, articles 5, 7, and 8), "The flesh or the blood that appear miraculously are neither consecrated nor converted into the true body and the true blood of Christ."

53. We are translating from the langue d'oc, Marie Rouanet, *Dins de patetas rojas* (Toulouse, 1975), p. 43.

54. Ramón J. Sender, *Requiem pour un paysan espagnol* (Lyons, 1976), p. 27. We find an echo of these sanctions in popular folktales: Paul Sébillot, *Traditions et superstitions de la haute Bretagne* (Paris, 1881), 2:45–48, in which the daughter of the king is sick because, after having received the host, she spit it into a pond. In the tale from lower Brittany, "Le pape Innocent" (Paul Delarue and Marie-Louise Ténèze, *Le Conte populaire français* [Paris, 1964], vol. 2, tale type 671) she profaned the host the day of her first communion.

6. Old Jews, Young Christians

1. In Lucette Valensi and Nathan Wachtel, *Mémoires juives* (Paris, 1986), pp. 212–213. This testimony echos that of the Greek novelists for the same period, in particular Dimitris Hadzis, *Le Cahier du détective. La fin de notre petite ville* (Paris, 1990 [1960–1963]). See also Henri Tonnet, "Sur quelques personnages de juifs dans la littérature néo-grecque," *Cahiers balkaniques* (1983), no. 5, pp. 77–91.

2. Quoted by Attilio Milano, *Storia degli Ebrei in Italia* (Turin, 1963), pp. 599–600; and Emmanuel Rodocanachi, *Le Saint-Siège et les Juifs* (Paris, 1891), pp. 153–154, 190–193, and 208–221. Michel de Montaigne describes the race in his *Journal*, in *Oeuvres complètes* (Paris, 1967), p. 493. On the Jews in the Roman carnival, see also Martine Boiteux, "Les juifs dans le carnaval de la Rome moderne, XVe–XVIIIe siècle," *Mélanges de l'Ecole française de Rome* (1976), 88(2):745–787; Paolo Toschi, *Le origini del teatro italiano* (Turin, 1955), sees the *giudiata* as a euphemized form of the old *palio*, the passage from a real execution to a symbolic killing of the Jew (pp. 333–338); see also notes 31 and 32 of chapter 4.

3. Giuseppe Pitré, *Cartelli, pasquinate, canti, leggende, usi del popolo siciliano* (Palermo, 1978), pp. 226–228; E. Sánchez, "Festividades y costumbres de primavera en la comarca de Calatayud," *Temas de antropologí aragonesa* (1983), no. 1, pp. 159–174.

4. We are summarizing from Joan Amades, *Costumari català. El curs de l'any*, 5 vols. (Barcelona, 1950), 2:758, a fine observer and no doubt a participant in the Catalan ritual.

5. According to Giuseppe Cochiara, *Il folklore siciliano* (Palermo, 1957), who describes the festival and provides a photograph of the *giudei* as they run.

6. Amades, *Costumari català*, vol. II, p. 758.

7. Antonio de Nino, *Usi abruzzesi* (Abezzano, 1879–1881), 1:174, 2:210–212.

8. The stories dealing with cursed or blessed artisans are in Joan Amades, *Folklore de Catalunya. Rondallistica* (Barcelona, 1950), pp. 1022–1026. We have developed the question of this equivalence between roles in the theater and the professions exercised in life in "Le jeu de la Passion," *L'Homme* (July-December 1989), no. 111–112, pp. 130–159.

9. See Sabaés de Balagué, *La Passió d'Esparreguera* (Barcelona, 1957).

10. Arnold Van Gennep, *Manuel de folklore français contemporain*, 8 vols. (Paris, 1943–1988), 1:1259–1263, established the cartography of this ritual, which is found in Spain and in the New World: Pilar García de Diego, "Censura popular," *Revista de dialectología y tradiciones populares* (1960), 16(3):295–333; and S. García Sanz, "La quema del Judas en Guadalajara," *Revista de dialectología y tradiciones populares*, 4(4):619–625.

11. Amades, *Costumari català*, 2:831.

12. We are summarizing from Valerio Gutiérrez Macías, "Retablo popular

de la tierra parda," *Etnología y tradiciones populares* (Saragossa, 1974), pp. 310–312.

13. Colin de Plancy, in Alphonse de Chesnel, *Dictionnaire des superstitions, erreurs, préjugés, et traditions populaires où sont exposées les croyances superstitieuses des temps anciens et modernes* (Paris, 1856), pp. 903–905. A similar violence can be observed in Manilla, according to Lucy M. J. Garnett, *The Women of Turkey and Their Folklore* (London, 1891), 2:9.

14. In Charles Bauby, *Coutumes de Pâques en Rousillon* (Perpignan, 1944), p. 22.

15. Miloslav Rybak, "Traditions et coutumes chez les Tchécoslaves," *Revue des traditions populaires* (1902), 18:327.

16. Amades, *Costumari català*, 2:814.

17. Ibid.,, p. 753.

18. *Arxiu de tradicions populars*, (1980), fasc. 6, pp. 356–357.

19. Rolland, *Flore populaire, ou histoire naturelle des plantes dans leurs rapports avec la linguistique et le folklore*, 11 vols. (Paris, 1967 [1877–1915]), 9:117–124, for the corneltree, and 9:124–129, for the dogwood tree.

20. In Bauby, *Coutumes de Pâques en Rousillon*, p. 23, citing a correspondent who further specifies that "the more the *fas* bleeds, the happier the child is."

21. Louis Stercky, *Manuel de liturgie et de cérémoniel selon le Rite romain* (Paris, 1940), pp. 285–287, 530, 578.

22. Cleto Corrain and Pierluigi Zampini, *Documenti etnografici e folkloristici nei sinodi dicesani italiani* (Bologna, 1970), reveals several occurrences, pp. 43, 88, 153, 237.

23. George L'Hôte, *La Tankiote. Usages traditionnels en Lorraine,* (Nancy, 1984), p. 162.

24. Ibid., p. 156.

25. Van Gennep, *Manuel de folklore français contemporain*, 1:1255.

26. L'Hôte, *La Tankiote*, p. 162.

27. Ramón J. Sender, *Requiem pour un paysan espagnol* (Lyons, 1976), p. 26.

28. The right they thereby assume was formerly a duty mentioned by Jules Corblet, *Histoire dogmatique, liturgique et archéologique du sacrement de l'eucharistie*, 2 vols. (Paris, 1885), 1:196, and, for other interesting details, 2:385–415; indeed, it was incumbent upon them to "taste" hosts and Mass wine in order to forestall any attempt at poisoning the prelate or pope whose servants they were (1:230).

29. Nicolas Théobald, *A l'heure des cloches de mon village, scènes d'un village lorrain du début du siècle* (Obernai, s.d.), pp. 78–79.

30. L'Abbé A. Collette, with *L'Histoire de la maîtrise de Rouen depuis les origines jusqu'à la Révolution* (Geneva, 1892); and Alex and Janine Béges, in *La chapelle de musique de la cathédrale Saint-Nazaire, 1590–1790* (Béziers, 1982), provided us with a wealth of information.

31. According to specialists in liturgical history, little is known about earlier centuries: Dom F. Cabrol and Henri Leclerq, *Dictionnaire d'archéologie chrétienne et de liturgie*, 30 vols. (Paris, 1924–1953), vol. 3, s.v. "Choriste," p. 1452.

32. Etienne Delaruelle, *La piété populaire au Moyen Age* (Turin), p. 737, examines the phenomenon of the exaltation of childhood and innocence in which this sudden rise in status is inscribed.

33. See Gustave Cohen, *Histoire de la mise en scène dans le théâtre religieux français du Moyen Age* (Paris, 1951 [1926]), pp. 32–40; Jean Mellot, "A propos du théâtre liturgique à Bourges au Moyen Age et au XVI siècle," in *Mélanges offerts à G. Cohen* (Paris, 1950), pp. 193–198; and Delaruelle, *La piété populaire*, p. 619.

34. The *Pro pueris*, included in the *Opera moralia*, was composed by Gerson between 1419 and 1429 in Lyons; see *Oeuvres complètes* (Paris, 1973), 9:423–491 and 4:686–689. On the rowdiness of the altar boys, see also Collette, *L'Histoire de la maîtrise*, pp. 18–27.

35. Cohen, *Histoire de la mise en scène*, p. 208.

36. Cleto Corrain, *Documenti etnografici nei sinodi francesi* (Rovigo, 1976), p. 135.

37. Jacques de Voragine (1265), *La Légende dorée* (Paris, 1942), 3:232–237; and Louis Réau, *Iconographie des saints* (Paris, 1958), 2:679–680.

38. Corrain, *Documenti etnografici*, p. 12.

39. The text cited by Giuseppe Pitré, *Spettacoli e feste populari siciliane* (Palermo, 1978), p. 138, is the following: "Ne permittant in Vesperis Innocentum pueros clericos induire vestibus sacris et agere ridicula." For Rouen, Holy Innocents' Day, though abolished in 1452, continued in great pomp until 1666, according to Collette, *L'Histoire de la maîtrise*, p. 18–27.

40. As was specified to us during a visit to the sanctuary. On the *escolanilla*, see M. Boix, *Montserrat* (Barcelona, 1978).

41. Robert Debrie, "Contribution à l'étude des cérémonies traditionnelles en basse Picardie," *Eklitra* (1969), no. 8, p. 73.

42. See the chapter "Kingdom of Childhood," *Le Carnaval*, with Marie-Claude Florentin (Paris, 1974). In Spain a similar displacement on the calendar is noted by Julio Caro Baroja, *El Carnival* (Madrid, 1965): the election takes place two days after Christmas, for Saint John's Day, but also on December 6 for Saint Nicholas's Day.

43. See Cohen, *Histoire de la mise en scène*, pp. 37–50; and Mellot, "A propos du théâtre liturgique," pp. 193–198. The massacre of the Innocents is always depicted by a group of carved wood figures in the Neapolitan manger.

44. In "De quelques livres populaires imprimés à Dinan," *Revue de Bretagne et de Vendée* (September 1884), pp. 289–300. In Romania the scene was dramatized and the text was established from it (Mihai Vulpesco, *Les Coutumes roumaines périodiques* [Paris, 1927], pp. 38–107).

45. Amades, *Costumari català*, 1:225 and 1:229.

46. According to Collette, *L'Histoire de la maîtrise*, p. 23. The painting by Gentile da Fabriano (1370) entitled *Adoration of the Magi* (Florence, Uffizi Gallery) bears a detail that can only be understood if we see the scene as a special service, with theater, in honor of the Magi with the kings dressed as warriors in the church. A crouching young boy detaches the spurs of Gaspard, thus maintaining the custom. It is also because he had entered the church of Saint-Etienne-de-Mer-Morte under arms on the day of Pentecost that Gilles de Rais was arrested. A great lover of song—in 1435 he founded a collegiate church dedicated to the Holy Innocents—he personally recruited the children for the choir school, some of whom mysteriously disappeared. He was accused of sacrificing them "by the hundreds" to his passion and to Satan, with whom he had a pact. René Villeneuve, *Gilles de Rais* (Paris, 1955), allows us a first approach to the "contemporary debates." It is also interesting to note that Salomon Reinach, "Gilles de Rais," in *Cultes, mythes et religions* (Paris, 1912), 4:276–299, basing himself on the accusations of ritual murder, argued for his innocence. The minutes of the trial are in Georges Bataille, *Le Procès de Gilles de Rais* (Paris, 1965).

47. According to the Abbé du Breuil, quoted by Paul Perdrizet, *Le Calendrier parisien à la fin du Moyen Age* (Gap, 1933), p. 280. The church of la Seu, in Barcelona, prides itself on possessing the heart of a "Holy Innocent."

48. We are summarizing and quoting from R. P. Caillau, in André Monniot, *Le Crime rituel chez les juifs* (Paris, 1914), pp. 164–165.

49. See chapter 5, note 40.

50. Joshua Trachtenberg, *The Devil and the Jews: The Medieval Conception of the Jew and His Relation to Modern Antisemitism* (New Haven, 1945), p. 50.

51. Armand Lunel, *Juifs du Languedoc* (Paris, 1975), p. 135.

52. Quoted by René Moulinas, *Les Juifs du pape en France* (Toulouse, 1981), pp. 210–212, who devotes several pages to this right of altar boys.

53. Ibid., p. 211.

54. Armand Lunel, *Nicolo Peccavi, ou l'affaire Dreyfus à Carpentras* (Paris, 1976), p. 55.

55. See de Voragine, *La Légende dorée*, 3:212–223.

56. Colette Méchin, *Saint Nicolas* (Paris, 1978), emphasizes the late appearance of this miracle and the ambivalence of the character within the mythico-ritual complex connected to his holiday. In Saint-Nicholas-de-Port the altar boys are the main actors.

57. Related by Amades, *Costumari català*, 1:435, and, for the design of glass trumpets, 1:405.

58. Guillaume Durand (Guillaume de Mende), *Rational ou Manuel des divins offices* (Paris, 1854), 3:236–242, develops the question. For a synthesis of the various positions of theologians, see Corblet, *Histoire dogmatique*, 1:108–158.

59. Abraham, the first circumciser and the last sacrificer, is one of the figures, which explains the deviations around the "sacrifice of Isaac" in the Middle Ages. This theme was studied by A. Moore Smith, "The Iconography of the Sacrifice of Isaac in Early Christian Art," *American Journal of Archaeology* (1922), 26:159–173, and readdressed in critical fashion by Aline Rousselle (unpublished work on "Le glaive d'Abraham").

60. In Gabrielle Sentis, *L'Art du Briançonnais, I: La peinture au XVe siècle* (Grenoble, 1970), p. 258; Bernhardt Blumenkranz, *Le Juif médiéval au miroir de l'art chrétien* (Paris, 1966), notes the manner in which the scene manifests "the anti-Jewish tendency" of the twelfth and thirteenth centuries: we see the infant Jesus attempting a gesture of resistance that increases the Virgin's fright at the oversized knife of the circumciser, who is wearing a Jewish hat (sometimes Joseph plays this role).

61. Damase Arbaud, *Chants populaires de la Provence* (Nyons, 1972 [1862]), 2:219.

62. P. Perdrizet, *Le Calendrier parisien*, p. 70.

63. E. Delaruelle, *La piété populaire*, pp. 621–680, analyzes the phenomenon. On devotion to the blood of Christ, see Luigi M. Lombardi-Satriani and Mariano Meligrana, *Il ponte di San Giacomo* (Milan, 1982), p. 321 and p. 423, n. 81.

64. Eugène Vacandard, "La question du meurtre rituel chez les juifs," in *Etudes de critique et d'histoire religieuse* (Paris 1912), pp. 313–377 (quotes from p. 332).

65. Zalman Shneour, *Le chant du Dnieper* (Paris, 1950), p. 46.

66. Cleto Corrain and Pierluigi Zampini, "Costumanze populari sull'uccisione dell porco nel Veneto," *Atti del I convegno di studi sul folklore padano, Mondo agrario tradizionale* (Modena, 1963).

67. E. Delaruelle, *La piété populaire*, p. 737, n. 58, emphasizes the role assigned to Christian children during this period.

68. We are taking these details from the work of Jean Delalande, *Les Extraordinaries Croisades d'enfants et de pastoureaux au Moyen Age* (Paris, 1962). The latest thinking on the question is found in Carlo Ginzburg, *Storia notturna, una decifrazione del sabba* (Turin, 1989), p. 9 and p. 28, n. 13.

69. Jean Duvernoy, *Le Registre d'Inquisition de Jacques Fournier* (Paris, 1978), 1:222–234.

70. Delalande, *Les Extraordinaries Croisades*, p. 95.

7. The Little Jew

1. Joan Amades, *Costumari català. El curs de l'any*, 5 vols. (Barcelona, 1950), 2:767–768 and 2:777; in Ripoll they are called "Hebrews." On the custom of having children appear as *pueri haebreorum*, see Noël Coulet, "Les entrées solonnelles en Provence au XIVe siècle," *Ethnologie française* (1977), 7(1):63–82.

2. Italo Sordi, *Teatro e riti. Saggi sulla drammatica popolare italiana* (Milan, 1990), pp. 64–85, based on fieldwork performed in 1982.

3. We are quoting from and summarizing Pasquale Marica and Franz Silesu, "La Settimana Santa a Sanluri," in *Atti del VII Congresso nazionale della tradizioni populari* (Florence 1959), pp. 237–249.

4. Testimony that appeared in *Enquêtes du musée de la Vie wallonne* (1928), 2:75.

5. Jules Lecoeur, *Esquisses du bocage normand* (Saint-Pierre-de-Salerne, 1979), 2:172.

6. In Paolo Toschi, *Le origini del teatro italiano* (Turin, 1969), p. 710, quoting Antonio D'Amato, 1928.

7. Geneviève Massignon, "La crécelle et les insturments des ténèbres en Corse," *Arts et Traditions populaires* (1959), 7(3–4):274–280; Arnold Van Gennep, *Manuel de folklore français contemporain*, 8 vols. (Paris, 1943–1988), 1:1209–1237, sees the appearance of as similar division between "playing the Jews" and "killing the Jews."

8. In Amades, *Costumari català*, 2:777, and according to a witness quoted in *Arxiu de tradicions populars* (1981), fasc. 6, p. 356.

9. Georges L'Hôte, *La Tankiote. Usages traditionnels en Lorraine* (Nancy, 1984), p. 161.

10. Van Gennep, *Manuel de folklore français contemporain*, 1:1229, 1:1253, 1:1261.

11. Arnold Van Gennep, *Le Folklore des Hautes-Alpes* (Paris, 1946), p. 217.

12. In S. Brandes, "Animal Metaphors and Social Control in Tzintzuntzan," *Ethnology* (1978), 23(3):207–215.

13. The expression has been noted by Ernesto de Martino, *Mondo populare e magia in Lucania* (Rome, 1975), p. 116; see also Charles Nyrop, *Linguistique et histoire des moeurs* (Paris, 1934), pp. 98–125.

14. Remarked by A. Cézerac (note on Faudoas) in 1899 for Antonin Perbosc (unclassified ms., B. M. de Toulouse).

15. Jean Duvernoy, *Le Registre d'Inquisition de Jacques Fournier* (Paris, 1978), 2:613.

16. In Vouk Karadjitch, *Contes populaires serbes* (Lausanne, 1987 [1853]), pp. 145–148; Valentino Ostermann, *La vita in Fiuli. Usi, costumi, credenze popolari* (Udine, 1978 [1894]), p. 443, who noted the formula sung by the ogre: "Nin, nin, mi sà di cristianin."

17. The expression was noted by Antonio de Nino, *Usi abruzzesi*, (Avezzano, 1879), 1:125–127; see also Gabriel Jeanton, *Le Mâconnais traditionaliste et populaire* (Mâcon, 1923), 4:13–14. On the Moor, see Joan Amades, *Folklore de Catalunya. Costums i creences* (Barcelona, 1969), pp. 57 and 65, who deals more broadly with beliefs related to the origin of children and baptism (pp. 37–73).

18. Jean Poueigh, *Chansons populaires des Pyrénées françaises* (Marseilles,

1977 [1926]), p. 49; and Alphonse Lamarque de Plaisance, *Usages et chansons populaires de l'ancien Bazadais* (Bordeaux, 1845), pp. 11–16.

19. On this ritual, see Poueigh, *Chansons populaires*, pp. 43–47; and, for a broader perspective, our article, "L'enfant, le four et le cochon," *Le Monde alpin et rhodanien* (1982), pp. 155–178. We will return to sorceresses and the transformed child in chapter 9.

20. For German data, see Edward Hoffmann-Krayer and Hanns Bächtold-Staübli, *Handwörterbuch der deutschen Aberglauben*, 10 vols. (Berlin-Leipzig, 1968 [1927–1942]), s.v. "Jude," p. 823.

21. In Jeanton, *Le Mâconnais*, vol. 2; and Patrice Bidault, "Les Superstitions médicales du Morvan," medical thesis (Paris, 1899). The formula against dry skin was noted by Raphaël de Westphalen, *Petit Dictonnaire des traditions populaires messines* (Metz, 1934), pp. 174–175 and 576.

22. According to Claude Seignolle, *Le Folklore de la Provence* (Paris, 1963), pp. 54–57 and 184–185; see also Chalres Gagnon, *Le Folklore bourbonnais* (Moulins, 1949), 2:62, where the ritual protects from smallpox.

23. We are translating the expression noted by Giuseppe Delfino and Aídano Schmuckher, *Stregoneria, magia credenze e superstizioni a Genova e in Liguria* (Florence, 1973), p. 37.

24. See Jean-Baptiste Thiers, *Traité des superstitions qui regardent les sacrements selon l'Ecriture sainte* (Paris, 1741 [1678]), 7:171–172; and Germain Laisnel de La Salle, *Le Berry* (Paris, 1902), 2:33.

25. Amades, *Folklore de Catalunya*, p. 72; and Hoffmann-Krayer and Bächtold-Staübli, *Handwörterbuch*, s.v. "Jude," p. 823.

26. See Jules Corblet, *Histoire dogmatique, liturgique et archéologique du sacrement de baptême*, 2 vols. (Paris, 1881–1882); and Agnès Fine, *Parrains et marraines, la parenté spirituelle en Europe* (Paris, 1994), who analyzes their role at the moment of the ceremony.

27. Achile Montel and Louis Lambert, *Chants populaires du Languedoc* (Paris 1880), p. 149.

28. On this custom see Gabriel Llompart, "Dos notas de folklore religioso levantino. Evangelios de bautizo y peregrinas de representación," *Revista de dialectología y tradiciones populares* (1966), 22(3, 4):7–25.

29. Noted and commented upon by Annabela Rossi and Roberto de Simone with regard to pilgrims in *Immagini della Madonna dell'Arco* (Rome, 1973), pp. 7–30.

30. In Poueigh, *Chansons populaires*, pp. 45–49. On the *rabalha*, see also Jean Delmas, *Autour de la table* (Rodez, 1983), p. 89.

31. Van Gennep, *Manuel de folklore français contemporain*, 1:1158–1206, established the geography of these patisseries. We have studied several in *Cuisine, alimentation, manières de table* (Toulouse, 1983), pp. 32–46.

32. Amades, *Folklore de Catalunya*, p. 63; and *Costumari català*, vol. 1,

which has rich pages devoted to children (see, among others, pp. 30, 34, 123, and 148).

33. Amades, *Costumari català*, 1:431.

34. Van Gennep returns to it, in fact, on several occasions, *Manuel de folklore français contemporain*, 1(1):143 and 1(2):21–22.

35. The bibliography of these pastries being large but scattered, we are citing only the articles and works that we used directly. For Italy, Bianca Maria Galanti, "Tradizioni gastronomiche d'Italia: uovi e dolci pasquali," *Lares* (1958), 24:17–41; for Sardinia, Alberto M. Cirese et al., *Pani tradizionali, arte effimero* (Cagliari, 1977); for Catalonia, Ramón Vioant i Simorra, *Obra oberta* (Barcelona, 1978), 1:272–330; *Archives suisses des traditions populaires* (1957), no. 53, collected several articles on this theme.

36. Vioant i Simorra, *Obra oberta*, 1:299.

37. Amades, *Costumari català*, 2:905. The cycle of stories on the red egg is collected by Venetia Newall, *An Egg at Easter* (London, 1971), which also shows the relationship between the egg and blood, the egg and the Eucharist (pp. 204–207). See also François Lebrun, *Le Livre de Pâques* (Paris, 1986), for complimentary material and testimonies.

38. Newall, *An Egg at Easter*, pp. 216–218, whom we are summarizing.

39. Ibid., p. 161.

40. Robert Debrie, "Contribution à l'étude des cérémonies traditionnelles en basse Picardie," *Eklitra* (1969), 8:50–51.

41. On *nebula*, see Jules Corblet, *Histoire dogmatique, liturgique et archéologique du sacrement de l'eucharistie*, 2 vols. (Paris, 1885), vol. 1, book 4; for the Sardinian *kokkòi de angùlla*, Cirese et al., *Pani tradizionali*, p. 31 and n. 30–31; on the *mona*, Joan Corominas, *Diccionari etimologic de la llengua catalana*, 5 vols. published (Barcelona, 1980), s.v. pp. 833–834: "*Mundus, a, um* is attested in the fourteenth century with the meaning of clean, clear, the opposite of the unclean—*mundar*, to purify. *Mona*, derived from *munda*, designates both the Easter cake garnished with eggs and, in old Portuguese, according to a document from 1220, an offering of bread to the poor; in Catalan *monda* is also attested in the sense of an offering of wax to the Virgin. In the south the *mona* has come by metonymy to designate Holy Week. Thus one may speak of the "first day of *mona*."

42. See Joan Amades, *Folklore de Catalunya. Rondallistica* (Barcelona, 1950), p. 791 and p. 1023, no. 1267, the story responds to the first question, "¿Perquè entre els esquerrans no hi ha cap home de bé?" (Why are there no good men among the left handed?).

43. We are using a part of the work of Roger Pinon on "Le jeu du Diable et de l'Ange en Wallonie," in *Le Folklore de l'enfance* (Brussels, 1982), pp. 33–71, which considers the variations in Europe.

44. François Marchetti, *Explication des usages et coutumes des Marseillais* (Marseilles, 1683), pp. 421–422.

45. Arnold Van Gennep, *Le Folklore de la Flandre* (Paris, 1935), p. 264.

46. Philippe Ariès, *L'Enfant et la Vie familiale sous l'Ancien Régime* (Paris, 1960).

47. Fortunato Pasqualino, *Mio padre Adamo* (Palermo, 1966), p. 48.

48. The ethnography of the ritual, the course of which is similar to the games with blood plants (see chapter 2), is in Maria Paraskevopoulou, *Recherches sur les traditions des fêtes religieuses populaires de Chypre* (Nicosia, 1978), pp. 51–54.

49. The Gironde belief is reported by Charles de Mensignac, *Coutumes, usages et chansons populaires de la Gironde* (Marseilles, 1982), p. 38. On the recurrence of the number seven in the representation of the ages of life, see Ariès, *L'Enfant et la Vie*, pp. 8–18.

50. As shown by Fine, *Parrains et marraines*.

51. *La Communion, quatre siècles d'histoire*, under the direction of Jean Delumeau (Paris, 1987), is the basic work.

52. Amades, *Costumari català*, 2:919 and 2:956.

53. For all these details, see chapter 6, n. 30.

54. Hans Niedermeier, "Die Rothaarigen in volkskundlicher Sicht," *Bayerisches Jahrbuch für Volkskunde* (Munich, 1963), pp. 76–106.

55. For that is the very name of the instrument in Alex, in Savoy, where it was noted by Van Gennep, *Manuel de folklore français contemporain*, 1(3):1237 (*jwhéro*).

56. The belief is an old one; Arturo Graf, in *Miti, leggende e superstizioni del Medio Evo* (Bologna, 1980), 2:253, mentions it. See also Amades, *Costumari català*, 1:93, 2:796–797; and Amades, *Folklore de Catalunya. Rondallistica*, the story, on p. 1124, on the island of Judas.

57. The question is posed like this in Catalonia: "¿Perquè no es pot donar truita de ceba als infants?" Amades relates several stories in *Folklore de Catalunya. Rondallistica*, p. 1023, no. 1268, for the one we are citing, no. 1267; no. 1270 and no. 1271 entitled "¿Perquè minjar pa sucat en Dies Sants fa jueu?" (Why eating bread soaked in sauce during the Holy Week makes you Jewish).

58. José Luis Morales, *El niño en la cultura española* (Madrid, 1960), 2:747–478.

59. Who, in the theater, always die sticking out their tongues. The Sardinian prohibition is related in *Archivio delle tradizioni populari* (1895), fasc. 6, p. 411, for Nuoro.

60. Charles Bauby, *Coutumes de Pâques en Roussillon* (Perpignan, 1944), p. 13.

61. The ritual is related by Giuseppe Pitré, *Cartelli, pasquinate, canti, leggende, usi del popolo siciliano* (Palermo, 1978), p. 233, and is practiced in Rosolini.

62. Valeri Serra i Boldù, *Calendari folkloric d'Urgell* (Montserrat, 1981 [1915]), p. 104; Giordana Charuty in "Le mal d'amour," *L'Homme* (1987), no. 103, pp. 43–72, for hysteria.

63. Amades, *Costumari català*, 2:753.

64. See *L'Instrument de musique populaire*, exhibit catalog of the Musée des Arts et Traditions populaires (Paris, 1977), pp. 44–45 and illustration 55.

65. According to Andreina Nicoloso Ciceri, *Tradizioni populari in Fiuli* (Udine, 1983), 2:750–767.

66. Alberto Catalan, "La Pasqua e il sepolcro nelle tradizioni popolari triestine," *Lares* (1943), pp. 165–168. The tradition of sepulchers is very lively on the Island of Procida (in the bay of Naples), where we were able to observe it in 1992. The young boys also prepare "mysteries" for the procession of Holy Friday.

67. In Edmonde Charles-Roux, *Fulco di Verdura. Une enfance sicilienne* (Paris, 1981), p. 200.

68. Nicolas Calmels, *L'Oustal de mon enfance* (Paris, 1985), devotes several pages to this experience, which should be situated in about 1914, pp. 64–66, 87, 105, and 120.

69. This expression is found in Rodolphe de Warsage, *Le Calendrier populaire wallon* (Anvers, 1920), p. 170. On the notion of Jewish "leftovers," see Cleto Corrain, *Documenti etnografici nei sinodi francesi* (Rovigo, 1976), pp. 14–15, and map, p. 147, in which *vinacium Judeorum* designates the marc of the grape harvest abandoned to the Jews. Several synods demand that one destroy this marc for fear that "Jewish wine" would later be mixed with the wine of the communion. Even in 1195 the bishop of Paris demanded, at the risk of excommunication, that the marc of Christian pressings be scattered or "given to the pigs." Again, it is to the pigs—along with the children—that the scraps of hosts and imperfect hosts are given when nuns make them in large quantity, see Claude Macherel and Jean Steinauer, *L'Etat de ciel. Portrait de ville avec rite. La Fête-Dieu de Fribourg* (Fribourg, 1989), p. 31; finally, according to Esther Fernández de Paz, *Los talleres del bordado de las cofradías* (Madrid, 1982), p. 89, in the slang of the ecclesiastical embroidery workshops, the box where the snippets of gold thread are kept, before being remelted, when the pieces are cut with scissors, is called *judío* (Jew).

8. The Return of the Pig

1. Quoted by Venetia Newall, *An Egg at Easter* (London 1971), p. 159, from Reuben Ainsztein, "The Jewish Background of Karl Marx," *Jewish Observer and Middle East Review* (London), October 23, 1964.

2. Antonio De Nino, *Usi abruzzesi* (Avezzano, 1879), pp. 35–36.

3. Joan Amades, *Costumari català. El curs de l'any*, 5 vols. (Barcelona, 1950), 2:725.

4. Quoted by Joan Amades and J. Tarin, *Leyendas y tradiciones marineras* (Barcelona, 1954), pp. 73–75, who adds that in its place they eat *pexpalo*—a kind of tough conger—which they "tenderize" to make a delicious dish. On the conger fair during Lent, see Amades, *Costumari català*, 2:644; for the stories relating to fish, Joan Amades, *Folklore de Catalunya. Rondalística* (Barcelona, 1950), pp. 934 (no. 925) and 942 (no. 958); Eugène Rolland, *Faune populaire de la France. Noms vulgaires, dictons, proverbes, légendes, contes et superstitions*, 13 vols. (Paris, 1967 [1877–1915]), 11:162 and 11:185; Paul Sébillot, *Le Folklore de France*, 4 vols. (Paris, 1968), 3:339–350. For an anthropological analysis of these "dualist creations," see Marlène Albert-Llorca, *L'Ordre des choses* (Paris, 1992), chapters 4 and 5, who has also translated and presented the corpus of Catalan stories, *L'Origine des bêtes* (Carcassonne, 1988). In Brittany, Saint Peter's Fish (*Zeus faber*) is marked by the hand of the saint, while in Catalonia it is sometimes accused of having furnished the Jews with the thorns of the crucifixion. It thereby rejoins the hammerhead fish (*Zygaena malleus*), in Italy called *pesce giudeo*, in Provence, *peyjudiou*, without there being any story to explicate these terms (Rolland, *Faune populaire*, 11:161).

5. Rolland, *Faune populaire*, 10:221–227.

6. See Carlos Lopes Cardoso, "O julgamento e o enterro do bacalhau," *Sintria* (1982), 1:753–802, who has assembled these texts, one of which is called "Supplicío do bacalhao e degredo de Judas em sabbado de Alleluia"; and Paolo Tschi, *Le origini del teatro italiano* (Turin, 1955), p. 239.

7. Amades, *Costumari català*, 2:705.

8. Joan Amades, in a curious text entitled *L'Escudella* (Barcelona, 1978), collected the elements of this confrontation. We learn, in fact, that during Lent, the conger replaces the pig in this culinary stew in which the chickpea and the bean are served with the meats and vegetables (p. 21).

9. Antoni María Alcover and Francesc de B. Moll, *Diccionari català—valencià—balear*, 2d ed., 10 vols. (Barcelona, 1977), 5:833.

10. Joan Coromines, *Diccionari etimologic de la llengua catalana*, 9 vols. (Barcelona, 1980–1992), 2:1072–1073.

11. See our article, "Le soleil des limaçons," *Etudes rurales* (July-December, 1982), pp. 63–93.

12. Alcover and Moll, *Diccionari*, 5:755–756.

13. Amades, *Costumari català*, 2:753, and Aurelio Capmany, *Calendari . . .* (Barcelona, 1982), 3:95.

14. While for the Holy Cross festival they use little stones; see Capmany, *Calendari*, p. 140).

15. Amades, *Costumari català*, 2:792, on oranges and vinegar; Amades, *Folklore de Catalunya. Rondalística*, p. 1007 (no. 1208), for the onion; and Amades, *L'Escudella*, p. 51, for lentils. A *Traité des dispenses du carême* (Paris, 1710), relates the belief according to which lentils make those who eat them "blind" and "leprous" (chapter 10).

16. On fasting and its importance in Jewish culture, see Léon de Modène, *Riti hebraici* (Venice, 1678), pp. 8–81; and Moses Maimonides, *The Guide for the Perplexed.* The treatise on Lent, *Traité des dispenses du carême*, cited in note 15 above, devotes seventeen chapters to the Christian fast, emphasizing its "spiritual" dimension in contrast to "pagan fasts" (vol. 2, chapter 5).

17. See Amades, *L'Escudella*, pp. 27–28, and our article, "Du cochon pour les morts," *Etudes rurales* (January-June 1987), pp. 181–212, on this dish and its place in the cycle of festivals of the pig and Saint Anthony.

18. Arnold Van Gennep, *Manuel de folklore français contemporain*, 8 vols. (Paris, 1943–1988), 1(3):1213–1239.

19. Amades, *Customari català*, 2:534 (for the bell of la Seu) and 815.

20. See *Traité des dispenses de carême*, 1:235–245, chapter 22. On carp in the Jewish diet, see Josef Erlich, *La Flamme du shabbath* (Paris, 1978), p. 197; Françoise Lebrun, *Le Livre de Pâques* (Paris, 1986), pp. 25 and 147; Laurence Bérard, "La consommation du poisson en France: des prescriptions alimentaires à la prépondérance de la carpe," *Anthropozoologica* (1988), pp. 171–179.

21. The story is in Amades, *Folklore de Catalunya. Rondallistica*, p. 909 (no. 826). Charles de la Morandière, *Histoire de la pêche française de la morue dans l'Amérique septentrionale* (Paris, 1962), specifies this detail of the tongue cut out and salted separately because it constitutes the fisherman's share and distinguishes two pieces of flesh that could be taken for a tongue, one of which, a cartilaginous piece, is still called *colibet* (see Littré, s.v.).

22. The text of one of these ritual scenarios appears in Léopold Schmidt, *Le Théâtre populaire européen* (Paris, 1965), pp. 425–451.

23. On this theater, of which we have already spoken in chapter 4, see Paolo Toschi, *Le origini del teatro italiano* (Turin, 1955), pp. 333–343; and Martine Boiteux, "Les juifs dans le carnaval de la Rome moderne, XVe–XVIIIe siècle," *Mélanges de l'Ecole française de Rome* (1976), 88:745–787, which discusses the antagonism between Christian and Jewish fishmongers (pp. 780–782).

24. Amades, *Costumari català*, 2:844.

25. According to *Le Ménagier de Paris*, written in 1393, in Paris "on absolute Friday between two and three thousands *lards* are sold" (Paris, 1846), 2:85. On the Bresse meal, see Dieudonné Dergny, *Usages, coutumes et croyances* (Brionne 1971 [1888]), 2:192.

26. On Rome see Robert Chambers, *The Book of Days* (London, 1967), 1:414; for Sicily, Giuseppe Pitré, *Spettacoli e feste popolari siciliane* (Palermo, 1978), p. 209.

27. Edith Durham, *Some Tribal Origins: Laws and Customs of the Balkans* (New York, 1979 [1928]), p. 292.

28. In Charles-Joseph Hefele, *Histoire des conciles d'après les documents originaux*, 4 vols. (Paris, 1907–1959), 2(2):1076–1077, quoting the Council of Antioch.

29. Chambers, *The Book of Days*, 1:429.

30. Quoted by F. Fertiault, "Des traditions populaires dans les Noëls bourguignons de La Monnoye," *Revue des traditions populaires* (1890), 5:487–499.

31. Lucien Guillemaut, *Les Mois de l'année* (Louhans, 1907), p. 46.

32. François Marchetti, *Explication des usages et coutumes des Marseillais* (Marseilles, 1683), pp. 358–364, to be compared with the work of the Abbé Jean Richard entitled *Agneau pascal, ou explication des cérémonies que les juifs observent en la manducation de l'agneau de Pasque, appliqueé dans un sens spirituel à la manducation de l'agneau divin dans l'Eucharistie* (Cologne, 1686).

33. On this polemic, see J. Van Goudoever, *Fêtes et calendriers bibliques* (Paris, 1967), pp. 217–225, and our chapter 5.

34. Amades, *Costumari català*, 2:902–903 and 2:919–921. It was the inquisitor Juan de Fontamar who emphasized the *xuetas*'s distaste for young goat (points 18 and 19 of his 1674 indictment of the descendants of the Jews, presented in an appendix to the Catalan translation of the work of Baruch Braunstein, *Els xuetes de Mallorca* [Barcelona, 1976], pp. 279–286).

35. According to Valerio Guttérrez Macías, "Retablo popular de la tierra parda," *Etnología y tradiciones populares* (Saragossa, 1974), pp. 283–319.

36. For Calabria, see Vittorio Teti, *Il pane, la beffa e la festa* (Florence, 1976); for Friouli, Bianca Maria Galanti, "Tradizioni gastronomiche d'Italia: uovi e dolci pasquali," *Lares* (1958), 24:17–41.

37. Margit Gari, *Le Vinaigre et le Fiel* (Paris, 1983), p. 310.

38. In Lebrun, *Le Livre de Pâques*, pp. 153–154. The custom is alive in Romania, where it was confirmed for us.

39. Newall, *An Egg at Easter*, p. 229.

40. Valentino Ostermann, *La vita in Friuli* (Udine, 1978), pp. 74–75.

41. The reference work on this ritual remains that of Solange Corbin, *La Déposition liturgique du Christ au vendredi saint* (Paris, 1960).

42. See, in the special edition (no. 53, 1957) of the journal *Archives suisses des traditions populaires* devoted to Easter pastries, the articles by E. Sánchez Sanz (p. 100); G. Perusini (p. 144 for Vénétie); Veiga de Oliveira (pp. 151–171, for Portugal).

43. Van Gennep, *Manuel de folklore français contemporain*, 1(3):1378–1379.

44. This is a story that appeared in the *Tabula exemplorum secundum ordinem alphabeti* (compilation dating from the end of the thirteenth century) ed. J. T. Welter (Toulouse, 1927), p. 49, no. 219. The text is the following: "Item hoc sacramentum munit contra temptacionem sicut castrum munitum armis et victualibus contra hostes, quia hic hospitatus est hic fortis in prelio, hic panis et vinum sc [ilicet] corpus et sanguis Christi; hic cara sumpta de lardario beate Virginis, sale passionum condita in patibulo crucis." The translation into French was done by Marie-Anne Polo de Beaulieu, to whom we give thanks.

45. In Jules Corblet, *Histoire dogmatique, liturgique et archéologique du sacre-*

ment de l'eucharistie, 2 vols. (Paris, 1885), 2:520, based on François-Maximilien Misson, *Voyage d'Italie* (1722), p. 71.

46. Van Gennep, *Manuel de folklore français contemporain*, 1(3):1356 ff, assembles many of these interdictions and "miracles," for what occurs is also a kind of transubstantiation: the water and wine changing spontaneously into blood. We find identical cases in Amades, *Costumari català*, 2:828.

47. We are summarizing from Luigi Pirandello, *Novelle per un anno* (Milan, 1944), 4:1927.

48. Notably in the region of Bragance, according to the testimonies of Giordana Charuty and Michel Valière, whom we thank.

49. Joan Amades returns twice to this heavenly body, in *Folklore de Catalunya. Costums i creences* (Barcelona, 1969), p. 1242, and in *Costumari català*, 1:78.

9. *Blood and Soul*

1. Georges L'Hôte, *La Tankiote. Usages traditionnels en Lorraine* (Nancy, 1984), p. 162.

2. The term and the function are in Oscar Keller, "La boucherie à domicile dans la Suisse romande," *Archives suisses des traditions populaires* (1946), 43:561–587. Valeri Serra i Boldù, "La matança del porc a Barcelona," *Arxiu de tradicions populars* (1980), fasc. 1, p. 43; Charles Beauquier, *Faune et flore poulaires de la Franche-Comté* (Paris, 1910), 2:157; and Jean-Claude Sordelli, *Soleil haut* (Paris, 1968), p. 55, sketches the portrait of this "helping woman," a pork butcher and midwife, also found in the Catalan Pyrenees (Louis Assier-Andrieu, "Anthropologie de la matança en Capcir," master's thesis, Université de Toulouse-Le Mirail, 1977, p. 35).

3. Antoni María Alcover and Francesc de B. Moll, *Diccionari català—valencià—balear*, 2d ed., 10 vols. (Barcelona, 1977), 9:724.

4. Gabriel Janer Manila, *Sexe i cultura a Mallorca, el cançoner* (Palma di Majorca, 1979), p. 133.

5. Sandra Ott, *The Circle of Mountains* (Oxford, 1981), p. 36.

6. Jesús Taboada, "La matanza del cerdo en Galicia," *Revista de dialectología tradiciones populares* (1969), 25:98.

7. Yvonne Verdier, from whom we are borrowing the expression "the men's share," gave meaning to this separation by showing that the "taking" of the lard in the salting tub is comparable to a gestation, *Façons de dire, façons de faire . . .* (Paris, 1979), p. 36. Ott offers another example based on the making of cheese by Basque breeders, *The Circle of Mountains*, pp. 13–27. See also "La fabrication mythique des enfants," under the direction of Nicole Belmont, *L'Homme* (January-March 1988), no. 105.

8. In Enrique Casas Gaspar, *Ritos agrarios. Folklore campesino* (Madrid, 1950), pp. 240–245.

9. For France one should refer to the rich ethnography published in the

revues *Etudes limousines*: Gérard Marsiquet (1964), pp. 15–19; and *Aguiaine*: A. Cadet (1972), p. 188; (1976), pp. 3–46; (1981), pp. 358–368). Michel Valière has noted the same practices in Poitou, and we thank him for sharing them with us. Georges Charachidzé, in *Le Système religieux de la Géorgie païenne* (Paris, 1968), p. 85, notes that any man who enters the room where the women are eating the ritual meal called *samalulo* (the "hidden meal") which brings to a close the winter fast and takes place on "piglet Thursday," exposes himself to losing his vision: "Stand back, go away, you'll go blind, we're eating the *samalulo*."

10. Marius Noguès, *Les Moeurs d'autrefois en Saintonge et en Aunis* (Marseilles, 1978 [1891]), p. 93.

11. It was Yvonne Verdier who alerted us to the article by Nils-Arvid Bringeus, "Food and Folk Beliefs: On Boiling Blood Sausage," in Margaret L. Arnott, ed., *Gastronomy: The Anthropology of Food Habits* (The Hague-Paris, 1975), pp. 251–273, of which she wrote a review (*L'Homme* [July-December 1978], 18(3–4):237–238), but which she didn't use, having found no echo of these beliefs and practices in Minot.

12. Bringeus, "Food and Folk Beliefs," p. 264.

13. See, on the status of the husband, Nicolas Richard, *Traditions populaires, croyances superstitieuses, usages et coutumes de l'ancienne Lorraine* (Marseilles, 1985 [1848]); and Dieudonné Dergny, *Usages, coutumes et croyances* (Brionne, 1971), 2:396, for the Bresse Louhannaise region.

14. Bringeus, "Food and Folk Beliefs," p. 265.

15. Ibid., p. 266.

16. Ramón Violant i Simorra, *Obra oberta* (Barcelona, 1935), 3:24.

17. Ziedonis Ligers, *Ethnographie lettone* (Bâle, 1954), p. 472.

18. Bringeus, "Food and Folk Beliefs," pp. 257–260.

19. On the spleen, its dangers and the prohibitions against it, see Casas Gaspar, *Ritos agrarios*; Taboada, "La matanza," pp. 97–100; Alcover and Moll, *Diccionari*, 7:334; on the lexicon, the maps of linguistic atlases are rich: Colette Dondaine, *Atlas linguistique et ethnographique de la Franche-Comté*, 3 vols. (Paris, 1972–1984), map 683; Henri Bourcelot, *Atlas linguistique et ethnographique de la Champagne et de la Brie*, 3 vols. (Paris, 1966–1978), map 984; Jean Lanher, *Atlas linguistique et ethnographique de la Lorraine romane*, 3 vols. (Paris, 1979–1985), map 305; Jean Séguy, *Atlas linguistique et ethnographique de la Gascogne* (hereafter *ALG*), 6 vols. (Paris, 1954–1973), map 1402; Pierre Nauton, *Atlas linquistigue et ethnographique du Massif central*, 4 vols. (Paris, 1957–1963), maps 537–538; Xavier Ravier, *Atlas linguistique et ethnographique du Languedoc occidental*, 4 vols. (Paris, 1978–1993), map 443, where the term *melsa* is used for the pancreas, which is also reputed to burst the bowels. Jean-Louis Fossat, *Le Vocabulaire gascon de la boucherie* (Toulouse, 1971), deals on several occasions with the etymology of the word (*rata/melsa*) and with the questions posed by this organ, pp. 77, 144–145, 158, 217–218, 237–238, 251, 272, 361.

20. Edward Hoffmann-Krayer and Hanns Bächtold-Staübli, *Handwörter-buch der deutschen Aberglauben*, 10 vols. (Berlin-Leipzig, 1968 [1927–1942]), 6:1087.

21. The document was published by Charles Joisten in the *Bulletin de la Société d'archéologie et de statistique de la Drôme* (September 1963), 75(349):369–380. On boiling see items 26, 33, and 118. We also found in it the belief according to which "when women make blood sausages no man must be present, which when it occurs, make the blood sausages burst" (item 82).

22. For Germany, see Hoffmann-Krayer and Bächtold-Staübli, *Hand-wörterbuch*, s.v. "Schwein," p. 1483; for Scandinavia, see Bringeus, "Food and Folk Beliefs," p. 259; for Calabria, Vittorio Teti, *Il pane, la beffa e la festa* (Florence, 1976), p. 330; for Corsica, Maurice Bigot, "Paysans corses en com-munauté. Porchers-bergers des montagnes de Bastelica," *Bulletin de l'Adecem* (Aix-en-Provence, 1991 [1889]). Claude Blazy, "L'identité paysanne. Recherches lexicologiques et sémantiques dans le Cantal," *Cahiers d'études romanes* (Université de Toulouse-II-Le-Mirail, 1979), pp. 31–74, noted the term *les astres* to designate the peritonium along with this commentary: "Oh! '*les astres*,' that's where one sees if the pig was killed right, if the slaughterer did his job well" (p. 49).

23. Note that in Catalonia, while one invokes Saint Rita so that the blood sausages won't burst because she was, in her lifetime, *botifarrera* (Joan Amades, *Costumari català. El curs de l'any*, 5 vols. [Barcelona, 1950], 3:655), the other protector of blood sausages is Saint Martha, "considered by the older women to be the patroness of witches" (ibid., 4:641).

24. In *Enquêtes du musée de la Vie wallonne* (1926), p. 301.

25. The ethnography of the *kalikandjarai* is in Maria Paraskevopoulou, *Recherches sur les traditions des fêtes religieuses populaires de Chypre* (Nicosia, 1978), pp. 26–30; and G. Georgeakis and Léon Pineau, *Le Folklore de Lesbos* (Paris, 1968), p. 349. The work by John Lawson, *Modern Greek Folklore and Ancient Greek Religion, a Study of Survivals* (Cambridge, 1910), pp. 190–255, remains fundamental. Daniela Perco, "Credenze e leggende relative a un essere fantastico: il mazarol/salvanel," in *Giuda al dialtte veneti* (1985), 7:155–179, presents and analyzes many contemporary stories and furnishes a bibliography for northern Italy. Algirdas Julien Greimas, *Des dieux et des hommes. Etudes de mythologie lituanienne* (Paris, 1985), shows that a bond between the souls of the dead and the pig is established by intermediary of the *kaukai* (pp. 29–78 and especially 51). The myths and beliefs of the Americas relative to the firing of pottery offers interesting analogies with Europe; see Claude Lévi-Strauss, *La Potière jalouse* (Paris, 1985), especially chapter 8.

26. The traditions relative to these child ghosts were collected by Eva Pócs, *Fairies and Witches at the Boundary of South-Eastern and Central Europe* (Helsinki, 1989), Folklore Fellow Communications, no. 243; and Juha Pentikäinen, *The Nordic Dead-Child Tradition, Nordic Dead-Child*

Beings: A Study in Comparative Religion (Helsinki, 1968), Folklore Fellow Communications, no. 202. Angès Fine proposed an anthropological reading of these unbaptized dead in "Le parrain, son filleul et l'au-delà," *Etudes rurales* (January-June 1987), no. 105–106, pp. 123–146.

27. Lawson, *Modern Greek Folklore*, p. 199.

28. Paraskevopoulou, *Recherches sur les traditions*, p. 19.

29. See Henri Labourasse, *Glossaire abrégé du patois de la Meuse* (Geneva, 1970 [1887]), p. 548, s.v. "Soutré."

30. On these piglet-ghosts, see Pócs, *Fairies and Witches*; and Pentikaïnen, *The Nordic Dead-Child Tradition*; Paul Sébillot, *Le Folklore de France*, 4 vols. (Paris, 1968 [1906]) 3:148–149, summarizes several variations on the legend in Brittany.

31. For an analysis of the symbolic logic uniting baptism and speech, speech and weaning, see Giordana Charuty, "Le fil de la parole," *Ethnologie française* (1985), 15(2):123–151.

32. On this *Gütel, Gütchen, Jütel* or *Jüdel*, see Hoffmann-Krayer and Bächtold-Staübli, *Handwörterbuch*, s.v. pp. 1233–1236; and Pócs, *Fairies and Witches*, p. 22.

33. Arnold Van Gennep, *Manuel de folklore français contemporain*, 8 vols. (Paris, 1943–1988), 1(7):2874–2981.

34. Simin Palay, *Dictionnaire du béarnais et du gascon modernes* (Paris, 1980), s.v. "Ahum," pp. 24–25.

35. The ritual is described by Giambattista Bastanzi, "Superstizioni religiose nelle provincie di Treviso e di Belluno," *Archivo per l'antropologia e la etnologia* (1887), fasc. 3, 17:271–310 (and 17:293–298 on the *massarol*).

36. William Carew Hazlitt, *Dictionary of Faiths and Folklore*, (London, 1905 [1870]), 1:116.

37. On this accusation see Henry Institoris and Jacques Sprenger, *Le Mareau des sorcières* (*Malleus maleficarum*, 1486), translated from the Latin by Amand Danet (Paris, 1990), pp. 246–247 and 403–406; and Jean-François Le Nail, "Procédures contre des sorcières de Seix en 1562," excerpt from the *Bulletin de la Société ariégeoise des sciences, lettres et arts* (1976), pp. 155–232; a midwife admitted this to the inquisitor of Aquilée in 1587, see Carlo Ginzburg, *Les Batailles noctures. Sorcellerie et rituels agraires en Frioul, XVe-XVIIe siècle* (Lagrasse, 1980 [1966, Italian]), pp. 108–109 and n. 15.

38. Lawson, *Modern Greek Folklore*, pp. 200–205.

39. M. Paraskevopoulou, *Recherches sur les traditions*, p. 27.

40. For all these stories, see C. Joisten, "Les êtres fantastiques dans le folklore de l'Ariège," *Via Domitia* (1972), vol. 10; José Miguel de Barandiarán, *Obras completas* (Bilbao, 1974), 2:420–480; for the Basque region and for western Europe, Elisée Legros: "Trois récits de lutins et de fées dans le folklore wallon et le folklore comparé," *Enquêtes du musée de la Vie wallonne* (1952), 6(65–68):129–227; (1964), 10(113–116):129–160; (1967), 11(125–128):129–159.

41. Legros, "Trois récits," 6:198.

42. Joisten, "Les êtres fantastiques" and Barandiarán, *Obras completas*; Greimas, *Des dieux et des hommes*, p. 57, emphasizes this mastery over boiling and fermentation—the *kaukai* are masters of *seré* (rennet) and of beer—in relation to the root of the word that designates them (pp. 40–45 for *kauka*, "furuncle" or boil; p. 71 for *aitvarai*, "to grow," "to boil").

43. On these prohibitions and the "patron of blood sausages," see Bringeus, "Food and Folk Beliefs," pp. 254–260. The term *lenga del ventre* is noted by Jacques Boisgontier, *Atlas linguistique et ethnographique du Languedoc oriental*, 3 vols. (Paris, 1981–1986), map 560, point 30.01.

44. Verdier, *Façons de dire*, pp. 136–137.

45. We offer an illustration of this in "La cuisine des sorcières," *Ethnologie française* (1991), no. 4, pp. 423–437, commenting on the scene in Macbeth.

46. Pierre Jakez Hélias, *Le Cheval d'orgueil* (Paris, 1975), p. 383.

47. For upper Provence, we obtained our information orally from Danièle Musset, who associates this rejection with Vaudois heresy. For Switzerland, see Oscar Keller, "La Boucherie à domicile dans la Suisse romande," *Archives suisses des traditions populaires* (1946), 43:575–584; the Scottish case is well analyzed by Alexander Fenton, "Pork in the Rural Diet of Scotland," in *Festschrift für Robert Wildhaber* (Bâle, 1973), pp. 98–110. In Romania, among orthodox Christians, where the interdiction against consuming the blood of animals is maintained, the pig killed on December 20 is the exception to the rule. Paul Henri Stahl, "Le Sang et la mort," in *Korper, Essen und Trinken im Kulturverständnis der Balkanvölker* (Berlin, 1991), pp. 167–182.

48. The Sardinian journal *Brads* devoted an issue (no. 9, 1979–1980) to domestic pork butchery.

49. In Laurent Joubert's second section of *Erreurs populaires au fait de médecine et régime de santé* (Avignon, 1578), chapter 12, pp. 85–89, he develops this thesis in the form of a dissertation and sees in it the origin of the "gift" of the pig.

50. See Claudine and Daniel Fabre, "Le testament du cochon," *Via Domitia* (1979), 14(2):121–156, in which the text is translated and commented in full.

51. Arnaldo Leal in his *Vocabulaire des bouchers de Saragosse et Santander* (Université de Toulouse-Le Mirail, 1976), returns to this several times (1:56; 1:95; 2:18).

52. Adam Maurizio, *Histoire de l'alimentation végétale depuis la préhistoire jusqu'à nos jours* (Paris, 1932), p. 459.

53. Séguy, *ALG*, map 742.

54. Alfons Nadal "Reminiscències àries en els costums funerals cristians," *Arxiu de tradicions populars* (1980), fasc. 2, pp. 92–93.

55. André Varagnac, *Civilisation traditionnelle et genres de vie* (Paris, 1948), p. 229.

56. Joisten, "Les êtres fantastiques," p. 50.

57. According to a communal monograph conserved at the archives of Toulouse (A.D. 31, b 2 4th 413), in Juzes, a canton of Revel, "the blood-red color that sometimes invades the porridge of corn flour is a subject of horror for the homemaker who prepared it and for the family as a whole.

58. We owe our knowledge on Sardinia to Andrea Mulas, whom we thank. The stories concerning the *súrbile*, the *coga* and the *pagana* present such analogies with those that depict the kalikandjarai that we tend to see these female "fantastical beings" as women who died in childbirth and who became "pagans" or "Jews" again without the benefit of the ceremony of churching to put an end to their "impurity." We return here to the belief according to which the Jews cannot give birth without an intervention of the Virgin, as stated in a medieval song noted on a manuscript of religious songs, *Romania* (1890), 19:297–299, with commentaries by Paul Meyer; see also Giuseppe Pitré, *Usi e costumi: credenze e pregiudizi del popolo siciliano*, 4 vols. (Bologna, 1978 [1870–1913]), 4:461. On Procida, an island off the bay of Naples, one threatens children with the *Giuritta* and the *Giovanna*, associated with Herodias and Salomé, a Jewish hero and heroine, murderers of Saint John the Baptist. See Maris Masucci and Mario Vanacore, *La cultura popolare nell'Isola di Procida* (Naples, 1987), pp. 122–124.

59. Maurizio, *Histoire de l'alimentation végétale*, p. 304.

60. On these characters, see Angelo Nardo Cibele, "Superstizioni bellunesi e cadorine," *Archivio per l'antropologia e la etnologia* (1885), 4:575–592, and (1886), 5:32–40; on the blood millet and the blood porridges, see Maurizio, *Histoire de l'alimentation végétale*, p. 294–307 and 456–460. Let us recall the role played by stews of sorghum stems in the struggles between Friouli *benandanti*, Carlo Ginzburg, *Storia notturna, una decifrazione del sabba* (Turin, 1989).

61. The English ethnography is in Robert Chambers, *The Book of Days* (London 1967), 2:723–724; for Germany, see Hoffmann-Krayer and Bächtold-Staübli, *Handwörterbuch*, s.v. "Schlachten," p. 1080.

62. Amades, *Costumari català*, 1:16.

63. The expression is in Gabriel Llompart, "Cabos sueltos de folklore religioso mallorquín," *Revista de dialectología y tradiciones populares* (1968), 24:35–36, which explains it by placing it in relation to the localization of purgatory on the island and its representation in the form of a chain of mountains "with sawlike teeth," the *serra*, which we find in the iconography.

64. Jean Duvernoy, *Le Registre d'inquisition de Jacques Fournier* (Paris, 1978), 1:254.

65. The anecdote of the "false Marrano blood sausage" was related to us by Matty Chiva, whom we thank. On the Christian *botifarras* of Majorca, see Kennett Moore, *Los de la Calle* (Madrid, 1987), pp. 147–148 and our chapter 4.

66. Rituals and beliefs relative to blood sausages should also be viewed within the context of a more complex series of gestures taking place the morn-

ing of Fat Tuesday, Hoffmann-Krayer and Bächtold-Staübli, *Handwörterbuch*, s.v. "Blutwurst," p. 1462, and s.v. "Schwein," pp. 1487, 1490, and 1493.

10. The Bone That Sings

1. Raphaël de Westphalen, *Petit Dictionnaire des traditions populaires messines* (Metz, 1934), p. 569.

2. Léon Zéliqzon, *Dictionnaire des patois romans de la Moselle* (Strasbourg, 1924), pp. 158, 378, and 380.

3. Refer to chapter 3 and to Oskar Dähnhardt, *Natursagen* (Berlin, 1909), 2:280.

4. On the *jeune fille*, see de Westphalen, *Petit Dictionnaire*, p. 602; Zéliqzon, *Dictionnaire des patois romans*, p. 434; Edward Hoffmann-Krayer and Hanns Bächtold-Staübli, *Handwörterbuch der deutschen Aberglauben*, 10 vols. (Berlin-Leipzig, 1968 [1927–1942]), s.v.; the original myth is in Dähnhardt, *Natursagen*, 2:280.

5. This connection was suggested by Claude Gaignebet, to whom I offer thanks. I have discussed it with Yvonne Verdier, who places Melusina, "the emblematic figure of the woman during her period," at the heart of the problematic in "Pouvoir du sang" (an unpublished text that accompanied the exhibition on blood *[Le Sang]* at the cité des Sciences et de l'Industrie in La Villette in 1988).

6. Dähnhardt, *Natursagen*, pp. 106–279.

7. The Germanic data relative to the lexicon of the vertebra and to the ritual uses of bones are in Hoffmann-Krayer and Bächtold-Staübli, *Handwörterbuch*, s.v. "Jude," pp. 831–833, "Schwein," pp. 1484–1486, "Schlachten," p. 1083.

8. Cleto Corrain and Pierluigi Zampini, "Costumanze populari sull'uccisione del porco nel Veneto," *Atti del 1° convegno di studi sull folklore padano, Mondo agrario tradiƶionale* (Modena, 1963), pp. 124–125.

9. In Mario Vicari, "Torchi e torchiatura in Valle di Blenio," *Folklore suisse* (1985), no. 3–5, pp. 84–95.

10. Ziedonis Ligers, *Ethnographie lettone* (Bâle, 1954), p. 468.

11. For the expression "to make the soul of the pig," *faire l'ame du cochon*, see Jules Lecoeur, *Esquisses du Bocage normand* (Saint-Pierre-de-Salernes, 1979), 2:136; Geneviève Massignon and Brigitte Hériot, *Atlas linguistique et ethnographique de l'Ouest (Poitou, Aunis, Saintonge, Angoumois*, 3 vols. (Paris, 1971–1983), map 571; Henri Bourcelot, *Atlas linguistique et ethnographique de la Champagne et de la Brie*, 3 vols. (Paris, 1966–1978), map 986. In the French Vexin "we shot a rifle to salute the soul of the animal" (quoted by Michel Bozon and Anne-Marie Thiesse, *La Plaine et la Route*, [Royaumont, 1982], p. 56). *Le Glossaire des patois de la Suisse romande*, s.v. "Boudin," blood sausage, gives *frakacha* for tripe, the spinal column, and the meal the day of the killing. Mariane Müller observes a same multiplicity of meaning in *Le Patois de Marécottes (commune de Solvan, Valais)* (Tübingen, 1961), p. 190.

12. Jean Delmas, *Autour de la table* (Rodez, 1983), p. 80.

13. The "edge of the world," "end of the world," etc., are attested in Pierre Nauton, *Atlas linquistigue et ethnographique du Massif central*, 4 vols. (Paris, 1957–1963), map 542; Pierre Gardette and Paulette Durdilly, *Atlas linguistique et ethnographique du Lyonnais*, 5 vols. (Paris, 1950-1976), maps 329 and 330 and commentaries, 5:238–247; Gérard Taverdet, *Atlas linguistique et ethnographique de la Bourgogne*, 4 vols. (Paris, 1975–1984), map 1158, where the *caecum* also bears the name of Jesus, *judru*, "bottomless sack"; it was sometimes the stomach, in fact, that was filled and eaten for carnival. Colette Dondaine, *Atlas linguistique et ethnographique de la Franche-Comté*, 3 vols. (Paris, 1972–1984), maps 681 and 687, notes the same oscillation as in French-speaking Switzerland (Oscar Keller, "La boucherie à domicile dans la Suisse romande," *Archives suisses des traditions populaires* [1946], 43:579); see also, on the names of the pig's stomach, Claudine and Daniel Fabre, "Le testament du cochon," *Via Domitia* (1979), 14(2):121–156. In Finland, pea soup, pigs' feet, and blood cakes are eaten for Christmas, carnival, and Easter; see Elsa Enäjarvi-Haavio, *The Finnish Shrovetide* (Helsinki, 1954), Folklore Fellow Communications, no. 146, pp. 9–10, 27, and 54.

14. I present this Andorran fieldwork in "Du cochon pour les morts," *Etudes rurales* (1987), no. 105–106, pp. 181–212.

15. On Saint Anthony, see Louis Réau, *Iconographie des saints* (Paris, 1958), 1:101–115; Henri Chaumartin, "Le compagnon de saint Antoine. Symbolisme du cochon, attribut caractéristique du saint," *Æsculape* (1930), no. 9, pp. 223–256. On the illnesses identified under the name of *Ignis sacer*, one should also refer to L. Laroche, *La Peste et la Lèpre dans la Bourgogne méridionale* (Mâcon, 1934), p. 68; and Victor Advielle, *Histoire de l'order hospitalier de Saint-Antoine de Viennois et de ses commanderies et prieurés* (Paris, 1883).

16. See the catalog to the exhibition *Religions et traditions populaires*, Musée des Arts et Traditions populaires (Paris, 1979), pp. 180–181, for the manuscript of one of these plays written for a puppet theater.

17. We are summarizing from Joan Amades, *Costumari català. El curs de l'any*, 5 vols. (Barcelona, 1950), 1:494–497. Dominique Blanc, in "Le chiffre du destin," *Etudes rurales* (1987), no. 105–106, pp. 167–179, established the relationship that the lottery created between the two worlds; Saint Anthony, who is said in Catalonia to have beaten the devil in cards, is the patron saint of gamblers.

18. Carmelo Lisón Tolosana, *Antropología cultural de Galicia* (Madrid, 1979), pp. 55–109, writes beautifully about the "parish of the dead," which, here, echoes that of the living.

19. Antonio d'Amato, "Nuovo contributo al folklore irpino," *Il folklore italiano* (1933), fasc. 3–4, pp. 141–167.

20. See Italo Calvino, *Fiabe italiane* (Turin, 1956), pp. 809–810; and Enrica Delitala, *Fiabe e leggende nelle tradizioni populari della Sardegna* (Sassari, 1985), p. 84.

21. Amades, *Costumari català*, 1:467–468.

22. Alfonso M. Di Nola, *Gli aspetti magico-religiosi di una cultura subalterna italiana* (Turin, 1976), p. 220.

23. This story, which appeared in *La Revue du monde invisible* (1899–1900), 2:92, was commented upon by Daniel Fabre in his seminar on "La parole des morts" (Toulouse, Ecole des Hautes Etudes en Sciences Sociales, 1980–1982). The messenger of the dead (*armassier*) constitutes one of the poles of *La Trilogie sorcellaire en bas Languedoc*, analyzed by Jean-Pierre Piniès (Toulouse, 1983). On the pig and death, see Marie-France Orsini-Marzoppi, *Récits et contes populaires de la Corse, I* (Paris, 1978), p. 140. We know that the Corsican *mazzeri* knew how to read deaths to come on pig's heads; see Georges Ravis-Giordani, *Bergers corses, les communautés villageoises du Nioulu* (Aix-en-Provence, 1983).

24. Ramon Violant i Simorra, *Obra oberta* (Barcelona, 1980), 3:16.

25. Rolande Bonnain, "Le pèle-porc dans les Baronnies," *Les Baronnies des Pyrénées, I* (Paris, 1981), pp. 195–218.

26. Théophile Janvrais, "Les offrandes aux saints," *Revue des traditions populaires* (1895), 10:178–179.

27. According to the books from the council of Roquefeuil (region of Sault); this information comes to us from Gaston Maugard, who analyzed them.

Oeuvre du purgatoire: an institution that, since the middle ages, has been responsible for gathering gifts in kind or money for Masses and prayers to be said for the dead in purgatory, that they might go to heaven.—Trans.

28. This detail is in Elisabeth Claverie and Pierre Lamaison, *L'Impossible Mariage* (Paris, 1982), p. 61; on the dues butchers paid to convents, see J.-L. Fossat, *Le Vocabulaire gascon de la boucherie* (Toulouse, 1971), pp. 18 and 143–144; on leper hospitals, L. Laroche, *La Peste et la Lèpre*, p. 74.

29. As established by Daniel Fabre in "Juvéniles revenants," *Etudes rurales* (1987), no. 105–106, pp. 147–164.

30. Valeri Serri i Boldù, "La matança del porc a Barcelona," *Arxiu de tradicions populars* (1980), fasc. 1, p. 47.

31. It was then that we clarified the enigmatic expression given us during a first visit. See "Carnaval, essai d'ethnologie culinaire," in *Aspects des collectivités rurales en domaine occitan* (Toulouse, 1972), pp. 31–65.

32. Giuseppe Pitré, *Usi e costumi: credenze e pregiudizi del popolo siciliano*, 4 vols. (Bologne, 1978 [1870–1913]), 3:406.

33. Charles Beauquier, *Faune et flore populaires de la Franche-Comté* (Paris, 1910), 1:165.

34. On this lexicon, see Colette Dondaine, *Atlas linguistique et ethnographique de la Franche-Comté*, 3 vols. (Paris, 1972–1984), map 693; Georges L'Hôte, *La Tankiote. Usages traditionnels en Lorraine* (Nancy, 1984), p. 42; Zéliqzon, *Dictionnaire des patois romans*, p. 710; de Westphalen, *Petit Dictionnaire*, p. 66.

35. Corrain and Zampini, "Costumanze populari," p. 122.

36. Giovanni Tassoni and Cleto Corrain, in Giovanni Tucci, "Premiers résultats d'une enquête sur le rhombe en Italie," in the sixth *Congrès international des sciences anthropologiques et ethnologiques* (Paris, 1960), 2(2):491–496; and Giovanni Tucci, "Contributo allo studio del rombo," *Reista di etnografia* (1954–1955), 8–9:1–16. All this research was undertaken at the initiative of the historian of religion Raffaele Pettazoni. Even though they bolstered the theory of relics dear to this period, they have the merit in certain cases of situating the instrument, its lexicon, and usage within the universe of practices and beliefs. This is the case for Raffaello Battaglia, "Sopra-vivenze del rombo nelle provincie venete," *Studi e materiali di storia delle religioni* (Rome, 1925), 1:19–217, which studied the fishermen of the Venitian lagoon.

37. See Daniel Devoto, "Rombo," *Boletín de la Real Academia española* (1972), 42:135–147.

38. Alberto Vecchi, "Il *frullo* in territorio modenese," *Lares* (1964), no. 34, p. 157.

39. Amades, *Costumari català*, 5:173.

40. Three typical tales illustrate this theme in Europe. A summary and bibliography of them can be found in Paul Delarue, *Le Conte populaire français* (Paris, 1957), 1:199–242 (T. 313); Paul Delarue and Marie-Louise Ténèze, *Le Conte populaire français* (Paris, 1964), 2:690–707 (T. 720); Marie-Louise Ténèze, *Le Conte populaire français* (Paris, 1985), 4(1):211–222 (T. 780). Daniel Fabre and Jacques Lacroix, *La Traditionorale du conte occitan* (Paris, 1974), 2:101–112, gathered several variants of T. 780. For northern Europe, see Paul G. Brewster, *The Two Sisters* (Helsinki, 1953), Folklore Fellow Communications, no. 147, which also collects more Mediterranean variants in which the theme of the pig appears (pp. 65–66). On the "bone that sings," see Léopold Schmidt, "Der singende Knochen, Kultergeschichtliche gedanken zur Musik im Märchen," in *Die Volkserzählung* (Berlin, 1963), pp. 48–54.

41. In *Coma de pèiras pels Camps, contes de la Maria* (Cantal, 1982), I.E.O., pp. 59–62.

42. Léon Pineau, "Contes du Poitou," *Revue des traditions populaires* (1889), 5;81–83.

43. Ernst Bargheer, *Eingeweide Lebens und Seelenkräfte des Leibesinneren im Deutschen Glauben und Brauch* (Berlin, 1931), p. 59.

44. In Achille Montel and Louis Lambert, *Les Chants populaires du Languedoc* (Paris, 1880), supplemented by "Petites compositions populaires," *Revue des langues romanes* (1873), 5:34–37, 60–61, and 92–104, for the relationship between children's couplets and the tale.

45. Camille de Mensignac, *Coutumes, usages et chansons populaires de la Gironde* (Marseilles, 1982), p. 42.

46. See Jean-Daniel Blavignac, *L'Emprô genevois* (Geneva, 1879), pp. 18–19; Martial-Blaise Régis de la Colombière, *Les Cris populaires de Marseille* (Marseilles, 1980 [1868]), p. 126, the Provençal expression appearing as a

development of the oath noted in *La Friquassée crotestyllonnée* (Paris, 1878 [Rouen, 1557]), 414–418, and commentary, p. 115.

47. Ernest Beyer and Raymond Matzen, *Atlas linguistique et ethnographique de l'Alsace* (Paris, 1969), vol. 1, map 144, is quite rich. Yet elsewhere, though the "little Jew" is infrequently represented (a single point in Jean Séguy, *Atlas linguistique et ethnographique de la Gascogne*, 6 vols. [Paris, 1954–1973], map 601), use of the term remains very much alive.

48. According to Albert Dauzat, "Les noms populares de la pointe du coude," *Le Français moderne* (July 1943), p. 174; it is also the name for the pinky in Lyons. We thank Jacques Boisgontier for having obtained this text for us, which appeared under the Occupation. See also Edouard Brissaud, *Histoire des expressions populaires relatives à l'anatomie, à la physiologie et à la médecine* (Paris, 1892), p. 78.

49. We owe these details to Jean Zammit, a radiologist and archeologist, to whom we give thanks.

50. According to the experience of Arnold Niederer, who shared this information with us.

51. Roger Pinon, "Le jeu du Diable et de l'ange en Wallonie," in *Le Folklore de l'enfance* (Brussells, 1982), 12:67.

52. Eva Pócs, *Fairies and Witches at the Boundary of South-Eastern and Central Europe* (Helsinki, 1989), Folklore Fellow Communications, no. 243, pp. 77–78; see also Luigi Lombardi Satriani and Mariano Meligrana, *Il ponte di San Giacomo* (Milan, 1982), pp. 140–141. Carlo Ginzburg, in the last chapter of his *Storia notturna, una decifrazione del sabba* (Turin, 1989), establishes a relationship between this bone defect and ambulatory asymmetry and lameness. The tale of Cinderella is the model for his analysis. In the oral versions the heroine acquires her magical gifts from the bones of an animal killed by her stepmother that she reassembled and preserved; see Margarita Xanthakou, *Cendrillon et les soeurs cannibales* (Paris, 1988), no. 28. For Ginzburg "lameness" constitutes a mythical and ritual trait designating the one who comes and goes from the other world. From this perspective it qualifies death, the ghost, as well as all those who are situated at the boundary and thereby occupy a position of mediator (the Siberian shaman, the Friouli *benandanti*, etc.). Fitting into this group are the psychopomps, animals that guide the souls of the dead and circulate between one world and the other, and marginalized groups: lepers, Jews and witches who are considered to have these same powers. Even though our analysis confirms these analogies on many points, we have focused solely on the context of the Jewish-Christian confrontation, in which they take on a particular meaning.

53. On the *ypping*, see Juha Pentikäinen, *The Nordic Dead-Child Tradition* (Helsinki, 1968), Folklore Fellow Communications, no. 202; on the burial, see Pineau, "Contes du Poitou," pp. 81–83; and P. Brewster, *The Two Sisters*, p. 59.

54. Gluckel Hameln, *Mémoires* (Paris, 1971), pp. 102–103.

55. Julian Stryjkowski, *L'Auberge du vieux Tag* (Paris, 1972), p. 169.

56. In Adam Cohen, *Le Talmud* (Paris, 1982), pp. 431–432.

57. In Louis Ginzberg, *The Legends of the Jews* (Philadelphia, 1987 [1925]), 5:184 and 63; s.v. "Luz" in the index.

58. On Jewish rituals see Eric M. Meyers, *Jewish Ossuaries: Reburial and Rebirth* (Rome, 1971), no. 24; and Sylvie-Anne Goldberg, *Les Deux Rives du Yabbock* (Paris, 1989), pp. 28–37 and chapter 7. The most famous Christian text on dogma is Tertullian's *De la chair de Jésus-Christ et de la Résurrection de la chair*, in particular chapters 29 and 30. On the treatment of blood and bone in relation to resurrection or life in other cultures, see Robert Hertz, *Sociologie religieuse et folklore* (Paris, 1970); Françoise Héritier, "L'identité Samo," in "L'Identité," a seminar directed by Claude Lévi-Strauss (Paris, 1977), and "Le sperme et le sang," *Nouvelle Revue de psychanalyse* (Autumn 1985), no. 32, pp. 111–122; Gherardo Gnoli and Jean-Pierre Vernant, eds., *La Mort, les Morts dans les sociétés anciennes* (Paris-Cambridge), 1982.

59. See Blavignac, *L'Emprô genevois*, p. 166; and William Carew Hazlitt, *Dictionary of Faiths and Folklore* (London, 1905), 1:62–63. Yvonne Verdier investigating the nature of the fuel used by the devil recalled this English name of the largest yearly fire in *Le conte, pourquoi? Comment?* (Paris, 1985), p. 377.

60. In *Un hiver à Majorque* (Palma di Majorca, 1971 [1842]), pp. 108–109, George Sand quotes Grasset de Saint-Sauveur. Garau's account of the death of Rafael Valls is in Baruch Braunstein, *The Chuetes of Majorca: Conversos and the Inquisition of Majorca* (New York, 1936). In a reverse trend Christians sometimes "adopted" anonymous bony remains that they named and kept— in order to ensure the remains and to ensure themselves a good metaphysical destiny, as revealed by contemporary fieldworld; see Patrizia Ciambelli and Paolo Guiotto, *Quelle figlie, quelle spose. Il culto della Anime Purganti a Napoli* (Rome, 1980); see also the journal *Quaderni storici* (1982), no. 50.

61. Milko Matičetov, *Sežgani in Prerojeni Clovek (Der Verbrannte und Wiederge Mensch)* (Ljubljana, 1961 [1956]), collected these legends for Europe and offers a bibliography of them.

62. This fourth-century text is in R. P. Baudot and Chaussin, *Vie des saints et des bienheureux* (Paris, 1935), 1:348.

63. In Roberto Partini, "Lu nimmice de lu dimoni, storia e leggende di Santo Antonio abate," *Lares* (1934), 5:119–153.

64. In Hungary we find stories in which a young swineherd rises to the sky thanks to his pig, leading some researchers to detect a "shamanistic theme"; see, on this point, Agnès Kovacs, "L'arbre qui pousse jusqu'au ciel," in *Le Conte, pourquoi? Comment?* pp. 393–413. A version of *L'Arbre merveilleux* can be found in Michel Klimo, "Contes et traditions populaires de Hongrie," *Revue des traditions populaires* (1897), 12:464–473. We also find fine examples

of swineherds following their animals and discovering "saints' bodies" in Elisabetta Gulli-Grigone, "L'innocente meditore nelle leggende dell'Atlante Mariano," *Lares* (1975), 41(1):5–27. And we are well aware that the patron saints of piglets—including Saint Blaise and Saint Nicholas to name only the best known—resuscitate and bring animals and children back from the beyond. Colette Méchin "Les saints gardiens de pourceaux, le porcher dans la tradition rurale," *Revue des sciences sociales de la France de l'Est* (1980–1981), nos. 9 and 10, pp. 286–292 and 148–163.

65. The belief is found in Jaume Aiats, *El Folklore de Rupit i Pruit* (Vic, 1984), p. 147 (*L'òme ve del porc*). The analogy is a subject of debate in archaic medicine, which displaces the question to the number of bones in a human hand (four or five metacarpals, according to Harvey Cushing, *A Bio-Bibliography of Andreas Vesalius* [London, 1962]). It should be noted that until the sixteenth century the pig's body was the one used by anatomists. The *De humani corporis* (Bâle, 1543) by Vésale, a fine example of which can be found at the Bibliothèque nationale, has frontispiece and chapter headings decorated with scenes of pig and sow dissections, but we find them again throughout the pages, leading us to assume that they were still used by the founder of modern anatomy.

The Time of Sacrifice

1. I am thinking of the beautiful work by Marcel Griaule and Germaine Dieterlen, *Le Renard pâle* (Paris, 1965); Charles Malamoud, *Cuire le monde, rite et pensée dans l'Inde ancienne* (Paris, 1989); Marcel Detienne and Jean-Pierre Vernant, *La Cuisine du sacrifice en pays grec* (Paris, 1979); Jean-Louis Durand, *Sacrifice et labour en grèce ancienne* (Paris-Rome, 1986); Luc de Heusch, *Le Sacrifice dans les religions africaines* (Paris, 1986). The founding text is that of Henri Hubert and Marcel Mauss, which first appeared in *Année sociologique*, 2d year (1899).

2. Reported by O. Szent-Ivàn, *Revue de traditions populaires* (1892), 7:487.

INDEX